PRAISE FOR *THE DEVIL AND BELLA DODD*:

"From Communism to Catholicism—and even politics—Bella Dodd lived an incredible life, and one lived against the odds. Mary Nicholas and Paul Kengor bring to life her walk from the dark side to the sunny path of faith in a Cold War saga of redemption that remains timely and provocative today."
—John Gizzi, White House Correspondent, *Newsmax*

"I couldn't put this book down. It seems timelier than ever as socialism continues to spread in our country and throughout our institutions. But more than anything, it is a beautiful testament to the peace and love offered not by ideologies but by Christ and his Church."
—Carrie Gress, Author of *The Anti-Mary Exposed*

"With impeccable research and riveting prose, readers of this book are introduced to the life of Bella Dodd, a former member of the Communist Party's national executive committee, and a woman who spent much of her time in the Party trying to weaken the Catholic Church from within. Mary Nicholas and Paul Kengor are a perfect team for this task as Nicholas has devoted much of her professional life to gathering and analyzing original data on Dodd, and no one understands the evil threat of Marxism and communism better than Kengor. Using years of research, coupled with Freedom of Information requests for formerly unpublished material on Dodd, Nicholas and Kengor expose the evil agenda of communists in America—and Dodd's malevolent role in it all. Dodd herself acknowledged that their most important demonic goal was to destroy the faith of the Catholic people by promoting a pseudo-religion of 'social justice' that looked like Catholicism but clearly was not. Nicholas and Kengor expose the many ways in which Bella Dodd appeared to be truly a 'lost soul.' But more importantly, this inspirational book reveals that even the wicked can be saved, as Dodd was saved through divine intervention and the support of the Venerable Archbishop Fulton J. Sheen."
—Anne Hendershott, Professor, Franciscan University of Steubenville

"Bella Dodd is a seminal figure of the Cold War, a brave American woman who fearlessly battled against atheistic communism. She should not be forgotten. Finally, thanks to this work, she won't be."

—Sebastian Gorka, PhD, *Newsmax* Host and former Deputy Assistant and Strategist to the President

"Through the fascinating life of Bella Dodd, Kengor and Nicholas offer readers a uniquely intimate window into the lure and trap of a demonic ideology. It is a gripping read. Far more than just historically valuable, this book is essential reading today, unmasking much of what led us here, and pointing to the real and robust hope that should animate us still."

—Noelle Mering, Author of *Awake, Not Woke*

"Paul Kengor and his newly discovered co-author, Dr. Mary Nicholas, have produced a tour-de-force analysis of the enigmatic former communist Bella Dodd. A thorough study of her writings and testimonies, along with in-depth interviews with people who knew Dodd, *The Devil and Bella Dodd* provides careful answers to important questions. Did Bella Dodd really place over 1,000 communist spies in Catholic seminaries? You'll have to read this fine book to find out!"

—Jennifer Roback Morse, Founder and President, The Ruth Institute

"If you've surveyed the wreckage from Marx's hellish ideas in *The Devil and Karl Marx*, you won't want to miss the storyline of escape and redemption in *The Devil and Bella Dodd*. Written by Mary Nicholas and Paul Kengor, this new biography of Dodd is formidable. In a world with much misinformation about Dodd, Nicholas and Kengor have rigorously researched their subject, allowing them to speak persuasively on questions as thorny as the possible communist infiltration of the Catholic priesthood. Masterfully analyzed, *The Devil and Bella Dodd* is a powerful book about what happens when pernicious ideas grip a soul—and what happens when grace snatches her back."

—Julia Meloni, Author of *The St. Gallen Mafia*

"There is nothing hidden that will not come to light. But hidden things may fester a long while, as Bella Dodd proved after her reversion to the Catholic Church by revealing the extent of the communist conspiracy in America that she had helped to spread. Mary Nicholas and the prolific Paul Kengor have performed a great service by shining a new and delightful light on this remarkable woman."

—Michael Knowles, *The Daily Wire*

THE DEVIL AND BELLA DODD

THE DEVIL AND

BELLA DODD

ONE WOMAN'S STRUGGLE AGAINST
COMMUNISM AND HER REDEMPTION

MARY A. NICHOLAS, MD
AND PAUL KENGOR, PHD

TAN BOOKS
GASTONIA, NORTH CAROLINA

Cover design by David Ferris—www.davidferrisdesign.com.

Cover image: Hammer and sickle by luma_art / Shutterstock, People's Republic of China CN by Dmitriy_KRD / Shutterstock.

Library of Congress Control Number: 2022914006

ISBN: 978-1-5051-2918-2
Kindle ISBN: 978-1-5051-2919-9
ePUB ISBN: 978-1-5051-2920-5

Published in the United States by
TAN Books
PO Box 269
Gastonia, NC 28053
www.TANBooks.com

This book is dedicated to the men and women who had the courage to leave the Communist Party; to those who had the courage to write about their odysseys; to the dedicated congressional committees that investigated the Communist Party; and to the publishers who had the courage to publish their stories.

CONTENTS

"Step by step, I retreated from God and went forth to meet the world, the flesh, and the devil. . . . I'd join the devil himself. . . . There is no doubt that I traveled with him at my side and that he extorted a great price for his company."

—*Bella Dodd*, Roads to Rome[1]

INTRODUCTION

This book is about conversion and recovery, about hope and redemption. It is about overcoming evil, about looking for a flicker of faith beyond the cold walls of a school of darkness. It is about one person's dramatic break from what fellow ex-communists called "the god that failed." That god was no angel. It was a fallen angel.

It is the story of a clever organizer who lived in a false utopian dream and, hearing faint rumblings in the dark, finally awoke and jumped up. No, none of it was true—what she saw, what they said. Their faux reality was a nightmare. It was always nighttime in their world. And morning never came. Her life changed drastically. She had finally put all the pieces together and had to tell others the truth. Describing it was the next part of her journey, draining the lies and hatred from herself. She had to tell her country and the world.

Hers was a struggle with the Communist Party,[2] with comrades, with the media, but ultimately with herself. Because she learned acutely that, in the end, communism is more than a crime against a country; it is a crime against the soul, the human spirit itself. It is a battle against the supernatural dimension of man, the spiritual element that makes each of us most human in the eyes and image of God—the God that does not fail. Sadly, communism totally rejected this belief in God, as it was a philosophy of pure materialism. Being trapped in communism, like being trapped in quicksand, makes extrication seem impossible, unless there is a helping hand to save you.

This book is about a woman named Bella Dodd.

Courageously, Bella reached into her inner self, the very depths of her soul, and changed course. The title of her autobiography alone, *School of Darkness*, captures the depth of the pit that is communism.

1

Her book—and this one too—describes the struggles, suffering, fear, and pain as she fought against the lies, deceit, propaganda, violence, and darkness of the Communist Party—dedicated to a system of absolute evil—to expose the truth even at the cost of her life if necessary.

From that evil, she would ultimately flee. She would cry for release from the depth of her heart and her deepest convictions. She needed the Church of her youth for the break, for the courage and the zeal to smash and even to unmask an atheistic criminal conspiracy operating on a global level. When Bella was asked if she could name and unmask the leader of this conspiracy, she put it succinctly and starkly: "I would have to say and have to identify that person as Lucifer."[3]

Bella came to that chilling realization so intimately. She saw how the devil drew in disciples to the communist movement by varied means. When a friend told Bella frankly that she was a communist, Bella shrugged: "I'm not afraid of labels. I'd join the devil himself to fight fascism."[4] That was a terrible excuse. One most certainly need not join the devil to fight fascism, or for any reason. Only later did Bella feel the full blow of this blasphemy, conceding: "Blasphemously, I would add, 'I'll join the devil himself if he is going in my direction.' There is no doubt that I traveled with him at my side and that he extorted a great price for his company."[5]

Many opened that door to the dark side and the devil's company, including many raised as Christians. Fulton Sheen, who lent Bella a hand as she struggled to pull out of the quicksand, flagged that danger. "He knew that a nominal Christian with a memory of the Cross can easily be twisted to the purposes of evil by men who masquerade as saviors," wrote Bella in *School of Darkness*. "Communist leaders achieve their greatest strength and cleverest snare when they use the will to goodness of their members."[6]

But a snare it is. Whatever it takes to capture a soul.

She would regrettably concede that she had once aggressively engaged in mass deception and manipulation on behalf of an ideology that her Church described at the time as a "Satanic scourge" enflamed by the "sons of darkness."[7] She eventually climbed out by carrying her cross through that cold night.

In Bella's unique case, that dark "school" that titled her memoir had special meaning related to her distinct work. Bella Dodd was the Communist Party's chief organizer of public-school teachers—the teachers' unions, the "education front." She in fact organized for the Party on many fronts, with more than one layer of infiltration. She lied and deceived.

And yet, Bella fought and beat the devil.

The devil, of course, has made many appearances in many titles, including stories, plays, and books, from *The Devil and Daniel Webster* to *The Devil and the White City* to *The Devil and Karl Marx* and more. In Bella's life, the Devil appeared in a form he has assumed for many decades, as the handmaiden of Marxist-Leninist ideology.

Bella Dodd did not engage with or even write about the devil in the way that others, like Karl Marx, did. Her story, unlike Marx's, is redemptive. Hers is a story of an inspiring Catholic convert who beat the demon of atheistic communism. She escaped the clutches of this diabolical system. Her agonizing sense of oppression under communism, only to come to the Church on her knees through the assistance of one of the greatest religious leaders of the twentieth century, one Fulton Sheen, is a wonderful story of reconciliation and redemption.

Bringing Communist Victory to America

Born in 1904, she came to New York by way of Italy. She came blessed with a pretty name, Maria Assunta Isabella Visono.[8] But she was brought into something ugly in the very country where her parents brought her for better things.

She was drawn to a particular location in lower New York City, 50 East Thirteenth Street, headquarters of Communist Party USA (CPUSA), which was committed to what founders such as William Z. Foster and Earl Browder called a "Soviet America." Or as poet

Langston Hughes put it, "Put one more 'S' in the USA to make it Soviet. The USA when we take control will be the USSA."[9] That was the way of CPUSA. And Bella Dodd made her way to the doors of the tawdry building that transmitted orders back and forth from the Soviet Comintern (Communist International) headquarters in Moscow to the United States.

In testifying to Congress, Manning Johnson, one of Bella's ex-comrades, described the basic and fundamental purpose of the Communist Party: "the complete destruction of the American Government and establishment of a soviet system of government in America. The system, of course, in America that we had planned and envisioned is a dictatorship of the proletariat in the transition from socialism to world communism." What would this entail? Johnson did not mince words: "This was based upon the complete liquidation of all forces of opposition, that is, the owners of industry, the heads of government, in fact, everyone in the whole political, economic, and social life who could be identified with the capitalist class. Those professionals who would not go along with us would go to concentration camps. The most rabid would be liquidated. The banks would be confiscated: the whole capital system, from top to bottom, would be destroyed. The Army and Navy would be liquidated and new armed forces would be created."[10]

Johnson's dire description should surprise no one, and it certainly did not surprise Bella Dodd. Communists behaved brutally wherever they took power. Stalin invoked Lenin: "The scientific concept of dictatorship means nothing more nor less than unrestricted power, absolutely unimpeded by laws or regulations . . . based on force and not on law."[11]

That was what members of Communist Party USA in the Stalin era (Bella's era) signed up for. New members swore a loyalty oath: "I pledge myself to rally the masses to defend the Soviet Union, the land of victorious socialism. I pledge myself to remain at all times a vigilant and firm defender of the Leninist line of the party, the only line that ensures the triumph of Soviet Power in the United States." This particular oath was issued in 1935, during the heart of Stalin's Great Purge that annihilated tens of millions.[12]

This unflagging allegiance to the Bolsheviks was the mission of American communists who joined the Party. It was printed on their membership cards. They carried it with them. Bella carried it with her. They did not question the Party or the Kremlin, from which the Party took its orders.

American Party members did not question the Soviet leadership. The Party was treated as an infallible authority. "None of us desires or is able to dispute the will of the Party," stated Leon Trotsky, one of the troika (along with Lenin and Stalin) that founded the Soviet state. "Clearly, the Party is always right. . . . We can only be right with and by the Party."[13] The esteemed diplomat and scholar George F. Kennan described this as the "infallibility of the Kremlin," explaining: "The Soviet concept of power requires that the Party leadership remain in theory the sole repository of truth. . . . The leadership of the Communist Party is therefore always right."[14] Their only guiding force was themselves and their Marxism-Leninism. That was what they answered to. That was their god; this was their faith. Ronald Reagan called it "that religion of theirs, which is Marxism-Leninism."[15]

In his "Evil Empire" speech, Reagan quoted Whittaker Chambers, who declared that Marxism-Leninism is actually the second oldest faith, first proclaimed in the Garden of Eden with the words of temptation, "Ye shall be as gods." The West could rise to answer that challenge of the serpent, affirmed Chambers, "but only provided that its faith in God and the freedom He enjoins is as great as communism's faith in Man."[16]

Bella Dodd, too, reached for that faith in God for answers, which trumped the false faith of communism. In fact, the full title of her memoirs, *School of Darkness: The record of a life and of a conflict between two faiths*, bears witness to her struggle among these two conflicting faiths.

Once she made her way into the light, Bella heralded the dangers ahead for the country that her mother and father had brought her to. And yet, compelling and courageous as her testimony to Congress had been, she has received scant attention from historians. This book seeks to right that wrong.

More Benign Labels

This is the first biography of Bella Dodd, over a half century after her death in 1969 and very public life. She was a household name at one time, one of the most high-profile Americans to leave the Party and communist lifestyle—akin to a female version of Whittaker Chambers. One modern observer lists Dodd and Chambers (as well as another key convert to Catholicism from communism, Louis Budenz) as the leading "apostates" from communism.[17] To borrow from the title of Chambers' memoir, *Witness*, they became witnesses, including to the truth of the Christian faith.

There were others, of course, as well as brave leaders of Congress, who recognized the dangers. They recognized it in the campaigns that bored into the school systems, the churches, the unions, and within various communities. The difficulty in recognizing the strategy in the United States is the fact that Lenin's violent revolution proceeded to a large degree under the guise of other forms. There was what Ronald Reagan described as "creeping socialism." There was also Fabian socialism, a passive but still relentless revolution of "boring from within." Fittingly, the official coat of arms for the Fabian Society is a wolf in sheep's clothing.

And for the record, socialism is, according to Marx, Engels, and Lenin, the final transitionary step to communism. In his definitive work on the subject, *The State and Revolution*, Vladimir Lenin, in his chapter titled "The Transition from Capitalism to Communism," quoted Marx and Engels: "And this brings us to the question of the scientific distinction between socialism and communism. What is usually called socialism was termed by Marx the 'first,' or lower, phase of communist society. Insofar as the means of production becomes common property, the word 'communism' is also applicable here, providing we do not forget that this is not complete communism."[18] Socialism leads to communism.

Bella Dodd certainly understood that. Nonetheless, like many communists who operated under deception, she was careful not to openly admit the deception to liberals and progressives. Once no longer a deceiver, she frequently shared with the world a quote from her boss, Alexander Trachtenberg, later identified by Whittaker Chambers as the "head of the GPU" in the United States—that is, the notorious Soviet military police.[19] "Trachtenberg once said to me," recalled Dodd in her memoirs, "that when communism came to America it would come under the label of 'progressive democracy.' 'It will come,' he added, 'in labels acceptable to the American people.'"[20]

These were benign labels like progressive, liberal, and democracy. She repeated this in slightly more detail in a speech in Utica, New York, in May 1961, where she said that Trachtenberg had told her in New York at the 1944 Communist Party national convention: "When we get ready to take the United States, we will not take it under the label of communism; we will not take it under the label of socialism. These labels are unpleasant to the American people, and have been speared too much. We will take the United States under labels we have made very lovable; we will take it under liberalism, under progressivism, under democracy. But take it we will."[21]

Again, wolves in sheep's clothing. Wolves operating in the cover of night.

Communism would march forward in the darkness, operating under other labels. It would find new forms of entry. When the economics/class-based revolution of Marx and Engels failed, a new breed of twentieth-century communist would turn to the "conveyor belts" of culture. Such became the destructive influence of the Frankfurt School[22] and the Marxism of Antonio Gramsci, a founder of the Italian Communist Party.

Gramsci recognized that the revolutionary Marxism of Stalin would not work in Western societies, which acknowledged individual rights and faith in the Creator. His goal is famously described as a "long march through the institutions" before socialism and relativism would be victorious.[23] That march continues to this day, well into the twenty-first century, where modern Marxists and even "democratic socialists" have turned not to farms and factories but matters of race and gender and whatever else works for them. The Marxism of these cultural revolutionaries like Gramsci and the Frankfurt School was nicely characterized by Cal-Berkeley professor Martin Malia as "Marxism without the Proletariat." It was Marxism applied to culture and even to sexuality, married to Freudianism—"Freudian-Marxism," of all things.[24]

The Communist Party of Bella Dodd's day recruited many intellectually gifted young women from the United States, a country that, as Chambers pointed out, was built on traditions of freedom and opportunity antithetical to the revolutionary struggles of Europe.[25] Yet, this idealistic person and future Party member heeded the communist call to replace injustices and hardships and the country's constitutional ways of resolving problems with its utopian solution. Hers was an early springtime enchantment: hands-on organizing experience and rising to a leadership role in the Party, followed by a bitter Moscow winter with much soul searching, a recognition of the stark deadliness of the communist revolution and finally leaving disillusioned.

Bella took the path of a hardened Bolshevik, what well-known ex-communist Frank Meyer called an "honorary title" for "which no higher praise exists in the Communist movement. . . . It is spoken with baited and admiring breath and it is a living and operative factor in the lives of the cadre."[26] Much better, she instead became an "ex-communist," eloquently described by Whittaker Chambers: "By ex-Communist, I mean a man who knew clearly why he became a Communist, who served Communism devotedly and knew why he served it, who broke with Communism unconditionally and knew why he broke with it."[27]

The reasons why people are lured to socialism or communism are as varied as the individuals. Called upon often by legislative committees, Bella testified about communism at length, each statement becoming part of the historical record; she left a gripping testament of her personal journey. Each testimony was a display of tremendous courage, exposing herself to character assassination, loneliness, ridicule and civil suits, uncertainty or inability to earn a living, and personal danger. Chambers described this loneliness after his break with the Communist Party as "annihilating," something only an ex-communist could understand.[28]

Dodd echoed those thoughts wholeheartedly.

Learning and Loving to Hate

This total self-surrender to the Party and the Kremlin meant that Communist Party members in the United States learned to hate when the Soviet Comintern ordained it, and as communists commanded.[29]

A defining characteristic of communism is hate. The Party expressed that hate both verbally and by its actions of murder, violence, and even deliberate starvation in countries like the Ukraine. Maxim Gorky actually penned a tribute to hate: "A genuine, sincere revolutionary of the Union of Soviet Socialist Republics must feel conscious, active, heroic hatred for his vile enemy. Our right to hate him has been well enough substantiated and justified. And equally well, equally thoroughly justified is our hatred towards all indifferent, lazy, vulgar persons and other ugly creatures who still live and tumble about in our country." This was pure Bolshevik hatred: "Our revolutionary, proletarian hatred for those who create misery and suffering of the people, must counter the brutal, selfish, sick hatred of the world capitalists, rotting from obesity, sentenced to death by history."[30]

Vile words, but all too typical. The founder of the Soviet state, Vladimir Lenin, put it concisely: "Hatred is truly the 'beginning of all wisdom,' the basis of any socialist and communist movement and of its success."[31] As stated by Harvard professor Dr. Richard Pipes, editor of the Lenin letters, quoting one of Lenin's collaborators (Peter Struve), "the principle feature of Lenin's personality was hatred."[32]

Lenin especially hated religion. "There can be nothing more abominable than religion," scowled Lenin.[33] Marxist-Leninist atheistic ideology was the fount of this hatred. The atheism is foundational. As Alexander Solzhenitsyn recorded in *The Gulag Archipelago*, "Within the philosophical system of Marx and Lenin . . . hatred of God is the principal driving force."[34]

Bishop Fulton Sheen felt that Marxist hate. It was a hatred of God Himself. "Marx was not first a Communist and then an atheist," noted Sheen. "He was first an atheist, then a Communist. Communism was merely the political expression of his atheism. As he hated God, so would he hate those who would own property."[35]

The Catholic Church felt this hate. Pope Pius XI's 1937 encyclical *Divini Redemptoris* called communism a "pernicious" ideology "replete with hate." Even Dorothy Day's *Catholic Worker*, often criticized by conservative Catholics for being soft on socialism, smelled the venom: "We Christians love Communists as human beings and potential fellows in Christ's Mystical Body," her publication stated in a September 1938 open letter to CPUSA head Earl Browder—Bella Dodd's Party boss. "Yet, you Communists hate capitalists as well as capitalism. We love men, hate their sins. You hate sinners against the 'Party Line.'"[36]

For the communist, hate was central.

After she left the Party, Bella Dodd recognized how this hate "was what distinguished me as a full-fledged Communist." She only later learned to love, as she broke free from communist hate. "I had to drain the hate and frenzy from my system."[37]

Of course, hating for a communist meant lying for communism. Lenin preached the "morality" of lying, so long as it furthered class interests. "We do not believe in an eternal morality," he explained in his famous October 1920 speech elucidating "communist ethics." "Communist morality is based on the struggle for the consolidation and completion of communism." This, too, meant rejecting God, as Lenin there again affirmed without equivocation: "We do not believe in God."[38]

As a teacher who was a member of the Communist Party, Bella Dodd was expected to lie, which made her uncomfortable in the classroom. "I think a teacher should have high ethical standards," she noted in Senate testimony, "and here again a Communist fails because, as we all know, the Communist organization definitely advocates lying if it will accomplish their purpose."[39]

Communism, as Vaclav Havel noted and experienced intensely, is the culture of the lie. Examples can be seen throughout this book of lies emanating from the Communist Party. Solzhenitsyn emphasized this in his remarkable essay, "Live Not By Lies." The Communist Party needed the lie. How could you tell the comrades that what they were doing would result in massive starvation, including of little children, or putting a prisoner on the train to Siberia for almost certain death?

For the communist, the hate and death also meant a lack of peace; it meant war and conflict.

"Marxism-Leninism states that you can't achieve peace as long as there is a capitalist country left," Bella Dodd explained in her US Senate testimony in March 1953. "In other words, war and revolution are going to be the fate of man until the Communists have taken over the entire world."[40] This, she noted, is what the American Communist Party believed and followed.

And in fact, Bella was merely echoing Lenin. "We live not only in a state but in a system of states," noted Lenin in March 1919 to the Eighth Party Congress, where he launched the Soviet Comintern, "and the existence of the Soviet Republic side by side with the imperialist states for an extended period is unthinkable. In the end either one or the other will conquer. And before this result, a series of horrible conflicts between the Soviet Republic and the bourgeois states is unavoidable."[41]

Horrible conflicts. Plenty of them. Bella saw them. "I was face to face with brutality, cynicism," she told the US Senate. There in the Communist Party, "I actually saw the things which are abhorrent not only to decent people but to anyone who has feelings for his fellowman."[42]

It eventually had the benefit of driving her away.

An Enormous Source of (Classified) Information

Bella Dodd is a person that most modern Americans have not heard of, although there are numerous documents and videos on the internet about her, some true, some dubious. Yet, as the highest female Communist Party official in the United States at one time, she was a very influential figure tasked with mass organization and infiltration. She was brilliant and charismatic, attracting many to herself and her cause. During the height of the communist movement and the start of America's lengthy battle with communism, in the 1930s and 1940s, you could say she was a willful agent of Moscow. She was a dutiful foot soldier.

And yet, Bella Dodd became even more prominent as an ex-communist. The degree to which that was the case is evident today in the likewise remarkable story of her FBI file, the contents of which are being shared here in this book for the first time.

Incredibly, Bella's huge FBI file remained classified for over a half century after her death. One of us (Paul Kengor) began the process of filing Freedom of Information Act (FOIA) requests in January 2019 for the release of her file. That process began a long period of waiting, with repeated appeals to the federal government submitted by our colleague Bill Marshall of Judicial Watch.[43] The subsequent inaction and delays were very unusual. "I'm wondering what possible reason the bureau could have for withholding it for so long," puzzled Marshall. "The only thing I can think is that she revealed shocking information about communist infiltration that could impact very important, still living people, or people who are somehow iconic figures (probably on the left) in American life."[44]

At long last, portions of that file began being released in March 2021. The first batch was 250 pages in length, of which 9 pages were withheld by the FBI. Several more batches followed, including one released April 1 that traversed another 250 pages (19 withheld), a 500-pager on May 1, another in June that covered 197 pages, and another in July that ran about a dozen pages. In all, we received several batches of what the FBI's Freedom of Information-Privacy Acts Section lists as a 1,281-page file for Bella V. Dodd, one of the longest that we have ever seen among FBI files of Cold War figures.

Revelations from that file will be shared throughout this book. For here in this introduction, a few brief points are worth underscoring from the outset:

Particularly striking, though not a surprise to those knowledge-able about the history of American communism, is that Bella Dodd's FBI file shows that she was placed on the federal government's Security Index, which meant that she could be immediately detained or arrested in the event of a national emergency, such as a war breaking out between the United States and USSR.[45] That kind of listing applied to people of Bella's level of impact in the Party. She was no minor member.

Bella's file attests to that influence at great length, from her work organizing "many hundreds" (actually, over a thousand) of teachers who were Party members into a "secret underground operation," to her work as New York State Communist Party Legislative Director helping her comrades attempt to capture "the entire American Labor Party throughout the state," to her testifying to Congress about her Party work toward "infiltration into important positions of public opinion, education, labor, Congress and congressional committees."[46]

The FBI was struck by Bella's rapid ascent up the ranks. An October 6, 1944 report by the FBI's large New York City office noted that Dodd had become no less than chairman of a "very important meeting" held that week in New York by the Communist Political Association,[47] where general secretary Earl Browder addressed approximately 150 trade union leaders.[48] Throughout the file, Dodd's voluminous efforts for the Party are chronicled at length.

Bella became a major source of information. By the early 1950s, according to the FBI, her code name during the McCarthy hearings was "the Falcon." This bird of prey had soared to heights that few ex-communists ascended to. Swift, powerful, and proud, she was not to be deterred on the witness stand. At the same time, publicly, Bella was always extremely discreet about what she said, often noting that she was a lawyer and thus extremely sensitive to and knowledgeable about the possibility of libel suits, which, she noted, could be extremely expensive and cost-prohibitive even when the truth was on your side.[49]

Even then, the material that we received as researchers from Bella's FBI files is, frustratingly, the mere tip of an iceberg that we cannot wrap our arms around. The 1,281 pages of material from this woman designated by the federal government as "an anticommunist informer from 1952–1969" were a scant glimpse of what was collected. For instance, the March 1, 2021 FBI cover letter on the first batch of released files states that Bella is referenced in hundreds of FBI files that are now stored at the National Archives. To begin trying to track those down requires navigating a winding maze of file numbers, each of which would require direct requests and visits to the National Archives and Records Administration. The task is overwhelming.

"I personally have never seen so many FBI files associated with one individual," observes Bill Marshall, a veteran of FOIA-FBI requests. "I suspect you're correct, that Bella was an enormous source of information. She probably appeared in many because she herself was such a powerful, well-connected communist, but probably also because she was diming out fellow Communists after she saw the light."[50]

Hundreds of files. One senses that all of these files on Bella, and thus a written record of what she knew, will never get reviewed nor fully presented. Testimony to that was a statement entered into the official

Congressional Record at the time of Bella's death by Congressman John Rarick: "Bella Dodd spent the rest of her life combatting the evil forces working for the destruction of the United States," stated Rep. Rarick. "She testified before Senate and House committees and gave information to the F.B.I. Much of her testimony was given in executive hearings and has never been made public. Some of this testimony was so damning to important figures that even the stenographic notes have disappeared. In open hearings she was warned again and again not to mention names, so careful were the legislators to protect the 'innocent.'"[51]

One wonders to what extent Bella's information on infiltration of Catholic seminaries might have appeared in those statements. Somewhere in those files might be the smoking gun on such tantalizing questions.

Infiltration and Infiltration

Once she broke from the Party and went public, Bella Dodd noted how the entire Party and its apparatus lived in fear that ex-communists like herself would testify and "begin to unravel the whole conspiracy."[52]

Bella's chief area of infiltration in that conspiracy was education. It was what she openly testified to during many hours in congressional hearings. The Party charged her with leadership on that front. Given her dazzling accomplishments in secretly infiltrating the teachers' union, the Party would not have hesitated to go to her for infiltration of other organizations.

The conspiracy of infiltration was multipronged, operating on many fronts. It was not a "conspiracy theory" but a real conspiracy to infiltrate US society, including the Catholic Church. That infiltration has been written about elsewhere, and usually without proper care and reliability. One of us wrote about it at length in his book *The Devil and Karl Marx*. Readers of that book were surprised to see that the longest section was not on the person of Marx but instead the extraordinary actions by the communist movement in the twentieth century to infiltrate churches worldwide, including in America, and especially non-Catholic denominations.[53] Some American Protestant churches were targeted aggressively, and with tragic success. The same was true, albeit even worse, for the Russian Orthodox Church. The Catholic Church was certainly not exempt from the effort, with everything from undercover thrusts by the Party to open public campaigns sugarcoated as olive branches, such as Earl Browder's infamous "outstretched hand" offered to Catholics.[54]

And why wouldn't the Church be in communists' crosshairs? Communists had a special hatred for the Catholic Church.

Bella Dodd's reported comments about her role in helping to infiltrate the Catholic Church in America with over a thousand "communist men" can be found all over the internet. And again, much if not most of the writing is scant in reliable documentation. It is, frankly, a mess. Here in this book, we have taken particular care to report what Bella both did say and did not say. Our primary interest in pursuing her FBI file was precisely in search of documentation for information regarding that alleged infiltration. We have been sorry to see, at least so far, that confirming information in her FBI file still has not been released. That is not a surprise. Of all the infiltration and deception that Bella Dodd dealt with in her flirtation with the devil of communism, this was the most pernicious. It remains the most sensitive. As we shall share, her confessor, Fulton Sheen, advised her to be extremely careful, if not to the point of silence, regarding the details of this infiltration. We were told that Sheen told Bella Dodd not to share names of any corrupted clergy.

Nonetheless, Bella and many priests alike were painfully aware of the Party's desire for infiltration. She recalled the words of Father Keller of The Christophers, the Catholic group with the apt motto, "It's better to light a candle than curse the darkness." She said to Keller: "You're forming The Christophers organization. Why don't you establish a national organization so everybody can join?" Keller looked her in the eye and said, "Bella, you should know better. In three months, they would infiltrate it, and either they would paralyze it or smear it, make it impossible for us to do anything."

Bella unhesitatingly agreed with Father Keller. She noted that communists were "the best infiltrators that God ever created."[55]

That is a bracing statement on these extraordinary deceivers, but with one crucial theological caveat: Though God created people, He does not create infiltrators. That is the devil's work. And besides, communists deny God the Creator.

Bella Dodd's explosive claim of a direct communist infiltration of Catholic seminaries was spoken to publicly by (among others) Bella's confessor at the time, Fulton Sheen—the man who brought her into the Church—and by Bella's close friend, Dr. Alice von Hildebrand, who passed away at age ninety-eight as this book was being finished.

During a dramatic talk in a church in Rome, Sheen's remarks were so explosive that the *New York Times* reported them on the front page of its April 28, 1952 edition under the headline "Sheen in Rome Says Red Agents Tried to Infiltrate the Priesthood." The article reported: "American Communists were under secret orders in 1936 to infiltrate the Roman Catholic priesthood, Bishop Fulton J. Sheen said today." The fifty-seven-year-old auxiliary bishop of New York spoke to what was described as an "overflowing congregation" in the American Catholic Church of Santa Susanna. "This was the beginning of the planting of forces of evil communism within the religious communities to destroy them from within," stated Sheen. "A call for volunteers to enter religious orders and make the great sacrifices of the life of a seminarian was made at a secret Red meeting in a large [American] city."

To the best of our knowledge, this was the first and only time that Sheen publicly spoke of such an infiltration. Sheen did not divulge his source. Tellingly, however, his revelation just happened to come less than three weeks after he baptized and heard the confession of Bella Dodd (April 7, 1952), after months of giving her personal instruction in entering the Church.[56]

Alice von Hildebrand, the acclaimed author and philosopher, repeatedly testified to Bella's claims of infiltrating the Church, including in an interview for this book. Bella admitted to doing so in a public talk in Orange, California, in the 1960s, at which she told an audience of six to eight hundred that she had personally helped to recruit 1,100 men to enter seminaries. (A notarized testimony from two witnesses present at Bella's talk is quoted in this book.)

These details, of course, will be explored in the pages ahead.

Deception and Deception

The infiltration, of course, depended on deception.

Aside from the question of whether a thousand communist men were slipped into seminaries, there is no question that socialism slid under many a parish door. It was always repackaged in some more palatable form, with those benign words like "social justice" and even "democracy." "They always use the word 'democracy,'" Bella said of American communists in Senate testimony.[57] Yes, always.

The Catholic Church warned of this deception. In 1937, as Bella was organizing a communist infiltration of the New York teachers' union, the Church released its most scathing indictment of communism, the encyclical, *Divini Redemptoris*: "In the beginning, Communism showed itself for what it was in all its perversity, but very soon it realized that it was thus alienating people," stated Pope Pius XI. "It has therefore changed its tactics [by] hiding its real designs behind ideas that are in themselves good and attractive." The encyclical noted that by using "various names that do not suggest Communism . . . they try perfidiously to worm their way even into professedly Catholic and religious organizations . . . they invite Catholics to collaborate with them in the realm of so-called humanitarianism and charity; and at times make proposals that are in perfect harmony with the Christian spirit and doctrine of the Church." Since God is love, and Christianity is a religion of love and not hate, it is diametrically opposed to Communism.

But whatever the deception, the devil is in the details. Pius XI explicitly warned: "Communism is intrinsically wrong, and no one who would save Christian civilization may collaborate with it in any undertaking whatsoever."

Whether in theory or practice, the Church has always rejected Communism on account of its errors, notably: its atheistic materialism, its doctrine and practice of class-war, its denial of the rights and liberties of the human person, including the natural right to possess some measure of private property. Quite remarkably, the Vatican issued a lengthy statement condemning communism in 1846, two years before the *Communist Manifesto* was even published. In November 1846, Pope Pius IX released *Qui Pluribus*, affirming that communism would "utterly destroy the rights, property, and possessions of all men, and even society itself." It was a "dark design" of "men in the clothing of sheep, while inwardly ravening wolves." Communists "make men fly in terror from all practice of religion, and they cut down and dismember the sheep of the Lord." The writings of communists teach "sinning," "widespread disgusting infection," are "filled with deceit and cunning," and "spread pestilential doctrines everywhere and deprave the minds especially of the imprudent, occasioning great losses for religion."

"As a result of this filthy medley of errors," *Qui Pluribus* warned, "we see . . . morals deteriorated, Christ's most holy religion despised, the majesty of divine worship rejected, the power of this Apostolic See plundered, the authority of the Church attacked and reduced to base slavery, the rights of bishops trampled on, the sanctity of marriage infringed."[58]

Yes, even marriage. In the *Communist Manifesto*, Marx and Engels wrote emphatically: "Abolition of the family! Even the most radical flare up at this infamous proposal of the Communists."[59] Bella Dodd painfully experienced that edict among her comrades. "The bourgeois family as a social unit was to be made obsolete," she explained. In

March 1943, as she gave herself totally to the Party, she longed for family life. "I often talked of adopting children," she wrote with a heavy heart in her memoirs. "But the comrades dissuaded me."[60] In later testimony to the US Senate, after she broke with the Party, Dodd said that "Communism is an all-embracing philosophy which embraces everything you do, which determines the kind of marriage you have, your relations with your children, your relationship to your community, your relationship with your profession."[61]

And yet, many misled Catholics fell for the more "benign labels" that Bella Dodd warned about, such as "socialism," as if that was milder and better than communism. Here, too, the Church knew better from the outset. In 1849, Pius IX issued another encyclical, *Nostis Et Nobiscum*, which referred to both socialism and communism as "wicked theories," "perverted theories," "perverted teachings," and "pernicious fictions."

All popes warned of this. On December 28, 1878, Pius IX's successor, Pope Leo XIII, the *Rerum Novarum* pontiff, started the first year of his twenty-five-year-long papacy with another stark Church warning on both socialism and communism. It was called *Quod Apostolici Muneris* (On Socialism), which warned: "We speak of that sect of men who, under various and almost barbarous names, are called socialists, communists, or nihilists, and who, spread over all the world, and bound together by a wicked confederacy." These men "leave nothing untouched." They even go so far as to seek to "debase the natural union of man and woman, held sacred even among barbarous peoples; and its bond, by which the family is chiefly held together."

So many such statements issued forth from the Magisterium. One more worth noting was Pope Pius XI's seminal 1931 encyclical *Quadragesimo Anno*, which stated emphatically: "Religious socialism, Christian socialism, are contradictory terms; no one can be at the same time a good Catholic and a true socialist."

And yet, many Catholics were roped in nonetheless. We saw in the 1970s the embrace of Marxist-influenced liberation theology. We see it still today. More recently, in July 2019, the Jesuit-flagship *America* magazine published a stunning article titled "The Catholic Case for Communism." The author, Dean Dettloff, is a Catholic—*America's* Toronto correspondent—and a member of the Communist Party of Canada. Jesuit priest Matt Malone, the magazine's editor in chief, provided a companion essay justifying *America's* reason for publishing this unapologetically pro-communist piece. In truth, there is no justification for such a piece in a Catholic publication.

"How could I be a communist when I am a devout Catholic?" a friend once heard Bella Dodd innocently ask on her road to Marxism.[62] Somehow, it happened. And she was not—and is still not—alone.

Socialism and communism have somehow managed to find supporters in a Church that once condemned these ideologies as "wicked theories." Bella Dodd would not be surprised. She became one of them.

Bella's Role in the Conspiracy

Bella Dodd was described as a woman of medium height and build, with grayish-black hair and brown eyes, who walked with a slight limp because of an artificial limb.[63] She was also described as charismatic, brilliant, energetic, and precocious from her earliest days arriving as a child in America. Her story, recounted in these pages, is not that of a simple woman who naively fell for the Communist Party line. Rather, her story is woven into the tale of a revolt launched in the early twentieth century against the world, the family, the school, the Catholic Church, and human nature itself.

Lenin and Stalin initiated an ideological war, one that seeped into numerous facets of western society through the cultural debasements imposed on our youth. Bella not only saw it coming; she helped facilitate it by spearheading the teachers' front. Years later, she harbored deep regrets and would endeavor to warn the world. She was especially concerned about how communists were manipulating children through the educational system.

"There is no doubt in my mind that the Communists will use the schools and every other educational medium," she told the US Senate. "They will use every educational medium . . . from the nursery school to the universities." They wanted children. "The youth are a very special target of the Communists," she told senators in open hearings. "They want youth because the youth are the government of tomorrow. . . . They want to indoctrinate and teach the people with whom they will take over tomorrow." Hence, the teachers, said Dodd, "were used on many different fronts" by the Party, both underground and above ground. This was fundamental, she said, "to establish a Soviet America," the designation used by CPUSA leaders to describe their new Comintern-directed country upon their "victory in America."[64]

Dodd became very disillusioned at the tentacles of this very real and very insidious literal "conspiracy." She could only take so much. But before she could leave the Party, her comrades expelled her in June 1949. In fact, it was June 19, 1949, to be exact.[65] A new birthdate, of sorts.

The revolution begun by Lenin and Stalin was deadly. The Harvard University Press volume *The Black Book of Communism* estimated that communism produced over a one hundred million deaths in the twentieth century (a conservative estimate).[66] And still somehow, communism is not widely condemned nor its crimes well known in our schools today. The sabotaging of the school system itself helps explain that. As popular commentator Jordan Peterson has noted, this unprecedented death and destruction is not widespread knowledge among students in the West, "And the reason I believe is that the communist system had extensive networks of admirers in the West, especially among intellectuals, and still, in fact, does." To Peterson, this absence represented "the absolute rot of the education system."[67]

Bella Dodd was responsible for an unhealthy portion of that rot in education that metastasized throughout the wider culture. Using striking metaphors, perhaps appropriate giving communism's killing capacity, she stated: "If I send you a machinegun and tell you it is a baby carriage, and I send it to you wheel by wheel and nut by nut and you do not know until you have assembled the thing that it is a machinegun and not a baby carriage, that is exactly what has happened to this country. We are being sold machineguns without knowing it is machineguns."[68]

This description vividly describes what took place during the Cold War and still occurs in culture wars of the West. Americans, focused on baby carriages, and brainwashed into believing that "they all lived happily ever after," simply could not imagine the deadly deception. After all, who could be against baby carriages?

That is how propaganda works. "The Communist cause is highly geared to propaganda," Bella testified to Congress. "They understood it even better than Dr. [Joseph] Goebbels did. Propaganda is the most effective weapon in the hands of the Communists in beclouding the minds of American people."[69]

Bella Dodd, though long gone, having died over a half century ago, helped bequeath today's post-modern, neo-Marxist world, a civilization both anti-Christian and anti-human. That is a sad legacy. But she also sought to make amends and to bequeath a better world. Her life took a happier course, toward faith, hope, and love. Finding God was key. "When did I really get myself completed separated?" she answered candidly to senators. "When I found myself a new philosophy of life, when I found something that I could believe. . . . I had to come to a belief in God in order really to achieve a reintegration of myself as a person."[70]

The "specter of communism," as Marx and Engels described it in the opening line of their *Manifesto*, one which they said all the powers of Europe, including the pope, hastened to "exorcise," had once filled a vacuum in Bella's heart. But as Saint Augustine said, there is a *God-shaped* vacuum in each of our hearts. Only God can fill it—not the specter of communism, not what the Church described as a "satanic" specter. "If you don't believe in God," said Bella to the senators, "there is a vacuum there, and where the vacuum is, the others will step in to take over."[71]

God intervened in Bella's life, and with the help of Venerable Bishop Fulton Sheen and grace, she reverted to the faith of her childhood and turned into an unexpected heroine and a model for us today. Here was an Italian immigrant, a little girl who arrived brimming with promise and innocence, who became a passionate Communist Party leader, and then eagerly sought faith and redemption.

We will show what made Bella Dodd choose communism over family ties, a professorship, country, and friendship, and then why she changed and looked for reconciliation. This is a woman who renounced the cold School of Darkness and re-embraced the warm light of the Catholic faith. Here, at long last, is her story.

CHAPTER 1

BELLA DODD'S PURGE FROM THE COMMUNIST PARTY

O n June 17, 1948, the phone rang. Bella answered.
"This is the Associated Press," said the voice. "We have received a statement from the Communist Party announcing your expulsion from membership. It says here that you are anti-Negro, anti-Puerto Rican, anti-Semitic, anti-labor, and the defender of a landlord. Have you any statement to make?"[72]

How intimidating, and how timely those words sound still today, perhaps even more pronounced in modern "cancel culture."

Words cut with sword-like tongues. And always the ubiquitous press. Present also was the reflexive Pavlovian charge of racism. But the usually gregarious Bella was subdued now and refused the bait: "No comment," she replied. She was eviscerated, with no fight left in her (at least not for now). She had no desire to look back on recent events.

This middle-aged American woman was once one of the most powerful divas in the US Communist Party. She was under FBI surveillance. She was an agent of the Kremlin. And now, one of the most important female Communist officials in America, who had served the Party faithfully for two decades, was being purged.[73]

What was her crime? How had she sinned against the Party? What apostasy?

Let the Violent Smears Begin

Among other charges, Bella was accused of the "anti-working class" crime of defending a landlady. It was so Bolshevik-like. It was a classic Party charge.

A reporter at the leading Socialist Party of America publication *The New Leader* captured the alleged transgression: "Frances Dzerlin, formerly a janitress at 1800 Lexington Avenue (New York City, N.Y.), had paid $200 down and taken the house as landlady. Like most of the neighborhood landlords (including the house's former owners), she ducked the rent law. As a result, she was hauled into court, charged with the violation, and ordered to refund the overcharges to her tenants."[74]

What was Bella's role and transgression in this?

Brought into court, Frances Dzerlin, who was actually a poor and struggling immigrant and far from a typical landlady, was unable to pay the $2,000 fine. Bella, who had befriended her, and who was a lawyer, offered to help. She made the landlady promise to pay back the $2,000 while she worked out an arrangement with the rent commissioner, waiving the sentence until the money was paid back. But since the tenants were Puerto Ricans and not white, the State Board of the Communist Party creatively and conveniently ruled Bella Dodd's efforts were "discrimination against Negroes."[75]

Or at least that is how *The New Leader* framed the story. Framing was always a delicately important job in the socialist and communist press, and it was rarely achieved without a heavy dose of Party propaganda. Bella herself had engaged in it.

Right on cue, the *Daily Worker* chimed in. The *Daily Worker* was the Party organ of CPUSA. Like CPUSA, it was New York-based and received an annual subsidy from the Kremlin. And like the head of CPUSA, the editor in chief of the *Daily Worker* was handpicked and approved by Moscow, a dutiful stooge of the Soviets. It was now ready to tear into Bella Dodd, by order of the Party.

The *Daily Worker* asserted that the charges against Bella were based on the constitution of CPUSA. First, there was Article 8, Section 2, which states that "conduct or actions detrimental to the working class and the nation, as well as to the interests of the Party . . . may be punished by expulsion from membership." Then there was Section 4: "The practice or advocacy of any form of racial, national or religious discrimination shall be grounds for expulsion from membership."[76]

Of course, the people who brought the charges tossed in "betrayal of the working-class struggle." This was a terrible sin. The Party organ explained that at this perilous period for the Proletariat, when "monopoly capitalism is utilizing the Department of Justice and the FBI to smash and outlaw the Communist Party of America as part of its drive toward war and fascism, the expulsion of Bella Dodd serves as a warning to all disrupters and anti-Party elements."[77]

She was a disrupter, a pawn of the landlords, the bourgeoisie, and much worse yet to come. No group could spout bile like the Communist Party. It was just warming up against Bella Dodd. Fascism, racism, and discrimination: these were the indictments brought against Bella in 1948—indictments very much in fashion still today, over seventy years later.

Bella was a tough woman, but the attacks stung. No question. Of course, she also expected this line of attack.

In her March 1953 US Senate testimony, Bella later explained how these smears worked, which is hauntingly similar to how political leftists in America wield the same tactics today when looking to purge—or in today's parlance, cancel—people they disagree with or who stand in the way of their revolutionary ambitions. "The Communists use the race situation in a very effective manner," she explained. "Since the Communists want to create a sense of fear among people, and a sense of hatred, what they do is to indicate that the majority of the people are against them. They will say to the Puerto Ricans, 'The white people are against you.' . . . They will say that to the Negro person. . . . In other words, they pit one racial group against another."

The communists cast aside America's "great strength" of being a racial melting pot. Instead, they divide. "They utilize this racial situation very effectively."[78]

They used it against Bella. Anyone who was against them was labeled as a racist. "For instance, when I was expelled," Bella told the US Senate, "I might have sued them for a couple of million dollars, because the resolution in the expulsion read that I was anti-Negro, anti-Puerto Rican, anti-Semitic, anti-working class, and degenerate. . . . Suddenly I found myself smeared in the most violent kind of way."[79]

And in these accusations—these accusations of "racism" or whatever worked—the communists could count on liberals to join in. "The Communist Party knew how to fight very effectively against anyone who touched the communist movement," Bella recalled of her expulsion from the Party. "If anyone tried to attack the Communist movement, the Communist Party immediately went among the liberals, among its allies, and on various bases got the support and help of these people to smear and to isolate the person who was hurting Communists."[80]

From there, the misrepresentation, disinformation, and character assassination would worm its way through the wider left-wing media and other progressives, starting with communists and too often picked up by duped liberals inclined to favor the smear of the targeted person and too easily misled from the outset by the initial Party misinformation campaign. Said Bella: Communists would often look liberals in the eyes and assert, "I am merely a progressive citizen."[81] Liberals were happy to believe them. Bella knew how it worked: "What we would do, of course, is, first of all, get it published in the Communist press, the *Daily Worker*, and [*Masses &*] *Mainstream*, *New Masses*, and whatever other publication the Party had. The Party would then publish the official attitude."[82]

That was step one. Then the next step: "The trade-union leaders reading that would understand that is the official [Party] attitude, and then, where they had the power within the trade-union movement, they would publish it in their newspapers, or, if they were part of the mass organization, they would publish it in the mass organization newspapers."[83]

After that came the next step in the circulation and attempted legitimization of the smear, as the slander worked its way up the media food-chain into the mainstream liberal press: "Then we had certain contacts with the newspaper world," continued Bella. "We had Communist Party members on various newspapers. We would contact them and see to it that they would use the publicity to smear the person."

Pause: At this point in our tracking of the process, we can see that *The New Leader* and *Daily Worker* had gotten the ball rolling. The Associated Press then followed suit.

After that, Bella furthered, came radio: "We had contacts with the radio world, and we would use them to see that they were smeared." Next came friendly left-wing intellectuals, professors, and ministers pulled into the calumny: "We had contact with the intellectual world. We had various committees, professors who could be called upon, or ministers who could be called upon."[84]

So, Bella Dodd knew of what she spoke. She had been a smearer herself for the Party. She actually spearheaded defaming campaigns against major legislators, such as Congressmen Hamilton Fish and Martin Dies and New York State Senator Coudert, the latter of whom she said, "We built him up into a pro-fascist, anti-Negro, anti-Semitic, anti-this and that kind of personality. . . . Everything which the man has done is blown up so as to create of him a monster and a horror."[85]

As for the slander campaign against Hamilton Fish, one of Congress' most brilliant and effective exposers of domestic communism, Bella set up shop in a hotel room on the Hudson River to coordinate the effort. "The liberals and the Progressive Party never knew I existed," she boasted. "We defeated Congressman Fish."[86]

It was standard operating procedure for the Party. In his *Manual of Organization*, the infamous "J. Peters," the top Communist representative in the United States (who Bella knew), described what methods loyal Party members could do to expose "stool pigeons" and "spies." He stated: "There is only one proper method of exposing the stool pigeons and that is *mass* exposure, creating and organizing mass hatred against these rats." The manual gave handy suggestions, such as photograph the "spy" and print his or her picture in the *Daily Worker*; mobilize children and women in the block in the part of the town where the "stool pigeon" lives to make his life miserable; let them picket the store where the spouse of the "rat" purchases groceries and other necessities; let the children in the street shout after the person or after any member of his or her family "that they are spies, rats, stool pigeons."[87]

This was brutal, but so was communism. So were Party members.

Now, the Party was smearing Bella. The Party considered her a heretic, and now it was her turn for defamation. She was denounced as a "stool pigeon," as an "informer," as "Judas," as selling out for "thirty pieces of silver," as "the most devilish kind of thing."[88]

Alas, here was the new Bella Dodd, hoisted on a petard for the world to see: bigot, racist, anti-Semite, fascist.

It certainly took its toll emotionally. But that was what the Party did to those who left. Bella told the senators: "Everything has to be done to destroy that particular person." Why? For the grand apostasy of leaving the Party, which really was like a church to the comrades. (Frank Marshall Davis and his comrades—Davis in the 1970s became a mentor to a young Barack Obama—referred to the Party as "the Church." Davis joined CPUSA the same year that Bella did.[89])

Bella described the method: "What you do is gather information and use it to affect him [the purged Party member] emotionally, you try to drive him into a breakdown, you try to destroy him economically by making it impossible for him to be employed, and you also destroy his personality as a person."[90]

Bella knew it all too painfully well. It was done to her. And it broke her down. But she did tell the senators during her testimony that fortunately, "I happen to have had special help in withstanding this thing."[91] That help was friends like Fulton Sheen, her Church, and her faith.

Purging Bella

But let's look more closely at the purge. The timing was everything.

Bella Dodd had by this time spent two decades working with communists, including six years as an open Party member. Among other things, she oversaw women's work for the Party, including the Women's Trade Union Committee for Peace, which was organized to encourage women to join unions. In turn, communists would infiltrate those unions and manipulate those women.

In 1952, Bella sat in the witness stand at the US Capitol to testify to subversive influence in the educational process. She testified about her work in the Party, affirming that her specialties included "legislation, labor, education, women's work, and youth organizations." She achieved a plum Party position as a member of the National Committee of the Communist Party, after having served on the state committee of the Communist Party in New York, which was by far CPUSA's largest state organization.[92]

The first public displays of Bella's purge were the attacks on her character. These were Party-orchestrated slurs and harassments which had begun before her actual expulsion.

"To the New York newspapers the story of the expulsion of a woman Communist was merely one more story," Bella wrote, but she winced "when reputable papers headlined the Communist Party charges using the words 'fascism' and 'racism,' even though I knew these words were only quoted from the Party resolution."[93]

But again, she knew how the food chain of smears worked, beginning in the gutters and sewers of CPUSA's propaganda network. She braced herself because she knew there would be more attacks, including financial threats, since some of Bella's law practice were referrals from trade union and Party members.

Bella's analysis was correct, as the Party took swift action, telling her there would be no more referrals. Many clients who were Party members came to her office, some with new lawyers, to withdraw their pending cases. There were also telephone calls, letters, and telegrams dripping with predictable hate and vituperation, many from people she did not even know. What made her feel desolate were the reprisals from those she had known best—those among the teachers whom she had considered friends. Once thinking she had hundreds of friends with strong ties that bound them, "now those bonds were ropes of sand."[94] Personal friends, some of whom she had lured into the Party, were lost to her, including many of her former students and fellow teachers.

She was now a non-person. Communists tightened the network and the noose. This was a complete excommunication. She was a "rat," vermin, a "Judas goat." Comrades in the Party knew to keep their distance, even if they had considered her a friend, lest they be purged and vilified themselves.

Only a Miracle

Of course, as we know well, and as Bella knew well, communists worldwide never stopped at mere character assassination. They engaged in actual assassination. High-level ex-communists in the United States (such as Whittaker Chambers) lived constantly in fear of a carefully arranged "accident" that could cost them their lives, especially once they went public and began naming names to Congress. Many went into anonymity and government protection programs.

Communists killed people. Could Bella Dodd become a victim?

In fact, the Party did make attempts on her life.

"I found myself in difficult positions because the moment the Party acted, I was followed," she later recalled. "I'd be on a subway stop, somebody would push. I'd be on a sidewalk and I'd find myself pushed in front of a car. I found I had a number of very difficult situations in which only a miracle, I think, made it possible for me to be here today."[95]

Later, a Party member told Bella the reason for the vicious resolution expelling her: "Bella, we had to make it impossible for you ever to have any credence or support from anybody. We had to make it impossible for you ever to rise and talk against us."[96]

What Bella had failed to understand was that the security she felt in the Party "was that of a group and that affection, in that strange communist world, is never a personal emotion. The psychology of the Party was that you were loved or hated on the basis of group acceptance, and emotions were stirred or dulled by propaganda made by the powerful people at the top." She explained that this was why ordinary communists got along well with their "groups," because "they think and feel together and work toward a common goal."[97]

Bella described this group rejection as "annihilating."

But she told herself that it was a big world and that there were many people other than communists in it. This brought no consolation, for the world was a jungle in which she was lost, in which she felt hunted. And really, she was being hunted. Worst of all, she felt a constant compulsion to explain herself. "I tried at first, but soon gave it up."[98]

She wrote letters to people, some of whom had lived in her house or had been frequent guests there, and in whose homes she had once been welcomed. Those who replied either were abusive or obviously sought to disassociate themselves from her. Two friends replied in one sentence on the back of the letter she had written them. They wrote only: "Please do not involve us."

Many did not answer at all.[99]

Communist Conversion—and Dehumanization

A witness to the rope tightening around Bella was John Lautner, who likewise dramatically left the Party. He testified to Congress about a 1949 meeting of the New York State leadership of the Communist Party at 100 Fifth Avenue in New York. It was held at the law office of Abe Unger, Dave Freedman, and Louis Fleischer, who were known as "the Party lawyers."[100] They met in the library room. The topic of the meeting was the expulsion of Bella Dodd from the Communist Party, "and what measures to take to destroy the influence of Bella Dodd, particularly among attorneys and in the teaching profession where she enjoyed a lot of influence." He said the meeting took place only a couple months before the end of the school year: "We had to race against time to meet with all the schoolteacher groups in the Party to explain why the Party had to expel Bella Dodd."[101]

It had become a necessity to get Bella and get her hard. With religious-like fervor, the communists set up their inquisition.

In order to get a better grasp of the devastation Bella was feeling after her expulsion, we should know that she had extensive one-on-one training when she first became a communist under the supervision of Harriet Silverman. Silverman was one of the first communists that Bella had met. She was an activist in New York City involved in labor and left-wing social and political movements in the 1920s and 1930s. As director and educational secretary of the Workers' Health Bureau of New York and executive-secretary of the People's National Health Committee, Silverman wrote articles, reports, and pamphlets regarding the rights of workers. It was Silverman who introduced Bella Dodd to Earl Browder.

Harriet Silverman would give Bella Marxist literature and instructions.[102] We can call this brainwashing, since that is what it was. An expert on that subject was a particularly high-ranking member of the communist cadre who supervised the process of brainwashing: Frank S. Meyer.

Meyer, too, would one day become a prominent ex-communist. So much so that he eventually joined the editorial board of conservative icon William F. Buckley Jr.'s *National Review*. He became a prolific writer and public speaker, traveling the country like Bella did throughout the 1960s warning Americans of the Marxist menace. In Bella's day, Meyer was a prolific communist, doing the foundational work of molding communists.

Meyer, in fact, was the author of just that, a book titled *The Moulding of Communists: The Training of Communist Cadre*. For over a decade, he was steeped in theoretical research, propaganda, and training communist activists, all prior to his defection. His magnum opus delineated the tactics and strategies used to recruit and train people to become dedicated Communist Party leaders and to transform their personalities as they became part of the "cadre."[103] He stressed the "profoundly different character of Communist consciousness. . . . For the Communist *is* different. He thinks differently. Reality looks different to him."[104]

Truer words were never spoken.

This transformation was purposely carried out in the training process, which began at the first moment of contact and never finished. Like a pious Catholic attending Mass, reading the Scriptures, partaking in the sacraments, and seeking to grow in holiness, so did the devout communist. According to Meyer, the "ideal type of Communist" was a person in whom "all individual, emotional, and unconscious elements have been reduced to a minimum and subjected to the control of an iron will, informed by a supple intellect."[105] Meyer described the intoxicating conviction of some members as a "special calling." There was a "common secular and messianic quasi-religion that inspires the Communists everywhere."

Meyer was not alone, of course, in observing this. Good communists sought always to grow deeper in the faith. It really was a religious-like conversion. For many communists, there was a Saul-like conversion into this atheistic ideology that, ironically, served them as a sort of religion. Another ex-communist, Arthur Koestler, strikingly conveyed this in his classic *The God That Failed*:

> To say that one had "seen the light" is a poor description of the mental rapture which only the convert knows. . . . The new light seems to pour from all directions across the skull, the whole universe falls into pattern like the stray pieces of a jigsaw puzzle assembled by magic at one stroke. There is now an answer to every question, doubts and conflicts are a matter of the tortured

past. . . . Nothing henceforth can disturb the convert's inner
peace and serenity—except the occasional fear of losing faith
again, losing thereby what alone makes life worth living, and
falling back into the outer darkness.[106]

For Frank Meyer, proper Party training, both theoretical and practical,
led to "absolute and uncompromising acceptance of the decisions of
the organization—not only in the face of prison, torture, and death
but in the face of what were yesterday one's firmest convictions. . . .
One must make those decisions one's own—even though one still
knows that they are wrong."[107]

One accepted this as an act of faith, a leap of faith.

According to Meyer, there were only two possible results of this
"moulding" process: "either failure of the will to enforce dehumanization, followed by revolt and break from the Party; or the triumph
of the will, fortified by cynicism and residual faith—the successful
moulding of a Communist."[108]

There you have it: the successful shaping of a communist results in
his or her (voluntary) dehumanization. It is a conscious decision to
subvert his conscience.

Bertolt Brecht, the German playwright known as the Marxist min-
strel to the Soviet GPU, commented on this developmental process
for the Communist Party: "Truly, it is not given to all to be members
of the Communist Party!" One must be uniquely gifted and blessed
in receiving the faith. Said Brecht: "The inner contradictions of a self-
reconstruction, which requires the suppression or destruction of the
best instincts and attitudes of the human being and demands complete
subordination of individuality, threaten at every moment to shatter
the acquired personality structure into a thousand bits. Only constant
exercise of the will holds it together."[109]

Bella had already submitted to this dehumanization before her
expulsion. Now, she was the recipient of a double dehumanization.
Booted from the Party, she was treated as a non-human altogether.

A Dark, Unpleasant Place

Bella now found out that her comrades shunned her. Her office was suddenly empty, except for snoopers and creditors. She lost her home and moved into a dingy room near her office.

Bella would wake and go to the office early, read the *New York Times* and *New York Law Journal*, and then sit and look out at Bryant Park and the New York Public Library. She had spent many hours in that library as both a student and teacher, hungry for knowledge. Unfortunately, she never really satisfied that hunger, because her reading in later years had been only communist literature and Party "technical material." That was part of the brainwashing. You were consumed and controlled in terms of what you could and could not read.

"There is no censorship of reading so close and so comprehensive as that of the Party," said Bella. "I had often seen leaders pull books from shelves in homes and warn members to destroy them."[110]

For all their claims of open-mindedness, and denunciations of fascist book-burners and narrow-minded "reactionaries," communists were completely closed-minded to viewpoints they disagreed with. They shunned those viewpoints, condemning them as stupid, even "superstitious" when religion was involved.

Ironically, that was where Bella turned. She had no desire to read as she had in the past, with one exception: "The one book I did open was the New Testament, which I had never stopped reading even in my days of starkest Party delusion."[111]

She stayed late in her office because there was no place to go other than her room, "a dark, unpleasant place, with the odor of a second-class hotel. I still remember the misery and darkness of the first Christmas alone."[112]

She stayed in her room all day that Christmas and the New Year that followed, when she listened with utter despair to the gaiety and noise from Times Square and the ringing bells of the churches. More than once, she thought of leaving New York and losing herself in the anonymity of a strange town. But she did not go. Something in her struggled against the wave of nihilism engulfing her. There was also something stubborn in her that told her she "must see it through."[113]

Slowly but surely, a sense of purpose called. She was asked by the *New York Post* to write a series of articles on why she had broken with the Communist Party. The editors made her a generous offer. She agreed, but when the drafts were finished, she read them over and decided not to have them published. She crafted an excuse for refusing the offer.[114]

Her discouragement came close to despair: "More than once," she recounted, "I wondered why I should go on living." She had no drive to make money, and when she did, she either paid creditors or gave it away, paying those who pressed her the hardest.[115]

By late 1949, her life had become monotonous. She observed several other Party acquaintances who had also been "displaced" and were struggling to find their way "back to the world of reality." One was in psychoanalysis and several were drinking themselves into oblivion. She went to visit her brothers and sisters but returned "more desolate than ever. I had lost my family; there was no returning."[116]

She walked along Sixth Avenue and Forty-Second Street and began to familiarize herself with all the characters there: petty thieves, prostitutes, and pickpockets.

Bella Dodd had come to a dark place.

And yet, Bella's life—before communism—had not always been full of such evil and dreariness. Her early life once had been very different.

CHAPTER 2

EARLY LIFE AND FIRST EXPOSURE TO UTOPIA

The beginning of Bella's life was sweet and simple, a total contrast to her existence as a Communist Party leader and the chaotic world she adopted as a radical. Born in 1904 on a farm in the quiet village of Picerno, Italy, you could say her early life was a kind of utopia—very unlike the Proletarian atheistic "utopia" aspired to by her Marxist friends in America decades later. That false utopia was full of hate; her years in Italy were full of happiness.

Bella's mother and father had unique backgrounds. Prior to meeting Bella's father, her mother, Teresa Marsica, previously had been left a widow when the youngest of her nine children was still a baby. With the help of the older eight children, she managed to run the family farm in the village of Potenza. Arriving soon in Potenza was a man named Rocco Visono, who came from a nearby village called Lugano. "If he had not come to Potenza," said Bella, "no doubt she would have remained there the rest of her life. But Rocco fell in love with Teresa Marsica who, despite her nine children and a life of work, was still attractive, with bright, dark eyes and lively ways."[117]

Rocco had actually come to visit his sister, who was married to a local government official. He first met the widowed Teresa in the nearby village of Picerno. He was a stonemason by trade. He and Teresa kindled a romance, and he found work in Potenza. She knew that he planned to leave Italy for New York, which gave her pause. That was not part of her plans. He waited while she made up her mind.

Like many Italians, Bella's father convinced his fiancée to set out for America. There, he and she and her nine children could find freedom and a chance to get rich. Rocco would take her three older sons to the United States until she joined them. Such an initial period of separation was common for Italian immigrants of that era.

So, in the spring of 1900, Rocco set out with the boys, traveling from Picerno to Naples. He and the boys boarded the *Augusta Victoria* for the ten-day journey to America. Teresa followed, probably in 1902, with her six younger children.

Bella, proud of her Italian ancestry, said her family came to America "for a crust of bread. They were hungry. They were part of the people who didn't have the advantages."[118] So many thousands of Italians left their beautiful country, with its traditions, its rolling hills, its food, its wine, its mirth, for an America that simply offered economic opportunities that the old country could not provide. Bella's parents were among them.

They landed in New York. After marrying Rocco in Saint Lucy's Church in East Harlem, Teresa made a return trip to Italy. It was there that she discovered that she was pregnant with Bella. Teresa delivered Bella there, in Picerno, in October 1904. The baby girl was baptized Maria Assunta Isabella Visono.

To say that Bella received a blessed name is an understatement. It carried much meaning. In Italian, "Assunta" means "Assumed," and is often coupled with the word "Madre." "Assunta Madre" means Assumed Mother, referring to the assumption of Mary, the mother of Jesus. Bella's mother made sure no one missed the point. With the name "Maria Assunta," Bella's name bore the title "Assumed Mother Mary." With such a name, Bella had a special start in life. The Blessed Mother was always part of her and her journey. It would seem hard to steer wrong.

Bella initially was left in Italy with foster parents, Taddeo and Mamarella, until her mother returned for her in 1909. Bella's description of her early upbringing in Picerno is sensitive and warm, with

Mamarella and Taddeo, a simple shepherd from Avialano, providing loving care. She remembered "the table drawn for supper, I in Taddeo's arms, his big shepherd's coat around me." He used to call Bella "carina," which in Italian is the feminine for "pretty."[119] Added atop "Bella," which means "beautiful," the little girl had wonderful names—Bella, carina, Assunta, Maria. Again, what could go ever go wrong?

Bella grew to love Taddeo especially, telling her mother she loved him better than anyone in the world. She remembered nights with the family sleeping in the open air in the hills while Taddeo watched the sheep. It was heavenly, and a stark contrast to the life she would later adopt.[120]

Bella's account of leaving Taddeo at age five to come to America is heartbreaking. "I don't want to go," she cried in panic. "I won't go, I won't!" He held her until she stopped sobbing and then he said, "Now I must really go. *Addio, carina*," and he handed her over to Mamarella and hurried from the house. Bella struggled free and ran after him, with her dress blowing in the wind on a bitterly cold day, wearing no shawl. She kept calling, "Taddeo! Taddeo!" She ran down the icy street until she came to the *piazza* and could see Taddeo and his fellow shepherd Filippi driving the sheep ahead of them. She fell in the snow, laid there, and wept.[121]

There, Mamarella picked her up and put her between hot blankets until she warmed up and fell asleep. The next day, she was dressed in her special red confirmation dress which was to have been saved to wear on the feast of the Blessed Virgin and *carnevale*. She was taken to the railroad station in Potenza, where Mamarella put her on the train and kissed her goodbye. "I could not cry for all the feeling was drained from me," recalled Bella in her memoirs, as if it were yesterday and the wounds still fresh. "Then I was alone on a train with strangers and on my way to Naples where my mother was to meet me."[122]

Looking out the train window at the changing landscape, she saw no more snow and mountains, only grass and plains, with scattered olive trees. She saw a flock of white sheep with a shepherd and thought of Taddeo, who was now forever far behind. "I was alone," she lamented. "I had left everything I knew and was going into the unknown."[123]

The little girl was frightened by what she saw in Naples, with its beggars and dirty children in the streets and noise and confusion. In her tiny village, the people were likewise poor, but they were clean and proud. She was glad when she set sail for America the next day.[124]

Though her father said the five-year delay was because there had been a terrible economic depression at the time and he could not raise enough money for Teresa's return, Bella later learned that her mother had hoped to persuade Rocco and the children to return to Italy. But he was settled in America and was staying put. It was 1909. Her mother returned to Italy, picked up Bella, then left for the United States, where the precocious five-year-old met her father, sisters, and brothers for the first time.

New Life in a New World

Little Bella, ready to seize life, spoke no English when she arrived. But her seventeen-year-old sister, Katie, took charge of her and, deciding Bella was smart, told the school she was born in 1902 instead of 1904, making her eligible for the second grade instead of the first. Bella loved her "new" family, especially Katie, and her foster family in Italy gradually receded from her mind. In four months, Bella spoke English and attended Public School Number One in East Harlem, formerly a charity school, and one of the last "soup schools."[125]

When she was ready for third grade, the family moved out of East Harlem to Castle Hill in the Bronx. Her mother, raised on a farm in Italy, had at last convinced her father that she could no longer bear to live a cluttered life in tenements. They moved several times. In the process, her entrepreneurial father established a successful grocery business, and then several years later, her mother took over a large house with tillable acreage near Castle Hill. "There were sixty-four acres of land and a big rambling house," recalled Bella fondly. "Mother had coveted this farm before we went to live on it." It was the property of two elderly women named Mattie and Sadie Munn, who lived nearby.

Teresa cared for Sadie, an invalid who grew to depend on her, and eventually the ladies left the house to her upon their deaths. Bella spent the rest of her childhood there. The land provided fresh produce for the family with enough left over for Rocco's store and some for the Washington Market in the Bronx. There was little money, but Teresa was creative and made ends meet, even "stretching snow" for a special dessert mixed with sugar and coffee.

At school, Bella was a brilliant student and a born leader. Reacting to "taunts of children in the community who were running into contact with a foreign-born child" for the first time, she plunged herself "into schoolwork with an unconscious determination to achieve superiority in the classroom."[126]

Bella's family members still considered themselves Catholic, but they no longer practiced their faith and likely received little catechesis. Although her home had no modern furniture, "we had a crucifix and pictures of St. Joseph and the Blessed Mother in our bedrooms."[127] Her mother burned votive candles in front of a statue of Our Lady, but the children thought these were symbols of their Italian past, and they wanted to be Americans.

This left a void in Maria Assunta Isabella, who had been religious as a young child in her days with Taddeo and Mamarella. "My mother, either because she didn't speak English, or because she didn't have the proper clothes or what not, stopped attending her church."[128] Bella insisted, however, that her mother's conduct was that of a "Christian woman and she sent her children to church."[129]

Later, Bella stated that the "deepest impressions made upon me by men and women in my school days were made by those who in their limited way tried to remind us of the real purpose of our lives." She remembered fondly "the dearly loved school principal" who insisted on opening every day by reading the Bible, "regardless of the indignation of some of the teachers and the indifference of many of the pupils."[130]

It was an indignation toward the Bible that she would later see at an entirely new level of vituperation among her comrades.

1917–1920: Key Moments in the Bronx—and in Portugal

Proud of how easily she went through the grades, Bella was anxious to start high school in 1916. All was going so well, until a terrible accident.

Traveling home one day, Bella caught her left foot in the trolley. Wedged under the wheel, it was crushed, requiring amputation. After spending nearly a year recovering in the hospital, she left for home, requiring a prosthesis for her foot. Her mother nursed her back to health on the family farm and brought her books from the local library. During this time, her mother instilled in Bella the belief that she could accomplish anything she set her heart on, despite her physical limitations, a mindset that would play a significant role in Bella's later struggles.

Armed with crutches, the now thirteen-year-old Bella entered Evander Childs High School in the Bronx, inauspiciously in the year 1917, the year of the Bolshevik revolution in Russia. It was also the year when notable events took place in Fatima, a small hamlet in Portugal, between May and October 1917.

In Fatima, three shepherd children claimed to receive apparitions of the Virgin Mary. The apparitions culminated in the world's most sensational miracle on October 13, witnessed by approximately seventy thousand people. A skeptical editor, Avelino de Almeida, from *O Seculo*, an anticlerical paper in Portugal, made the journey to the tiny village simply to record and denounce and make fun of what he thought were fake events. He was shocked at what happened. He witnessed a miracle. He immediately published an article the following day, headlined:

ASTOUNDING THINGS!
HOW THE MIDDAY SUN DANCED AT FATIMA

The apparitions of the Virgin – What the sign from heaven consisted of – Many thousands of people affirm a miracle occurred – War and peace

This hardened cynic had trekked to Fatima with the intent of mocking the wild expectations of the *silly and stupidly superstitious-minded*. His atheist readers were ready for a good laugh in the newspaper. Instead, they were taken aback by what Almeida reported to them:

> From the road where the wagons were gathered and where stood thousands of people who did not have the courage to traverse the terrain made muddy by the rain, I saw an immense crowd turn toward the sun which appeared at its zenith cleared through the clouds. It seemed like a disc of silver, and it was possible to fix one's gaze upon it without problems. It did not burn the eyes or blind them, as if there had been an eclipse. Then there was heard a loud cry, and the people nearby began to shout: "Miracle! Miracle! Marvel! Marvel!" Before my eyes, ecstatic people were amazed . . . as the sun shook, performing strange and abrupt movements beyond all the laws of physics.[131]

It would thereafter be known as the Miracle at Fatima.

In one of the messages at Fatima, the Blessed Mother asked the three little shepherds, Lucia, Jacinta, and Francisco, to pray and do penance. Otherwise, Russia would "spread her errors throughout the world, causing wars and persecutions of the Church."[132] Fatima scholars and Church officials came to understand the "errors" to be those of communism.[133]

In another city, on the very day as the Miracle of the Sun, a significant and related event allegedly occurred. Fulton Sheen told the story:

Maria Alexandrovich was teaching religion to a group of 200 children in Moscow, in the Church of the Iberian Virgin. Suddenly, numerous men on horses entered the front door and came riding through the middle aisle. Jumping off their horses, they began to destroy the communion rail and the altar and smashed statues as the children and Maria watched in horror. Unpredictably, those men then turned their rage on the children, beat them, and murdered several. Maria, in utter loss and fear, ran out of the church screaming. She knew of an imminent communist revolution but was completely unprepared for this sort of violence.

Maria went out to one of the revolutionaries with tears in her eyes, and screamed: "I was teaching the catechism to my children and men came in and killed some of them!" That revolutionary was Lenin who said: "I know it. I sent them."[134]

Sheen shared this story as a preamble to the communist overthrow of the Russian government, which indeed transpired within thirteen days of the Miracle of the Sun. By October 26, 1917, Bolshevism was seizing Russia. Everyone would suffer, especially the religious.

When these horrible events enflamed Russia, Bella Dodd was a thirteen-year-old girl living a happy life in a new country, a nation that loved freedom, including religious freedom, and whose leaders would never support breaking into a church and destroying it and its precious altar and people. Bella and her family would have been horrified. This would never have happened in Italy either, but it was tragically transpiring in Russia—the start of a long stream of communist "errors" and "persecutions" predicted that very year by Our Lady of Fatima.

Sadly, Bella's new home, notably New York, would become a political-educational corridor of Marxist-Leninist propaganda, as more communists hailed from New York City than any other part of America. As stated in a now-declassified March 2, 1948 FBI report titled "Redirection of Communist Investigations," there were "approximately 30,000" Communist Party members in the New York City area alone,[135] organized and "controlled" through "1,016 clubs." They were spread out among the four boroughs of New York City. Remarkably, the document reported that "almost 50% of the Communist Party members in the United States are located in the New York area."[136] The document further noted that the New York Office of the FBI had accumulated 1,168 Security Index cards on these CPUSA members in New York.

Bella Dodd would become one of them.

For now, however, while these major events were unfolding an entire world away, Bella was a "happy girl" (as she later described herself) who "loved life dearly and found pleasure in many little things." The students at Evander Childs were Scottish, Irish, and German as well as Italians, Russians, and other Europeans. They were from all faiths—Protestant, Catholic, Jewish. All from modest circumstances, no one tried to exploit their differences. In her fourth year of high school (1921), Bella "had a teacher who insisted on taking ten minutes of our time each day to remind us of the existence of God. Only four years after the Bolshevik revolution, he was stopped by a complaint to the principal."[137]

It was clear that the tentacles of Marxism-Leninism were reaching further into New York City, ready one day to seize Bella Dodd.

A Battle for Bella's Mind

In addition to severing her Italian Catholic roots, Bella also lost her Italian cultural roots. Finding a new cultural foundation was difficult.

Fortunately, Bella was talented and accepted as a leader at Evander Childs. Others were attracted to her. Unfortunately, that included budding political radicals.

Sadly, Bella walked into an ideological minefield at Evander Childs. It would become known as a center for communist propaganda. One New York newspaper later reported: "There have been disquieting rumors for a considerable time that the institution is more or less a hot-house of school Communism."[138] A leading communist at the school was Tima Ludins, a teacher at Evander Childs. Bella Dodd knew Ludins (also a graduate of Hunter College). As noted by the lead counsel in Senate hearings in March 1953, Ludins "had been a leader of a move by the Communist Party in late 1949 and early 1950 to organize 500 Communist teachers into an underground, the plan for which had been imported from Europe by the leaders of the Communist Party." Bella said she knew that Ludins was "a Communist member of the coordinating committee of the Communist teachers of New York City. She represented one of the boroughs. . . . She had been assigned actually the chairmanship of this coordinating committee of the Communist teachers of New York."[139]

All of that would come later, the bitter fruits of seeds being sown by communists at Evander Childs when Bella was there as a young girl. This was the corruption to come.

At Evander Childs, a girl from the East Bronx approached Bella about politics, something that interested Bella, and gave her a copy of *The Call*, a leading newspaper of the Socialist Party of America, which ran from 1908 to 1923, precisely the period to catch the eye of the inquisitive high school girl. The full name was *The New York Call*, and it billed itself on the masthead as "A Newspaper for the Workers" and "an organ of international socialism."[140] Excited as she read the articles on "social justice," Bella recalled that "even the poetry on the conditions of the poor, on the inequalities of their lives, held my interest."[141]

For the first time, she felt what she described as "a call, a vocation. Unconsciously I enlisted, even if only emotionally, in the army of those who said they would fight social injustice, and I began to find the language of defiance intoxicating."

A battle for Bella's mind thus began at an impressionable age in her life, with *The Call* being a major instrument in that battle. The publication ran articles celebrating the glorious Bolshevik revolution taking place. She saw headlines like "Bolsheviki Power Comes from Masses" by leading communists like Louis Fraina[142] and John Reed,[143] the latter celebrated with headlines such as "John Reed Named Consul General to NY by Bolsheviki."[144] In short order "John Reed Clubs" sprung up around America as communist clubs to study the gospel of Marx and Engels.

There were other headlines like "Russia Is Free!"[145] To the thinking of *The Call*, Russia was "free" because it had been "liberated" by Marxism-Leninism, by emergent murderous dictators like Lenin, Stalin, and Trotsky. Other articles written at the time by early leaders in the American socialist/communist movement carried titles like "Poverty and Brains Made a Socialist of Rose Pastor Stokes"[146] and "Bolshevism v. Democracy in Education."[147] One wonders if articles like the latter struck the teenage Bella, the future Bolshevik educator.

The magazine advertised meetings against the wartime draft and publicized information on the labor movement. Other contributors to the publication included Elizabeth Gurley Flynn, Margaret Sanger (founder of Planned Parenthood), Eugene Debs, and Agnes Smedley.[148] The newspaper was a who's who of American left-wing radicals.

The *New York Call* was pivotal in shaping Bella's views and instilling in her an interest in fighting for "social justice," something that she would retain throughout her life.[149] Reinforcing the message of *The Call* was the political atmosphere at Evander Childs, which was decidedly to the left. Politics was beginning to take the place of religion. Was it becoming her religion?

Speaking of her now fading Catholic religion, Bella wrote that during high school, the only religious exposure she had was through her gym teacher, who reminded her that she had been born a Catholic and invited her to meetings of a girls' club at the Cenacle of St. Regis on Riverside Drive in Manhattan. There they had spiritual readings, sewed clothes for the poor, and said prayers with Benediction. Later, she said the hymn "Tantum Ergo," sung at Benediction, was to haunt her for a long time. She admitted that she "already had an encrusted pride" in her own intellect and rejected what she felt was "unscientific." She noted that she had come to reflect the thinking "prevalent in educational circles at that time, about science being opposed to religion."[150]

Bella observed that she had become "a logical product of my environment, my emotions, and my education." Though religiously inclined as a child, a "distorted sort of pride made school seem more important to us than church."[151] Bella described the evaporation of her religion and how it opened the portal to a darker world:

> Step by step, I retreated from God and went forth to meet the world, the flesh, and the devil. First, there was a lack of belief in the Sacraments and in the dogmas of the Church. I lost the Blessed Mother in the vulgarity of sophisticated jokes and the divinity of Christ in my worship of the superficialities of science. Then I believed in God merely as a force—as nature—but not as a personal God who cared about me and whom I might offend by my conduct. It was one short step to the prevailing fashion of agnosticism.[152]

Rather than walk with God as a child of light, Bella chose to slow dance with the devil as a child of darkness. This was not good preparation. This was what the little Italian girl's public-school education in America was doing for her. This was a disservice.

Bella's anti-religious attitude continued throughout high school, where she got the idea "that religion was for old ladies who couldn't stand on their own two feet."[153] Later, Bella remarked, "to mention God was to invite sneers or polite rejection and embarrassment. From 1920 on we just didn't talk about God."[154]

During high school, Bella became conscious of the secular educational principles that were "underlying the curriculum." There was a "great deal of emphasis" on the development of sound mind and body, and the development of an "open mind." She became a "passionate advocate of the 'open mind.' Indeed I would constantly state that the mind 'must be open and let'—like an empty apartment."[155] She said the books that she and her peers read during this period, "both in the schools and outside the schools, left us with no belief in God, in patriotism, or in goodness. Love of God was for the Babbitts, some love of country was 'spread-eagle jingoism' and 'dollar diplomacy.'" As for goodness, it was "just plain dull."[156]

At Evander Childs High School, Bella earned good grades in English, history, and science and was awarded a state scholarship. When graduating, she clutched her diploma and her prize copies of Shelley and Keats. But her chief prize, the one she treasured most, was being chosen as the "most popular girl" in her class.[157]

But what had this popular, precocious girl really been prepared for? What had her education given her? In many ways, she had been steadily indoctrinated, primed and readied to deepen her dedication to socialism and Marx and Lenin instead of deepening her devotion to Catholicism and Christ and Mary.

What awaited her next in her "education?"

CHAPTER 3

HUNTER COLLEGE—
EDUCATION FOR THE
REVOLUTION (1921–25)

In 1921, Bella entered Hunter College, a public city college in New York, one of the largest colleges for women in the United States at that time. It was founded in 1870 by Irish immigrant Thomas Hunter, who served as president of the school during its first thirty-seven years. Hunter founded it originally as a women's college for training teachers (men were not admitted until 1946, after World War II), which made it an ideal choice for Bella.

The college, whose faculty and students fancied themselves as champions of the Proletariat, is located on the extremely expensive Upper East Side of New York, gracing East Sixty-Eighth Street, Lexington Avenue, and the posh commercial district of Park Avenue, lined with America's top high-end fashion stores. The official address is 695 Park Avenue, a wealthy section of the city filled with multi-million-dollar brownstone buildings—not exactly the heart of the downtrodden suffering poor and working class. Among the genteel accommodations adorning Hunter is a luxurious historic townhouse formerly owned and dedicated by Franklin and Eleanor Roosevelt. It was here, far removed from what Marx sneeringly called the "*lumpenproletariat*," that limousine liberals, champagne socialists, and mansion Marxists gathered to bemoan the plight of the toiling masses they purported to represent. It was here that New York's pampered professoriate and elite educated classes eagerly awaited idealistic students like Bella to indoctrinate about the evils of private property.

It was here, too, that one such brownstone Bolshevik welcomed Bella with open arms. It was at Hunter that an enthusiastic member of the Communist Party took an immediate interest in Bella Dodd. Her name was Sarah Parks.

A Bella Mentor: Sarah Parks

The influence on Bella by English professor Sarah Parks was significant. Bella met her on campus right away, in her freshman year, as a student in one of her courses. Thereafter, in the years ahead, she often talked with her, both at the college and at Parks's home. "She invited some of us to her apartment," recalled Bella, "and we sought her advice as if she were a kind of unofficial dean." Bella said that "so many of us wanted to consult her. She was an important factor in preparing us to accept a materialist philosophy by mercilessly deriding what she called 'dry rot' of existing society. . . . She questioned existing patterns of moral behavior and diverted some of us into a blind alley by her pragmatic approach to moral problems."[158]

Parks had an open slate with Bella from her freshman year. Bella's first course in English literature was taught by comrade Parks, who provided less a course on English literature than the literature of revolution. Said Bella: "My first teacher in English literature was a woman by the name of Sarah Parks. A wonderful human being who had become a communist. It was Sarah Parks who introduced me to the literature on revolution. She was the one who praised and glorified the French Revolution as a method of freeing man from what the communists termed 'the medieval spirit.' What they really meant is from the spirit that has been part of civilization of the Western world for the last 2,000 years."[159]

That was indeed what they meant. Vladimir Lenin had sneered at what he called this "medieval mildew"—that is, religion, Christianity.

Lenin explained how the true revolutionary needed cleansing from this medieval spirit: "The revolutionary proletariat will succeed in making religion a really private affair, so far as the state is concerned. And in this political system, cleansed of medieval mildew, the proletariat will wage a broad and open struggle for the elimination of economic slavery, the true source of the religious humbugging of mankind."[160]

That was how the revolutionaries viewed religion: medieval mildew, Marx's "opiate of the masses," what Lenin called "spiritual booze."

Sharing this condescension, Bella's new English professor was proving herself a good Bolshevik. She was eager to make Bella a good revolutionary as well. That meant trying to purge from Bella's mind any residual respect for the religion of her youth. In her memoirs, Bella shared a painful example of how the heavy-handed Parks sought to expunge these religious sentiments:

> During my first year with her as my teacher I wrote two term themes, one on how to grow roses, the other on monasticism. She gave both good grades, but the one on monasticism bore the ominous little order, "See me." She was too honest not to give a good grade if the work was well done, but she also had to speak her mind on the subject matter. When I came in, she seemed sympathetic and asked how I came to choose such a topic. I tried to tell her about my reading in the medieval history course and how impressed I had been with the selfless men and women of the Middle Ages who served mankind by putting self aside. "And does that seem a normal manifestation of living to you, a seventeen-year-old girl?" she asked scornfully. It was a question I could not answer, and her clever scorn raised doubts in my mind.[161]

For Sarah Parks, monasticism was bad, whereas Bolshevism was good. Parks was showing herself to be an astute follower of Karl Marx in rejecting the monastic selflessness that appealed to Bella. Marx himself was a horribly selfish man, and he despised Christianity's selflessness:

"The social principles of Christianity preach . . . submission, humility," scowled Marx. "The social principles of Christianity are hypocritical."[162] Marx preferred selfishness: "The more of himself that man gives to God," Marx groaned, "the less he has left in himself."[163]

In addition to seeking to purge Bella's respect for religion, Parks also took aim at any respect that Bella might have had for market freedom—the very freedom that had drawn her family to America and allowed her father to build a business and send Bella to a school like Hunter with tuition dollars that paid the salaries of professors like Sarah Parks.

Parks, said Bella, "was the one who began telling me how terrible the American capitalists were." Already indoctrinated with such thinking by *The Call* and her socialist-communist classmates in high school, Bella conceded that she already "agreed with some of these things" that Parks said. The ground had been ploughed. Comrade Parks, a true revolutionary committed to the global cause of Bolshevism, went further, expanding Bella's horizon to the wider world of alleged American exploitation: "She was the one who kept on saying that American leaders were sucking the life blood out of the South Americans, out of the Chinese, out of all the African countries, and so forth and so on. She emphasized all that was wrong with America, never once telling about the blessed things that America does, never once pointing to the great generosity of the American people . . . and the way they go at it by helping others."[164]

For American Bolsheviks, there was nothing good about America, even as they all lived in America and enjoyed its wealth and opportunity, its freedom of enterprise, the freedom of its extraordinary Constitution.

Bella stated that Parks "emphasized all that which was wrong, and being a child with a heart which was big, I fell in with her plans. By the time I was out of Sarah Parks' class, I did not believe in patriotism. I considered myself a citizen of the world."[165] Parks gave Bella some books on the Russian Revolution, comparing it to the French

Revolution, saying the Russian Revolution would do the same for the Russian people. The French Revolution was taught to her as a glorious adventure in which the "archaic and barbaric" was wiped out and new principles of freedom were unleashed.[166] Unlike the erroneous American Revolution, where unalienable rights were mistakenly said to come from God, the enlightened men of the French Revolution knew better: "government was the most important thing and . . . man derived his rights from government."[167] In Bella's description, Parks taught her pupils that the French Revolution "had had a great liberalizing effect on European culture, something which the revolution in Russia would also one day accomplish."[168]

Of course, the French Revolution was a bloody catastrophe, with forty thousand people guillotined in year one alone, as the Jacobins launched their war on religion, beheading nuns, priests, and anyone else in the way of Robespierre's "republic of virtue." But Lenin, not surprisingly, loved it, referring to his Bolsheviks as "glorious Jacobins." American Bolsheviks like Sarah Parks were fully on board.

It was Parks, said Bella, "who had brought to class books on communism and loaned them to those of us who wanted to read them."[169] Parks loaded up Bella and classmates with books on the glories of Bolshevism. "The books she had given me," said Bella, "had quickened my interest in the communist movement. Those books had been in praise of the change in the world brought about by the Russian Revolution."[170]

Parks said, "Here, Bella, you have an active mind. Read this." It was a book about communism, *I Change Worlds: The Remaking of an American*, by Anna Louise Strong, a devout socialist/communist who lived in Russia from 1921 to 1940. Strong was enamored with the Soviet Union, and even more smitten with Chinese communism. The political pilgrim became a close friend of Marxist tyrant Mao Zedong. She settled in Beijing, staying there until her death. Bella somehow found Strong's crazy screed "exciting."[171] No doubt Parks framed it that way for the impressionable eighteen-year-old.

Parks took her wide-eyed freshmen under wing, pushing forward with the aggressive indoctrination of young Bella. They discussed in English literature "the whole question of the new Soviet experiment, and while she didn't say she was for it, she left all the implication, and thereafter a number of us became attached to her and discussed these problems with her."[172]

And so, while the Bolshevik revolution was underway in Russia, tilling up a vast field of slaughter, students in the United States, such as Bella, were targets of Russia's subversion by professors who were effectively Soviet agents, either as communists or fellow travelers. And that was precisely the conclusion of a congressional subcommittee: "World communist leaders have made schools and colleges of the United States a target of infiltration and activity as part of their program to destroy the United States."[173]

By the time Bella left Sarah Parks's class, she had taken a crucial political-psychological step toward communism: "Sarah Parks did to me what communists do to young people throughout the world. They make them unhappy, and dissatisfied, and ashamed of their own country. If their country is strong and powerful like ours is, in a country like the United States, the communists constantly press on the fact that the American government, the American system has been imperialistic. . . . When I left Sarah Parks's class, I regarded myself as a citizen of the world, no longer somebody who had a duty towards the people of my own town, my own city, my own country."[174]

Sarah Parks had a lasting impact. She was clearly a mentor to Bella.

Parks was a graduate of Northwestern University and received her MA from Columbia University, America's worst hotbed of communist influence in higher education. She was active in the National Women's Trade Union League of America, which viewed women workers primarily from the perspective of oppressed workers. Women workers were shoehorned into communists' reinforcement of victim-oppressor status.[175] Parks was in charge of Hunter's Discussion Club and also played a role in the Debating Club.

Regarding the Debating Club, a look into the archives of the *Hunter Bulletin* from this period is revealing. An October 1924 issue described those in charge of the club as feeling "very strongly against the old-fashioned method of debating by which lots are drawn for either of two sides. . . . There is a so-called progressive movement in colleges throughout the world, which attempts to get away from this strict point of view and to encourage debates in which no definite side is taken."[176]

As for the Discussion Club, an April 1924 issue of the *Hunter Bulletin* reports that Sarah Parks addressed the club on "The Significance of Race in the World Today."[177] Parks spoke on the matter of "class collaboration"—not classrooms, but working classes.[178] Few of the underclasswomen, of course, would object to the use of the word "collaboration." It sounded noble to them. The majority who took part in Parks's "discussion" favored making "the present system more perfect through class collaboration, and advocated employees' representation, profit-sharing, arbitration and trade-unionism." The students discussed and debated. The second largest group of debaters advocated collaboration "as a road to socialism," and the third largest group contended that "while capitalism had rendered valuable service to society, it had outlived its use."[179]

Here was a prime example of Marxism in action in the field of education. This was manipulation by a communist teacher further influencing her students with notions of socialism. Bella would both learn this art of manipulation as a student and one day leverage it herself as a professor at Hunter College.

Sarah Parks was grooming Bella well.

Warm, Sincere, Charming—and Brainwashed

New ideas are often accompanied and championed by influential or charismatic people. Bella Dodd was that person. Bella was elected president of her class at Hunter in 1923. Those who remembered her later recalled her warmly.

A former peer of Bella at Hunter, Mildred Garvin, who herself later became a teacher, remembered her as a "very warm-hearted person" who took her under her wing. It was a custom at Hunter for every freshman girl to have a junior big sister. "When I entered college I was told that Bella Dodd was my big sister," said Mildred. "It is a long time since I went to college, but the feeling that I had for Bella Dodd was that she was a warm person who tried to make me feel at home at college."[180]

Bella formed a small group of friends at Hunter. With agnosticism as their religion and pragmatism as their philosophy, they considered themselves the avant-garde of a new culture.[181] After only a year at Hunter, Bella said her thinking had changed. She talked of science and evolution and was skeptical of religious concepts, something she had noted about herself in high school. "I had drifted into an acceptance of the idea that those who believed in a Creator were anti-intellectual, and that belief in an afterlife was unscientific. I was tolerant of all religions."[182]

But what did she really believe?

A sad illustration took place when she was a senior at Hunter. She had a flashback to one Sunday afternoon when she was eighteen. Sitting at her desk, she wrote on a blank sheet of paper, "What I believe." She struggled to find the answer. The sheet remained blank.[183]

Her belief system had been so purged that she was ready to believe anything. The brainwashing was in full force. Her mind had been cleansed of its religious "mildew."

Her intellectual circle was interested in social reform, the equivalent of today's "social justice warriors." At the time, Hunter had many foreign-born students whose parents had taken part in the first Russian Revolution of 1905. Bella later observed that these students grew up hearing their parents discuss socialist-Marxist theories and became "the nucleus of the communist activities to come."[184] They spoke of ending the concentration of wealth in the hands of a few families and of the glories of the Russian Revolution. "Many of the students who came to us were immigrants," said Bella. "Some of them had been active in the Russian revolution of 1905, and some, of course, were already aware of the whole Communist movement in Europe [that] had had some contact with their parents. The parents imported these ideas when they came from Europe, and the children were conditioned already to this approach."[185]

These students had experienced European high culture and were interested in good music and European literature. They had also experienced European left-wing politics. Now, in America, they read left-wing opinion magazines such as *The Nation* and *The New Republic*.[186]

These students had an impact on Bella's American-born friends who were happy and carefree. In a time of flappers and bobbed hair, Bella said her group grew "vocally indignant as we read of fortunes amassed by people whose hardest labor was pulling the ticker tape in a Wall Street office. It was a period of almost ostentatious vulgarity in the city, and our group became almost ascetic to show its scorn of things material."[187] The group was well intentioned and wanted to help build a better future for the poor and troubled of the world but lacked any solid foundation of man's nature and destiny upon which to build it. They possessed feelings and emotions as a basis for judgment, which were easily exploited by both communists and fascists alike.

Amid this very left-wing milieu, there were professors who had not been sucked in, and who tried to break through to Bella. One day, Hunter professor Hannah Egan stopped Bella and asked why she had left the Newman Club. Noting her confusion and concern, Egan said sternly: "Bella Visono, ever since you were elected to Student Council and became popular, you have been heading straight for hell."[188] Flabbergasted at the time, Bella tried to throw off what the professor was "trying to load on me." Later, however, Bella conceded, "Although I was disturbed by her goading, I did nothing about it, for the poison was already working within me."[189] She reassured herself that she did not need the old-fashioned creed, since she was a follower of science and was going to spend her life serving her fellow man.[190] Her new creed was the creed of fellowship, and so she rejected the "opium of the people."

Bella was drawn to the revolution. Her life was empty of religion, and her family no longer practiced the faith. Rather than leaving this emptiness, she became anti-religious. That blank piece of paper spoke volumes.

Though professor Egan noticed Bella's downward spiral, Bella turned elsewhere to other professors, like Sarah Parks. To someone like Bella, Sarah Parks was the real thing, a member of the Communist Party, and she would follow her. This was a turning point, and the Communist Party would soon fill up that empty paper she had been staring at.

Bella said Sarah Parks was important in preparing the students to accept a materialistic philosophy, the heart of Marxism. She pulled in those "who were already so emptied of convictions that they believed in nothing. These could only turn their steps toward the great delusion of our time, the Marxist socialist philosophy of Karl Marx."[191]

It was a utopia the youngsters would need to learn did not really exist.

Seeking Power and "Any Standard of Right and Wrong"

Bella's interest in social reform turned into a drive for power. This change can be seen in her ambition for leadership in student government at Hunter. She even called herself a politician.

In 1924, Bella attended an Intercollegiate Political Conference at Vassar College. The conference organizers made the students feel at home, and their time in the dormitories was filled with various talks and an invigorating exchange of ideas. They discussed the abolition of sororities, which they considered a social problem; the value of an honor system under student supervision; and whether punishment for crime should be treated as a penalty or deterrent. They also discussed the presidential election that year, which was a dominant issue at Vassar. The *Vassar Miscellany* said the school's healthy interest in the presidential campaign of 1924 was "demonstrated by carrying the arguments of each of the presidential candidates including the Republicans, the Democrats, and the Progressives."[192] It carried a camouflaged description of Norman Thomas, the perennial socialist candidate for president, writing that his party was going to "establish 'industrial democracy,' and get rid of the tyranny of profit over use."[193]

Bella took some of the ideas discussed at Vassar and led a movement to establish the honor system at Hunter. She conducted the first straw poll for the presidential elections and insisted on a series of lectures on social hygiene.[194] Supported by a group of school politicians, she later recalled that this incident exhilarated her by "the power it gave."[195] Recounting that political high, Bella once described one of the chief motivations for her subsequent work for the Communist Party and for many others with whom she worked—namely, raw personal power: "At first, I joined the movement out of a will to goodness. . . . There are millions of human beings throughout this world who are joining the communist movement out of a will to goodness, who will make very bad mistakes. . . . However, those who remain in the Communist Party, like myself, who joined out of a will to goodness, actually stay because it gave us a sense of power. As time went on, I got more and more power.[196]

By this time, Bella Dodd was a full-blown radical, influenced by teachers and students at Evander Childs and Hunter. She would later characterize herself at this point as a "perfect product of the public schools"—a sponge. "I took in everything, both its good parts and its errors."[197] She was part of an intellectual proletariat at Hunter, where they discussed religion, politics, revolution, sex, philosophy, and religion unguided by "any standard of right and wrong. We talked of a future 'unity of forces of the mind,' a 'new tradition,' a 'new world' which we were going to help build."[198] Reflecting later, Bella said it seemed peculiar that

a philosophy which believes in nothing except that which one can see or feel, and which has enthroned itself as a Messianic ideal dedicated solely to the purely animal well-being of man, should have captivated so many young people. Yet, as I think back, it is not so strange. In our country we have always been proud of the extensive reach of our free public school system, but we now recognize that our children have been deprived of their right to beliefs based upon the accumulated wisdom of the race, which has been gathered over thousands of years. As children we were told that we must make up our own minds about every subject. The result was not independence of thought, but an almost total lack of belief in anything. Into this picture the communists fitted naturally.[199]

And a power-seeking Bella Dodd, with no clear standards of right and wrong, ready to believe in almost anything, was being fitted nicely by communists.

Readied for Revolution

Bella was elected class president as a junior. In remarks she gave to the class at the beginning of the year, she noted that "it was rather nice to be a freshman and felt it was rather a curious experience to be a sophomore but it was great to be a junior."[200] One of her duties was to introduce college officials and alumnae at official college events.[201] By her senior year, 1924–25, she became president of the Student Council.[202]

In all of these efforts, Bella was becoming not just a leader but a master organizer, a skill that would serve her greatly later in organizing for the Communist Party.

Closing the year as president of the Student Council, Bella presided over the Council Day Chapel. There, she discussed the accomplishments of her Student Council. She drew attention to the Student Curriculum Committee, noting that many of the faculty and student body were opposed to it, but arguing that it was nonetheless an advance in self-government. She also discussed the honor system which had been implemented under her watch. Curiously, she concluded that there was "more cheating but not therefore, more dishonesty."[203]

Toward the end of college, Bella's personality was almost completely shaped. Many described her as a warm person and an idealist, a brilliant lady "with a genius mind."[204] She readied to graduate with honors as one of the school's outstanding students. She had a lengthy list of academic accolades, from Phi Beta Kappa to many leadership posts. She graduated from Hunter in 1925, the same year that Whittaker Chambers, another intellectual from New York, joined the Communist Party. Chambers had received his college brainwashing at Columbia University.

Four years at Hunter had completely changed Bella Dodd, as had four years at Columbia for Whittaker Chambers. Vladimir Lenin would not have been surprised. "Give me four years to teach the children," asserted Lenin, "and the seed I have sown shall never be uprooted."[205]

It would take many years to uproot what Bella Dodd had learned at Hunter College. She had been readied for revolution.

CHAPTER 4

INTELLECTUAL INFLUENCES ON BELLA'S PROFESSORS

B ella Dodd's exposure to Marxist socialism at Hunter College with radical professors was not an anomaly. There were significant numbers of socialists and Bolshevik professors active on campuses throughout the United States during this time, influencing many students. The radical turn of the colleges began not in the 1960s, as is commonly believed today, but in the 1920s.

We have seen that Bella was influenced by communism in both high school and college. There is, however, a more fundamental question that should be asked: where did Sarah Parks and other professors learn about Marx? Who influenced the professors who in turn influenced Bella Dodd? How did the idea of utopian states emerge in America when the first Communist Party was not founded in the country until 1919?[206]

There were, in fact, several early socialist-collectivist settlements in the United States long before the 1917 Russian revolution. The outcomes of these ideological colonies, planted in soil at places ranging from New Harmony, Indiana, to Oneida, New York, were disastrous and their ideas rejected. Many of these communities took a keen interest in education. There were also socialist influences from abroad, such as the Fabian Society in England. The two main intellectual streams that influenced Bella's professors were 1) the work of Charles Fourier and Robert Owen, brought to American soil from Europe, and 2) the work of the Fabians from England.

Fourier and Owen and Friends

Robert Owen (Wales, England) and Charles Fourier (France) are important names as they formulated socialist schemes in the early 1800s. From 1824 to 1846, the United States—ironically, an emerging beacon of freedom and liberty, established in 1776 by founding fathers like Madison, Adams, Jefferson, and Washington—became a kind of "theater" for socialist experimentation.[207] Socialists within the United States were pursuing the path of Owen and Fourier.

Owen, a wealthy philanthropist who lost his belief in Christianity, traveled to America in 1824 to invest in an experimental colony, New Harmony, in Indiana. This was to be a utopian society, and Owen twice addressed the US Congress on the subject of the glories of socialism.[208]

Owen, as one historian noted, developed into a "full-fledged communist."[209] Karl Marx himself knew of Owen and praised him in connection to education: "From the factory system budded, as Robert Owen has shown in detail, the germ of the education of the future, an education of the will, in the case of every child over a given age, combine productive labor with instruction and gymnastic, not only as one of the methods of adding to the efficiency of production, but as the only method of producing fully developed human beings."[210]

Owen's ideas of a socialist paradise wormed their way into American public education. Owen outlined a plan for a national system of education based on the philosophy that man is perfectible through the process of education and that man's character is formed by the environment. According to this philosophy, rational education would have to precede a socialist society. There is, in fact, a continuous link between socialism and education in the United States from this period, of which Owen was a crucial thread.

On July 4, 1826, as Americans in their young nation celebrated the fiftieth anniversary of the Declaration of Independence, Robert Owen made his own unique "Declaration of Mental Independence."

The former had acclaimed the unalienable rights of life, liberty, and the pursuit of happiness. To the socialist Owen, the natural and even biblical rights extolled by the founders were nothing to celebrate. Instead, he stood at his ideological colony in New Harmony and denounced what he considered a trinity of monstrous evils: "private property," "absurd and irrational systems of religion," and "marriage combined with some of these irrational systems of religion."[211]

"I now declare to you and to the world," proclaimed Owen, "that man up to this hour has been in all parts of the earth a slave to a trinity of the most monstrous evils that could be combined to inflict mental and physical evil upon the whole race." Yes, these monstrosities were property, religion, marriage—Robert Owen's unholy trinity. The socialist called for no less than a "revolution" to deliver mankind from "this hydra of evils." Of course, American communists a century later would likewise seek a revolution that undermined property, religion, and marriage.[212]

Owen's work was taken up by his son, Robert, and also by Frances Wright, a feminist and education reformer who helped organize the Workingmen's Party in New York in 1829, which called for "educational communism."[213] It is obvious that communists were working within the United States long before the 1917 Russian Revolution.

Later, in 1841, Brook Farm, one of America's most prominent utopian experiments, was established outside Boston. Its purpose was to foster an environment where intellectual and agrarian life would flourish together. John Van der Zaes, a resident, hoped the principles professed by each "would do away with all evil in the world and bring about a return to the Golden Age." During the age of transcendentalism, it attracted Nathaniel Hawthorne, Horace Greeley, Charles Dana (who would have a prominent influence later), and Orestes Brownson, a significant writer and philosopher who was associated with Owen for a brief time, only later to denounce socialism in the harshest terms as a pernicious ideology.[214]

Another notable ideological colony of the period was the commune started in Oneida, New York, by John Humphrey Noyes (1811–86), who dubbed himself a "Bible Communist." The Puritans had booted the Ivy League educated Noyes from New England, where he first ramped up his vision, leading him to relocate. The Oneida experiment actually lasted longer than most communes of the era because economically it found products to produce and sell. But what undermined it were its social values, including its redefinition of marriage. Noyes conjured up a communal arrangement that he called "Complex Marriage," where he married hundreds of his ideological colonists together in collective marriages.[215] Noyes governed a group of some three hundred men and women who divined that monogamy was impure. Many of the younger girls disapproved of his marriage arrangements, especially those with older men.

These were just a few of the dozens of ideological colonies that sprung up on American soil in the nineteenth century. Historian Daniel Flynn called them and their pioneers, residents, and enthusiasts the "Yankee Utopians."[216] They tilled the soil, making it fertile for the next generation of American communists in Bella's day in the early twentieth century, who would hail as their ultimate model the "great experiment" (as Columbia education professor-pioneer John Dewey put it) in Moscow.

There were other powerful intellectual forces at work in America at this time. Among these was Fourierism, a philosophy of social reform originating with French social theorist Charles Fourier (1772–1837). It advocated the transformation of society into self-sufficient, independent "phalanges," and claimed that communism was a remedy for all social ills. This philosophy spread through Albert Brisbane, a native New Yorker who studied under Fourier in France. He translated Fourier's works, publishing *The Social Destiny of Man* in Horace Greeley's *New York Daily Tribune*—the first detailed account in America of Fourier's utopian theories.[217]

Brook Farm, which shortly after its founding began to founder, was transformed into a Fourierist establishment. The philosophy of Fourierism came under heavy criticism, with some of the most insightful critiques originating from Nathaniel Hawthorne, who summarized: "Our feeling was, that Fourier had skipped no fact but one, namely, Life. He treats man as a plastic thing, something that may be put up or down, ripened or retarded, moulded, polished, made into solid, or fluid, or gas, at the will of the leader; or, perhaps, as a vegetable, from which, though now a poor crab, a very good peach can by manure and exposure be in time produced."[218]

The most important critic of the commune experiments was Orestes Brownson, who disapproved of its educational aspect, noting that utopian education promised to cure society's evils: "The age is as mad in its worship of education as it is in its worship of radical or socialistic democracy." He singled out the "enemies of religion" who "seek to control the education of the young who only have to exclude religion from the schools, under the plea of excluding sectarianism."[219] Brownson said of Frances Wright and her friends:

> [They] were the great movers in the scheme of godless education, now the fashion in our country. I knew this remarkable woman well. . . . I was for a brief time in her confidence, and one of those selected to carry into execution her plans. The great object was to get rid of Christianity, and to convert our churches into halls of science. The plan was not to make open attacks on religion, although we might belabor the clergy and bring them into contempt where we could; but to establish a system of state—we said national—schools, from which all religion was to be excluded, in which nothing was to be taught but such knowledge as is verifiable by the sense and to which all parents were to be compelled by law to send their children. Our complete plan was to take the children from their parents at the age of twelve or eighteen months, and to have them nursed, fed, clothed and trained in

these schools at the public expense; but at any rate, we were to have godless schools for all the children of the country, to which the parents would be compelled by law to send them.[220]

Brownson's insight was keen and evidenced throughout the coming decades in the US public school system.[221] Though there was diminished support for Brook Farm after it converted to Fourierism, it still had an influential impact on the United States, chiefly through Horace Mann.[222] Horace Greeley, who founded the *New York Daily Tribune,* was one of the people who pushed Fourierism. Charles Dana, a follower of Robert Owen, was instrumental in turning New Harmony into a communist society. And it was also Dana who visited Marx in England and hired him as European correspondent for the *New York Daily Tribune.* Under its auspices, Marx was kept with pocket change and wrote articles on American slavery, as well as contributing to the *New England Zeitung* in Boston, the *New York Democrat,* and the *National Workingmen's Advocate* in Washington. These articles included subjects such as "Parliamentary Debates—The Clergy and the Struggle for the Ten-Hour Day—Starvation;"[223] "Revolution in China and In Europe;"[224] "On Strikes and the Value of Labor;"[225] and "Trade or Opium?" among many others.[226]

It is crucial to understand that the ideas of Frances Wright and other American socialist utopians regarding public education perfectly accorded with the ideas of Marx and Engels. In their 1848 *Communist Manifesto,* Marx and Engels excoriated the "exploitation" and "home education" of children by their parents. "Do you charge us with wanting to stop the exploitation of children by their parents?" they asked rhetorically. "To this crime we [communists] plead guilty. But, you will say, we destroy the most hallowed of relations, when we replace home education by social."[227] They raged against "the bourgeois claptrap about the family and education" and sniffed at "the hallowed correlation of parent and child," a notion they found "disgusting." The tenth and last point of the crucial ten-point plan in the *Manifesto* called for "Free education for all children in public schools."[228]

Marx and Engels and subsequently Lenin and all communists wanted those children out of the harmful reach of their parents' home education, as well as religious education, which the Bolsheviks immediately banned. They instead pushed and herded children into the public-education collective. American progressives cheered that goal, especially Columbia's John Dewey—whose work, as we shall see, was adored and implemented by the Bolsheviks in establishing the Soviet education system.[229]

And as for Frances Wright and friends' goal of taking children from their parents at the age of twelve or eighteen months to have them nursed, fed, clothed, and trained at public expense, it echoed the goals of Marx and Engels. Their views are most clearly seen in their collaborative works *The Origin of the Family* (1884) and *The German Ideology* (1846). They advocated for a system in which a woman's/wife's private housework would be supplanted by social labor in the communist state. Women would not only be forcibly channeled into factories and onto farms, to work there, but private housework would be nationalized by the state. Housework would become a public industry with communal childcare, cooking, cleaning, and so forth. Children would be raised communally.[230] This dovetailed nicely with their striking goal in the *Manifesto* of "abolition of the family!" Engels wrote with excitement: "With the transfer of the means of production into common ownership, the single family ceases to be the economic unit of society. Private housekeeping is transformed into a social industry. The care and education of the children becomes a public affair; society looks after all children alike."[231]

The nurturing and care and education of children would become a public affair, a social industry.[232] Society would look after all children. The public schools would have a grand function in this brave new world. In America, socialist-collectivist educational "reformers" and progressives were excited about the prospects.

Bella on Bringing in Marx

These were the destructive ideas that Bella Dodd's socialist-Marxist professors had learned, and now in turn inculcated in her and other students. Bella spoke to Marx's early influence in a 1954 speech:

> From 1848 to 1855 was a period in which propaganda was unleashed and unleashed to the intellectuals of Europe and England, but the United States was not to be free of this kind of propaganda. . . . The first measure was to send Karl Marx to the United States. Karl Marx lectured in New York, Philadelphia, and Boston, and wrote a weekly column for the *New York Tribune* from 1852 to 1862, so this disease is not a new disease. You and your fathers may not have been aware of the same, but the plans were already made for taking over the powers of this world and the execution of the plans is now being put into shape.[233]

The United States had early on experienced functioning Marxist parties, such as the Workingmen's Party of the United States, which was organized on July 19–23, 1876, in Philadelphia, and the New York Communist Club, which was set up in 1857. A decade later, in 1868, the New York Communist Club affiliated as "Section 1" of the International Workingmen's Association.[234]

By the early twentieth century, courses were initiated and socialist clubs were formed on elite college campuses. For example, the *Vassar Miscellany* of 1915 (recall that Bella attended a major conference at Vassar) noted that faculty had approved the Student Association's request for a socialist club on campus and the same year published an article, "Socialism in a Nutshell," which claimed that the advocates of socialism are just beginning to realize that "upon their shoulders rests the tremendous responsibility of upholding the principle of universal brotherhood."[235] Columbia University listed topics for graduation theses that included the Brook Farm Experiment.[236] Various book reviews and news articles in college newspapers mentioned the commune.

The *Vassar Miscellany* in 1929 carried a column on the publication of Brook Farm letters.[237] Popular leftist publications read by these professors, such as *The Nation*, had long published positive articles on Brook Farm.[238] Thus, Sarah Parks and other faculty members had many opportunities to become familiar with Marxist socialism and these experiments.

In addition, utopian novels such as those by Edward Bellamy, *Looking Backward* and Laurence Gronlund, *The Cooperative Commonwealth*, exercised a strong influence on American socialism.[239] Most of these were available in campus libraries.

The Fabian Influence (1883–Present)

Among these ideas, Fabian socialism played a key ideological influence in the United States, with a special appeal to intellectuals. While appearing less deadly than Marxism and its intellectuals, who talked of revolution and "overthrow" and abolition, Fabian socialism had the veneer of a dazzling new toy, albeit likewise an ugly beast with lethal implications. It had the same goal of building socialism, but its costume was more cunning—a wolf in sheepskin was the Fabians' coat of arms. The Fabian socialists wanted to achieve socialism gradually and by stealth, by deception. Some members of the Communist Party moved seamlessly between the two.

To get an idea of the importance of Fabianism in the United States, the most courageous and famous ex-communist in America, Whittaker Chambers, described his experience with the Fabians:

> The simple fact is that when I took up my little sling and aimed at communism, I also hit something else. What I hit was the forces of that great socialist revolution, which, in the name of liberalism, spasmodically, incompletely, somewhat formlessly, but always in the same direction, has been inching its ice cap over the nation for two decades. . . . No one could have been more dismayed than I at what I had hit, for though I knew it existed, I still

had no adequate idea of its extent, the depth of its penetration or the fierce vindictiveness of its revolutionary temper, which is a reflex of its struggle to keep and advance its political power.[240]

The influence of the Fabians far surpassed their numbers, which were always restricted. The Fabian Society of London was a revolutionary secret society, hiding behind a false front. The Fabians spelled out their goals in an unequivocal pledge signed by candidates prior to admission: "The Fabian Society consists of socialists. It therefore aims at the emancipation of Land and Industrial Capital from individual and class ownership, and the vesting of them in the community for the general benefit. In this way only can the natural and acquired advantages of the country be equitably shared by the whole people."[241]

Thomas Davidson, an American, and E. R. Pease, a British psychic researcher and stockbroker, started the Fabian Society in London in 1883. The Society attracted such illustrious persons as George Bernard Shaw, Sidney Webb,[242] and Joseph Fels.[243] Though it gained a reputation for "respectability," Rose Martin, author of *Fabian Freeway*, concluded that the demise of "Great Britain," which is no longer great or an empire, was in large part due to Fabian Socialism. In 1949, Sir Stafford Cripps, minister of the Crown, announced the necessity of this demise: the "liquidation of the British Empire is essential to Socialism."[244] The Fabians accomplished what no foreign force for a thousand years could achieve—not Phillip's Spain, Napoleon's France, not the Kaiser or Hitler. Where they had failed, said Rose Martin, "a group of home-grown socialists peacefully accomplished [their goal] in approximately three-quarters of a century."[245]

The destructive nature of Fabian socialism was hidden from the British people by the good manners and "humane" reforms of the society's members. Such things veiled their revolutionary purpose and rendered it improbable to all but the initiated. Concealing its will to power behind a series of apparently benign social welfare programs, the society preached the brotherhood of man for the attainment of

purely material ends.[246] Though they preached and practiced socialism, its practitioners "escaped the censure directed at socialists of the
catastrophic school."[247] In 1948, George Bernard Shaw (whose play,
Pygmalion, was the basis for *My Fair Lady*) announced that the Fabian
Society was "still alive and doing its work, which is to rescue socialism
and communism from the barricades." Cunningly, Fabian socialism
represented itself through a series of parliamentary measures as "a constitutional movement."[248]

Were there direct links between the Fabian Society and Karl Marx?
Pease listed the philosophical sources of Fabian socialism: John Stuart
Mill, Henry George, and Karl Marx.[249] Shaw was asked to clarify the
socialism discussed in one of the tracts and remarked: "The answer did
not amount to much either way; for the tract contains nothing that
was not already to be found better stated in the famous *Communist
Manifesto* of Marx and Engels."[250]

In fact, Shaw liked Stalin. He met with him in Moscow in July
1931 during a ten-day pilgrimage to the Soviet Union. He defended
Stalin against the dictator's critics. He even excused Stalin's purges,
making the shocking assertion: "We cannot afford to give ourselves
moral airs when our most enterprising neighbor [the Soviet Union]
. . . humanely and judiciously liquidates a handful of exploiters and
speculators to make the world safe for honest men."[251] This was not
a sarcastic statement by Shaw. He was deadly serious. He praised the
dictator's "utilitarian killing," which he deemed necessary to fulfill the
USSR's "gifted" "economic conscience."[252] He dismissed reports of
famine in the Ukraine as a "lie" and "inflammatory irresponsibility"
and "slander" of Stalin's beneficent Five-Year Plan.[253]

Shaw was hardly alone. A fellow Fabian, H. G. Wells, met with
Stalin in 1934, at the start of the Great Purge. He traveled there with
his girlfriend, Planned Parenthood founder Margaret Sanger (who was
married with children). "I've never met a man more candid, fair, and
honest," marveled Wells after meeting the Soviet mass killer. "Everyone trusts him." Wells had likewise been impressed by Vladimir Lenin,

whom he called a "frank," "refreshing," and "amazing little man," who had "almost persuaded me to share his vision."[254]

Wells's primary vision was Fabian socialism, like Shaw.

Of course, Shaw and Wells were very prominent names among the Fabians, known worldwide for their written works. Less known to the world was the Fabians' dedication to deception. The stained-glass window for the Fabians at the London School of Economics illustrates the deception at the heart of their society. It depicts Sidney Webb and E. R. Pease helping to build the new world, along with a depiction of the society's coat of arms. Beneath the sheepskin, its creed was radical: nothing less than the "reorganization of society" with the extinction of private property and industrial capital from individual and class ownership, redistributing them to the "community." To conceal its philosophy, the society shrewdly decided to leave out the word "socialist" and stick solely with "Fabian."

Fabian Socialism in America

British Fabianism brought its deception to the United States through college campuses, exerting a prominent role in higher education.

A group of intellectuals in the Northeast established American Fabianism,[255] developing a set of techniques tailored to the country's diversity of religions, national origins, and races.[256] The schools were a central part of the techniques developed. It was a prime illustration of what Bella Dodd herself once emphasized—namely, that the "Communist Party acts in different ways in different parts of the world at different times. . . . Everything is going to be done to utilize the schools for convincing the minds of children so they will behave as the conspirators want them to behave."[257]

Bella addressed the subject of Fabian socialism during her talks around the country after she left communism. For example, at an address in Detroit in 1961, Bella was asked: "Is Fabian socialism a forerunner of communism or is it the same thing under a different name?" Her reply was illuminating:

Well now, the question should have been is Fabian socialism a forerunner of communism or an ultimate objective of communism? Because, my dear friends, there are four or five different strands working towards world government. One of them is socialism. One of them is communism. Now there are those who say you may have to have communism first. But ultimately what they want is a Fabian socialist society. It was easy to sell Fabianism in the nineteenth century as a response to the social evils which existed. And many of the Fabians were well-intentioned people and hard-working people. But now the communists live in a collective society for what purpose? So that those on top can have the power over those below. And that therein lies the great difficulty.[258]

At another address in 1954, Bella compared communism and socialism during a question-and-answer period: "Does this mean I am going to oppose every socialist? Well, it means that basically I am opposed to the principles of socialism as I am the principles of communists because they are the same."[259]

The Fabians made initial contacts with the American intellectual community. For example, Beatrice Webb met with the presidents or trustees of several Ivy League schools, including Columbia, Cornell, and Yale. In 1889, Webb's *Socialism in England* was circulated at Harvard and other schools in the United States.

The chief route for the migration of Fabian socialism into America, however, was the Intercollegiate Socialist Society (ISS), founded in New York in 1905.[260] There were Fabian chapters at Harvard, Princeton, New York University, Columbia, the University of Pennsylvania, and other universities. By 1916, the number had grown to approximately seventy colleges and universities, with an estimated membership of eleven thousand, more than two thousand of whom were members of the faculties of leading schools and universities.[261] While the Intercollegiate Socialist Society existed ostensibly to "promote an intelligent interest in socialism among college men and women,"[262] only a few of its hundred or more founding members were primarily involved in college activities.

What, then, was the function of the ISS with reference to its adult founders and to the successive generations of college alumni who remained so firmly attached to it over the years? According to Rose Martin, the true purpose of the ISS officially was disclosed some fifty years later: "By that time a substantial number of its trainees and 'cooperators' had achieved influential posts in education and the U.S. government. Others controlled the expenditure of multi-million-dollar labor union funds. Their combined influence was widespread, and their personal respectability was assured. Only then was it considered safe to admit, in literature designed for student recruitment, that the ISS had actually been founded as an American Fabian Society—a secret society of intellectuals, that would 'provide the leadership for a Fabian Socialist movement devoted to gaining political power in America, directly or indirectly.'"[263]

Like the London Fabian Society, says Martin, "individual members were expected to be politically active in their chosen spheres, while the ISS itself remained aloof from public controversy on electoral and policy matters."[264]

Universities became virtual beachheads for Fabian socialism, penetrating the United States through them—that is, via higher education. Socialism also spread through lectures and exchange groups between the United States and the United Kingdom. The British socialist and Fabian Harold J. Laski, an icon at the London School of Economics, taught at Harvard from 1915 to 1919.[265]

There is no record of Bella Dodd being a member of ISS. Her attendance, however, at Columbia University (which had an ISS unit) coincides with ISS ideas which were then permeating the campus like osmosis through articles in campus newspapers.[266] ISS and other socialist groups were active on campuses during the years that Bella's professors attended. Sarah Parks, for example, received her BA from

Northwestern University in 1907, which had an ISS chapter, and then received her MA from Columbia in 1910, which also had a branch of the ISS as early as 1905–6.

Notably, the League for Industrial Democracy (LID), from which the 1960s student-radical group Students for a Democratic Society (SDS) eventually sprung up, was developed out of ISS. In 1921, ISS recognized that the term "socialism" had become extremely unpopular in the United States after the violent Russian revolution. Shrewdly, it dropped "socialist" from its name, as Shaw himself had recommended.[267] Suddenly, the words "socialism" and "communism" were nowhere to be found in its platform and mission statement. So, without changing its objective—to promote socialism—the society changed its name to the League for Industrial Democracy. And despite the name change, the British Fabians maintained an informal association with US socialists, as indicated in the correspondence of Harry Laidler, the first paid organizer and officer of the ISS.

Bella Dodd later mentioned the LID suddenly springing up at Hunter in 1938 after President Franklin Roosevelt formally extended US diplomatic recognition to Bolshevik Russia.[268] The organization brandished its slogan of "Production for Use and Not for Profit."[269] It was, as noted by one history of the organization, "officially anti-capitalist, condemned the profit system, and proposed that the community be the 'instrument and arbiter of social change.'"[270]

These organizations and individuals were just some of the influences that left-wing intellectuals inhaled on college campuses in Bella's day. They were operating during the time when the best students of Marx—Lenin and Stalin—violently destroyed a (religious) country to build the first socialist state in Russia. Until then, such utopian pipedreams had remained buried as theory on the pages of textbooks. Now, the dreams were reality.

At Hunter College in Bella's time, professors like Sarah Parks were leading purveyors of these new ideological creeds. To Bella and other students, Parks was living proof that socialism was no longer theory but a new reality. Bella was precisely the type of middle-class intellectual whom Whittaker Chambers mentioned as being prone to Marxism-Leninism: those who feel a natural concern, "one might almost say a Christian concern," for underprivileged people.[271]

But sadly, they expressed their concern by adopting an ideology that was anti-Christian, violent, and dangerous.

CHAPTER 5

COLUMBIA UNIVERSITY PROGRESSIVE EDUCATION— TOOL FOR THE REVOLUTION

Columbia University, the Ivy League school in New York City, was a hotbed for these ideologies. Young students as diverse as Whittaker Chambers and Thomas Merton entered its confines wide-eyed and innocent, only to leave the place as communists.[272] "I can say," acknowledged Merton, "that there were, at that time, quite a few communists or communist sympathizers among the undergraduates."[273]

Bella Dodd would later attest to that as well. She, too, was headed to Columbia, and at the worst of times.

As Bella began her graduate studies at Columbia in 1925, she discovered other intellectual influences around her. Among the most important, in terms of her profession, were the progressive educators on campus. Many of these progressive instructors were promoting socialism in the United States through education. Leading them was Dr. John Dewey.

Dewey had an enormous impact at both Columbia and well beyond the campus in the larger world of public education. As to his influence at Columbia, Merton wrote with sarcasm: "Poor Columbia! It was founded by sincere Protestants as a college predominantly religious. The only thing that remains of that is the university motto: *In lumine tuo videbimus lumen*—one of the deepest and most beautiful lines of the psalms. 'In Thy light, we shall see light.'. . . . It might profitably be changed to: *In lumine Randall videbimus Dewey*."[274]

For many at Columbia, Dewey was a guiding light in their new moral-spiritual universe, especially those committed to a revolution in education.

Dewey's philosophy was that public schools' ultimate social objective was the transformation of society through the creation of a mass of new "socially-minded" individuals.[275] A child would, little by little, come into an understanding and "consuming zeal of social concern."[276]

Professor Dewey's mark on education over the past one hundred years is difficult to overstate, especially through the instruction and training of college students to become public-school teachers. He is the father of modern public education, and no less than honorary president for life of the National Education Association. In fact, Dewey is often claimed as "father" of a number of concepts, some of which overlap or are confused, from "pragmatism" to "experimentalism." We see the spirit of Dewey in the constant experimentation that prevails in the classroom, the never-ending, always-changing search for new methods, programs, terms, fads and fashion, and "research" into "improving" education.

Not only does such thinking maintain a hold on educators, but so does the sharp secularism and post-modernism. Dewey favored that too; when it came to rampant repudiation of moral absolutes in public schools, Dewey was ahead of his time. Most telling and lasting for Dewey was the role of "environing forces." He trumpeted the formative role of the "collective," the "public," and "socialization." The individual student is subsumed by the "collective."

This Deweyan view conformed to his broader vision for society and the world. Reality itself, the environment itself, *progress* itself, is always moving onward, never satisfied at its present state. A process of constant, ongoing flux and "reform" is always at hand. This is the essence of the political progressive, as is the belief in the possibility of utopia. John Dewey even penned a book called *Schools of Utopia*. He said that the "most utopian thing in Utopia is that there are no schools at all. Education is carried on without anything of the nature of schools."[277]

In all, Dewey's specter thrives. Especially significant in light of today's politics and education, Dewey judged that pursuing change through politics was frustratingly slow; doing so via education could be much quicker. This was a central theme of his best-known work, *Democracy and Education* (1916). The schoolhouse could be more efficacious than houses of legislatures. Education was a vehicle for revolution.

The Progressive Education Association

Bella Dodd quickly discovered the John Dewey Society and the Progressive Education Association while at Columbia, where professors from the Teachers College led the movement for radicalism in education. John Dewey gathered similarly "open minded" progressives around him, including George Counts, Harold Ruggs, and William H. Kilpatrick. Calling themselves the "Frontier Thinkers," they became some of the most prominent people in US education circles.[278] Dewey was, in turn, influenced by Horace Mann, whom he viewed as the patron saint of progressive education.

A graduate of Harvard, Mann is likewise considered a "father" of the American public education system and a contemporary of the socialist utopians of New Harmony and Brook Farm. He became the most influential American activist for compulsory state-funded public schools. He believed that religion, particularly Christianity, was harmful to education and fought to create a system of secular public schools that would be administered, staffed, and funded exclusively by the state. He saw public schools not only as a public good but as the most effective means of establishing an egalitarian, democratic utopia here on earth. He enthused: "The common [public] school is the greatest discovery ever made by man. . . . Let the common school be expanded to its capabilities, let it be worked with efficiency of which it is susceptible, and nine-tenths of the crimes in the penal code would become obsolete; the long catalogue of human ills would be abridged; man would walk more safely by day; every pillow would be more inviolate by night; property, life, and character held by a stronger tenure; all rational hopes regarding the future brightened."[279]

It was the idealism of utopia yet again. Mann was secretary of the Massachusetts Board of Education and had a profound effect on education, guiding it into a statist philosophy. He criticized the traditional alphabetic teaching method and endorsed the experimental. He and his well-connected colleagues established the first state-owned and operated teacher-training school at Lexington, Massachusetts, and looked on children as "hostages to our cause."[280]

In addition to being influenced by Horace Mann, John Dewey was taught by G. Stanley Hall, who studied at the University of Berlin, and who readily admitted that he "half-accepted" what he understood of Karl Marx.[281] Tracing back, Hall was inspired by Wilhelm Wundt, spending time in Wundt's laboratory in Leipzig, Germany. Dewey used the work developed by Wundt and his animal psychology, and believed that through a "stimulus-response approach" (like Pavlov, if not like lab rats), students could be conditioned for an altogether new "social order."[282] Wundt, the founder of experimental psychology in Germany, laid the basis for much of the contemporary mind-bending programs found in American public schools today. He believed that a thing made sense and was worth pursuing if it could be measured, quantified, and scientifically demonstrated.

Wilhelm Wundt was the source of dozens of American PhDs who came back from Leipzig. Daniel Coit Gilman was a member of the Skull and Bones secret society at Yale University and the first president of Johns Hopkins University, the first institution of higher learning in the United States built on the German model. G. Stanley Hall, who was the first American to study in the laboratory of Wilhelm Wundt, was appointed professor under Gilman.[283] Educators in America wedded education and psychology, established laboratories, and generated hundreds of PhDs to teach the new educational conditioning system to students, including John Dewey. From this point, it was a short step to a "new education." The new education became the process of exposing the student to "meaningful" experiences (stimuli) so as to ensure desired reactions.[284]

Among the philosophers who influenced Dewey was George Sylvester Morris—a Hegelian philosopher who became his mentor, and through whom Dewey discovered Hegel.[285] Morris sought a method of combining empiricism with idealism. This had an impact on Dewey, who adopted the Hegelianism of Morris.[286] Here was a direct intellectual line from Hegel to Karl Marx to Morris to Dewey. That line was clear. Sidney Hook, the famous socialist-atheist who was very close to Dewey and later became an ardent anti-communist, put it this way: "There was a strong philosophical kinship between Karl Marx and John Dewey."[287]

The philosophy of Dewey gave education a social mission. Rejecting competition, he thought the classrooms with "their moveable chairs helped to make each period a social occasion. In all classes teachers and children started off the day's work with a face-to-face discussion of cooperative plans for individual and group activity." And, expressing a pantheistic secular humanism, he said, "The things in civilization we most prize are not ourselves. They exist by grace of the doings and sufferings of the continuous human community. . . . Here are all the elements for a religious faith that shall not be confined to sect, class, or race."[288]

Dewey's influence can be seen in the National Education Association's (NEA) startling 1913 manifesto regarding the teaching of history, printed by the US Bureau of Education: "High school teachers of social studies have the best opportunity to influence one and one third million high school pupils to acquire the social spirit. The time formerly spent in the effort to understand the process of passing a law under the President's veto is now to be more preferably used in the observation of vocational resources of the community. The committee recommends that social studies in the high school shall include community health, housing, homes, human rights versus property rights, impulsive action of mobs, the selfish conservatism of traditions and public utilities."[289]

In *Democracy and Education*, Dewey stated that the aim of progressive education is to "take part in correcting unfair privilege and unfair deprivation, not to perpetuate them."[290] He also described the individual in a progressive society: "The emancipated individual was to become the organ and agent of a comprehensive and progressive society."[291]

Some claimed that Dewey "supplied the intellectual weapons for a 'non-totalitarian Marxism.'"[292] There was no question that he favored Marxism. John Dewey had long been pro-communist, albeit later conflicted, especially after he eventually split with the Soviet leadership in the late 1930s as Stalin and Trotsky split, even as he had been a great enthusiast for the Bolshevik regime early on (as we shall see below).[293] In April 1934, he penned an essay titled "Why I Am Not a Communist," published in *Modern Monthly*, which was reprinted (that same year) in hardcover in a printed symposium edited by Sidney Hook.[294] Dewey actually wrote the piece in 1933, and he said it was the culmination of "reservations" that had begun to swirl in his mind back in 1931. It was clear from the essay, however, that Dewey's problems were not so much with "communism" as a philosophy as much as official "Communism" as it was being pursued by communist regimes at the time—a reference to Soviet Russia. As he put it, he objected to "Communism, official Communism, spelt with a capital letter." According to Dewey, it was not so much the ideology but the way in which the ideology was currently being practiced.[295]

Even then, at first, Dewey was a cheerleader for the ideology both in theory and in practice.

John Dewey: Inspiration to Bolshevik Educators

Not taught in our teachers' colleges today, amidst the eternal veneration of John Dewey, is the alarming extent to which the Bolsheviks venerated the work of John Dewey. The Soviets embraced Dewey for their schools. The Bolsheviks were big fans of his work, and Dewey was clearly—initially, in the 1920s—a big fan of them and their work.[296]

From the beginning, the Bolsheviks had studied and experimented with Dewey's educational ideas, not to mention those of American educational progressives Helen Parkhurst, Edward Thorndike, John B. Watson, and Dewey's close Columbia pupils/colleagues William H. Kilpatrick and Thomas Woody—all of them within Bella Dodd's orbit at Columbia.[297] As celebrated by another educational colleague, William Brickman,[298] who wrote a gushing introduction to Dewey's book *Impressions of Soviet Russia*, published by Columbia's Teachers College in 1964, "The number of translations of Dewey's works was quite impressive during the initial decade [of the Russian Revolution]."[299]

The Bolsheviks wasted no time getting Dewey's words into Russian. In 1918, only three years after it was published in the United States, Dewey's *Schools of Tomorrow* was published in Moscow.[300] Given what was happening in Russia at the time, this is staggering. The Bolshevik Revolution had begun only months earlier, and the devastating Russian Civil War was in full swing. Millions of people were on the verge of poverty, starvation, and murder by war and execution. The Bolsheviks were as preoccupied with survival as they did not have money.

The Bolsheviks did not have the money to be translating American educational books into Russian. Of course, they saw education as foundational to building the communist state; it was a very high priority. Thus, the fact that they allocated such time and resources to Dewey's work at such a perilous moment is a remarkable testimony of how indispensable Lenin, Trotsky, and Stalin considered John Dewey to be in raising the communist state.

Indeed, only a year after *Schools of Tomorrow* was published came a Russian translation of *How We Think* (1919) and then, in 1920, *The School and Society*.[301] Again, this was at the height of the misery unleashed by the Russian Civil War (1918–21), which, according to historian W. Bruce Lincoln, snuffed out the lives of *seven million* men, women, and children. Nonetheless, Dewey's ideas were too crucial to receive short shrift, apparently judged as formidable to the revolution as any weapon in the arsenal of the Red Army.

Several more translations immediately followed, including, in 1921, a sixty-two-page pamphlet excerpted from Dewey's *Democracy and Education*, done by Professor Stanislav T. Shatskii, a leading Soviet educational "reformer."[302] This classic of American public education was a Bolshevik phenomenon before the Russian Civil War even ended.

This thought deserves special pause: As noted, *Democracy and Education* remains Dewey's most significant work; it remains the most common (approved) choice by schools of education as an introduction to Dewey's thought. It became the bible of Columbia Teachers College. It became the guidepost of numerous educational students, teachers, programs, departments, and colleges. It was the book in which the philosopher himself said he attempted to summarize his "entire philosophical position."[303] And it was a Bolshevik favorite.

Dewey's impact was immediate and pervasive. A witness to this was Anna Louise Strong, whose communist book, *I Change Worlds: The Remaking of an American*, was given to Bella Dodd by Sarah Parks. Strong made a visit to the USSR in this early 1920s period, where she closely observed Soviet education.[304] As she did, she recorded that contemporary school reform in Stalin's state had been "modeled more on the Dewey ideas of education than on anything else we have in America. Every new book by Dewey is seized and early translated into Russian for consultation. Then they make their own additions."[305]

The Soviets themselves stated this quite candidly. In a 1929 book, Albert P. Pinkevich, rector of the Second State University of Moscow, stated that Dewey had a "tremendous influence" on Soviet education.

Pinkevich compared Dewey's impact to that of leading educators in Germany, where Marxism was prevalent; German was often the first Western language of translation for Soviet documents. Compared to even the Germans, "Dewey comes infinitely closer to Marx and the Russian communists," asserted Pinkevich.[306]

The Soviets heaped praise upon Dewey. The likes of Stanislav Shatskii told Thomas Woody that he "drew greatest assistance" from Dewey, and was "deeply impressed by his [Dewey's] 'philosophy of pragmatism.'"[307]

A testimony to this achievement was mailed to Dewey in 1928 by Professor A. G. Kalashnikov of the pedagogical department of Moscow Technical University. He sent Dewey a two-volume set of the most recent *Soviet Pedagogical Encyclopedia*, which owed a great debt to Dewey's progressive work.[308] Kalashnikov included a warm personal note to Dewey that read, "Your works, especially 'School and Society' and 'The School and the Child,' have very much influenced the development of the Russian pedagogy and in the first years of [the] revolution you were one of the most renowned writers." The "concrete shapes of pedagogical practice" that Dewey had developed, wrote an appreciative Kalashnikov, "will be for a long time the aim of our tendencies."[309]

The apparatchiks commandeering the Soviet educational bureaucracy were dizzied by Dewey. Thus, they were begging John Dewey to come pay them a visit. That would happen in the summer of 1928.

Dewey's "Impressions"

Dewey became a literal fellow "traveler" to Stalin's Soviet Union in the summer of 1928 as part of an unofficial delegation of twenty-five American educators from various universities, including, naturally, Columbia Teachers College, where colleagues like Dr. J. McKeen Cattell joined the voyage. According to State Department records, Dewey and crew sailed for Europe on June 23 and left Russia to return home on or around July 20.[310]

Dewey should have known the obvious: the purpose of these invitations from the Soviet government was to try to dupe high-level American/Western leftist intellectuals into favorable impressions of the Great Experiment in Bolshevik Russia, and, in turn, to get the US government to officially recognize Stalin's state. This was a standard practice by General Secretary Stalin in the late 1920s up through the 1930s.[311] The progressives were paraded from Potemkin Village to Potemkin Village in the hopes of being suckered into false impressions of Soviet Russia, which they could gleefully report in dispatches to Americans back home. And Dewey swallowed it hook, line, and sinker, proclaiming the Bolshevik Revolution "a great success."[312]

Not disappointing his handlers, Dewey filed a six-part series of gullible reports in the gullible pages of *The New Republic* from November 14, 1928 through December 19, 1928, which eventually were compiled into an entire book on his "impressions" of the "revolutionary world." That book was titled *Impressions of Soviet Russia* (published in 1929).[313]

Revisiting all of those Dewey dispatches here is beyond the scope of this book.[314] We will, however, focus briefly on those dealing with public education.

To that end, the professor provided lengthy treatises on Soviet education. He perceived in Russia nothing short of an "educational transformation," of which he wholeheartedly, enthusiastically approved—in fact, envied. He would conclude that "the Russian educational situation is enough to convert one to the idea that only in a society based upon the cooperative principle [Bolshevik Russia] can the ideals of educational reformers be adequately carried into operation."[315] In other words, Dewey seemed to have viewed Bolshevik Russia as the ideal sort of system where his kind of educational reform could be implemented.[316]

Dewey understood that Russian schools were the "ideological arm of the Revolution," as he rightly put it, and that they indulged in propaganda, but he did not seem to care or sense the dangers. Rather, given his own views about how public schools must serve a socialization function, derived from society, the group, and the collective—all superior to the individual—and, in addition, that these schools be devoid of a religious foundation, he appeared highly impressed with what he witnessed in Russian education. A wide-eyed Dewey thrilled, "The activities of the schools dovetail in the most extraordinary way, both in administrative organization and in aim and spirit, into all other [Soviet] social agencies and interests."[317]

The father of experimentalism in American public education was thrilled with the "experimentation" thriving in Russian public education, which he saw as "flexible, vital, creative." He longed for the same in America. It was here that Russia earned the tag "The Great Experiment." Dewey projected: "I think the schools are a 'dialectic' factor in the evolution of Russian communism."[318]

Professor Dewey raved about all of this to students at Columbia—to pupils like a young Bella Dodd. In fact, Bella knew all about Dewey and his fellow political pilgrims and their voyage to the Soviet motherland. She told an audience in September 1961: "Once the [Russian] revolution was made in 1917, they brought over to Russia some of the leaders of the progressive education school. They brought John Dewey over there for a while. They brought George Counts over. They brought Kilpatrick over there. They brought them over there to establish a school system. But that progressive education lasted only while the Russian leaders and the Communist leaders were establishing hegemony and control over the Russian people. The moment Stalin, after the death of Lenin, had established control over the people, he threw them all out kit and caboodle."[319]

Bella knew all about Dr. George Counts, who she described as a "cooperator" in the League for Industrial Democracy.[320] He was an associate of John Dewey, a leading professor at Columbia, an author of pro-Soviet books, and a frequent fellow traveler to Moscow.[321] His first pilgrimage to Bolshevik Russia was in 1927. The Columbia professor of education enthusiastically helped the Russian government set up its

Marxist-Leninist educational system. He translated the Russian Primer into English for the benefit of American teachers. He hoped that the Soviet education system could be a model to remedy "class inequality" in the American education system.[322]

Counts was just one of many Dewey comrades at Columbia fighting for the revolution under the banner of "education reform." These were the experts training future teachers like Bella Dodd.

Bella and Friends Expanding the Social Frontier and the NEA

Bella became familiar with the so-called "Social Frontier" thinkers at Columbia, who had a publication by the same name. It was a cutting-edge organ of militant progressive educational thought. Published independently at Teachers College, these intellectual hucksters urged educators to use schools as agents of "social change."[323] They went so far as to say: "This new journal . . . has an important, even strategic, role to play in the reconstruction of American society."[324] William H. Kilpatrick, a disciple of Dewey, and also chairman of the board of the League for Industrial Democracy, was the editor of *The Social Frontier* from 1934 to 1939, and he wanted teachers to become social partisans using classrooms to mold "the values and ideas of the students in accordance with a socialistic society."[325]

In one issue, *The Social Frontier* examined the applicability of Marxism-Leninism to American education. Left-wing revolutionary Theodore Brameld proposed that "when the ruling class is once replaced, a period of oppression will continue to be necessary until gradually the citizenry honestly comes to agree that collectivism is a better solution of our troubles than capitalism." Violence was not to be ruled out: "Let us never resort to it [violence] indiscriminately. Meanwhile, let us achieve by the vote what rights we can. But let us not characterize violence categorically as immoral under all circumstances."[326]

Here was yet another distinguished professor admitting that violence is acceptable, for the proper reasons. The progressive changes in education at this time were striking. Many students were taking it all in, including Bella Dodd, who frequently visited Teachers College while at Columbia.[327]

The Frontier Thinkers were influential at the very time that communists in the Teachers Union were consolidating power and simultaneously capturing the top jobs and control of John Dewey's NEA. Bella fell right in.

Bella Dodd would later observe that the main source of the change in the philosophy of American education came from the NEA. She admitted that she was instrumental in laying the basis for "affiliation of the Teachers Union with the NEA."[328] She would do this at Hunter College as a faculty member in the 1930s and then through a heightened role throughout the 1930s and into the 1940s organizing the "teachers front" for the Communist Party.

In an address in 1961, Bella admitted frankly that back in the 1930s, educators "made up their minds that the schools were to be used to train the students for the new world, for the new civilization. They would not train the children in *their* minds, they were not training the children's minds, they were not training their intellects. They were not passing on the cultural heritage of the last 2,000 years." And the NEA became a mass vehicle for this training: "The NEA at that time went along with the idea that the school must become the agency where you train the children for the new world, for the new society." This was fully consistent, she noted, with the goals of communists: "The communist Teachers Union advocated principles locally that within a few years the NEA was advocating on a national basis. I'll make it even more definite than that, I had a good deal of success as a lobbyist in Albany and I went to Washington. I was consulted by the national lobbyist for the NEA as to methods he could use for their program before Congress. In other words, the Columbia progressive education crowd used the communist Teachers' Union to spread ideas locally that they used NEA 'to effect nationally.'"[329]

Bella went further, speaking about the effect of such ideas: "And so the parents began to lose their children. They were being trained for a new society and the old values were allowed to slip away. . . . So that from 1932 on in this America of ours, unfortunately the progressive education based upon the philosophy of pragmatism unfortunately has catapulted our schools into great propaganda agencies. They've become an institution for the purpose of taking care of children according to the new world."[330]

During another of her later lectures, in Indianapolis in 1954, a person in the audience asked Bella just how "far to the left were John Dewey and Kilpatrick at Columbia?" She provided a lengthy answer, proving her familiarity:

> Well, there is no doubt—you see what happened to John Dewey, John began by being a Christian gentleman when he was at the University of Vermont. He shifted in his allegiance when he was at the University of Chicago and by the time he reached the University of Johns Hopkins and became the student of the professor who had studied under Hegel in Germany, who was the teacher of Karl Marx, Dewey had discarded the Christian principles or the religious principles upon which this civilization was established. Therefore, Dewey became a communist even though he was not a communist in the sense of a Party member.
>
> He became a person who believed that man is nothing but material. Therefore, his philosophy of education brings the principle of education in which he says the child can only learn through his senses; seeing, hearing, touching, and what not. Those are the attributes of the animal, aren't they? Now we, as human beings, are part animal. We do learn partly through seeing, hearing, touching, feeling, smelling, but John Dewey

denied the existence of the mind, which is something that is part of the soul.[331]

Bella said that although "not all the sins of modern progressive education are on John Dewey's shoulders," his "fundamental error" was his "concept of what a child is."[332]

A major advocate of the NEA and Dewey's preference for consolidation and centralization of children into mass public-school collectives was William Z. Foster, general secretary of the American Communist Party. In his 1932 book *Toward Soviet America*, Foster, a founding board member of the ACLU, claimed that "schools, colleges and universities will be coordinated and grouped under the National Department of Education and its state and local branches. The studies will be revolutionized, being cleansed of religious, patriotic, and other features of the bourgeois ideology. The students will be taught on the basis of Marxian dialectical materialism, internationalism, and the general ethics of the new Socialist society."[333]

In this, he and John Dewey were two peas in a pod. And in this, budding Bolshevik educators, like Bella Dodd and some of her colleagues, would find their calling to transform the children of America.

The Role of Progressive Education

Much will be shared in the pages ahead on how Bella proceeded in that task. For now, in this chapter, a few closing words on Bella and "progressive education" as it was viewed by the likes of Columbia professors, by various educational "reformers," and by the Communist Party.

During her later testimony to the US Senate in the early 1950s, Bella was asked specifically about progressive education, and if there was a prescribed "Party line" for teachers in that respect. She stated the "Communist Party as a whole adopted a line of being for progressive education. And that would be carried on through the [Party] steering committee and into the Teachers Union."[334] Party leaders like herself, who infiltrated and hijacked the Teachers Union, would bring this "progressive education" into the union.

At her addresses in Indianapolis in 1954, Bella noted that the Communist Party "did not develop progressive education," but it certainly embraced it.[335] She likewise spoke of this in a January 1953 address to the American Education Association: "The communists were using progressive education as a manner of freeing students from discipline and encouraging them for the day when they could take matters into their own hands." She added that "this new education says that truth is only relative," and she admonished teachers to "restore God and basic truths to the schools."[336]

On still another occasion, in September 1961, Bella spoke out against the "pragmatic philosophy which says there is no such thing as right and wrong. That which is successful is right. That which is successful is good. That pragmatic philosophy, which became the basis of progressive education, has done more damage to American education than anything else in the history of America."[337] She said the communists inside the New York State Teachers Union were progressive education's most vocal and enthusiastic supporters.[338]

Bella Dodd's exposure to Columbia Teachers College was important. She understood the ripple effect of one communist teacher influencing countless more: "If you have a communist teacher in a school of education and he teaches, say, 300 teachers who go out all over the United States to spread their ideas to thousands of children, he's a very valuable asset to the communist cause."[339] The label "progressive education" became the Trojan horse to make this happen; it became the "Party line." And so it happened that, besides "learning that the *Communist Manifesto* was among the great works of literature and that the Soviet Union was an 'economic democracy,'" a small group of educators, chiefly based at Columbia Teachers College, within twenty years had turned "thousands and thousands of teachers into mission-aries of the collectivist, i.e., socialist creed."[340]

How cynical and how convenient it was. The communists did not need to evolve any new educational theories themselves. They instead merely "injected themselves into the campaign to develop 'progressive education' and sometimes pushed it to ridiculous extremes to make it conform to a program of preparing American youth for acceptance of a communist regime."[341]

This was one of many ways, Bella commented, that communists usurped the positions of the wider progressive left in order to accomplish their goals.[342] At Columbia University, Bella Dodd, a communist revolutionary in training, was learning well.

CHAPTER 6

BELLA AT COLUMBIA, NYU, AND ABROAD (1925–30)

Following graduation from Hunter College, Bella and her friend, Ruth Goldstein, enrolled in the 1925 summer session at Columbia University. She was determined to get a master's degree.

An energetic student, Bella was excited when she enrolled.[343] While studying there, she was affected not only by her classes but by institutions around campus. She became a frequent visitor at International House, whose members, she said, met on a "level of equality and tolerance" with the hope of creating a world where all people "could live and work on free and equal terms."[344] Bella noticed that some of the Columbia professors were "fresh from the London School of Economics"[345] and from the Brookings Institution.[346] She read about imperialism and became critical of the role the United States was playing in the world.[347]

During this period, Bella also started teaching at Hunter College. She later admitted that at this time she did much damage to her students, since a teacher transmits to her students something of what she is and what she believes. And what Bella was being taught to believe was damaging. "But," she said later, "the saving grace of my destructive teaching of that time was that, in my personal relationships with these students, I retained within me something of the essence of what God had meant me to be—a woman, a mother. I loved my students, all of them, the dull, the weak, the strong, the conniving, the twisted. I loved them because they were young and alive, because they were in the process of becoming and had not yet been frozen into a mold by a cynical society or by a conniving power."[348]

Unfortunately, Bella herself was being molded by a cynical ideology and conniving power.

Bella's Professors

At Columbia graduate school, Bella studied with Adolf A. Berle, who later was appointed assistant of state for security at the Department of State by Franklin Roosevelt. In 1939, after Whittaker Chambers defected from the Communist Party, Isaac Don Levine arranged a meeting between Berle and Chambers. At the meeting, Chambers gave Berle a list of the names of people working in the State Department and other agencies of the government connected with Soviet espionage, either as Party members or fellow travelers, all working for the Kremlin apparatus. During his testimony before the House Committee on Un-American Activities in 1948, amid the heat of the Hiss-Chambers trial, Berle's testimony was more than misleading.[349] Significantly, Berle worked with Harry Dexter White, a major Soviet spy within the Roosevelt Treasury Department.[350]

Bella also studied treaty-making powers of the US Senate with Lindsey Rogers, an associate professor of government and part of the Advisory Committee for the Institute of Social Sciences, which had close ties to the Frankfurt School. (As will be sketched out below, the Frankfurt School, better known as the Institute of Social Research at Goethe University in Frankfurt, Germany, would move to Columbia in the 1930s.) Rogers's course examined European political institutions and the governments of Canada, Australia, Austria, Germany, and Switzerland.[351]

Raymond Moley, another one of Bella's professors, lectured at the Rand School and became another Roosevelt brain-truster.[352] As the Carlton J. H. Hayes Professor of History in the Department of History, he taught "The Rise of Nationalism." The course was described as a "study of the more important problems of state, country, and township government in the United States such as state administrative reorganization, county reorganization, the administration of the criminal law, election laws, and the relation to government of private organizations and associations with civic purposes."[353] Initially in favor of Roosevelt's New Deal, Moley went on to become a bitter opponent. Other professors in the department at Columbia at that time included James T. Shotwell, a member of the Intercollegiate Socialist Society, who was connected with the Institute for Social Sciences and became director of research at the Carnegie Endowment for International Peace.[354]

Robert S. Lynd, author of *Middletown*, also taught Bella and was on the letterhead of the Institute for Social Sciences and a member of the National Committee of the ACLU.[355] A lifelong radical known as an apologist for "drastic collectivism with rigid state controls," he was instrumental in inviting the Frankfurt School to Columbia, encouraged by John Dewey. Though described in FBI files as a "fellow traveler" by one source, prominent communist defector Louis Budenz stated: "In the 1940s Eugene Dennis and Jack Stachel instructed me to consider Lynd as a communist. This was equivalent to stating he was under communist discipline and I so regarded him during my entire time as managing editor of the *Daily Worker* since these instructions were official in character."[356] Lynd collaborated with the Frankfurt School's empirical research.[357]

Philip Jessup, another controversial professor in the Department of History at Columbia, with a background in international law, was also connected with the Institute of Social Research.[358] He was a character witness for Alger Hiss, served as chairman of the American group of the Institute of Pacific Relations (IPR), and was a major figure in the State Department in charge of China policy, where his damage was immense, helping to make possible victory for Mao Zedong and forces in China in 1949.[359] M. Stanton Evans, who spent a good part of his life doing exhaustive research on these subjects, said Ambassador

Jessup would become the most visible and eminent leader of the IPR holding federal office. He served as chairman of the American group, leader of the international body, and head of the IPR research committee. He eventually became ambassador at large and played a pivotal role in US-China policy during the time when America abandoned Chiang Kai-shek, the vehemently anti-communist leader of China from 1928 to 1949.[360]

The Frankfurt School

Most notably, while Bella was at Columbia and not yet a formal member of the Communist Party, some of her professors were in the process of inviting a lethal Marxist group into the country as "refugees." That group was the Frankfurt School and its destructive band of Freudian Marxists.

In 1922, a group of German communists in Thuringia were dissecting an unpublished manuscript "Marxism and Philosophy," which became the blueprint for creating what would come to be known as the Frankfurt School.[361] They proposed the founding of a Marxist discussion and research institute modeled on the Fabian Society.[362] That same year, at the Marx-Engels Institute in Moscow, a similar plan was hatched by the likes of Karl Radek, Felix Dzerzhinsky (head of the Soviet secret police, the NKVD), Hungarian Georg Lukács, and Willi Münzenberg from the Comintern. It would morph into the so-called Institute of Social Research, eventually planted at Frankfurt University and dedicated to neo-Marxism, which would blend Marxism with Freudianism.

Since the Marxist Proletariat revolution was not going according to plan, the intellectuals needed to re-examine why and to reformulate Marxist theory and prepare for future action. Their goal was to become a major force in the "revitalization of Western European Marxism in the postwar years."[363] The Frankfurt School developed a new strain of Marxism that gave priority to the radical transformation of the cultural foundations of Western civilization.

The Frankfurt School was formally established in 1929 at (fittingly) Goethe University in Frankfurt, Germany, as the Institute of Social Research.[364] Amid Hitler's madness, its founders and members by 1934 looked to escape Nazi Germany, given that many to most (if not all) were Jewish and faced terrible persecution at home once the Fuhrer became chancellor in 1933. Where would they relocate to? What respectable institution in the West would willingly accept a crazed cabal of fugitives of Freudian-Marxism? What academic institution would dare play host to the distillation of such toxic ideas? The answer was Columbia University.

"Over the years, the Institut had made several contacts with prominent figures in the American academic world, such as Charles Beard, Robert MacIver, Wesley Mitchell, Reinhold Niebuhr, and Robert Lynd, all of whom were at Columbia University," notes Professor Martin Jay in his seminal history of the Frankfurt School.[365] Lynd and MacIver particularly pushed Columbia to roll out the red carpet for the Frankfurt Marxists. MacIver, professor of political science and chairman of the Department of Sociology at Columbia, made a direct pitch to the Ivy League college's acclaimed president, Nicholas Butler Murray, writing a letter in which he went so far as to urge Butler to offer housing facilities for the Frankfurt clan, in addition to offices.[366]

When the left-wing radical Robert Lynd was asked by the Columbia brass if there were any red flags in bringing these Freudian-Marxists to Columbia, Lynd conceded: "The only possible entanglement in the whole affair lies in the fact that the Institute is on the liberal-radical side." No worries, however, said Lynd: "I think it is fair to conclude that they are a research agency with high standards and not interested in propaganda."[367]

Dr. Butler was Columbia's patriarch. He was an establishment Republican with a liberal bent. He was easily swayed by his far-left colleagues' endorsements. Thus, when the Institute of Social Research's head, Max Horkheimer, made his first trip to America in May 1934, he easily got access to Butler to make a pitch. "Much to his surprise," writes Martin Jay of Horkheimer's reaction, "Butler offered the Institut affiliation with the university and a home in one of its buildings, at 429 West 117th Street." Horkheimer was so taken aback by Butler's speedy and generous offer that he feared he misunderstood him, given his limited command of English, and hence wrote a four-page letter seeking clarification. "You have understood me perfectly!" clarified a thrilled Butler.[368]

And just like that, the institute and its poisonous ideology—which became known as "critical theory"—established a foothold in the United States of America, courtesy of its dutiful comrades at Columbia University.

The first Frankfurt professors to join Horkheimer in New York were its two most infamous extremists: Erich Fromm and Herbert Marcuse, the latter of whom arrived in July 1934.[369] He would one day become the guru to the 1960s New Left, and his most infamous student remains Angela Davis, the leading female Marxist in the United States to this day, the onetime proud recipient of the Kremlin's Lenin Peace Prize, which she glowingly accepted in Moscow in 1979. Columbia gave Marcuse the space to cook up his noxious ideas, which he published in bizarre bestselling books such as *One-Dimensional Man* and *Eros and Civilization*, which were extremely influential among '60s revolutionaries.

Columbia housed the Frankfurt School until its safe post-war return to Germany in 1950.[370] During that crucial period, Columbia allowed the school and its practitioners to survive, thrive, and establish a stronghold for their ideas to invade America through academia. The likes of Marcuse never left. Once in America, he spread his wings, from college to college and coast to coast, from New York to Los Angeles, carefully training a future generation of Marxist critical theorists. The Frankfurt School became one of the chief routes for cultural Marxism to gain entrance to the United States.[371] It would give rise to more than a few ideological madmen on the extreme left.[372]

Thereafter, the communist revolution took flight not only in Soviet Russia but also in the United States. However, the revolution here was cultural, even sexual, with the universities as the seedbed. A great misconception in America is that when the Soviet Union "collapsed," communism ceased to be a threat. The ideology, in fact, has been one of the biggest Trojan horses in history, especially through its perverse offspring of critical theory, which has spawned a whole legion of rot and hate, from critical gender theory to "queer theory" to critical race theory. The Frankfurt School is responsible for a large part of this. It started there.

The presence of the Frankfurt School at Columbia is significant, since it and Fabian socialism have been handy hammers and sickles to pound and chip away at the US Constitution and the very foundations of not only US society but Western civilization. Lenin's lieutenants left the army and went back to school.

Bella as Professor and at Law School

As for Bella Dodd, she lived in New York while all of this transpired. Many of her professors at Columbia were on the board of or associated with the Institute of Social Research and had even lobbied to bring it to New York. They were the professors who would help make her a professor.

Bella began teaching in 1926. That year, while studying for her master's degree at Columbia, she was hired to teach political science at Hunter. Both Bella and Ruth Goldstein became assistants to Dr. Dawson, chairman of the Political Science Department at Hunter. She would teach there for the next twelve years, intersecting with the Frankfurters arrival and establishment at Columbia, as she too influenced a generation of students with Marxism.

Bella was an enthusiastic professor, and comments from friends and students indicate that she was effective and popular.[373] She was once described as "the most popular professor at Hunter College."[374]

Bella exposed her students to *realpolitik* and, applying the theories she was absorbing at Columbia, sent them out to political clubs, socialist groups, courts, jails, legislatures, and institutions to gather and spread information. As a result of her studies and involvement in local politics, Bella admitted that she began "to tear apart before my students many respected public groups—charity, church, and other organizations," and later conceded that she "had a destructive effect." She regretted: "If they followed where I led, there was nothing left for them to believe in."[375] Her teaching, in fact, applied the very elements of what came to be tenets of critical theory.

Bella received her MA in history from Columbia in 1927. She stayed on to do an additional graduate year at Columbia in economics.[376] She thought of herself as a teacher above all and loved teaching, later reflecting that "there is in teaching a continuing renewing, and in that renewal there is always the promise of that freshness which brings us nearer to perfection." The incoming students were especially inspiring to her: "To me, freshmen were always a delight as students. They came to school with high resolve, many of them caught by a sense of dedication to learning, and they were not yet pressured by practical considerations of jobs and careers, not yet having to accommodate themselves to the status quo."[377]

After graduating from Columbia in the spring of 1927, Bella and her friends Ruth Goldstein and Beatrice Feldman rented a cottage on Schroon Lake in the Adirondacks for the summer. They had luxurious discussions long into the night on the theories of John Dewey and Justice Oliver Wendell Holmes, and they debated many of the things their parents had accepted. She said this group was like a new kind of family, the "social family of the like-minded."[378]

The following autumn, Bella made a sharp turn in her career and enrolled in New York University Law School. Her friend Ruth entered with her. While continuing to teach at Hunter, Bella took law classes in the afternoon. The classes at NYU were large, attended by several hundred students. She found the case system boring, but she was driven to study law as a discipline worth mastering, and she earned her JD from NYU. (Often referred to as "Dr. Dodd," Bella did not have a PhD but a juris doctorate.)

Her decision was caused not by any interest in legal procedure, which focused on the status quo, but by her desire to change the status quo. In her memoirs, she did not say much about her work at law school except that it was mediocre.[379] In her personal life, she was meeting men and women leading unorthodox lives who had an interest in literature, the arts, and the Russian revolution, which was fresh in the public's mind. During this time, she left home and lived in a cramped apartment in Greenwich Village. She said her group spent endless hours, night after night, sitting before fireplaces in some village loft discussing politics.[380]

The Suicide of Sarah Parks

A pivotal episode in Bella's life came unexpectedly. While teaching at Hunter, faced with what she termed "conflicting currents" among intellectuals, she decided to consult her old teacher from Hunter, Sarah Parks, but found her preoccupied with salary and promotion controversies. Bella sensed an emptiness in Parks's life—the Parks who had helped cleanse Bella's mind as a pallet for Marxist propaganda. That impression proved correct, as Sarah Parks committed suicide the following year in 1928.

Parks had been such a popular professor and a mentor to Bella. She had imbibed socialist-communist politics and transmitted that dark worldview to her impressionable young students. She had helped form Bella. The English professor had provided the young Bella and other freshmen with less a course on English literature than the literature of revolution, as she denounced America, capitalism, the "medieval spirit" of Christianity, and praised the atheistic views of the French and Bolshevik revolutions. She loaded them up with tracts on communist Russia. She pushed Bella away from positive thinking about something like monasticism and instead prodded her toward Bolshevism. She invited students to her apartment for further indoctrination off campus. She was their unofficial dean.

But as with so many far-left intellectuals, these ideas proved empty for Sarah Parks. These were the gods that always failed. They failed Sarah. And so, Sarah Parks killed herself.

What happened to Parks pained Bella. She would later remember her as someone of a "bright intelligence wasted because she had no standard to live by." She was empty inside. "In the end," said Bella, "she took her own life rather than face its emptiness."[381]

The revolutionary students influenced by Parks were unsurprisingly unforgiving. Rather than offering understanding, they seemed to feel that comrade Sarah had not been steadfast enough in accepting the ideas of the revolution. If only she had been a more committed Bolshevik. Parks's disciples felt that although having the "intellectual courage" to believe in the "coming collective society," she had lacked "the practical boldness to become a disciplined member of the group," something they perceived as a failure.[382]

The *Hunter Bulletin* tried to summon up a remembrance more uplifting. It paid tribute to Parks's "selfless courage which was the keynote of her character. She always felt the inward urge of a passion for truth in the intellectual realm and for justice, against anything which she conceived to be false or unjust."[383]

Sarah's suicide left a deep impression on Bella. Reflecting on it later, she said she herself took a longer, more deceptive road to annihilation. She said the years of 1928 and 1929 were filled with "confusion and ugliness," and she turned "more and more to the literature of despair. . . . For the first time in my life, I viewed the future with apprehension and found little pleasure in anything."[384]

The same had been true for Sarah Parks. Was Bella Dodd destined for a similar course of emptiness and self-destruction?

Bella Abroad

Fortunately, Bella still had her Italian family to escape to when life became confusing. It was a happy family, even as her education was tugging her away from the mirth of her youth.

In 1930, after Hunter, Columbia, and NYU, and as she had prepared to take the bar exam, Bella sought respite in a return visit to Europe. But this was a different Bella than the lovely little girl filled with hope and joy who had left Italy two decades earlier. This was a Bella who was now a cynical left-wing intellectual molded by American universities like Hunter and Columbia.

Instead of going into the smaller villages of Europe or to the centers of spiritual strength, such as Florence or Rome, Bella headed first to the University of Berlin,[385] traveling with her friend Beatrice Feldman.[386] Rather than visiting sites like Vatican City and St. Peter's Basilica and Assisi and Siena, Bella engaged the dark forces of the enlightened "seats of learning" at German universities. At the University of Berlin, "We talked with university students and professors. The university was torn with strife. Socialists, Communists, National Socialists were battling each other." She saw that "acts of violence" were common in the city and around the university, and she was made "conscious of the fact that here politics had become a matter of life and death." She also witnessed the decadence of Berlin, which in the interwar years had become a modern European Babylon: "In Berlin we saw more pinched faces and more blatant lavishness. We were alarmed at the frank and open evidences of sexual and moral degradation flaunted in the night spots and exhibited to the tourists everywhere."[387]

It was the same sexual-moral degradation that the Frankfurt School theorists would work into their perverted Freudian-Marxist philosophy and bring to America.

This trip was critical in Bella's development, and she was never the same afterward. She saw fascism firsthand, its effects visible. This was six years before the Reichstag fire of 1933, when Hitler seized power.

It etched an indelible mark on her. She visited Hamburg, "filled with merchant seamen, longshoremen, soldiers. There were the *nouveau riche* with pockets bulging with the country's wealth. There were Communists everywhere, marching, singing, meeting."[388]

In Berlin, professors, intellectuals, and scientists were arrogant in their pride but "lacked the inner strength to play a positive role in Germany's hour of need, and were ready to join the forces of violence." Only later did she realize that, for nearly a century, the educational world of Germany had been subjected to "systematic despiritualization," which had resulted in an obvious dehumanization. Students and professors she met said fascism could never come to Germany, but the universities and the civil service would be the first to serve Hitler.[389]

She could not wait to leave Berlin. Interestingly, she felt a lingering for the faith of her youth, beckoning her out of this European hellhole that would soon become the capital of Hitler's Third Reich. Said Bella: "I was happy to leave Berlin. And now I insisted on a trip which was not on our schedule. I had hitherto generally refused to spend much time in museums and churches but I wanted to go to Dresden and see the Sistine Madonna. It was worth the long trip to see the lovely Virgin and Child and the cherubs at their feet looking like gay little urchins. The day I spent in Dresden was my happiest in Germany."[390]

Then they visited Italy, filled with even more churches and images of the Madonna, the Virgin Child, and cherubs. But Bella was less interested, and her friend Beatrice Feldman did nothing to persuade her otherwise. Her "education" back home had pulled her too far away. "When I reached Rome I was more interested in the ruins of classical times than in the monuments to the living spirit at the heart of Christianity," Bella later lamented. "It was evidence of how far I, through my education and my own perverse pride of mind, had traveled from the past of my own people and from the accumulated wisdom and safety which two thousand years of Christianity could provide for the modern children of the Western world."[391]

The student of Sarah Parks and Columbia University was drawn elsewhere.

In Italy, Bella was disappointed as she searched in vain for the memories of the country she had treasured during her childhood and that her "imagination had embellished." The spiritually uplifting quality of Italy that she cherished was not there (or she was not looking hard enough), and she realized "she did not belong to the country she had left as a child." She now saw the "tangible evidence of the blight of fascist philosophy."[392]

What she had seen in Germany, she also saw in Rome: It was filled with men in uniform. Fascism was taking hold there as well. Europe was brimming with fascists, socialists, and communists.

Bella tried to visit Picerno, where she had been born, to see her foster parents, Mamarella and Taddeo, but an earthquake prevented travel. That must have been crushing to her. One wonders how such a reunion might have affected her at that crucial moment in her life.

It was in Rome that Bella received the news that she had passed the bar exam, and her mother asked her to come home. "My mother and father wrote, 'Come home. We are lonely without you.'" Bella was excited to hear the good news. She prepared to voyage back to her new country.[393]

After witnessing fascism firsthand, Bella returned to America on the aptly named *Leviathan*, which departed from Cherbourg, France, in September 1930. Here again, she had another political encounter that would impact her life for the worse. On board the ship, Bella met a group of teachers who urged her to join the Teachers Union. A union member convinced her that anyone interested in education ought to be interested in trade unions. She objected that the union consisted largely of public-school teachers and did not think college teachers had a place in it, but they persuaded her, and she promised to join to show her willingness to throw in her lot with the working class. She also knew there were some familiar college teachers in the union, such as Dr. George Counts and other professors from Columbia University.[394]

Upon her return to New York, she went to meetings of the Teachers Union, which she found "disconcerting because there was so much strife between groups seeking control." She struggled to comprehend how "intelligent adults should struggle so hard to control an organization which in numbers was small and insignificant." She was also "dumbfounded" to find the names of distinguished professors like Counts and John Dewey embroiled in these imbroglios. "It was only later, when I better understood left-wing politics," she noted, "that I became aware of the significance of control of this beachhead."[395]

She would become a leading lieutenant on that left-wing beachhead. Bella Dodd came back to the United States with a new direction and commitment.

Chapter 7

Bella, the Family, and Communism

After returning to the United States from her trip to Europe, Bella Visono married John F. Dodd, whom she met abroad. It was one of the few moments she had in Europe that seemed to have created something loving. Sadly, however, it would not be permanent.

When she arrived back in America that year, in 1930, she saw a "great deal" of John Dodd. "At first it seemed we had little in common, for John had an engineer's mind and I was disinterested in all machinery, regarding mechanical devices as a kind of black magic," said Bella. "But we soon discovered topics of common interest, such as our love for this country and an awareness of its problems."[396]

She and John were married in a civil ceremony in the Bronx in September 1930. Apparently, John's views on religion were as negative as Bella's comrades. "We did not plan to be married in a church, since John was bitterly anti-clerical," said Bella. "I did not mind the civil marriage; like John, I thought of myself as a freethinker." So, one morning in late September, they were married at the county clerk's office in New York City. It was just Bella and Dodd and two of Bella's friends who served as witnesses—Beatrice Feldman and Dr. Louis Finkelstein.[397]

John was a southerner. Born in Floyd County, Georgia, he was the youngest of six children and an electrical engineer. John had blonde hair and was much taller than Bella and ten years older. He had served in the Royal Canadian Air Force and later in the American

Air Force and was a reserve officer in the Army. After watching her time-consuming activity with the Teachers Union and the Communist Party, one day John said to her: "Bella, I am not sure where you would stand if America is on the spot."[398]

Though he clearly must have harbored left-wing sympathies, John seems to have also been patriotic, with deep roots in military service by both him personally and his family, the latter going all the way back to the Battle of Shiloh during the Civil War, where his grandfather had lost an arm. The intensely political Bella was angry with John's suspicions of where she might stand if America was on the spot, even though John's suspicions were fully justified (Communists swore to defend the Soviet Union over the United States if war ever broke out between the two nations). She bristled. "I became very haughty as a woman," Bella remarked, "and said he had no right to ask me that question. Well, as a result of that question, my husband divorced me, because he felt there was too much cleavage between us."[399]

That seems quite abrupt, but it must have been a culmination of many fissures in the relationship. Bella had some hesitation prior to the marriage. Still, she "grew to love John more than I thought I was capable of loving anyone." The divorce came nonetheless, and later she heard that he had married again.

In her memoirs, Bella did not say a lot about the marriage, nor even meeting John. She did, however, talk about how the perspective of the Communist Party drove a wedge into her marriage and many other marriages. She spoke of this in her memoirs, in speeches, and even in congressional testimony. Remarking upon the situation in a 1961 speech, she stated:

> But so deluded was I that I was helping the world, as I say, I gave
> up my freedom as a woman for a mess of pottage. And so, you
> will see that in every Communist establishment, everything is
> done to promote a circulation of wives and husbands, a looseness
> of the marital relationship. The relationship of sex as the only

important relationship between the man and the woman. The relationship of provider from the father to the son but not the relationship of obedience or the relationship of helping the child as the guardian sent there by God himself.[400]

This applied to her relations with her family, not just with her spouse. Bella said that because of her work in the Party, she became "completely separated" from her parents and siblings, who did not approve of what she was doing. "My husband had become estranged from me."[401]

Bella, of course, had come from a large, intact Italian family. Hers was likely the first divorce in her family.

Communism "Permeates Everything"

When it came to marriage and family and even the entirety of tradition, Bella knew what the Party taught, what the Bolsheviks taught, what Lenin taught, and what Marx and Engels taught. The latter, in their *Communist Manifesto*, stated candidly that "communism represents the most radical rupture in traditional relations, in traditional ideas," seeking to abolish nothing less than "the present state of things." Communists, stated the close of the *Manifesto*, sought "the forcible overthrow of all existing social conditions."

That included everything from religion to family to marriage.

A change in doctrine toward the family was at the root of Marxist socialism. The *Communist Manifesto* itself asked: "On what foundation is the present family, the bourgeois family, based? On capital. On private gain." It predicted a great triumph: "The bourgeois family will vanish when its complement (prostitution) vanishes, and both will vanish with the vanishing of capital." It referred to marriage as a "system of wives in common" among the bourgeoisie.[402]

The personal marriage history of Bella reflects communist ideals perfectly. The ideology was not just a system of economics, politics, or foreign affairs, or about the support of the Soviet Union. In her own words, "Communism is a whole philosophy of life that permeates everything that you do."[403]

Bella saw and felt how communism became "part of your bloodstream." It "determines the kind of marriage you have, your relations with your children, your relationship to your community, your relationship with your profession. It decides and makes decisions for you."[404] As noted, Bella's Catholic Church had stated and warned of this from the very beginning, in encyclical upon encyclical. Marxism was no mere economic philosophy. It was an all-encompassing way of life, later prompting popes like John Paul II and Benedict XVI to state that communism failed above all "anthropologically" because it failed to properly understand human nature.

This was a thoroughly comprehensive worldview, so much so that the atheistic philosophy actually became a religion itself.

Bella described communism as just that—a religion. It was a religion that served as your new family. Frank Vasile, who knew Bella for eight years, and was interviewed for this book, told us something quite remarkable about Bella: "Her husband told her to leave the Communist Party. She had a family, she had a son." But she told her husband that the Communist Party was her family.[405]

Particularly notable here is the statement that Bella had a son. Did she?

Whether Bella Dodd had a son is a great mystery that we as her biographers have not been able to pin down, even as one of us (Mary Nicholas) spent years trying to track down information. Mary became convinced that she had a child, a boy, who went to one of the military academies, but could not locate his identity. Various acquaintances of Bella said she had a son but that her husband retained custody after the divorce. Bella herself reportedly rarely mentioned it, and even then, not directly. That child today would be roughly ninety years old. We do not know if he is alive. It was no doubt a hole in Bella's life and in her heart.

We do know that the Party deterred Bella from having children. Bella longed for a family, and at one point after her divorce from John, she thought of adopting children, but her comrades "dissuaded me. They reminded me that I could not overcome the legal handicaps of adoption for a woman living alone, and I knew, too, that irregular hours and my limited income would make it difficult."[406]

The Party was her family.

In 1955, after her purge from the Party and her reversion to her Catholic faith, a sad twist occurred in Bella's life, one that must have hurt her deeply. Bella attempted to adopt five foster children who had been abandoned by their mother and neglected by their father. Chief Justice Laird Henry, in Juvenile Court, said she was turned down because "the New York Welfare Department would not approve Mrs. Dodd's New York City apartment as a home for the youngsters."[407] The department found the physical facilities inadequate for a family of that size, rather than ruling against Mrs. Dodd's character. She was highly recommended by a former state senator and by Bishop Fulton Sheen, who later was made archbishop of the Titular See of Newport, Wales, by Pope Paul VI.

But it was not to be. Bella Dodd was not to have a family life, though she hungered for one.

"One of the things that Communism has sworn to destroy," Bella said, "is the so-called bourgeois family life in which the father, the mother, and children are related to one other." The bourgeois family, Marx and Engels insisted, would be made "obsolete" in their new classless utopia.[408]

Bella's life was a testimony to that.

Postcard Divorces and Easy Abortions

On a practical level, how was the destruction of family life achieved in the Soviet Union? The Matrimonial Codes of Russia in the years of 1918 and 1927 proclaimed that "all children belong to the State."

The family code of 1918 invalidated all Church marriages and declared that any marriage "could be dissolved at the will of either party, simply by sending a post card to the registration office, which in turn sent another postcard dissolving the union."[409]

The Russian Orthodox Church's long-standing prohibition against divorce was forcibly lifted by the Bolsheviks as soon as they seized power. The result was total havoc, leading to an explosion in divorce rates and utter mayhem upon the Russian family.[410] The dramatic combined effect of an immediate full liberalization of divorce laws and institution of so-called "red weddings" (i.e., state-approved, fully secularized weddings) became especially calamitous with the corresponding complete legalization of abortion in 1920, which was an unprecedented action anywhere in the world at the time. With those changes and the squashing of the Russian Orthodox Church and its guidance in marriage, families, children, education and more (all schools were removed from the Orthodox Church and fully secularized, with religion banned), Lenin and his allies dealt a severe blow to marital and family life in traditionally religious Russia. Right out of the gate, within the first months and years after they seized power, the Bolsheviks had initiated these jolts to society. Consider the data on both divorce and abortion:

The number of divorces exploded in Bolshevik Russia. One Russian man, painfully recalling his boyhood years from the late 1920s, stated: "The years 1929 to 1932 were the unhappiest period for my family. At that time there were many cases of divorce. Many of our acquaintances got divorced. It was like an epidemic."[411]

The numbers grew worse decade by decade. As was reported by Professor H. Kent Geiger, who in 1968 published *The Family in Soviet Russia* through Harvard University Press, probably the seminal scholarly work on the subject, it was "not unusual" to meet Soviet men and women who had been married and divorced upwards of fifteen times.[412] The world certainly took notice of this domestic carnage. It is instructive that the influential American magazine *The Atlantic* published a 1926 piece with the title "The Russian Effort to Abolish Marriage."[413]

If divorce was an epidemic in the USSR, abortion was a black plague. The Bolsheviks legalized abortion shortly after they seized power. Like divorce, it was a rare area where the communists allowed for total individual freedom. Here they enacted full privatization. You were not free to own a farm or factory or business or bank account or go to church or print your own newspaper, but if you wanted a divorce or abortion in Bolshevik Russia, there were no obstacles—not when it came to abolishing the family.

As for abortion, Vladimir Lenin quickly made good on his June 1913 promise for an "unconditional annulment of all laws against abortions."[414] As his partner Leon Trotsky insisted, "Revolutionary power gave women the right to abortion." For a communist woman, this was "one of her most important civil, political and cultural rights." "You cannot 'abolish' the family," lectured Trotsky, looking for a better description of their goals. "You have to replace it."[415]

By 1920, abortion was made fully and legally available and provided free of charge to Russian women. The number of abortions skyrocketed. By 1934, Moscow women were having three abortions for every live birth, shocking ratios that American women, in the worst throes of *Roe v. Wade*, never approached. In the Soviet Union, abortion rates ascended to heights heretofore unwitnessed in human history. One authoritative source from the late 1960s reported: "One can find Soviet women who have had twenty abortions."[416] By the 1970s, according to official statistics from the Soviet Health Ministry, the Soviet Union was averaging seven to eight million abortions per year, annihilating whole future generations of Russian children. (America, with a similar population, averaged nearer 1.5 million abortions per year after *Roe* was approved in 1973.)[417]

Family life was being revolutionized, especially for women. Housekeeping, for instance, became a state industry, as mothers were pushed out of the home to factory floors and farms. Marx and Engels most clearly articulated those goals in two books, *The German Ideology* (1846, published two years before the *Manifesto*) and *The Origin of the Family* (published in 1884, a year after Marx's death). They advocated for a system in which a woman's private housework would be supplanted by state-run social labor. In the communist state, private housework would be nationalized. Housework would become a public industry with communal childcare. Children would be raised communally. Engels wrote in *The Origin of the Family, Private Property and the State*: "With the transfer of the means of production into common ownership, the single family ceases to be the economic unit of society. Private housekeeping is transformed into a social industry. The care and education of the children becomes a public affair; society looks after all children alike."

The nurturing and care and education of children would become a public affair, a social industry. Society would look after all children.[418]

One of the most influential Bolshevik theorists on the family was Aleksandra Kollontai, the regime's leading feminist. A sort of Soviet version of Eleanor Roosevelt, Kollontai was appointed People's Commissar for Social Welfare by Lenin. She became the most prominent woman in the regime. In 1919, she founded Lenin's "Women's Department." An early sexual feminist, Kollontai, like Margaret Sanger, was an advocate of so-called "free love."[419] In her 1920 Marxist classic *Communism and the Family*, Kollontai wrote: "There is no escaping the fact: the old type of family has had its day. The family is withering away not because it is being forcibly destroyed by the state, but because the family is ceasing to be a necessity."[420]

This became the official propaganda of the communist state. Bella Dodd knew it all too painfully well. So did her Church.

About the time that Bella was suffering from her ideology's assault on her family life, Pope Pius XI issued his 1937 encyclical *Divini Redemptoris*, which said of communism:

[It] makes of marriage and the family a purely artificial and civil institution, the outcome of a specific economic system. There exists no matrimonial bond of a juridical-moral nature that is not subject to the whim of the individual or of the collectivity. . . . Communism is particularly characterized by the rejection of any link that binds woman to the family and the home, and her emancipation is proclaimed as a basic principle. She is withdrawn from the family and the care of her children, to be thrust instead into public life and collective production under the same conditions as man. The care of home and children then devolves upon the collectivity.[421]

The pope and his Church clearly knew of which they spoke. That assessment was unerringly correct. It was precisely how Marx and Engels and the Bolsheviks applied their communist philosophy. It was exactly why Bella's personal life suffered. Such was a consequence of choosing to become a communist.

Artificial Birth Control

The Bolshevik approach to the family included rigorous birth control. The biggest advocate for birth control in America was Margaret Sanger, a socialist, who joined the Women's Committee of the New York Socialist Party.[422] Sanger's Planned Parenthood was originally founded as the American Birth Control League.

Margaret Sanger had a keen interest in what the Bolsheviks were doing to promote birth control, so much so that she made pilgrimage to the Soviet motherland in the summer of 1934, where she fell in love with the Stalinist state's birth-control policies. Once she returned home, Sanger eagerly shared her findings in the June 1935 edition of her *Birth Control Review*, in an article titled "Birth Control in Russia." She raved: "Theoretically, there are no obstacles to birth control in Russia. It is accepted . . . on the grounds of health and human right. . . . [W]e could well take example from Russia, where there are no legal restrictions, no religious condemnation, and where birth control instruction is part of the regular welfare service of the government."

"Free-love" progressives like Sanger, the matron of Planned Parenthood, joined American communists in their love affair with Bolshevism's support of birth control. Birth control was about advancing not just "free love" but also population control. (Sanger was a radical eugenicist who preached "race improvement.") Communist Party leader William Z. Foster said, "Man will free himself, under Socialism. . . . Man, too, for the first time disregarding foolish religious taboos, will boldly solve the population problems both in respect to the size of his own individual family and that of the number of people in the nations generally."[423]

Bella Dodd spoke to these things—birth control, the family, the communist view of human beings—in speeches and in congressional testimony. During a congressional hearing in November 1953, Representative Kit Clardy (R-Michigan) asked Bella about a claim that communists believed that "killing off 100 million people would be a good thing." (Ironically, 100 million dead is precisely the most common estimate of how many people communism did kill by the end of the twentieth century, including by Harvard University Press' *The Black Book of Communism*.) Bella answered: "There is no doubt in my mind that this is a program for reorganizing and rebuilding mankind, according to their peculiar pattern. The basis of the Marxist socialist approach to the family is its philosophy that persons are only material, with no spiritual dimension, no soul."[424]

In such a ruthless world of division, communism's rejection of any spiritual dimension was crucial. Under communism, noted Bella, man is solely a material animal, and this view had a profound effect on how communists viewed human beings. She told her audience in Utica:

> Now the communist concept of man is materialistic. Man is
> born, he grows, he dies, he decays, and that's the end of him. And
> if that is true, then everything the communists say is correct. But

if the Christian concept, the Judeo-Christian concept of man as embodied in the Old and New Testaments, is true, if that man is a creature of God, then, as David said in that beautiful eighth psalm of his, "Oh, God, what is man that Thou art mindful of him and the Son of Man that you visit him." If you believe the words of David—"Thou hast created man, a little less than the angels, to have dominion over all the other pieces of the earth," to "serve God in this world, and to know him and be happy with Him in the next world"—if you believe that concept of man, then each one of us, no matter how crippled, and how deformed, how weak, no matter what we are, each one of us has that divine spark trying to find its way back to God. Each one becomes, then, a sacred person, an individual, a person important to respect, a personality. Then it follows as night follows day, that you can't kill off those who are sick, those who are deformed, without violating the great rules of life.[425]

Of course, in turn, this distorted image of human beings cut deep into communists' views on what Pope John II called the core of civilization: the family.

Bella spoke of the family in another address in Indianapolis in 1964, where she described the communist attempt to eat at the family as a "worming" away at civilization as a whole: "This whole concept of breaking up the family and fragmentizing family life is the worm, really, at the heart of civilization there. We ourselves are guilty of changing in that direction." She also touched on the subject of equality: "It isn't equality which women are seeking. Women are seeking the right of fulfillment of their lives as women and men as men. Under the Communist regime, you begin to have masculinized women and feminized men."[426]

In all, it was nothing short of a war on the family, an abolition of the family. And Bella Dodd felt it most personally.

CHAPTER 8

BELLA OPENLY JOINS THE COMMUNIST PARTY (1943)

Due to personal financial difficulties, Bella in 1932 returned to Hunter College to teach. She had stepped away from Hunter in 1930 to accept a clerkship for admission to the New York Bar, working for a nominal salary in the office of Howard Hilton Spellman, who Bella remembered as an "excellent lawyer" who at that time was writing several texts on corporate law. But her cut in salary became a major liability when the Great Depression hit. It hurt her family especially. "My father's business had come to a standstill," she recalled. "John, too, was meeting financial difficulties. I, therefore, decided to return to my post at Hunter College."[427]

But as the Depression jeopardized the jobs of non-tenured teachers such as herself, Bella earnestly looked to a career in educational politics and activism, which became her passion and her world. Her activism left little time for teaching. Her gift and vocation as a dynamic teacher were almost abandoned, though she did hang on at Hunter, even as her priorities were shifting. Where would she go from here?

At that point, Bella Dodd turned to the Communist Party.

By her own account, Bella had started working "very closely with the Communist Party from the time that I first became interested, in 1932, until the time that I became the legislative representative of the Communist Party in New York City." By 1935, she was invited to Party meetings—"secret meetings, and caucus meetings, unit meetings. . . . Wherever the work which I was doing was going to be discussed by the Communists at their meetings, I was invited and made part of the movement." It was in 1943 that she agreed to join the Party as an open member, to serve as its legislative representative, and to do other work that the Party asked her to do.[428]

In reality, Bella had been effectively a secret communist since 1935, when she was given assignments, and even earlier when she had been placed under infamous "Party discipline."[429] She later testified under oath to Congress that from "1932 on . . . I was under discipline from the Communist Party."[430]

Not until later, however, was she given a Party card. The lack of a card theretofore was standard procedure by the Party. As Bella herself explained, "It was a uniform rule [for the Party] throughout the United States that professional people were to be protected. In many cases, they did not receive cards. If they were in very high and important positions, such as Government positions or civil service, no cards were issued."[431] Not having an actual card allowed Party members deniability if and when they were asked by federal authorities if they were members.

Since Bella continued to teach at Hunter until 1938, she continued to cloak her evolving loyalty to the Party and the movement. She also began working for the teachers' union in 1936 (through 1944), where she was careful to hide her communism, especially as she started pushing the ideology through deceit. She had infiltrated the union.[432] This means that Bella, like many others in the communist ranks, was an agent of the Kremlin during her time teaching at Hunter and when serving as legislative counsel for the New York Teachers Union.

Bella, however, eventually became so committed to the Party that she did not bother to hide her affiliation. In 1943, Bella made a choice that ensured that her life would never be the same: she openly joined the Communist Party.

The Fight against Fascism (Sort of)

Anti-fascism was one of the main reasons that Bella chose to become a communist. Europe, and Germany in particular, with its fascism on display, made a strong impression on Bella and made her a confirmed anti-fascist. This was an important bridge for many into the Party, as she later explained:

> The communists were very clever in giving us two alternatives, which really were not alternatives. They put themselves at the head of the anti-Fascist movement. They said, "We are the great anti-Fascists" and, since you wanted to fight fascism, you fell into the trap of working with the communists. They first approached me in 1932 on the question of uniting in the fight against fascism, and since I had been to Germany and seen it in action, I fell for the propaganda line of the communists. I know now, as practically all Americans are beginning to realize, that these alternatives are false propaganda alternatives, that actually the communist movement is nothing but a more intensified kind of fascism, but at that time it was difficult to tell.[433]

Orchestrated by Stalin, the Party presented the choice for communism as the moral good in the fight against Nazism, even though Hitler himself had remarked that "the whole of National Socialism was based on it [Marxism]."[434] And of course, as Bella and many Jewish American communists would one day learn to their horror, World War II would be launched in September 1939 through a pact between Hitler and Stalin, which committed both sides to mutual invasions of Poland that month.

The truth is that Hitler and his National Socialist German Workers Party had much in common with Stalin and the Bolsheviks. The commonalities stemmed from each supporting socialism and championing the worker to their willingness to eliminate entire categories of human beings based on hate. For the Nazis, it was racial hatred. For the communists, it was class hatred. The Bolshevik view was described by Martin (M. Y.) Latsis, who Lenin appointed to his Cheka and who orchestrated Lenin's Red Terror. Latsis affirmed the Bolshevik approach with deadly candor: "We are exterminating the bourgeoisie as a class. In your investigations don't look for documents and pieces of evidence about what the defendant has done, whether in deed or in speaking or acting against Soviet authority. The first question you should ask him is what class he comes from, what are his roots, his education, his training, and his occupation. These questions define the fate of the accused."[435]

As Lenin's and then Stalin's disciple (before Stalin had him purged in 1938), these were Latsis's orders to the comrades in the killing field: *We are exterminating the bourgeoisie as a class.* Like Nazism, Bolshevism was fueled by hatred—again, one based on race, and the other on class.

Bella would come to understand that, but only after a moral realization and reckoning years later. She explained in congressional testimony: "Nazis betrayed the individual man by the synthetic use of a mystical thing called the race. They said in the interest of a pure German race everyone was expendable who did not fit into that goal. The Communists use another mystical thing. They teach a mystical thing called the proletariat, the race of proletariats, the industrial class will rule, and in the interests of that everything else is expendable, farmers, professional people. As a matter of fact, they make appeals to the youth and the minority national groups which they played havoc with."[436]

Bella spoke in one of her addresses about the connection between fascist-socialism and communism: "And so, now we know, after having captured the documents from Berlin and other sections, that there was a close interrelationship between this national socialism, with, what was established in Germany and Italy and began spreading, and communism. After all, when you have the Soviet-Nazi pact, it was not to say an accident, nor was it unusual."[437]

It most certainly was not. Bella's later spiritual mentor Fulton Sheen understood this too. In fact, quite prophetically, throughout 1939,

Sheen had openly expressed his suspicion of a possible emerging alliance between the two devils, one in Berlin and one in Moscow.[438] "There is not a vast difference between them," he said in the summer of 1939, just before the Hitler-Stalin Pact was finalized. "What class is to Russia, race is to Germany, what the bourgeois are to the Russians, the Jews are to the Germans."[439] "As Americans," said Sheen at a huge January 1939 rally hosted by the National Council of Catholic Men, "we are not concerned with whether a dictator has a long moustache or a short moustache; or whether he invades the soul through the myth of race or the myth of the class; we are concerned only with the fact that there has been an invasion and expropriation of the inalienable liberties of man."[440]

As Sheen summed up, Hitler and Stalin were "two gangsters."[441] Both were "assassins of justice."[442] One punished and stole and killed for race and the other for class. Above all, there was their joint contempt for God. "The anti-God regime is always the anti-human regime," said Sheen. "What more clearly proves it than the Red Fascism of Communism and the Brown Fascism of Nazism which, by denying the spirit of God as the source of human rights, makes the State the source?"[443] Sheen sized up the two dictators as the modern equivalents of "Pilate and Herod—Christ haters."[444]

But this was not how the international communist movement had been busily framing things throughout the 1930s, or at least until it was forced to do an about-face once Stalin forged a formal partnership with Hitler. Prior to the signing of that alliance on August 24, 1939, communists told the world that they represented the grand movement against fascism. If you truly wanted to fight Nazism, communists insisted, their movement was your only genuine choice. This became a mass campaign for communist recruitment.

Willi Münzenberg, a crucial high-ranking propagandist for the Communist Party, was ordered to transform the "peace" movement into a worldwide anti-fascist movement in 1933, the year Hitler came to power. This new myth helped to attract many converts to communism as they made their choice for what appeared as "the good." The myth alleged that whatever the failings of the Marxist-Leninist state, it had the virtue of being opposed to Nazism.[445] This propaganda was so effective that it lured thousands of the best and brightest, who thought they were fighting for intellectual freedom and against fascism.

The fraud of anti-fascism continued to work throughout the 1930s and even throughout Stalin's Great Terror. In this light, it is easy to see why fighting fascism became Bella's primary entrée, as well as the entrée of several generations of intellectuals, into the Communist Party.[446] When Bella returned to the United States, she said, "The communists were on my doorstep with the question, 'We hear you are an anti-Fascist.' They asked me to join a committee. I did—not knowing how they were functioning." So, Bella joined the Anti-Fascist Literature Committee.[447]

Some of the most successful communist front-groups ever in the entire history of the movement were forged around this campaign—organizations such as the American League Against War and Fascism and the American Peace Mobilization, the latter of which Congress later termed "one of the most seditious organizations which ever operated in the United States," "one of the most notorious and blatantly Communist fronts ever organized in this country," and an "instrument of the Communist Party line."[448] They were enormously successful in pulling in both communists and non-communist progressives (so-called "dupes") unaware that they were being lured by communist front-groups.

Of course, the absurdity of all this is that there were a million ways to oppose fascism. One certainly need not become a communist to do so. Over 99 percent of people realized that, but others did not.

Around this time, Bella met Harriet Silverman. Harriet's husband was John Louis Engdahl, yet another Socialist Party of America member who joined the Communist Party, serving as editor of the Soviet-funded and controlled *Daily Worker*.[449] Silverman's apartment was lined with bookshelves filled with works by Lenin, Marx, and Stalin, with Lenin's picture draped with red flags and hammers and sickles. Silverman admitted she was a communist and Bella said to herself: "Let it be; I am not frightened by labels. If they are for the people, I am for them." Bella Dodd then let forth a chilling concession: "Blasphemously, I would add, 'I'll join the devil himself if he is going in my direction.' There is no doubt that I traveled with him at my side and that he exhorted a great price for his company."[450]

By this point, it was the devil and Bella Dodd. She was willing to travel with him at her side. Her path was taking a dark turn.

Silverman organized a group to ostensibly fight fascism.[451] She suggested that the college teachers form an anti-fascist literature committee to do research, raise funds, and write pamphlets, and asked Bella to join them.

Bella was extremely anxious to join, and said she did almost nothing else from 1932 to 1935, aside from teaching, with her name mentioned on one of the group's flyers.[452] She also met Margaret Schlauch, a professor from NYU. Schlauch and Silverman were probably Bella's first official contacts with communists. Among the committee's publications were "Who Are the Aryans?" written by Schlauch, and "The Fate of Trade Unions under Fascism."[453] The group noted that "Fascism, and its blood-brother Nazism, are the enemies of the people. We also know that Fascism means war."[454]

Perhaps as a pretense, Silverman asked Bella if she wanted proof that the money the committee raised was getting to where it should go. Bella said she did. Silverman arranged for her to meet Earl Browder, then head of the Communist Party of America.[455] Introducing Browder and Bella at Party headquarters, Silverman said, "Here are two people who are for the anti-Fascist movement." Bella recalled: "He greeted us very cordially. I didn't say much. We talked about the evils of fascism and we left."[456]

The Anti-Fascist Literature meetings pretended to be nonpartisan— the trademark of a classic front group. The group raised thousands of dollars for the cause and Bella embarked on a fund-raising campaign supervised by Silverman, who hosted meetings and social affairs at her home. Silverman began bringing many well dressed, sophisticated communists—doctors, lawyers, and businessmen, as well as functionaries of the Party—to the meetings. In this bourgeois mix were longshoremen, painters, plumbers, sailors. The common ground on which they met was that past society was corrupt, and the future would be "worthwhile only if it became collective."[457]

The fight against fascism was the bait, a major propaganda tool that morphed into various fronts, used to entice many to either work with or join the Communist Party—not only Bella Dodd but Elizabeth Bentley, Eugene Lyons, Manning Johnson, and a number of well-meaning Americans. Said Bella of this diverse lot of recruits: "Since 1932, the Communist Party had publicized itself as the leading opponent of fascism. It used the emotional appeal of anti-fascism to bring many people to the acceptance of communism, by posing communism and fascism as alternatives, with its propaganda machine grinding out an endless stream of words, pictures, and cartoons. It played on intellectual, humanitarian, racial and religious sensibilities until it succeeded to an amazing degree."[458]

Willi Münzenberg

A key player in this tactic of mass deception through front groups was Willi Münzenberg.

In 1925, during Bella's senior year at Hunter, and the year she entered Columbia for graduate studies, the Communist International tapped Münzenberg, who owned several newspapers and a publicity firm in Germany.[459] His propaganda machine was charged with a little known but large role in giving CPUSA its shape and function with the artillery of propaganda and deception.

Münzenberg's operation made no attempt to form a political party capable of viably challenging constitutional government. Rather, as noted by historian Stephen Koch, the apparatus of the American Communist Party was directed toward discrediting American politics and culture while assisting the growth of Soviet power. It sought moral authority developed through the propaganda of "righteousness politics," with a practical influence on culture.[460] No guns or tanks, it was a deceptive strategy aimed at the culture proposed by practitioners such as Georg Lukacs, Antonio Gramsci, and the Frankfurt School, often in the guise of "human rights."

Münzenberg, noted Arthur Koestler, was "the original inventor of a new type of Communist organization, the camouflaged front; and the discoverer of a new type of ally: the liberal sympathizer, the progressive fellow-traveller."[461] These fronts would influence public opinion and spread pro-communist propaganda to the unsuspecting. Rather than personally write propaganda, he organized it via hundreds of committees and front organizations, inspiring intellectuals to become fellow travelers and manipulating innocent and ignorant intellectuals as dupes. These front groups were created by communists in order to serve a specific purpose, almost always through a strategy of carefully employed deception. The front groups became "transmission belts" used to convey the current Party line to many people who would not accept it if communists themselves openly and directly presented it.[462]

It was all about deception and manipulation.

The Special Committee on Un-American Activities of the House of Representatives explained that "by its nature a Communist-front organization must have persons who are willing to front for it. If the organization were made up exclusively of persons who are professed Communists, it would be simply one more open-and-aboveboard Communist organization." Thus, "The genius of a Communist-front organization is to secure the services of distinguished persons whose very names aid in concealing the real nature of the organization."[463]

In the following years, especially under the management of Willi Münzenberg, the Comintern sponsored the development of hundreds of these "innocent clubs" all over the world. From 1933 to 1953, front groups were particularly active in the United States, some of which Bella joined and helped to organize.[464]

Bella Dodd was influenced by this organized manipulation of public opinion, especially Munzenberg's successful exploitation of the so-called Sacco-Vanzetti campaign, which was a massive, aggressive effort by the American Communist Party, which attracted many converts. The effort was constantly pushed in Party newspapers and magazines that Bella read, like the *Daily Worker*, the official Communist Party organ, which ran headlines like "Americans of All Races, Colors and Creeds Honor Sacco and Vanzetti." The *Daily Worker* carried a story with photographs of Sacco and Vanzetti in the August 23, 1940 edition.[465] While Bella was attending Columbia University graduate school, the *Columbia Spectator* announced that the Social Problems Club would "discuss Sacco and Vanzetti." The speaker was Elizabeth Gurley Flynn, identified as an International Labor Defense member.[466]

The cultural magazine *New Masses*, for which Bella was later a contributing editor, had several articles on Sacco and Vanzetti in 1927, the year she graduated from Columbia. The editor wrote at the time: "Sacco and Vanzetti had guts. What a dramatic, what a heroic episode! Two men before our eyes, walk calmly to death for the sake of an idea."[467] And the *Nation* headlined the Sacco and Vanzetti story with "Massachusetts the Murderer."[468]

To this day, the pair are considered "class war heroes" and their execution a "legal lynching."[469] Their case and execution created tremendous excitement and became a *cause célèbre* throughout the world. The Sacco and Vanzetti case even brought a comment from a future Supreme Court justice, Felix Frankfurter, then a professor at Harvard.[470]

By every measure, Münzenberg's accomplishments were above expectations.

Bella on the Communist Conspiracy and Its Wealthy Patrons

These front-group "transmission belts" were tied into the larger global communist conspiracy. Bella Dodd was adamant about making a distinction between the communist conspiracy, the Communist Party, and communist movement. Thus, she might refer to someone as a "communist" when he or she was not a card-carrying member of the Party but, in fact, was working for its goals. She gave a detailed explanation:

> The communist conspiracy . . . is a secret organization of a group of people who are determined to be in control, or are determined to accomplish something illegal, sometimes in legal ways, and sometimes in illegal ways. The communist conspiracy consists of men and women who are located in New York, in Moscow, in Paris, in London, in Saigon, in Hong Kong, and throughout the world. . . . It consists of a group of people who cooperate with each in moving toward a world government, moving towards statism, moving toward a totalitarian system moving toward a complete monopoly of industry and so on. The conspiracy is made up of men who are determined to control the natural resources of the world . . . in controlling oil, and controlling iron, steel, uranium, yes, timber, and land itself. The communist conspiracy is as simple as all that and in order to control these, they have to control the two and a half billion human beings who stand in their way. If there weren't a conspiracy, there wouldn't be this symphony of movement, of people and events which leads almost diabolically and in a very planned way, towards the elimination of freedom on a worldwide basis.[471]

This communist conspiracy, she emphasized, was a "world conspiracy on a worldwide basis," operating "under different labels at different times. Sometimes it uses the communist label, sometimes it uses the socialist label, sometimes it uses the humanist label, sometimes it uses the goodwill label."

As for the Communist Party's role in this, Bella described the Party as the "organizational blueprint of the new organized society, which they will establish when they come to power. It is like the skeleton of the new form of government which they hope to establish . . . sometime in the future." In this new world, each nation would have its own Communist Party, though all would answer to the Soviet Comintern in Moscow: "The Communist Party in America was established in Chicago in 1919 as a result of certain Russians who came here," said Bella. "And so, the Communist Party . . . sometimes they're called Labor Party, or Socialist Labor Party, but the answer to whether they're Communist Parties or not is to whether they are affiliated, whether they are sympathetic, are they cooperative with the Soviet system."[472]

That was how the global conspiracy would operate. The Comintern, situated in Moscow, would conduct the worldwide Marxist-Leninist symphony.

Bella explained that the Communist Party is not a political party in the sense that we typically understand it. This was something she only came to understand once becoming a member. That was most clearly so because no other group of individual country parties were all coordinated by a single source headquartered in one country, a source that dictated to all the others to overthrow their native government and align with the Kremlin.

Moreover, Bella came to understand that this was not "a poor man's party" but a party of "certain men of wealth." The communist movement sought to create the "illusion of the poor man's party; it was in reality a device to control the 'common man' they so raucously championed."[473] Bella came to the realization that some capitalists, the wealthiest people in the world, actually believed in and financed communism. Why would they support what appeared to be the pathway to their own destruction? It was strange, but they did so nonetheless.

A friend of Bella, Frank Vasile, recalled that she had told him that the "higher she got in the Communist Party, she dealt less and less with communists, and dealt more and more with representatives of the Rockefellers, Lehmans, Harrimans. And at that time, they were dealing with Russia even though we didn't recognize Russia. The Harrimans were making deals for the magnesium to take the magnesium mines and the products from the magnesium mines from Russia, and the Rockefellers with the oil and the gas, and so on and so forth."[474]

Bella emphasized this in an interview with Facts Forum in 1955. She discovered that the "really wealthy people in the political front are those who are on the left. Those are the ones whom the national committee of the Communist Party feed and promote and help. Those are the ones who have the estates in Westchester County. Those are the ones who are making the money. It's a delusion to think that the Communist Party is only made up of poor people. The poor people are the suckers; they're the ones who are used over and over again against their own interests." These money-people were the mansion Marxists, the champagne socialists, the limousine leftists.

They were not actually the working men and women of the Proletariat; instead, they were men and women of wealth.

Bella Dodd emphasized that this was one of the "hardest things to get across to the American people and yet unless they understand this, they won't understand communism." She said that communism "would fall by the wayside if it were not supported and promoted by people who had something to gain materially by the promotion of communism."[475]

While Bella Dodd was still in the Party and a member of the national committee, she began to get suspicious about the chain of command inside the Party. Bella could see webs and patterns that formed a picture, a picture quite different from the accepted "official" explanations.

W. Cleon Skousen, a former FBI special agent, attorney, and researcher, interviewed Bella several times in the 1960s. Once, he asked her the question "Who is trying to take over the world?" She replied, "I think the communist conspiracy is merely a branch of a much bigger conspiracy!"[476]

She meant that the tentacles of cooperation went even further than people realized, sometimes snagging even wealthy capitalists. It was a mess.

Bella's Associations and Alliances, and the Cloak of "Academic Freedom"

By this time, Bella was becoming fully enmeshed in various associations and alliances.

While at Hunter, Bella joined the Instructors Association and helped establish the short-lived American Association of University Teachers. As noted, she also joined the pro-communist Anti-Fascist Literature Committee. At the time, her interests and those of the American Communist Party appeared mutual: anti-fascist, anti-war, and a commitment to working-class rights. After helping pass a bill on college teachers' tenure, she became legislative representative of the Teachers Union Local 5 in 1936 and thus an officer of the American Federation of Labor (AFL).

Through these organizations, Bella came to admire the dedication of "many who belonged to the Party. They took me into their fraternal circle and made me feel at home. I was not interested in any long-range Party objectives, but I did welcome their assistance on immediate issues, and I admired them for their courage. Most of all, I admired how they fought for the forgotten man of the city. So I did not argue with them about the 'dictatorship of the proletariat' which they talked about."[477]

She also worked with the Classroom Teachers Association, which communist teachers were using as a front group.[478] Bella was invited by a number of communist teachers to meetings organized in every school. Membership by "supervisors" was forbidden. It was labeled the "best example of the Rank and File's mass organizing strategy."[479] (As will be shown ahead, "Rank and File" was the name of a militant communist faction of the Teachers Union.) Bella said the Classroom Teachers Association learned "the techniques of mass action and were carefully organized on the basis of the class-struggle philosophy. They were a disciplined band secretly associated with the Trade Union Unity League (TUUL) led by William Z. Foster, future head of CPUSA."[480]

"Mass action" was something the Rank and File flaunted in a way that suggested they were fighters for "academic freedom." Here is a typical information sheet prior to the New York Teachers Union elections of June 1934: "No longer do members of the union recoil at the words 'Mass Action.' They vote at membership meetings for our resolutions calling for mass action." The group lobbied for "Academic Freedom," saying, "We have won a large part of the membership of the Union to our program of mass action in defense of 'victimized teachers.'" The members of the "academic freedom committee [continue] the fight waged by the rank and file all year."[481]

As we shall see repeatedly, this rallying cry of "academic freedom" served the comrades mightily. When some of these communist teachers were called before the US Senate to testify on whether they were Communist Party members dedicated to subverting the educational process and supporting the overthrow of the US government in favor of creating a "Soviet American Republic," they self-righteously lectured the senators about the sanctity of their "academic freedom," and also invoked the Fifth Amendment of the US Constitution—a document that they secretly pledged and battled to replace with the Soviet Constitution. They were being trained well, especially as these sanctimonious appeals always found support among easily duped progressives.[482]

In her testimony to the House Committee on Un-American Activities in November 1953, Bella was asked: "Does the Communist Party have any respect for academic freedom?" Her answer was succinct and to the point: "The Communist Party doesn't know what academic freedom means. If a person criticizes the Party or raises a question, that person is suspect. It is academic freedom for the Communists to say what they want to say, but not academic freedom for anyone else."[483]

Bella spoke of this phenomenon often. On another occasion, she told the US Senate in sworn testimony:

> The communists will use academic freedom as a cloak or as a shield to protect themselves in the spread of any idea which they are determined to spread. I think that academic freedom has to be the right for the professor or the teacher to make a search for the truth; but, by heavens, he must then find the truth and label the truth, and let the student and other teachers know what the truth is. You can't just ask for academic freedom in general and under the shield just to promote anything you want. That is not academic freedom.[484]

She added: "I think that the history of this country would say that we are all interested in freedom of thought. But what goes by the name of academic freedom very frequently is not freedom of thought."[485]

By her description, Bella and the Classroom Teachers Association had two tasks: "to convert a considerable number of teachers to a revolutionary approach to problems, and to recruit as many members as possible to the Communist Party. Some were also members of Teachers Union Local 5, forming an organized minority opposition to the prevailing noncommunist leadership."[486] Bella said the Classroom Teachers Association, like all Red unions, publicized popular problems such as the large number of unemployed teachers in the city and substitute teachers hired at low wages. It engaged in mass action such as sending delegations to the Board of Education and the mayor's office, meeting with the group at City Hall that "opposed further cuts," and demanding "a restoration of salaries to the 1932 level."[487] The technique of mass action was fully displayed when a group of four hundred "besieged" City Hall in 1934 to protest cuts and payless furloughs.[488]

Bella had become an aggressive activist. By this time, even her old friend Ruth Goldstein was alarmed and warned Bella of her associations and alliances. She cautioned: "You are getting too involved, Bella . . . you will get hurt. Wait and see!" Bella laughed it off, saying, "Oh, Ruth, you are too concerned about promotions and tenures. . . . These people are about the only ones who are doing anything about the rotten conditions of today. That is why I am with them, and I will stay with them."[489]

During later congressional testimony, Bella said that during this time in the 1930s she thought that communists were "for the working class" and "for the underdog."[490] They were "fighting hunger and misery and fascism then, and neither of the major political parties nor the churches seemed to care. I was the kind of person who was interested in the underdog. I was interested in people who were suffering. I was interested in people who had problems."[491]

When Bella began teaching, the US Depression was in full swing. The promise of a better country—a utopia—was enticing, and she recalled how party intellectuals lied and how this "was made plausible by my desire to see man-made perfection in this imperfect world."[492] She later reflected: "Unconsciously I enlisted, even if only emotionally, in the army of those who said they would fight social injustice, and I began to find the language of defiance intoxicating."[493]

Convinced that the Party cared for the little guy and fought fascism, Bella Dodd became an official member in 1935. But this was kept secret. "It is not advisable for people like yourself, for people who are in strategic positions, to become members of the Communist Party," she was told, "to have cards or to attend meetings."[494] The Party bosses gave her specific instructions: "We will have you attend private meetings. We will instruct you personally."[495]

But while embracing the underdog, Bella at this time turned her back on her friends, family, religion, "people close to me." She became completely separated from her family, which did not approve of her activities. Though feeling a twinge of regret, she found a "poignant sense of kinship" elsewhere.[496]

Bella's family was no longer the locus of strength it had once been. Her parents had lost touch with the culture of Italy. Her family also stopped going to church or having any connection with Catholicism. Bella would later say:

> But instead of being proud of that heritage and true to being in this country, my mother, the 10 children, the family, my father, worked so hard at making a living and in trying to increase their material welfare that we looked not with great pride on Italy. And we allowed the great heritage to just slip from our hands. My mother, either because she didn't speak English or because she didn't have the proper clothes or what not, stopped going to her church. And when she did, so did the children, and I say to them, that one of the first steps that I took towards communism was when I stopped going to my church.[497]

Bella had her new family and her new church. It was the Communist Party. It was there that she turned.

Bella and Famine in the Ukraine

Ironically, at the time of Bella Dodd's statement that only communists were fighting hunger, misery, and fascism, and as the Party and progressive left were engaged in agitprop "hunger marches" across the United States,[498] there was extremely severe hunger taking place in the Ukraine, where the people were too weak to march. They were starving to death. The "hunger marches" in America coincided with the beginning of the *Holodomor* in the Ukraine, which took place from 1932 to 1933.

This was one of the worst famines in history, orchestrated on the Ukrainian people by Joseph Stalin, who employed the starvation in part to crush the kulaks, the land-owning farmers. Some five to ten million starved to death. Stalin made it a crime to talk about the fam-ine. "The party has succeeded to the extent that the kulaks as a class have been crushed," stated Soviet authorities. "In carrying out the five-year plan for agriculture, the party has carried out collectivization at a rapid pace. Was the party right in doing so? Yes, the party was absolutely right, even though we did get carried away a bit. In carrying out the policy of liquidating the kulaks as a class and exterminating the nest of kulaks, the party could not stop halfway but had to take everything to its logical conclusion."[499]

Communists everywhere dutifully covered up the mass crime. That included the shameful work of the *New York Times'* infamous "Man in Moscow," Walter Duranty, who scandalously would be awarded the Pulitzer Prize, despite his woefully misleading journalism. In arti-cles with titles like "Russians Hungry, but Not Starving," Duranty reported: "Here are the facts. . . . There is no actual starvation or deaths from starvation, but there is widespread mortality from dis-eases due to malnutrition. . . . These conditions are bad, but there is no famine."[500] Duranty wrote a story blaming the famine on "peasant hatred of new ways, peasant conservatism, and peasant inertia." The stubborn peasants thought they "could change the Communist Party's collectivization policy by refusing to cooperate."[501]

This was not simply erroneous reporting. Duranty knew otherwise. He told William Strang at the British embassy on September 26, 1933, that as many as ten million people had already died in the Ukraine. He also personally told Eugene Lyons (UPI's Moscow correspondent) that he estimated the total number of famine victims around seven million. Malcolm Muggeridge would call Duranty "the greatest liar of any journalist I have met in fifty years of journalism." Even the esteemed man of the left, Joseph Alsop, denounced Duranty as a "fashionable prostitute" in service of communists.[502]

Bella recalled the famine later and said her personal life at the time was meaningless and chaotic, and "my spiritual life was void. So blind was I that the murder of 5,000,000 farmers (called kulaks) in

Soviet Russia in the name of a classless society and a planned economy aroused only a twinge of conscience. And the word liquidation meant not the murder of those who did not agree with the leaders of World Communism, but the purification of the Party."[503]

Her comrades in the Party were silent about the famine. No statement. No protests. No collective ads in the *New York Times*.

Historian Robert Conquest called the famine a deliberate act of "mass murder, if not genocide," committed as part of Stalin's collectivization program. The *Holodomor* was monstrous, and but a single example of the Soviet Union's misinformation peddled to Bella and other American communist teachers, who no doubt taught the misinformation to their pupils. The great "humanitarian" and Fabian Socialist George Bernard Shaw said in a statement to the Russian press, "I did not see a single under-nourished person in Russia, young or old. Were they padded? Were their hollow cheeks distended by pieces of India rubber inside?"[504]

That is because such people were hidden from Shaw and his fellow "progressives." They were taken by their Soviet guides to happy and tidy "show places," not to the killing fields. They were shown caviar, not cannibalism.

Bella admitted during testimony that she was "one of the sorriest examples I can give you," referring to her lack of knowledge of true events in Russia. Commenting on the US press at another time, she said, "Unfortunately, the same press which exposed the things which Hitler did, has refused to . . . expose the terrible things being done in the Soviet world."[505]

These were all lies, and lies that hit Bella hard, given that she was not by nature and upbringing an easy liar.

In fact, an ironic twist to Bella's reasons for joining the Communist Party was that she had good moral values. That showed in her honest work for the Party, such as refusing to steal Party funds, a standard practice by many Party members, especially Gus Hall, the longest-serving head of CPUSA ever, who always lined his wallet with pilfered

Party dollars.[506] Bella was loyal to the Party, and Party officials trusted her. She based the activity she was doing for the Party "on my own standards of goodness, of honesty, and of loyalty. I failed to understand that the Party, in making alliances, had nothing whatever to do with these qualities, that it was not out to reform the world, but was bent on making a revolution to control the world."[507]

If only Bella had read more Lenin. She confessed that she would have known about communists' ethics had she reflected on Lenin's speech at the Third All-Russian Congress of the Russian Young Communist League: "Is there such a thing as communist ethics?" Lenin asked. "Is there such a thing as communist morality? Of course, there is. . . . In what sense do we reject ethics, reject morality? In the sense given to it by the bourgeoisie, who based ethics on God's commandments. . . . Our morality stems from the interests of the class struggle of the proletariat."[508]

How long would Bella's own moral standards last in the Party? Would there be a reckoning, a choice between her high moral standards, anchored in God's commandments, and those of the Party, anchored in the commands of Marx, Lenin, and Stalin?

CHAPTER 9

THE COMMUNIST PARTY TAKES OVER THE TEACHERS UNION

Shortly after she joined the Communist Party, Bella Dodd was catapulted into the work of organizing unionized teachers, where the Party was looking to make great headway. She quickly learned of the communist infiltration and deep penetration.

Bella knew later that warning people about this subversion of teachers would always be sensitive. It was not what people wanted to hear, and it always invited accusations of hyperbole and conspiracy-mongering. She knew, however, the truth. She sounded the alarm. She had to because she had partaken in the infiltration and saw the immense damage done. "Now I don't object to anyone joining the teachers union," she would hasten to tell audiences with a caveat, "[but] the teachers unions on a nationwide basis, the American Federation of Teachers, unfortunately was utilized by the socialists first and then the communists, by Marxists as a whole, for the purpose of creating a new approach toward education on a nationwide basis."[509]

As we shall see, and as Bella laid out repeatedly in sworn testimony, that assertion was unerringly correct.

In a sense, the Communist Party viewed teachers unions like other unions: an opportunity to fulfill the Marxist vision for mass action, to draw the lines between workers and their oppressors, to create class consciousness, and to provide the leadership of the vanguard that would do the thinking for the working class.[510] That approach was in lockstep with the guidance set forth in Vladimir Lenin's crucial 1902 essay "What Is To Be Done?" which called for a vanguard or "party of a new type" capable of organizing and imbuing the working class with "revolutionary consciousness."

But the Party saw teachers as offering a special part in that effort. It was teachers who most influenced the next generation.

The Teachers Union's Battle in the "Class War"

In Bella's day, the generically named "Teachers Union" was a dominant force in US education, and its largest affiliate was Local 5 of the New York Teachers League, forerunner of the New York Teachers Union. It was thus also known as "AFT Local 5" of the American Federation of Teachers (AFT). It was organized in 1913 by socialist Henry Linville. Very Dewey-like and very "progressive"-like, Linville said, "We can learn democracy from Soviet Russia."[511]

Linville, a left-winger and early board member of the ACLU, was another big promoter of "academic freedom." Bella noted that Linville participated in the preparation of the union's original statement on academic freedom.[512] For Linville's comrades, "academic freedom" was a Trojan horse to teach socialism. Linville eventually, in 1931, became president of the AFT. And to Linville's credit, as we shall see, he also became anti-communist, even testifying to Congress about the problems of communist infiltration into education.

The Teachers Union was the first New York labor union for teachers, and its connection to socialists and communists was so clear that even Wikipedia acknowledges it in the opening line of its entry for "Teachers Union."[513] The US Senate, in its September 1952 investigative report *Subversive Influence in the Educational Process*, summed up concisely: "The history of the communist movement in the New York City school system [is primarily] the history of the so-called Teachers Union of the City of New York, formerly Local No. 5 of the AFT, and of its subsidiary, the College Teachers Union, formerly Local 537 of the AFT, which was founded by Local 5 in 1938."[514]

Communism gained a foothold in New York public schools in the 1920s. Linville dated the beginning of problems with the communist faction to 1922.[515] Bella would point to a crucial development in the years 1924 or 1925, when a group of "would-be revolutionaries," assembled under the leadership of Scott Nearing, crafted a treatise titled *The Law of Social Revolution*.[516] Their chief instrument for introducing communism directly into the schools was the New York Teachers Union.

The communist capture of the New York (City) Teachers Union is at the root of this history. Communism is, of course, based on the theory of class war, and to communists, the events that took place in the union represented a major front in that war. Linville, in his 1939 testimony to Congress, quoted from documents stating that "the Board of Education and other high authorities in the school system represented the employing and oppressive class. The Union should not only join in the class war to fight with the working class for 'economic and political demands,' but must also fight the people above them, from the Board of Education through the Superintendents down to principals and supervisors." Linville noted that in the communist view, "any let-up in this struggle, to say nothing of cooperation with supervisors, even for educational purposes, would be 'betrayal' of the workers' cause."[517]

War was, therefore, the strategy they followed. Communist tactics involved war at all times—between employers and employees, between teachers and the administration, between supervisors and teachers, between parents and teachers, between teachers and students. This was how class conflict was raised. This was "permanent revolution."

In 1923, the Profintern (the Communist International's Trade Union body in Moscow) ordered a portion of the communist membership in the Teachers Union to go underground, while a communist nucleus of about ten members above ground began to organize. The underground section of the Communist Party served as the "directing organ" of the open Communist Party. Going by the innocuous name the Research Study Group, it was operated by Benjamin Mandel, a typing teacher from Julia Richman High School in New York City, who was the first communist in the Teachers Union, and by Scott Nearing, a member of the National Committee of the ACLU and a professor dismissed from the University of Toledo for his radical views.[518] The Research Study Group was affiliated with the Educational Workers' International (EWI), a radical group created in 1923 by the Red International of Labor Unions, operated from Moscow. How radical the EWI was can be seen in two of its articles in its Constitution and Rules:

Article 2 of the EWI Constitution and Rules stated that "under capitalism, the school serves, above all, the interests of the propertied and governing classes, with a view, on the one hand, to the formation of an isolated stratum of privileged persons, and, on the other hand, to maintaining the great majority of the people intellectually enslaved as blind instruments of capitalism."

Article 3 of the EWI was similar: "In such a society, teachers cannot be the bearers of a higher culture for the young, and fall themselves into a state of intellectual dependence on the capitalist system, becoming bureaucratic officials and badly paid wage slaves of capital and its State."[519]

According to Bella, Dale Zysman, vice president of Local 5, became "the top liaison man between the Communist Party and the teachers."[520] He had lots of help. Myra Page, author of "Fascism in American Education," asserted that the AFT needed more militancy to prevent the onward march of fascist imperialism in American schools.[521] EWI's organ, the *Teacher's International*, labeled teachers as workers exploited by bosses. It assured teachers that they stood behind them as long as they had no illusions about being professionals.

Mandel, the chairman of the EWI Membership Committee, dreamed of making the union a militant mass organization and affiliating with the EWI, but since the communists were still a minority, the motion was defeated. The new Party line for the schools was announced by EWI in the November 1924 issue of the *Daily Worker*.

Since the Party viewed American public schools as "a weapon in the hand of the capitalist to poison the minds of the working-class children," it called for "councils of working-class parents, students, and teachers to fight capitalist domination of the schools," and teachers were urged to join the fight for the "complete abolition of capitalism." Their strategy included the following: combat "capitalist control" of the schools, develop separate educational institutions for working-class organizations in the spirit of the "revolutionary struggle," and emphasize that teachers "are exploited by capitalists and must instill in children the idea of the class struggle."[522]

At that time, there were two warring factions in the Teachers Union: the Progressive Caucus and the "Rank and File" of Local 5. The latter were the militant communists gunning to capture the union from Linville and Dr. Abraham Lefkowitz, and became the strongest caucus in the Teachers Union. They were widely known as Stalinists.[523] It was that militancy that helped Linville, Lefkowitz, and others recognize the Rank and File's true Marxist origins; it was the first definitive indication of the presence of communist elements in the Teachers Union.

The militant "Rank and File" group aligned against Linville and Lefkowitz included radical activist Isidore Begun, who first appeared on the scene in 1931. Serving as a New York State Communist Party official, Begun was on the payroll of the Party by 1935.[524] Linville and Lefkowitz tried to fight back, declaring that the membership had no desire for mass action advocated by "the protégés of an exotic dictatorship."[525]

By 1925, the communists in Local 5 had gained some respectability, and Mandel and Nearing were elected to the Executive Board. Strategically placed, they could now introduce and second motions and present their demands. They appealed to members through a sense not of communism or socialism but of "liberalism." Because members were afraid of appearing "reactionary," many appeals were approved by a majority of members who were not in sympathy with the general policies of the communist members.[526] Responding, Linville and

Lefkowitz published "Do You Want Your Union to Die?," which accused the radicals of soliciting funds for the Communist Party, seeking affiliation with the Communist Workers Party and the Education Workers International, pushing a "no confidence" vote among officers, eliminating the merit system in education, and of seeking the "admission of unqualified or doubtfully qualified teachers."[527]

In May 1931, the first issue of *Education Worker* was distributed, published by the Education Workers League of New York and the Educational Workers International. It claimed that there was a need for a "militant fighting organization" because of "the decay of capitalist 'civilization,'" and the "helpless future," urging every teacher to "take up the struggle." The *Education Worker* stated that the "AFT was a symbol of decay and falsity of the present economic system" and had failed to marshal the teachers, the workers' children, and others "for the overthrow of capitalism and establishment of a republic of hand and brain, workers and farmers."[528]

The "immediate demands" of the Education Workers League included improvement in the salaries of teachers, elimination of unsanitary conditions in some of the schools, free lunches and clothing for children of the unemployed, low-paid workers, and unemployment insurance for all workers. The league demanded the abolition of "anti-labor propaganda in the schools;" a presentation in the curriculum and texts of "working-class interests, problems, and struggles;" and the "abolition of all religious and militarist practices."[529]

Working underground, the Education Workers International continued to criticize the AFT.

The communists in the Teachers Union stepped up their activity from 1932 to 1935, just as Bella was entering the scene. To expand the union, they used one of communism's common techniques: (1) broaden the definition of something to include the class you want to manipulate, and (2) add to the membership of the class. With this new rubric, the word "teacher" now included unemployed teachers, those who indicated a desire to teach, even those without a license, and the unappointed. The communists organized and pulled in the substitutes and unappointed teachers. They established the Unemployed Teachers Association, and by January 1932, substitute teachers were permitted to join the union, thus increasing their overall representation.

Clearly, these shenanigans had a sinister purpose. As Bella would later concede, it was clear that "by organizing the unemployed teachers and fighting to have them in the Union," before long "the Teachers Union would be controlled by Reds."[530]

That is precisely what happened.

Bella's Role in the Struggle

During this time, Bella was already developing into "quite a power" in the Communist Party, functioning as the lobbyist for the Teachers Union.[531] The union became a dominant force in her life. (There are some seventy references to "Teachers Union" in Bella's memoirs.)

Bella later stated that a primary vehicle for the Communist Party's manipulation of the Teachers Union was the so-called "faction meetings." These were groups of some sixty to one hundred people from the Teachers Union composed of individual communist units, which were tightly controlled by the Communist Party. "At the beginning of the year," said Bella, "you would have a program laid down for the Party," dictating what the Party was hoping to accomplish among schools.[532] "The executive committee of the Teachers' Union," she said, "had a majority of communists. As a matter of fact, it was deplorably large . . . as many as 80 or 90 percent of the executive board were communists."[533]

Bella said that when she was the legislative representative for the Teachers Union, she "soon got to know [that] the majority of people in the top leadership of the Teachers Union were communists or, at least, were influenced by the communist organization in the city." Within the union, there was a "caucus of the executive board fighting various groups who were struggling to gain power over the union."

Nonetheless, the communists "were successful in taking control." When later asked by the US Senate, "So there was no doubt at any time that that was strictly a Communist Party operation operating within the executive board of the teachers' union?" Bella answered an unqualified "yes."[534]

Bella pointed to the Rank and File group's adoption of the factions technique, which made it especially effective with noncommunist groups. Bella said they "were prepared, organized, trained, and disciplined with a program worked out in detail. . . . In other organized blocs the communists had 'sleepers,' assigned to protect Communist Party interests. These 'sleepers' were active members in noncommunist blocs for the purpose of hamstringing and destroying the power of the opposition."[535] Within the American Federation of Labor, "the few communists who were in there were strongly organized, and this is the secret of the communist movement: centralization and organization."[536]

Again, that was especially true of the Rank and File.

Purging the Rank and File

Over time, the Rank and File became increasingly belligerent, constantly agitating and causing rancor and division. Because of their continuous disruptions at union meetings, Lefkowitz wanted "every member of the Rank and File Group in the union" brought up on charges for expulsion.[537] As a result, a "Joint Defense Committee" was formed by the Rank and File faction, which charged the administration of the union with conducting expulsion campaigns and of publicly accusing teachers and union members of being communists— charges that could result in loss of their jobs—and of "outlawing and suppressing minority opinion."[538]

Eventually, this led to a major report, which was publicized on April 29, 1933, at a chaotic meeting of eight hundred teachers. John Dewey himself was present at the meeting, and by that point, he had become very suspicious of Stalinists. Dewey himself recommended that six teachers be expelled. Isidore Begun, one of those accused, protested: "A member of the Teachers Union has the right to belong to any political party that he wishes."[539] The meeting was a battleground.

One former member of the union, Rebecca Simonson, later testified, "These meetings were described as a 'riot.' Floor fights erupted all the time. The fights were wild, absolutely wild. It was worth your life to go through it. If you rose to vote against their position, [the communists] literally took you by the coat and pushed you down to your seat."[540] Simonson continued: "When they weren't warring, the wily foes were boring each other into a mind-numbing stupor. Meetings gaveled to order at 4 o'clock dragged on till after midnight as various factions used parliamentary tactics to frustrate one another's planks. Prepared to burn the midnight oil, the highly disciplined communist faction often passed resolutions in close-to-deserted meeting rooms."[541]

This rabid demeanor and outright thuggery were critical to communists' advances.

Several years later, an investigator asked Linville how the communists succeeded in getting control of the Teachers' Union. He replied that the number of communists in the union was not "anywhere near a majority." The key to their success was not their numbers but their tactics, their dedication, and their fanaticism: "In our general meetings, where anybody could come, the communist elements . . . came early and stayed late, and by their disciplined maneuvering of introducing motions and having supporters bob up all over the meeting and confusing the situation, they often were able to carry certain motions . . . but the fact that they kept up this constant attack, month after month . . . they wore our people out."[542]

This was their cause, their life, their religion. They gave it everything they had, all the time.

In 1933, a Delegate Assembly was formed by the union's executives based on proportional representation. Within a few months, the Rank and File claimed that it was undemocratic, and meetings again became chaotic. The Rank and File slate for 1934 included Isidore Begun for president, demonstrating its tactic of putting someone up for a leadership role who had been previously attacked, now characterizing him as a "victim."

And yes, as Linville stated, the communists eventually wore out the other side. They were hell-bent on success, possessed by their cause. They eventually persevered. By 1935, the Communist Party had captured the Teachers Union with approximately 1,500 members through a feverishly united front of dedicated fanatics.

The Educational Vanguard

Later commenting on the takeover of the Teachers Union, Bella Dodd said: "The communists did not take over the union all at once."

As seen, first they captured the executive positions. The AFT investigated Local 5 on charges of communist control but did not lift the charter, allowing just enough room for the comrades to survive. After the investigation was over, seven hundred of the anti-communist teachers left the union and established the Teachers' Guild. The old Teachers Union retained the charter and continued to organize. The communists were the leaders, and their attempts at control, said Bella, "continued to make headway."[543]

From there, they steadily chipped away, day and night, week after week, month after month, year after year.

Bella emphasized that "the communist members of the executive board met together before union meetings, went over the agenda, decided how to clear away the obstacles, and how to achieve the end which we were trying to achieve. We caucused not only before executive-board meetings, but before membership meetings."[544]

Thus, a small, disciplined minority took over the union.

Later, Bella commented on these years of upheavals: "The communists were successful in taking control of the board. And while preaching 'tolerance,' 'intellectual freedom,' and 'academic freedom' to express individual political opinions," teachers who were not communists "didn't have a chance really of expressing their opinion or of really being heard."[545]

Bella Dodd testified that from 1936 to 1944, the top leadership of the Teachers Union was communist.[546] By May 1937, eleven of the twenty-seven executive board members of the Teachers Union could be identified as Party members, and by December of that same year, fifteen of the twenty-four members were in the Party, with communists in key positions, including Dale Zysman, Isidore Begun, and Bella herself, who was not known to be a communist at the time.[547]

The takeover by the communists was significant, since the Teachers Union was a major focal point for educators, especially college professors. According to academic historian Ellen W. Schrecker, a sympathizer, "for academic communists, the most important organization was the Teachers Union. Almost everybody belonged." One former professor recalled that it was practically "mandatory" for every member of his unit.[548]

Bella was a leader in the Teachers Union and recruited comrades for the classroom and for leadership roles. She later said of these comrades: "They touched practically every phase of Party work. They were not used only as teachers in Party education, where they gave their services free of charge, but in the summer they traveled and visited Party figures in other countries. They provided the Party with thousands of contacts among young people, women's organizations, and professional groups. They were generous in helping finance Party activities."[549]

The Party turned its sinister gaze to college campuses—the fertile soil for communist vocations—especially those institutions training future public school teachers. In fact, during this time, several college campuses were home to groups of communists and not at all shy about it. Many of them ran their own publications, which did not conceal their sympathies.

For instance, *Educational Vanguard* was published by the Teachers College and organized by Columbia University units of the Communist Party. One of the publication's articles, titled "Who are the T.C. [Teachers College] Communists?" gave some insight into the composition of the group: "Many of these forward-looking students are members of the Communist Party because they realize that progressive education includes a minimum of theory and is based on active participation, the working for better living conditions, and educational opportunities for ALL Americans." It emphasized that communism is "the friend of education."[550]

And while teachers were indoctrinating their students during the school year, the communist units at Teachers College and Columbia sponsored summer schools for intense indoctrination. According to *Educational Vanguard*, during the summer of 1936, ten thousand teachers, principals, and superintendents from all over America participated in these sessions.[551]

Teacher-Worker was another shop paper that appeared on campuses and carried water for Stalin: "The Soviet plans for 1936 call for more than 4,000 more schools and a 20 per cent increase of students in pedagogical schools," said *Teacher-Worker*, asking: "Why can we not 'plan' for obviously necessary expansion here at City College? Is it not because the only planning done here is to increase the flow of profits to the bankers? How else was the city budget planned?"[552]

Naturally, *Teacher-Worker* supported class war: "To be for class war in the communist sense means using the class war to destroy capitalist power, to transfer it to the proletariat, which, as Soviet Russia is showing in a relatively short time wipes out class distinctions and conflicts.'"[553]

They were bringing the class war home, from Moscow to New York City.

August 1939: the AFT Convention
and the Hitler-Stalin Pact

Of course, not all was well in communist utopia. That became painfully clear with events abroad in Moscow and Berlin in the summer of 1939.

The annual convention of the AFT took place on August 21, 1939, at the Hotel Buffalo in upstate New York. As usual, it brimmed with the usual political propaganda, especially with communists fervently politicizing everything. The college section of the convention held panels on various issues. During the discussions, Bella, as representative of the New York State Federation of Teachers, placed the "responsibility for the cut in the school budgets squarely on the Republican Party."[554] Franz Boas, one of Bella's contacts, delivered the keynote address, which was described as a "stirring appeal to democracy and intellectual freedom." He concluded his remarks with a rejection of "Red-baiting" attempts to split the Teachers Union.[555] The convention endorsed the Boas Committee for Cultural Freedom, which opposed "Nazi and fascist totalitarianism, but again, refused to include the Communists in the same camp."[556]

Then the convention received the bombshell: the news of the Nazi-Soviet pact.

As noted earlier, the Hitler-Stalin pact was signed that August 1939, only two days after the start of the AFT convention. Joachim von Ribbentrop, the Third Reich's minister of foreign affairs, had just flown to Moscow to conclude the negotiations.[557] CPUSA, which had excoriated Hitler and the Nazis for a decade, now lined up behind them, given that their leader, Stalin, was now the Fuhrer's partner. Thus, CPUSA quickly endorsed the pact without reservation the very next day.

The *Daily Worker* headline on August 23 heralded, "The Soviet Union and Non-Aggression," and complained that most news agencies had not only "failed to report the news correctly" but had given it "distorted and wrong meanings." The *Daily Worker* condemned what it called the media's "lack of fairness and correctness in reporting such a first-rate development in the international situation."[558] The day after the pact was signed, Earl Browder, with a straight face, told the *New York Times* that the deal "made a wonderful contribution to peace."[559]

Communists everywhere followed their new marching orders from the Kremlin. That included loyal teachers.

Stalin wanted CPUSA members in the Teachers Union to swallow this. Some choked on it. It outraged many, causing numerous members of the Party to leave. Whittaker Chambers was one of them. Hypocrisy and changes of the Party line were twisting and frequent. This one was maybe the worst ever. How could these stoic anti-fascists in the Communist Party suddenly stand behind Adolf Hitler? No way!

After the Stalin-Hitler pact, Bella said Party groups began shamelessly making alliances with the "most vicious pro-Hitler" groups in America.[560] Those who left the Party were praised (rightly) for their honesty; those who remained were blasted (rightly) as "allies of fascists."[561] Many who had stayed with the Party through even the Ukrainian famine and Stalin's purge trials now bolted, especially those among the Jewish membership, outraged at the picture of Molotov shaking hands with Ribbentrop. That photograph brought a wave of defections. After all, the Communist Party line called for a Popular Front against fascism, and Local 5 leaders, including Bella Dodd, had pushed a campaign against fascism since 1935.

Commenting on the Nazi-Soviet Pact, Celia Lewis Zitron, a stalwart member of CPUSA and chair of the Academic Freedom Committee of the Teachers Union, regretted that "the Nazi-Soviet nonaggression pact of 1939 intensified hostility to the Soviet Union."[562] It most certainly did.

Local 5 had once run campaigns to boycott all German goods. But now, overnight, with Stalin's new partnership with the Fuhrer, these activities were halted.[563] As Bella later derisively put it, "We used to have the American League Against War and Fascism" (identified as a communist front by Congress).[564] The "used to" referred to past tense. "Overnight," said Bella, "we had to change the name."[565]

Bella personally reacted to the Hitler-Stalin pact by staying in the Party, in spite of the fact that one of her earliest attractions to the Party was its supposed stand against Nazism and fascism, and that she had been drawn to groups like the Anti-Fascist Literature Committee. Actually, she joined the Party still later, in 1943.[566]

What of the anti-fascist committee's line that "Fascism, and its blood-brother Nazism, are the enemies of the people?" Those who stayed, said Bella, "rationalized the event on the ground that the warmongers of the West wanted to destroy the Soviet Fatherland, so in self-defense it had outfoxed the Western 'warmongers' by making an alliance with their enemy."[567] That was a highly creative excuse.

On a personal level, Bella said she was "too busy with the teacher problem to give much attention to this outrage, though it troubled me."[568] It no doubt did. But she found a way to keep busy and keep her conscience clear on Hitler-Stalin by diving even deeper into her Party's educational activism. In October 1939, after the pact was signed and after Poland had been carved in half by the Nazis and Bolsheviks, with World War II now on, Bella organized a campaign calling for one million signatures against the New York governor and legislature protesting cuts to education.[569]

And so, Bella stayed, doing "busywork" for the Party along with many others who had once signed up to fight fascism. She was apparently determined to renounce her own thoughts in favor of the Party line. Obedience, all for the Party.

How long could she keep going down this path?

CHAPTER 10

BELLA AND THE PARTY INVADE EDUCATION

"We have developed schools which spend millions of dollars," noted Bella Dodd in a speech in Detroit in September 1961. "We spend more money on education than we do on anything else. . . . We spend a tremendous amount of money on education, and the end result is that we do not have an educated populace."[570]

The results are certainly clear in America today. Every year, over 1.2 million students drop out of high school. That equates to a student every twenty-six seconds.[571] Less than a quarter of high school seniors are proficient in math,[572] and only 37 percent of twelfth graders read at a proficient or advanced level.[573] Many manage to graduate without basic reading abilities. And of course, students are saturated with sex education and destructive ideologies and theories, including critical race theory and gender ideology. They do not learn about America and its Judeo-Christian roots. They learn about "Amerikkka," about the slave-centered America of the 1619 Project. They learn that America at its roots is "racist" and sexist and imperialist.

This was a system that Bella helped corrupt. She and her Party. They did it by infiltrating public schools and universities and poisoning the well. Their America was not the Shining City on a Hill.

When they were not tearing down America's traditional schools, Bella and her Party had its own schools that trained teachers in toxic ideas and in the principles of communism. CPUSA was zealous in training new recruits and in the continuing indoctrination of comrades. There were district training schools and then national training schools, the latter of which sought to develop higher Party functionaries, such as section organizers, "agitprop directors," and other types of activists.[574] The Party ran the so-called Abraham Lincoln Schools and Jefferson Schools—yes, egregiously and deceptively named not after Marx and Engels but Abraham Lincoln and Thomas Jefferson—and the intense Workers School in New York City. The Communist Party of New York State stated unequivocally: "We decided that the concentration of the whole educational apparatus would be the Party schooling and inner Party education."[575]

Bella Dodd was part of the apparatus spreading communism's ideologies directly into the public education system. Later, to Congress, she spoke often of the Party's work in education. Here is an exchange from 1953 with Senator Olin Johnston, Democrat of South Carolina, which was entered into a full Senate report titled "Orientation and Training of Communist Teachers:"

> Johnston: Then it is true that you have meetings at intervals where the teachers come and where they are indoctrinated in the Communistic doctrine?
>
> Dodd: There is no doubt about it. They are given the Marxist-Leninist training. As a matter of fact, most teachers who join had to go to a school. They are sent to a school to learn how to become Communists.
>
> Johnston: Is it not true that they also report the success they are making?
>
> Dodd: They report both successes and failures, and they are praised and scolded, and they are given new directions as to how to make the change. Where they have failed, they are shown how to get success. Where they have succeeded, they are told to go on and make some more.

Part of the communist doctrine they learned was the role of discipline, better known as the infamous "Party discipline" that members

of CPUSA adhered to with religious-like fervor. Stalin had emphasized: "The achievement and maintenance of the dictatorship of the
proletariat is impossible without a party which is strong by reason of its
solidarity and iron discipline."[576] This discipline was rigidly enforced
by the Party's disciplinary committee and a separate apparatus.

In June 1953 congressional testimony, Bella was asked about one of
the enforcers of Party discipline, the notorious "J. Peters," well-known
back in the day and to historians of American communism. He and
his role were described by congressional counselor Robert Kunzig in
his questioning of Bella Dodd:

> Kunzig: Dr. Dodd, while you were in New York, while you were
> a member of the New York State Committee of the Communist
> Party did you know an individual by then name of J. Peters—
> and before you answer, I would like to say something on the
> record about J. Peters. J. Peters, as you know, was the author of
> the instruction book on espionage.[577] He has been established
> as head of the Soviet-controlled espionage organization which
> operated in America. Did you know J. Peters? If so, how did you
> know him?
>
> Dodd: Well, that is an interesting question, because I knew
> the J. Peters manual before; I had read it. It had been given to
> me to read and study and I knew a man by the name of Steve
> Miller, but Steve Miller was an insignificant little fellow who used
> to help with the mimeographing at party headquarters. He was
> attached to the New York County committee. He was assigned
> from time to time to teach communism to some of the teachers,
> kind of take individual teachers who were rising in the party
> movement and give them special instructions. I thought he was
> just an insignificant little fellow until one day the authorities
> picked him up and I discovered he was J. Peters. He was engaged
> in using teachers throughout the United States for maildrop

purposes, for revolutionary mail that was going back and forth, from the Soviet Union into the United States.[578]

Those special instructions, of course, related to revolution, to rules and methods for disciplinary cases, and to the particular role and function of the communist teacher. Bella put it this way in March 1953 testimony to the US Senate:

> The communist teacher has a very definite function to perform. He must not only make himself an agent of the class struggle; he must indoctrinate other teachers in the class struggle, and he must see that their students are indoctrinated in the class struggle. That doesn't have to be in four-syllable words. In the classroom, the class struggle means that the schools are regarded, for instance, as part of the apparatus of the bourgeois state, and therefore the student is considered to be in rebellion against the bourgeois state. It is the function of the teacher to fan that rebellion and to make the student recognize that only by establishing a Soviet system of government will you be able to be free.[579]

That was a remarkable task. It meant undermining the notions of the American system of government in favor of the preferred Soviet system of government. The members of Congress who asked these questions to Bella and her comrades knew that. They also knew how communists crammed their philosophy into every subject, regardless of whether the topic had anything to do with issues of class.

Not unlike radical teachers today, including Marxist "critical theorists" who shoehorn notions of gender and sexuality and race into the teaching of Shakespeare, Dickinson, and Austen (with subjects like "the white maleness of Shakespeare" and "the queering of Jane Austen"), communists in Bella's day did the same with Marxism—that is, shoving their ideology everywhere and anywhere. When answering a question from Senator Johnston about slanting teaching, even Shakespeare, toward communist ideas, Bella answered:

Dodd: Yes. communism is a total philosophy. If you believe in it, you live it, you breathe it, you teach it. You can't separate yourself and say, "Now I am a teacher of mathematics; now I am a communist." You are a total personality with your total philosophy, and you take it with you seven days a week, twenty-four hours a day, as long as you believe in that philosophy.

Johnston: It would be impossible, then, to keep from rubbing a little off on the students you came in contact with.

Dodd: They wouldn't recognize it as communism; nobody else might recognize it as communism. But there is no doubt in my mind that the communist teacher teaches the communist way.[580]

And just like Marxist-based critical race theorists teaching in schools today, the key was to hammer groups into categories of oppressed versus oppressor. Said Bella, using the teaching of John Milton as an example: "What happened in the time of Milton? What were the struggles then? Which was the class that was going down?" She added: "The whole question of teaching the class struggle, teaching the need for a classless society, teaching the fact that there was always an oppressed and an oppressor, becomes the theme of every teacher."[581]

Thus, material had to be reframed into a Marxist superstructure. But this had to be done delicately. Deception was integral to this form of "education." The communist teacher dare not openly name and quote Marx and Lenin, which would immediately expose the teacher's concealed bias, but the communist teacher nonetheless was duty-bound to find subtle ways to include its founders' teachings. According to Bella, the professional communist, particularly the teacher, must indoctrinate others with its party's philosophy.

Despite their claims of "academic freedom," sung loudly and sweetly to sympathetic liberal media, at teacher conferences, and in the halls of Congress in noble tones, they were completely beholden to orders from the Party, which acted as a direct extension of the dictates of the

Soviet Comintern. In truth, they were not acting freely at all; rather, they were fully subservient to Marxist-Leninist ideology, willingly shackling themselves to Party discipline. Bella explained this in an exchange with Senator Herman Welker, Republican of Idaho:

> Dodd: No communist who knows he is a communist can be a free agent. He is a soldier in the international army of world communism, and he has a devotion to that principle over and above anything else there may be. It is not like just being an ordinary liberal or an ordinary radical. You are part of an international movement, and you are coordinated with your committees and your organization. You meet at least once every two weeks with the people who are the party apparatus. There is no such thing as freedom for a communist college teacher.
>
> Welker: Dr. Dodd, is such a teacher or professor free to pursue the highest ideal of academic freedom and freedom of inquiry?
>
> Dodd: I will give it to you from two points of view. From the information we have from the Soviet Union and from the satellite countries, certainly we learn that the physicians, biologists, the linguistic professors, were not free to pursue their own inquiry into the truth. They had to accept the Communist Party determination as to what was the truth. Within our own country, we have any number of illustrations of both professors and writers who, from time to time, have been called up before the control commission because they have either written or spoken or done that which was contrary to the Marxist-Leninist philosophy.[582]

Bella frequently addressed academic freedom and freedom of inquiry when testifying before Congress. On another occasion, the Senate committee asked Bella whether communists should be allowed to teach, and whether she personally would hire a known communist teacher. She answered:

> If I were the president of a university today, and I knew definitely that a certain person was a communist who was applying for a job, and it was told me that this person was impartial in the classroom, I would simply laugh at the statement. I have never known any communist, no matter how apparently impartial they seemed to be in the classroom, who was really impartial in the classroom. In addition to that, it is always the case that even in the selection of material to be discussed or references to be read, there is a very considerable slanting.[583]

This was not a matter of whether a communist could legally hold a teaching a job in the United States. They could and did. But as Bella explained it, teachers who were members of the Communist Party could not be expected to withhold their ideology from their students in their teaching. Just as a Christian professor's Christianity was an integral part of him or her, so was a communist professor's communism.

The most reasoned response to the question of permitting communists to teach came from Sidney Hook, a professor of philosophy at New York University who studied Marxism in the Soviet Union and taught courses on its philosophy.[584] Hook was an intellectually honest man and became disillusioned with the Soviet Union when he learned of Stalin's purges. His complete break came with the Nazi-Soviet pact in 1939. Even before that agreement, he and his close colleague John Dewey began pulling away from the USSR as Stalin started showing his colors by the latter 1930s.[585]

Hook was disenchanted by the reality that the college section of the Teachers Union consisted of communists, making it a dangerous organization. He wrote that in any college "where you have a group of people who take their instructions from a foreign power, the basic allegiance of the communist power is oriented toward Russia. Where you have such a group that publishes newspapers, organizes the students, aims to inculcate a point of view laid down by a foreign power, the very pre-supposition of educational freedoms is undermined." And thus, "There can be no question that if groups of that sort existed on the campus, it would make it impossible to fulfill the work of education of the university or college as such."[586]

Hook explained that members of the Communist Party are committed to a grave and systematic violation of their threefold academic trust: "for their responsibility to help their students to mature intellectually and emotionally; for their responsibility to their colleagues in the quest for truth; and for their responsibility to the democratic community to develop free men, they have substituted a blind and partisan loyalty to the objectives of the Communist Party."[587]

Hook, a committed socialist, knew many members of the Communist Party, in America and around the world. He knew of which he spoke.

How They Taught—and the Lesson of Juliet Poyntz

Bella was a professor at Hunter College for twelve years, 1926 to 1938, and worked with the Communist Party from 1932 on. She was under Party discipline beginning in 1935. During that time, she followed communist instructions without a Party card and later acknowledged that her teaching reflected that philosophy. At the same time, she helped organize the Hunter College Instructors Association and worked with the American Association of University Teachers.[588]

Consequently, Bella Dodd was beholden to the Communist Party for at least half of her Hunter teaching career.

After breaking with the Party, Bella spoke throughout the country about her experiences, including the Party's discipline and iron-hand treatment of its members and anyone who dared to break ranks. In relating to her audiences, she sought to bring in items of local interest whenever possible. One day in Omaha, Nebraska, May 1962, she said:

> I searched my brain for some connection which I might be able
> to talk to you about in the city of Omaha. In the city of New

York, teaching at Hunter College, which is the same college where I taught, was a member of the Communist Party who came from Omaha. She was a very attractive, a very lovely person, full of eagerness, full of understanding and yet she was as zealous as I was in my youth. . . . She was a person who joined not only the Communist Party but served the conspiracy, the world conspiracy. She was part of the Soviet espionage system. She taught economics and history at Hunter College. And when she changed her mind about doing certain things they wanted her to do, she disappeared. And there are those in the Party whom I have known who said that she was killed by the Russian espionage system, the Russian underground system.[589]

Modern readers figure that Bella's audience in the American heartland must have collectively gasped when she said this, but they likely did not. They surely knew exactly who Bella Dodd was referring to. She was referring to the high-profile case of Juliet Poyntz.[590]

Poyntz was a graduate of Barnard College and Columbia University. Initially a socialist, she quickly turned to communism, becoming one of the early ground members if not founders of the Communist Party in America. Poyntz was a well-known radical director of the International Ladies Garment Workers Union, and one of the most prominent women in the CPUSA. She left a prestigious faculty post at Columbia to pursue full-time Party work, including CPUSA's women's department, the New York Workers School, and the League for Industrial Democracy, and became an intelligence agent for the Soviet Comintern and OGPU/NKVD.

Eventually, Poyntz became disillusioned, especially after a trip to Moscow amid Stalin's Great Purge. She sought to defect, for which she would pay a price, dearly so. She disappeared in 1937 without a trace, and both Elizabeth Bentley and Whittaker Chambers (among others) said she had been killed for her desertion. (Bentley, who was another convert to the Catholic Church through Fulton Sheen, wrote about Poyntz in her autobiography, *Out of Bondage*.) News of her disappearance was reported in the *New York World-Telegram* and the *New York Times*. Carlo Tresca, a leading Italian-American anarchist and anti-Stalinist, wrote:

> Miss Poyntz was for years an outstanding Stalinist leader. In 1934 she retired from public political activity. She became an OGPU agent.[591] Witnesses are available who knew her through her work as an agent of the GPU. As late as 1936 she was seen in Moscow in the company of George Mink. George Mink is a GPU agent. . . . Although we differed politically, Miss. Poyntz was a personal friend of mine for twenty years. In May of 1937, I met her on the street and at that time she told me that she had become disgusted with the Soviet regime and the Communist Party in this country. Her attitude was known to the Stalinists. They had reason to fear her because she might break with them and disclose secret matter.
>
> About a year ago, Miss Poyntz took a room in the American Women's Association headquarters. She was seen by friends as late as June 4 or 5, 1937. She has never been seen since. Her attorney noted that her absence was involuntary: "It is my belief that the Russian secret police were seeking to put Miss Poyntz out of the way."[592]

They were indeed, and that it precisely what they did. Whittaker Chambers wrote of Poyntz in his book, *Witness*:

> She was living in a New York hotel. One evening she left her room with the light burning and a page of unfinished hand-writing on the table. She was never seen again. It is known that she went to meet a communist friend in Central Park and that he had decoyed her there as part of a G.P.U. (OGPU) trap. She was pushed into an automobile and two men drove her off. The thought of this intensely feminine woman, coldly murdered by two men, sickened me in a physical way, because I could always see her in my mind's eye.[593]

The bright girl from Omaha, radicalized by the elite academic institutions of New York, was "liquidated" by Soviet intelligence.[594]

What is notable is that nothing about Juliet Poyntz was mentioned in the communist press. It is as though there were a missing negative which contained more information than the developed photo. Louis Budenz, former editor of the *Daily Worker*, spoke of the case of Poyntz when underscoring this Communist Party-Soviet illegal apparatus that had no hesitation in purging (i.e., killing) those who dared to betray the Kremlin. These comrades engaged in the "assassination of those who disagree." Said Budenz:

> One of these instances was of the former American school teacher, Julia Stuart Poyntz, who disappeared from the streets of New York into thin air. She had been at one time very active in the Communist Party, had then worked with the secret apparatus, but was turning sour. When she disappeared, the party was assailed for this act, and I said in an editorial board meeting that a public defense should be made. But [Clarence] Hathaway drew me out of the office, I remember that one day, and said: "This is hot cargo. It might injure some of our comrades, and we cannot discuss it." And it was never discussed by the Communist press.[595]

That included the headquarters of the communist press—Louis Budenz's *Daily Worker*. The fate or even mere mention of Juliet Poyntz was verboten. Moscow said so, and thus the Party said so.

Again, Juliet Poyntz taught at Hunter College with Bella Dodd. Bella knew Juliet. What happened to Juliet surely terrified Bella; the same could happen to her.

Yes, the mysterious disappearance of Juliet Poyntz indicated to any sober-minded and rational reader that the Communist Party was clearly different from any other party in America. Such was precisely the point of people like Bella Dodd, Louis Budenz, Elizabeth Bentley, Whittaker Chambers, and others who left the Party and testified to

Congress. It was precisely what Congress strove to illustrate to American citizens.

Targeting Professors for the Party

Bella described how the Party's educational wing courted professors for the revolution. Bella's wing thus helped spearhead this key task.

Members of the Party carefully planned for conventions and meetings of learned societies of history, social studies, and modern language associations. According to Bella, this was like a Panzer division assembling. One group searched for Party members and friends. Then the national office would call the leaders of communist teachers and discuss the nature of the targeted academic organization, asking if it had Party members in it. If their response was affirmative, they would decide which resolutions to oppose and which to introduce at gatherings. If there were no Party members, they would send someone to make contacts. Issues of key concern were federal aid to public schools, separation of church and state, and many others.[596]

Bella said the conventions were "invaluable in bringing together the growing group of scholars who were not members of the Party but who followed Marxist ideology idealistically." At the end of the convention, "they returned with lists of new conquests, the names of men and women who would go along with us. They gave the names and addresses to the district organizer of the Party and made follow-up visits to flatter him and establish closer ties to the Party."[597]

At the conventions, the comrades also made sure that (1) no resolution was ever passed against the Soviet Union; (2) no resolution was ever passed against the Communist Party; (3) any resolutions on curriculum move in the direction of "progressive education."[598] The behind-the-scenes level of control and manipulation was very dictatorial—Soviet-like. Some non-Party observers understood exactly what was going on. Remarking on these tactics in congressional testimony was George Hartman of Columbia University: "They are drilled in tactics of parliamentary law. For example, an unfavorable motion which they want to suppress arises, and they move to table. They demand that a motion to table is not debatable, and so on, and it sort of intimidates the rest of the group . . . the communists are experts at that particular procedure."⁵⁹⁹

Before long, said Bella, a professor recruited at these conventions would be pulled into in the "proletarian class struggle and his name would be used to support communist public demonstrations, etc. He would then start identifying himself with a particular 'side' and all good people were on his side." In turn, this affected hiring and promotion decisions. Said Bella: "The strength of the Party was increasing in high positions; and job getting and job promotions are a *sine qua non* of academic gatherings. . . . The Party and its friends were assiduous in developing the job-getting and job-giving phase of these meetings."⁶⁰⁰ From there, the new contacts were courted. According to Bella, "you made it your business to socialize with them . . . to take them to lunch."⁶⁰¹ With that, effective units could be built: "As soon as you had three people who were committed with you, who felt that the communist movement was a good movement . . . you established yourself as a unit. That unit then became attached to the district or section or the city which had a communist movement, and the District Organizer was always very sensitive to what was happening on the campuses."⁶⁰²

From there began the process of "boring from within" at the very "nerve centers" of American colleges.⁶⁰³

In her position, Bella influenced both New York City and New York State educational policies for decades after, when some of the most critical issues and debates took place, including the issue of communism in the schools. She published the legislative newsletter of the New York State Federation of Teachers Unions, with a prominent column "Bella Dodd Reports," in the publication *New York Teacher*. It summarized legislation affecting teachers as well as the union's philosophy of education: "The opportunity to go to school, to learn, to know the traditions, purposes, and aspirations of this country, to become the master of a vocation, is the inherent right of every child."[604]

One can see that Bella was more careful with her language in that publication. She had to be. Concealment was paramount. But when Bella was in the presence of fellow true believers, she took the gloves off.

For instance, in 1944, Bella was assigned to speak at a meeting of more than five hundred communist teachers and their friends at the Jefferson School in New York City. The topic was new communist perspectives applied to education. "I held out the prospect of a new approach to education soon to be disclosed by American leaders who controlled the purse strings of the nation," said Bella. "I urged the communist teachers to unity . . . and pointed out that the NAM (National Association of Manufacturers) had established a tie with the NEA and had pledged itself to help build education and to support a nationwide school-building program. . . . To those who questioned this perspective I said that the progressive businessmen were playing a revolutionary role."[605]

Here, she urged her teacher comrades to break bread and find ways to work with the NAM and NEA, all the while, of course, hiding their true philosophy.

Targeting Students and Protecting Communist Teachers

Of course, beyond the targeting of professors was the ultimate prize: the targeting of students. That was the chief objective.

How did this militant organizing and communist activity by some unions and their members translate to students in New York City schools? Bella Dodd later explained: "The educational system of New York City has become completely geared toward a dictatorship pattern in which the people, the intellectuals at the top, tell the lower animals what to do." And despite the comrades and their progressive friends' honeyed words about "democracy" and "freedom," "it has become a completely socialist system in the sense that there is very little appreciation for the rights of the freedom of choice for the individual." That socialist system sweetly sells "revolution" under the guise of "strawberries and cream." But in reality, "they're eating socialism whether they like it or not."[606]

For hardened American communists operating in the school system, this meant communist ideology, though again, done with a cautious degree of subtlety to avoid exposure. Said Bella:

> As far as the teaching of the children was concerned, there would have to be a certain ideology. The children would have to be taught in accordance with the directives of the Communist Party. If the Communist Party directives are to eliminate the private ownership of property, children would have to be taught in that direction. If the Communist Party believes—and it does—in eliminating all religion and all belief in God, then the communist teachers would have to promote the Communist Party program as far as they possibly dare to do so and of course it was a question of judgment as to how far you could go without getting fired.[607]

Of course. That was always the goal—to go as far as a communist teacher could without being so aggressive as to be transparent and risk getting fired. There was no manual for that; it was a matter of judgment—very careful judgment. Bella explained: "There was not, and I presume there still isn't, any standard plan for teaching communism in American schools. Any teacher who is a member of the party or a close sympathizer knows the effect he or she wants to achieve. In various subtle ways students are led to believe that everything communistic is admirable and everything democracy stands for is dogmatic, illogical or outmoded."[608]

In reply to a question on whether a communist teacher could instruct children and be free to teach all sides of every question, Bella flatly said no, "It is absolutely impossible."[609] Should a communist teacher be fired? Bella was often asked that question. At a speech in Detroit in September 1961, she answered:

> A lot of parents are asked the question should you permit a teacher who is a communist to teach in your high schools, your elementary schools, or in your colleges. And there is a great deal of argument. The American Association of University Professors has said that though a person is a communist, that's no reason why they shouldn't be allowed not to teach, they may be great mathematicians or great physicists. But my dear friends, communists don't just teach subject matter, they teach human beings. Which is essentially of course the correct thing. But they teach them as the communist principles call for, and therefore a communist teacher can have a tremendous effect upon the future of your child.[610]

Bella addressed this matter again in a 1954 speech in Indianapolis, there stating her belief that teachers who are actual Party members should be fired: "I think actual members of the Communist Party should be dismissed. . . . I don't think we should be sentimental about it, and that would apply to me when I was in the university as well as anybody else. There is no obligation to use the taxpayer to support men and women who are doing everything they possibly can to tear down. If they want to be communists, nobody is putting them in jail, but certainly we have no obligation to keep them in positions."[611]

Bella understood that communist teachers were indoctrinating students. Taxpayers need not subsidize that. Communists should not be jailed, but they should be dismissed.

For the record, communists did train their teachers to deceive, to conceal their underlying motivations. Richard Frank described the technique for introducing Marxism into education in a landmark article circulated in 1937, titled "The Schools and the People's Front."[612] According to Frank, communist teachers must take advantage of their positions "without exposing themselves," and all teacher comrades must be given a thorough education in Marxism-Leninism. Only when they have mastered it will they be able to skillfully "inject it into their teaching at the least risk of exposure."[613]

Professor Enrico Ferri also explained the methodology at a meeting of the International Congress of Socialist Students and Graduates: "No need of making a direct propaganda, which would frighten many of the listeners." Ferri excelled at this craft of deception. He admitted, "Without pronouncing the word 'Socialism,' once a year, I make two-thirds of our students Socialists."[614]

It was also best to peddle communism under a more benign label. The comrades knew that very well, whether targeting students or teachers.

CHAPTER II

BELLA DODD'S
MULTI-FRONT ACTIVITY

To fully understand Bella Dodd and communism, it is crucial to see that perjury, lies, Aesopian language, false names, disinformation, and deceit were not the exceptions but the *modus operandi* of the Party, the coins of the realm. Fabians like H. G. Wells and George Bernard Shaw made glowing references to the likes of Lenin and Stalin and the USSR. The Fabians deliberately left out the word "socialism" in the title of their organization. This was typical. We have seen that when the Intercollegiate Socialist Society changed its name, the word "socialist" disappeared.

As part of their propaganda, all communists were adept at the use of Aesopian language (Orwell's doublespeak), which is the use of lying and double-talk that looks innocent to the uninitiated but conceals a different meaning to the disciplined. Lenin explained that one of his pamphlets was written "with an eye to the tsarist censorship . . . with extreme caution, by hints, in that Aesopian language—in that cursed Aesopian language—to which tsarism compelled all revolutionaries to have recourse whenever they took up their pens."[615]

Even outside of an environment of censorship, communists constantly concealed their intentions with deceptive language.

Bella on the Remaking of Language

Bella Dodd commented on this manipulation of language. She spoke of a linguistic conference in the Soviet Union that declared that the remaking of language was essential to the revolutionary change of mankind. Those professors of linguistics who dared to disagree "were sent off to the salt mines. They were sent off to Siberia, they disappeared. And after a while all the professors refused to accept the Chairs of Linguistics in any of the Soviet countries, so Stalin was made professor of all the Linguistics Chairs in the Soviet Union."[616]

This carefully chosen language—including the language of violence—was used in the Party's propaganda. For example, in 1942, there was a celebration for the new board of contributing editors, including Bella, for the publication *New Masses*, an organ for the cultural front of CPUSA.[617] The slogan for the affair was "Words Can Be Bullets."[618] Bella gave other examples of Aesopian language, saying, "the right not to incriminate myself" meant the "right not to incriminate the communist group," "freedom of speech" meant freedom of the communist group to speak through the mouth of the individual who had been selected by the higher intelligence, and "peace" meant world socialism.[619]

Bella made an appeal for *New Masses* in 1943, claiming that financial contributions were needed to ensure the "winning of the war." She described the magazine as extremely important to those involved in organizational fields who have to face the problem of "molding public opinion in the interest of the people." The right language could mold public opinion.[620]

The most egregious use of Aesopian language was the word "democracy." Bella said that during the World War II period, the communists appropriated the word, and "it became very difficult to oppose them because they posed everything in terms of the word 'democracy.'"[621] Stalin himself described his dictatorship as the "highest form of democracy." "Democracy" had several meanings, and Lenin admitted that "there was no contradiction between the Soviet (Socialist) democracy and the use of dictatorial power by individuals."[622] Lenin wrote plainly in his 1917 classic *The State and Revolution*: "Democracy means equality. . . . But democracy is by no means a boundary not to be overstepped; it is only one of the stages on the road from feudalism to capitalism, and from capitalism to communism." During these stages, said Lenin, as did Marx and Engels, institutions such as democracy (as well as property, the state, capital, and even religion and the family) would "wither away." "Democracy" was a temporary means to an end, and even then, communists most certainly did not mean democracy as Americans have long understood democracy.

For communists, "democracy" from the outset was a word to abuse and a tool to exploit. Way back in 1847, Friedrich Engels wrote in his *The Principles of Communism*: "Democracy would be wholly valueless to the proletariat if it were not immediately used as a means for putting through measures directed against private property." The cry of "democracy" would be used to remove property rights. Engels made direct reference to the United States, where its democratic constitution could be exploited: "In America, where a democratic constitution has already been established, the communists must make common cause with the [Communist] party, which will turn this constitution against the bourgeoisie and use it in the interests of the proletariat." That was exactly what American communists would do a century later, invoking and exploiting the US Constitution for their Soviet purposes—a constitution they planned to replace with the Soviet constitution.[623] They incessantly appealed to the freedoms of the US Constitution to protect themselves and their communist ambitions.

Bella understood this deception very well. "They always use the word 'democracy,'" she said of American communists in Senate testimony. The communist movement was engaged in a "great campaign . . . to proclaim that they were for democracy . . . to make everyone realize that the *real democrats* in this world were not the members of the Democratic Party here or not the Americans, but the *real democrats* were the Communists" (emphasis original). She spoke of how when communists used the word "democracy," they meant "economic democracy," and they also meant to use the word among gullible liberals and Westerners in a misleading way to cloak their Marxist-Leninist goals.[624] Bella recalled a Party convention in 1944:

> I remember that the chief of the communist publishing company of the Communist Party, Mr. Trachtenberg, speaking to us that night and one of the things he said I will never forget. Everybody was feeling in good humor. You know wine, whiskey had been around, good food, pleasant surroundings. And he got up and said: "A toast to the Communist Revolution comrades." And then he said—when we take over this America we will not take it over under the slogans of communism because that is unpleasant to the American people, and we will not take it over with the slogan of Socialism, because that has been made unpleasant to the American people, but we will take over with the slogans which have been made lovable to the American people. We will take over with the slogans of democracy and liberty, and of progressivism and liberalism.[625]

Bella recalled the Trachtenberg incident often, including during a speech in the early 1960s, where she said that Trachtenberg had told her at the Communist Party's 1944 national convention in New York: "When we get ready to take the United States, we will not take it under the label of communism; we will not take it under the label of socialism. These labels are unpleasant to the American people, and have been speared too much. We will take the United States under labels we have made very lovable; we will take it under liberalism, under progressivism, under democracy. But take it we will."[626]

Louis Budenz, a defector from the Party, also commented on this tactic. The Communist Party "takes over the terms of the nations it means to conquer and uses them to describe its own purposes. . . . The word becomes a convenient means to deceive the people as to communist purposes." The people of the wider community understand the term in its genuine sense, but the communists always "have in mind the advancement of Soviet rule."[627] "Democracy" was used liberally in

Daily Worker headlines and articles, especially when referring to the revolution in Spain.[628]

Propaganda Instructions from the Daily Worker

During her time in the Communist Party, Bella, like all conscientious Party members, read the *Daily Worker*, which was not only a propaganda sheet, but also contained instructions for mobilizing the comrades. According to *Daily Worker* editor Louis Budenz: "Each one of these articles contained directives. . . . The communists read each article to find the directive. . . . They modified the line or interpreted the line or explained the communist conditions in various countries. . . . Immediately, the *Daily Worker* not only published these communications but adjusted its editorial policy . . . in order to be able to know what phrase to use, what attitude to take, and how to push forward the cause of the communists in various countries, here in the United States."[629]

The *Daily Worker* was more than a newspaper; it was a manual of instructions for what today we would term "politically correct" thought and language. Everything in it was approved by Moscow, and Moscow could and did change its mind the next day. The *Daily Worker* guided Party members in the titles of books to read, plays to see, and movies to watch, a totalitarian strategy that sought cultural control over individuals and societies.

Studying the *Daily Worker* at this time, Bella would have read about the unjust abuses toward Negroes in the South and the Party's defense of the Scottsboro plaintiffs,[630] another campaign orchestrated by Münzenberg; about the horrors of the Nazis; of assistance for the communist side in the "civil war" in Spain, which American communists cleverly (if not laughably) named the Abraham Lincoln Brigade.[631]

Bella would also have read of appeals for the help of women in the Party; of constant strikes, demonstrations, and protests supported by the Party; of the "lies Hearst was spreading" (newspaper editor

William Randolph Hearst) about the Party, and so forth. She would have read about a celebration given by the Party in New York City to honor the release of Antonio Gramsci from prison.[632]

Create a Victim and Showcase Him

As noted, a major component of this propaganda was the fig leaf of "academic freedom." For communists, this was a vital appeal to peddle their philosophy with utmost subtlety, especially in infiltrating classrooms. The case of the pro-communist and pro-Soviet Jerome Davis showcased the Teachers Union's battle for "academic freedom."

Jerome Davis was born in Japan of American parents. He became an enthusiastic student of the Soviet experiment, living in Russia from 1926 to 1927, and he wrote approvingly of what he observed. Together with the so-called "Open Road," he took young college students on political pilgrimages to Russia. A graduate of both Union Theological Seminary and Columbia, he was a "progressive" and active trade unionist. His writings included *Christian Fellowship Among the Nations, Business and the Church, The Russian Immigrant, The New Russia, A Sociological Interpretation of the Russian Revolution*, and his controversial *Capitalism and Its Culture*.[633]

In 1936, the Yale Corporation voted Davis, who at that point had been on faculty at Yale Divinity School for twelve years, a one-year terminal contract. He did not receive tenure and was effectively being let go. Liberals and leaders of the AFT were convinced that this was because of his pro-Soviet views and turned him into a martyr, embracing him, and making his termination a *cause célèbre* for the Teachers Union. Davis was elected president of the AFT at the August 1938 convention. (Upon his election, Davis received a telegram from FDR saying: "I hope that your deliberations will result in stimulating the teachers of the country and the public in general to redouble their efforts to secure for all the children the kind of schools to which they are entitled.")[634]

The Communist Party wasted no time exploiting Davis's situation. Bella and her comrades swung into action, staging first-class demonstrations, with two hundred teachers and students picketing Yale: "We were an unusual group of pickets, for we wore caps and gowns and paraded with dignity on the beautiful campus."[635]

Demonstrating their mass-action skills, they asked Columbia, Harvard, NYU, Smith, Vassar, and other schools to join.[636] After several hours, the Yale Corporation agreed to see the committee, including Bella. Once inside, the agitators outlined their demands and sermonized about the role of American educators and their right to participate in community problems.[637] The president of Yale Corporation responded: "Mr. Davis has always been accorded full freedom of speech and action both in the classroom and outside."[638] Davis received a year's salary but was not reinstated.

The Yale officials stood firm. The comrades, however, were undeterred. They never let a good crisis go to waste.

In truth, of course, there was grand hypocrisy in these Party members, who swore a loyalty oath to Stalin and his Soviet Union when they joined CPUSA, claiming to be great advocates of academic freedom. The status of intellectuals and professors in Stalin's "utopia" was anything but utopian. There were mass arrests of professors, teachers, doctors, and directors of academic and scientific research institutions.[639] Bella would later often note just this in speeches and in later testimony to Congress, once she was no longer a shill for the Party.

But for now, a shameless shill she was.

Bella's Role in Setting Up Fronts

Bella Dodd became very active on many fronts for the Party. In fact, she both joined and organized numerous front groups. Many of them. For instance, to protect notions like academic freedom, Bella served on the executive committee of the constitutional-sounding National

Federation for Constitutional Liberties, launched by communists in the Teachers Union.[640]

That was but one area. Another was her work on the communist-feminist front.

For the record, feminism was another mass movement that communists got behind. The role of women in the revolution was of special interest to Vladimir Lenin. Especially close to Lenin was German socialist Clara Zetkin, founder of International Women's Day and a leader of the international "worker women" movement. Lenin frequently spoke to her about the "women's question." She quoted him: "We must create a powerful international women's movement, on a clear theoretical basis. . . . The thesis must clearly point out that real freedom for women is possible only through communism." This "woman question [is] a part of the social question, of the workers' problem, and so bind it firmly to the proletarian class struggle and the revolution." Lenin said that women "must realize what the proletarian dictatorship means for them: complete equality with man in law and practice, in the family, in the state, in society; an end to the power of the bourgeoisie."[641]

An early iteration of this in the United States was the Congress of American Women, which was vigorously supported by the international communist movement, and of which Bella was a member. The House Committee on Un-American Activities named the Congress of American Women as part of a "solar system" of international communist-front organizations.[642] In a 1948 report, the California Senate examined "a number of Communist fronts for women" that had been "established as out-and-out Communist sections. Some of these had been directly affiliated with the International Congress of Women, with headquarters in Moscow. Others were affiliated with the Women's International Congress Against War and Fascism." It noted that leaders of these included the likes of Clara Zetkin, the Bolshevik feminist leader Aleksandra Kollontai, Elizabeth Gurley Flynn, and many others.[643]

The House Committee on Un-American Activities went so far as to sum up the Congress of American Women as "just another communist hoax" that, rather than arising from a long-established women's group, "could be traced to the Soviet-dominated Women's International Democratic Federation Congress, held in Paris in November 1945."[644] The committee said that "the administrative and policy-making core of the Women's International Democratic Federation consists of leading women Communists, beginning with Nina Popova, Soviet deputy and president of the Government-sponsored Soviet Women's Anti-Fascist Committee, down to the Congress of American Women, led by Elizabeth Gurley Flynn and Margaret Cowl, representing the Communist Party, U.S.A."[645]

This organization's fakeness was just one front for communists like Bella. In congressional testimony, she explained the strategy in creating propaganda fronts:

> When the Party created propaganda to persuade people, they first set up committees and everything is geared toward building that line. Assume that they set up a committee to fight the Velde committee, the Un-American Activities Committee. They have for a long time. Then all you do is build up a number of seemingly nonpartisan people.
>
> For instance, you might get a college professor who is a Party member but not known as a Party member. He then sends a telegram to one or two or three other professors and they establish themselves as a temporary committee to fight the Un-American Activities Committee. To facilitate that, they send out 1,000 or so communications to different names they have and ask a question such as, "Will you join us to fight this?"...
>
> For example, you send a telegram or a letter saying: "Dear Professor, we are setting up such-and-such committee. May we hear from you? If we don't hear from you we will add your name to the list."... Then the committee does publicity work and it

appears in the *New York Times*, the *Herald Tribune*, and all the
leading papers, and this would have a tremendous impact on
the public, the publication of the list of names of 1,000 or 500
college professors all across the country.[646]

Bella was asked by Congressman Kit Clardy (Republican, Michigan)
for an example of how this tactic was used against Congress itself when
it dared to investigate communists' and their front activity: "Is it the
general idea, through that apparatus you have described, to, then, by
the mere punching of a button, so to speak, make it appear that all over
America there is a concerted desire, for example, that this committee
be abolished or that McCarthy be condemned to perdition, and so
on?" Bella responded: "You can set up a committee like that in a week
and have the newspaper publicity for it almost immediately. You can
have 500 names listed in a week of people who support you."[647]

Bella had become a master at these techniques. She was learning the
crass art of how a small group of organized individuals could manipulate the masses.

Bella's Rise in the Party

Bella's skills indicated to CPUSA officials that she was a bright and
talented woman who could take their party to another level. She was
a rising star.

Thus, Bella became a member of the National Committee of the
Communist Party from 1944 to 1948 and a member of the Party's
New York State Committee. She became the legislative representative
of the New York State district of the Communist Party and a member
of the State secretariat of the New York District. She was the Party's
official legislative representative, a major job, and a very impressive
one. She served on committees for labor, education, women, and
youth. She was not only an organizer but an outstanding speaker.[648]
She was called on for Party gatherings, such as membership drives.[649]

During this time, Bella was a Party member doing its bidding, albeit comparatively safe from exposure. In reality, there was little or no difference in belief or actions among a card-carrying member, a non-card-carrying member, and a fellow traveler. A "Party member" usually meant someone was an active card-carrying member of the Communist Party. "Fellow traveler" meant a person who sympathized, wittingly or unwittingly, with the goals of socialism or communism and was complicit in the ends and means used to attain these goals, but safe, as technically, he "didn't have a card."[650] Bella also called such people "non-Party Bolsheviks"—that is, "a person who was not a member of the Party, but who attended all the meetings and was given assignments."[651] Speaking of this later in a 1961 address in Detroit, she explained: "One of the problems has been that we have put too much attention on card-carrying members." She advised, "If it looks like a duck, acts like a duck, and speaks like a duck, it's a duck."[652]

As for Bella's card-carrying status, it had been irrelevant. "From 1935 on," she recalled, "I was invited to Communist Party meetings, secret meetings, and caucus meetings, unit meetings. Wherever the work which I was doing was going to be discussed by the Communists at their meetings, I was invited and I was made part of the movement."[653] But she was not to be known as a communist. And just as communists were ordered, she would deny if asked. As noted in congressional testimony by Dr. Abraham Lefkowitz in September 1948, "Bella Dodd, their clever legislative representative, indignantly denied she was a Communist. Within a few weeks of such denial she appeared and spoke as the spokesman for the State Communist Party."[654]

Significantly, when Bella was legislative representative for the Communist Party, she demanded that the New York Board of Examiners cease asking people applying for a teaching job if they were affiliated with "communist" movements. In letters to the Board of Education and the Board of Examiners, she branded the question "misleading and notoriously perverted." She said it was a shock to find this question asked of applicants: "Are you now or have you ever been affiliated with any organization or group endorsing the Communist, Fascist, or Nazi movements?"[655]

Bella certainly changed her position on that a few decades later, after she had left the Party. At that time, however, she was a full-blown communist, actively representing the Party's and the Soviet Comintern's interests wherever possible, shoehorning them into the Teachers Union agenda at every turn. A good communist found a way to politicize everything. For teachers, communists made sure the agenda included not just pencils but politics. That included international events far outside the classroom, such as a significant conflict erupting in Spain.

The Spanish Civil War Campaign

The Teachers Union inserted itself into the bloody Spanish Civil War (1936–39), thanks in part to the bidding of its closet Party members. The union's College Section came to Spain's aid on the side of the "loyalists." Explaining their position, New York teachers said: "Just as fascist governments throughout the world work together to stifle democracy, so believers in the democratic form of government are tied by a common bond which must not be broken. . . . The Union is supporting the activities of the committees to aid the Spanish people formed by many professors in the New York colleges."[656]

As usual, the terms "democracy" and "democratic form of government" meant something entirely different to communists, even as they kept those meanings carefully concealed. American communists framed the Spanish communists as pursuing democracy and the democratic form of government. The Soviet Comintern organized a vast International Brigade worldwide to join the Spanish communists in their fight against Franco and the fascists.

Propaganda and demonstrations took place in support of Spanish "loyalists" and against fascists. Today we know that the American Committee for Spanish Freedom, the Emergency Committee to Save Spanish Refugees, and the United American Spanish Aid

Committee were all listed by Congress as "subversive" or communist front groups.[657] At the time, however, all operated as slick Party
front groups.

Bella noted that the terminology of "loyalist" vs. "fascist" was
another literary coup for the Communist Party, using "loyalist" for
their side of the campaign and "Franco-fascist" for the people who
opposed them. They lumped all the Catholic clergy on the side of the
"fascists" and, using this technique, sought to further undermine the
Church by attacking its priests, driving a wedge between the clergy
and the laity.[658] The Church, in truth, did not like Franco and the fascists but viewed them as the lesser of two evils, the only viable option
that avoided Spain becoming a communist state under the thumb of
atheistic international Stalinism.

Many humanitarians and progressives fought together against
Franco, including artists, teachers, singers, preachers. According to
Bella, "they gave the Party tremendous assistance in conditioning the
mind of America."[659] Many writers, in Hollywood and elsewhere,
including closet communists like Ernest Hemingway (who we now
know served the KGB under the code name "Argo") and Hollywood
Ten screenwriters like Alvah Bessie and Albert Maltz, took up the
cause for the Spanish communists, and sometimes even literal arms.

Moscow ordered CPUSA to organize an American contingent of the
International Brigade for Spain, and the Party obeyed. Accordingly,
the communist port agents of the National Maritime Union along
the East Coast provided false passports and expedited the shipment of
this secret army. Various Party members also operated out of Europe
to send Brigade volunteers to Spain.[660] The American contingent,
the so-called "Abraham Lincoln Brigade," requested volunteers. Each
national subdivision had national commissars who, in turn, served
under Soviet commissars. Teachers in New York City recruited soldiers
for the Lincoln Brigade. For example, Sid Babsky, a teacher in the fifth
grade in Public School 6 in the Bronx and a classmate of Bella's in law
school, went and never returned. Neither did Ralph Wardlaw, son

of a Georgian minister from City College, who left without packing his clothes.[661]

The estimation of the number of volunteers in the Abraham Lincoln Brigade was 3,300, of which "1,800 were killed in action and more than half of those who were returned were wounded at least once."[662] The Abraham Lincoln Brigade was correctly listed as a communist front by Congress.[663]

Later addressing the deception of the Abraham Lincoln Brigades, Bella said: "We must never deny our heritage even if the communists begin to adopt it as their own because the communists have a way of taking our heroes. They have pre-empted Lincoln and made him the leader of the Lincoln Brigade that went to Spain to fight against the Christian concept as against the communist concept."[664]

What an irony: here was Bella organizing teachers, many who never taught in local classrooms, but instead, served Moscow's international causes, such as the Spanish Civil War. She was dutifully doing the work of the Soviet Union.

Teachers Union—How They Operated

According to Bella, while the actual number of communists in the Teachers Union was small, they were "strategically placed and were so instructed and so alert to the problems which the party wanted to bring forward, that you cannot count their number. You must see the intensity with which they work and the training which they had in revolutionary techniques."[665]

Like a virus, the Gang of Ten in the Teachers Union multiplied. In fact, it multiplied to a factor of 1,500. The influence of just one person, Bella herself, is a prime example.

Someone like Bella would launch a campaign in the union. The campaign would start by getting certain people elected or have volunteers seek out a core of dependable representatives. A plan of action would detail what measures to put through and which to defeat. The goal was to defeat anything that did not "conform to Marxist ideology."[666] Among teachers, said Bella, the goal was a "professional leveling" to fit teachers into the "class-struggle philosophy" and bring them to "identify with the proletariat."[667]

To that end, the first AFT convention that Bella attended was in Philadelphia in 1936. She and her comrades were primed for infiltration. The communists, in fact, were so well organized that they were in complete control of the convention. As Bella later recalled, the Party assigned its ablest trade union functionaries "to hold continuous secret sessions in a room at the convention hotel to aid comrades on all questions."[668]

Bella later remarked in her memoirs that she was "overwhelmed by the sense of power which this convention manifested."[669] She was in awe at the degree to which closet communists dominated. She offered a remarkable summation: "The convention was entirely swallowed up by the Communists. They passed every resolution they wanted and I began to feel that we had enough votes to pass a resolution for a Soviet America."[670]

Bella's "Soviet America" observation was surely sarcastic, but it was not far from the truth. The American Federation of Teachers convention was so controlled by communists that they could pass almost anything they wanted, short of electing Earl Browder (or Stalin) the next head of the AFT. They did, however, settle for the "progressive" Jerome Davis. Bella noted that in her next line: "Jerome Davis was elected president of the Federation and his cause became the rallying point around which we fought during the next year."[671]

There on full display, Bella noted, was "the secret of the communist movement: centralization and organization." Thus, "you might have five delegates to the American Federation of Labor Convention who were communists, but they met in advance, decided what they could accomplish at that convention, and they, at least, would be armed and would get something out of that convention when the others might not know what they were driving at."[672]

More than anyone else, Bella helped to structure the Teachers Union "into a social protest organization."[673] She helped to politicize and ideologize its work. (To this day, annual conventions of the AFT and NEA are heavily political and ideological.)

The Committee on Legislative and Teachers Interests was headed by Dr. Abraham Lefkowitz, but after the split with the union, it was renamed the Legislative and Political Action Committee, signaling more direct political involvement and also more militant tactics. With Bella Dodd as its head, it became the union's most important committee. She was the union's "real power."[674] As a leader, Bella broadened the union's concentration on lobbying to include political action strategies to pressure lawmakers, conduct rallies and mass demonstrations, dispatch delegations and create committees to shakedown legislators in Albany, lobby for legislation, edit newsletters, organize mass direct-mail campaigns to schools and parents, and more.[675] All of it spearheaded by communists.[676]

This militant approach of the union was displayed in its fight for substitute teachers. Bella admonished the Board of Education to "fulfill its moral obligation to thousands of substitute teachers who had been in the schools during the Depression as per-diem employees."[677] The substitutes, the WPA teachers, and instructors' associations were "goaded by a sense of injustice and a fear of failure. This was the lush soil in which the Communist teachers' fraction in the Teachers Union flourished."[678] Bella said the substitute teacher campaign attracted thousands of non-union teachers. And in a "quiet way they began to be grateful to the Communists."[679]

The Teachers Union in April 1937, under Bella's leadership and numbering one thousand, went to Albany to lobby for the Neustein bill to increase substitutes' pay.[680] Bella said she hoped Democrat Governor Herbert Lehman "would have the courage and vision to sign the bills now before him."[681] Six educational groups joined forces in this demonstration against "exploitation" by the Board of Education. The group also claimed that the Board of Education deliberately failed

"90 to 95%" of teachers sitting for the license exam simply to save money. A key bill at the time (the Fischel Bill) would have allowed any substitute teacher who had been working for five to seven years as a regular teacher to obtain tenure and benefits. Bella backed it, saying: "These men and women have proved their fitness to teach through many years of faithful service."[682] Bella, representing the Classroom Teachers Association, said more teachers were needed than the number provided in the state budget, and teachers could not continue to handle fifty or sixty students in a class. Those numbers would result in "turning out illiterates."[683]

The substitute teachers' bill, the most controversial bill of the 1939 legislative session, was passed by the New York state legislature but was vetoed by Governor Lehman. Despite this loss, said Bella, the "union and the communist group grew immeasurably in stature and prestige among the new crop of teachers and among other civil-service employees. Even politicians and public officials respected us for our relentless campaign."[684]

And with the loss, the fight would continue anew in different areas of penetration. Bella began to build new Party leadership not only in the Teachers Union but in the state Board of Education. In later testimony, she admitted that there were secret members of the Communist Party on the curriculum committee of the Board of Education: "Information was available from them. Also, there were clerks on the Board of Education who kept us informed as to what was happening, so we had advance information about what was going on."[685]

The tentacles of the Party continued to dig still deeper.

Bella Joins the Labor Movement

Bella Dodd had clearly become a labor activist. Her activism was all-consuming. She did more and more.

In 1938, Bella ran for State Assembly from the Tenth Assembly District on the American Labor Party line.[686] As she was popular with students, the American Student Union chapter of New York City held a torch-light parade in her honor and helped raise funds for her campaign. That same year, 1938, she was made legislative representative for the college teachers union, Local 537 of the AFT, an affiliate of the AFL.[687] This also made her the organizer for the New York Federation of Teachers.[688] Because of her leadership skills, she developed strong ties with labor leaders, state and city political figures, and civic leaders, using these ties to improve education for children and working conditions for teachers.

It was no surprise that by 1938, Bella decided to leave her job at Hunter College because she felt she could be of "more help to my fellow Americans if I became more active and worked with the trade union movement." When she informed the Hunter College president, Dr. Eugene Colligan, of her decision, he replied, "Bella Dodd you're crazy. These people will use you and then throw you out." She replied, "I don't worry. 150,000,000 Americans don't have any pension, don't have any security, and I'll take my chances with them."[689]

President Colligan tried to persuade her otherwise, telling her: "We don't always like all your ideas but we think you are a good teacher. Why don't you stay here and save your pension?"[690] He could not convince her. "And so," said Bella later, "I threw overboard what I had and went into the labor movement."[691] She gave up her position as assistant professor at Hunter.

This meant more activism and organizing, including some major efforts.

In February 1941, for instance, Bella rallied 1,500 teachers from nearly every teachers' group in New York City, plus 300 parents, to protest cuts in state aid at Albany. Photographs show her speaking to a large group of teachers at the capital. She, Charles Hendley, and Robert Speer spoke at the hearing.[692]

Of course, this was not just about the classroom; it was also about communist ideals. Bella later said of this effort: "You also have to train people into action, direct action. There is no doubt in my mind that, for instance, when you conducted a mass delegation of 1,000 or 1,500 teachers to Albany and just kind of landed on the poor legislator and you brought students—and brought parents—that was schooling in direct action." She said that one must politicize people to take direct action so they will understand the "feeling of illegality" allegedly repressing them.[693]

Creating a sense of repression and oppression was crucial for communists, who thrived on antagonism. Divisive issues were sought out and blown up and politicized. The more exaggeration, the better. The more explosive, the better.

As Bella later put it, communists were "unerring in attaching themselves to explosive situations, and had their answers for troubled young teachers. Their chief answer was that we had reached the 'breakdown of the capitalist system.' To those who were self-conscious on race or religion, they said that 'religious or racial discrimination' was the cause." The answer was always some form of alleged oppression. Bella explained that "when individual instances of bigotry and discrimination arose, the Communists were quick to note them and to exaggerate them."[694]

The Party absorbed Bella's enormous energy. When Bella was first recruited, she was overwhelmed with activity. As soon as she finished one assignment for the Communist Party, she would be given three more. She said she had no time to stop and think and reason. At first she was happy because "I escaped the nothingness of my own life. But the activity grew in alarming proportions. There was activity to save this situation or that, for world peace, against discrimination, for better schools, for better working conditions, for youth, for the Negro people, for the foreign born, now for the war against Fascism, and so on, with tactics endlessly changing until there was no principle except that of obedience to the service of a mythical 'class.'"[695]

The intensity and complete commitment became self-destructive. She added that "in an act of self-destruction I subjected my will to ambitious men high in the Party apparatus—men who were climbing the ladder to the political power of world Communism. I was to learn that all this led directly from my own country into the walls of the Kremlin and spiritually into Red Square, where a mummified Lenin lies as a cruel mockery to the people of Russia—a would-be saint."[696]

The Split Becomes Official

As was predictable, the infiltration of communists tore at the fabric of the Teachers Union. As radical elements took over, a break-up ensued. In 1940, George Counts and some of the Old Guard organized the Committee for Free Teachers Unionism to make formal charges against Local 5 and other locals and to consider the revocation of its charter. In December 1940, the Executive Council of the AFT met and heard evidence from the committee seeking to investigate Local 5 for conduct "not in harmony with the principles of the American Federation of Teachers."

The allegations focused on trade union matters, and no explicit mention was made of the communist issue. In response to the charges, three representatives of Local 5, Charles Hendley, Dale Zysman, and Robert Speer, said that the allegations of the council were purely of a trade-union nature and criticized the council for allegedly playing into the hands of New York State Senator Frederic Coudert, the leading anti-communist legislator in the state, and vowed that they would oppose "Couderism both inside and outside the American Federation of Teachers."[697] Prior to ousting Local 5 from the AFT, the council ordered its officers to appear and present their case against the revocation of their charter (that included both Local 5, New York City, and also the College Teachers Union Local 537).

The matter of communist control over Local 5 was couched as "political and other activities" that had been prejudicial to the labor movement. Both sides knew that this was the crux of the complaints. But both sides also knew that this would be extremely difficult to prove. As expected, the accused challenged the constitutionality of the proceedings, the admissibility of evidence, and other aspects without success.

The council charged that the internal affairs of Local 5 had been conducted "to bring disharmony to the membership," that factionalism within the Local had resulted in loss of membership, and that Local 5 could probably never become a "satisfactory organization of teachers of New York City." The leaders who expected to take over the Teachers Union did not want to do so except on the "basis of the ideologies which they respectively hold."[698] The council spelled out the claims of the Communist Party itself, which "bragged about how [it] had recruited enough members to control the Local and dictate its policies."[699]

The following is from an affidavit by Manning Johnson, a defector from CPUSA, who highlighted the Communist Party's use of teachers, mentioning specifically Locals 5 and 537: "At a number of meetings of the Central Committee and of the political bureaus which I attended, reports were given on the work among the teachers, specifically the work of the Communist Party faction in Locals 5, 537, and 453. Particular emphasis was placed upon the fact that the editorial staff of the *New York Teacher*,[700] also the executive boards of Locals 5 and 537, were, in the main, controlled by the Communist Party faction. Moreover, numerous issues among the teachers were used in order to form the basis for the successful establishment of the 'united front.'"

Johnson here described "united front" as "issues utilized to get persons who were not in the Communist Party to work with the Communists to front for them in the Teachers Union." The Party made use of non-Party persons placed in leading positions in the unions who could be easily influenced.[701]

Clearly, many non-communist liberals in the field of education had begun to wise up. They saw how the Party used teachers on international issues from the Spanish Civil War to the Hitler-Stalin Pact. The pact had immediately followed the end of the civil war, which was won by Franco, a devastating defeat to communists in America and abroad. The pact was a huge wakeup call to non-communist left-ists. They were now, at long last, increasingly suspicious of American communists and their meddling, antics, and tactics. The Communist Party watched closely to see how the Teachers Union would carry out the Party line on the Nazi-Soviet pact.[702] Also watching closely were the non-communist liberals.

Having seen the news of the purge trials in Russia and the bolshe-vization efforts of Local 5 in the union, there was by now a counterof-fensive by anti-communists comprising several elements. Of course, many still remained socialists. Dewey, Counts, and Kilpatrick fit into the Fabian category. So, while they repudiated communism, they did not repudiate the socialism of Marx. Still, they now openly opposed the communists. Bella later said: "The Communists had been kicked out by George Counts, by John Childs, by William Kilpatrick. In other words, the Socialists had kicked out the Communists."[703]

Around 1939–1940, as part of these efforts, George Counts became a leader in the anti-communist faction of the AFT.[704] He was one of the "frontier thinkers," along with Dewey and Kilpatrick. The Teachers Union that had organized the Teachers Guild formed another offensive against communism and was strongly supported by officials of the A. F. of L. However, a two-fold dilemma arose: The old-guard socialists who built the Teachers Union were friends with many of the old com-rades. Also, Dewey and others detested the tactics of the communists in the Teachers Union, but not its philosophy. For Counts, it was personal, as some of his old Soviet counterparts in the USSR had been purged and possibly executed.

In fact, back in the USSR, Stalin was not finished with his show trials.[705] In 1937, he also ordered the murder of Trotsky. This presented unique problems to the American wing of the Communist Party and to liberal intellectuals, who wanted to see a fair hearing for Trotsky.[706] The American Committee for the Defense of Leon Trotsky was set up in 1936, with Dewey as director. Its findings, titled "Not Guilty," concluded that no attempt had actually been made by Stalin and his cronies to ascertain the facts about Trotsky.[707] (That, of course, was hardly a surprise.)

Meanwhile, a small group in the union formed the unauthorized Committee to Save the American Federation of Teachers, headed by Professor Speer of NYU. The AFT Executive Council put the issue of revocation of Local 5's charter to a referendum. By a vote of eleven thousand to eight thousand, the Locals voted for the revocation of Local 5's charter and Local 192 of Philadelphia. As described in the April 1941 issue of the *American Teacher*, the Executive Council of the AFT said it could not "have the confidence and support of organized labor or the general public so long as important locals are in general disrepute." It now faced the issue of communism in the unions directly: If the AFT is to "conduct a vigorous campaign to protect teachers, schools and democracy, it must not be handicapped with the eternal necessity to deny, to equivocate, or to apologize for Communist influence." To the contrary, it must "eliminate this influence."[708]

The Radical Transformation of America—a "Soviet America"

Throughout this book it is clear that the purpose of the communist infiltration of education was nothing less than to radically transform the United States. Education was just one more institution to be penetrated. And yet, it was particularly critical because it was about capturing and indoctrinating American youth—that is, the future generations.

On March 10, 1953, Bella Dodd elaborated on this in an exchange with Senator Pat McCarran, a prominent anti-communist Democrat from Nevada, in perhaps the single most important hearing on the infiltration of education by communists in America:

> McCarran: Doctor, from your observation, is there any more fertile field for the implanting of doctrine for conspiracy than in the minds of youth?

Dodd: The youth are a very special target of the communists. They want youth because the youth are the government of tomorrow. The people of today are pretty well through, as far as they are concerned. They want to indoctrinate and teach the people with whom they will take over tomorrow.

McCarran: The youth during those (school) hours is a subject for the activities of this conspiracy to train the mind of the youth along the lines that would eventually lead to the destruction of our form of government, is that not true?

Dodd: There is no doubt in my mind that the Communists will use the schools and every other educational medium, whether it be comic books or the radio and television; they will use every educational medium.

McCarran: They go to every level in the schools, is that not true?

Dodd: From the nursery school to the universities.

McCarran: From the primary schools, the grade schools, the high schools, and then into the academies, is that right?

Dodd: There is no doubt about that.

McCarran: To get back at it, Dr. Dodd, the object of this conspiracy and the object of all of this movement in the schools is to build up over a long period of time, if necessary, the tearing down of the American way of life?

Dodd: To establish a Soviet America. [709]

That had been the goal of American communists: a Soviet America. And few fronts in the battle for that sweeping objective were as critical as Bella Dodd's educational front. Would anyone stop her and her comrades from this fundamental transformation of the schools and the United States of America?

CHAPTER 12

COMMUNISTS MAKE
A SHOW TRIAL OF THE
RAPP-COUDERT HEARINGS

There were many brave legislators throughout America, at the national and local levels, including in Bella's home state, that sought to expose and stop the fundamental transformation of the United States of America into what CPUSA sweepingly envisioned as a "Soviet America." One such group was the Rapp-Coudert Committee, set up by the Legislative Committee of New York to investigate whether fascism, Nazism, and communism had penetrated New York schools.

American communists and leftists were, of course, fully supportive when these committees investigated fascism and fascist sympathies in various American institutions, but they drew an uncrossable line when legislators dared to concern themselves with communism, even as communism was committed to a "forcible overthrow" of America. Once these legislative committees began looking into communist influence in addition to fascist influence, American communists and many of their progressive allies and dupes ferociously objected. And here in particular, long before she became an ally of legislators looking to expose communism after she left the Party, Bella Dodd made her mark, as she served as counsel and tactician for the Teachers Union to protect communist teachers.

Of course, as she did so, Bella never dared publicly admit that she herself was a communist teacher. Instead, Bella and her secret comrades and their liberal allies insisted that they were protecting not Marxism-Leninism but "democracy." As they did with the House Committee on Un-American Activities, which they labeled "HUAC" (the "House Un-American Committee"), these American Bolsheviks sworn to Stalin's Soviet Union accused the committees of being "un-American"—and fascist.

As for the Rapp-Coudert Committee, Bella and her comrades claimed that its real purpose was to "cut aid to education." They urged New Yorkers to "visit people in their homes" and "tell them our story. There is no more worthy cause than the preservation of democracy."[710] Rapp-Coudert was a threat to "democracy."

Rapp-Coudert Established

The subversive work of Bella and her comrades to radicalize education during the 1930s and 1940s did not go unnoticed. As a result, the Rapp-Coudert Committee, named for two New York Republican state legislators, Assemblyman Herbert Rapp and Senator Frederick Coudert, was formed in 1940–41 to investigate socialist-communist and fascist philosophies in the New York education system.

This was not the first such investigation in New York. The Lusk Committee had already investigated seditious activities back in the 1910s and exposed the history, purpose, and tactics of radicals embedded in education. This occurred while Bella was still in high school. Lusk laws were approved by the legislature over Democrat Governor Al Smith's veto and required public-school teachers to be "loyal and obedient to the government of this State and of the United States" and denied certification to any teacher who "has advocated, either by word of mouth or in writing, a form of government other than that of the United States or this State."[711]

The Lusk Committee was followed in 1930 by the first large-scale congressional investigation of communist activity in America, with a focus on the communist threat to education, chaired by Hamilton Fish, a prominent congressman who likewise hailed from New York. The Fish Committee labeled the communist threat the "most important, the most vital, the most far-reaching, and the most dangerous issue in the world."[712] At a hearing in July 1931, the congressional committee heard school superintendents and principals describe the communist influence on students in their schools.[713]

Influenced by the public battles within the Teachers Union in New York, on March 29, 1940, the New York legislature established the Rapp-Coudert Committee to "investigate whether left- and or right-wing movements—Communism, Fascism, and Nazism—had penetrated New York City public schools and colleges."[714] The model for Rapp-Coudert was the US Congress' Dies Committee, the predecessor to the House Committee on Un-American Activities and the successor to the Fish Committee. At this time, twenty-two states required loyalty oaths for teachers. These oaths arose because of the radical Marxist goals advocated by some teachers and their threat to American liberties. The Rapp-Coudert investigation was considered fair and laid down strict rules for both sides. And, contrary to the negative publicity stoked by the Teachers Union, it said that neither "the Committee nor its staff will tolerate any invasion of civil liberties, of academic freedom, or of the right of any man to his own political beliefs."[715]

The Rapp-Coudert Committee had evidence showing that there was an "organization, a majority of whose members are employed in the institutions under the Board of Higher Education, which is under the influence or domination of the Communist Party U.S.A."[716] It named the College Teachers Union of the City of New York and Local 537 of the AFT. This was no idle accusation. Years later, Bella would admit that this was accurate. Though at that point, she would never dare divulge the truth because she was committed to serving a deceptive Party.

Bella later recalled how everything went down: "Local Five was served with a demand, a subpoena *duces tecum*, by the Rapp-Coudert Committee to produce all our records, membership lists, and financial reports. There was general consultation."[717] That meant general intense consultation within the Party. How would it respond to this threat to smoke out the truth about those concealed in the Teachers Union?

The Party, said Bella, responded by establishing a "joint chief-of-staff group" made up of hardliners from the "teachers' faction." This included Party apparatchiks such as Israel Amter,[718] Jack Stachel,[719] and Charles Krumbein,[720] all straight from Party headquarters, plus several lawyers. In all, they constituted the top command in charge of operations.[721] No city or state had as many communists as New York to draw from. But communists would call on the full force of Party members nationwide to descend upon the Rapp-Coudert Committee and its exposure of communist teachers. This was ground zero, and every Party supporter was summoned to help. The Communist Party brought in reserves from the northwest, California, and the south, in addition to its forces in the east and New England.[722] Bella referred to her efforts as legal counsel and those of the Communist Party as "a well-trained army."[723]

These American Bolsheviks were ready for combat.

The Party placed its forces at the teachers' disposal, "since the teachers were now in the vanguard holding the line in defense of the Party itself."[724] Most rank-and-file teachers in the union did not know that they were part of a vanguard for Marxist educators. They had no idea that they and their union were a Trojan horse for the Party. The unaware and innocent non-communist teachers were the Party's dupes. Following typical propaganda procedures, the Party established a front group called the "Committee to Defend the Public Schools."

The comrades were primed for ideological warfare. As an opening tactic, they decided to start by fighting any seizure of their Teachers Union membership lists, all the way to the Court of Appeals. "This would gain time and enable us to continue organizing the mass campaigns against the legislative committee," said Bella. "It would also serve to wear out the investigating committee." Thus, as legal counsel, Bella's starting point was to refuse the Rapp-Coudert Committee's request for the membership lists.[725]

What ensued was an epic combat in the annals of anti-communists' battles with what Whittaker Chambers would later dub "the concealed enemy." A decade later, the US Senate would look back at the Rapp-Coudert Committee as having "provided the Teachers Union with an opportunity for its greatest 'struggle.' . . . The leadership of the Teachers Union saw in the creation of this Committee an opportunity to conduct a 'struggle' on the highest possible plane, i.e., against an agency of the Government, and to link that struggle with the economic self-interest of the teachers. Such a 'struggle' would be in the best Bolshevik tradition."[726]

Like fighting for Stalingrad, these American Bolsheviks readied their political bayonets for the struggle.

Based on previous statements and actions by the undercover Marxist agitators within the Teachers Union, it was perfectly logical for the Rapp-Coudert Committee to want to obtain the lists, minutes, and financial records of the union in order to find out who was really pulling and controlling the strings, including the purse strings. The union nonetheless refused, successfully stalling for three months.

"The membership files were turned over to me and I was ordered to refuse to turn the lists in, preferring jail if necessary," said Bella later in her memoirs. "I happened to be out of the office when the Committee came to demand them, and Miss Wallas, in whose custody were the public schoolteacher lists, gave them to the representatives of the Committee." What did Bella do with the lists in her possession? She destroyed the evidence: "I burned the lists of the college Union teachers which were in my possession. We were afraid that through them the Committee would be able to trace a pattern of membership, since our cards showed who sponsored each individual and the date on which he joined."[727]

In the meantime, Bella said that both she and the Committee to Defend the Public Schools advised non-Party members to appear before the Rapp-Coudert Committee and to tell the truth: "We instructed those teachers who were not Party members to appear before the Committee and to tell the truth."[728] To repeat: *non*-Party members.

Since they were not Party members, they could be truthful. It was Party members who would either lie or plead the Fifth Amendment and refuse to speak. And in fact, Bella and comrades went the route of lying. They advised Party members to lie. Later, during US congressional hearings, one teacher, Harry Albaum, testified to this dedicated tactic of perjury. Here is Albaum's exchange with Senator Homer Ferguson:

> Albaum: Before the Rapp-Coudert Committee, when we were advised as to what to say by the then representative of the Teachers' Union, the legal representative, Bella Dodd, her advice was, "if you are asked the $64 question, you say you are not."
> Ferguson: In other words, if you were asked whether you were a member of the Communist Party, you were advised to say that.
> Albaum: By the attorney—to say you were not.
> Ferguson: Even though you were?
> Albaum: That is right.[729]

The once nice, honest immigrant from Italy, that sweet little girl from Picerno, was now a hardened Communist Party attorney, an American Bolshevik advising her clients to perjure themselves to protect the Party and the cause of international communism. This is what communism had brought her to.

The Party was playing for keeps. It placed CPUSA's full intelligence apparatus at the Teacher Union's disposal. This meant that the Teachers Union's legal defense was made up of clandestine Communist Party intelligence officials. The legislators of the Rapp-Coudert Committee knew there were serious problems at the Teachers Union, but surely they could not have imagined that it was this bad. The Party was secretly running the Union's entire response operation.

Bella said: "No sooner did the Rapp-Coudert Committee begin to issue subpoenas than I got a message from Chester, in charge of Party Intelligence, assuring me that he had arranged for a liaison who would meet me regularly with information on what was going on in the Rapp-Coudert Committee."[730] Bella later described her unnamed contact as an "attractive, aristocratic blonde, well-dressed and charming," who would hand slips of paper to Bella with the names of those who would be called by the committee. This mysterious woman herself highlights just how long were the tentacles of the Party and its underground network. Years later, in a 1962 speech in Seattle, Bella recalled how this woman served to show that "the Communist Party arm is everywhere." They had in this woman someone from "the subpoena process service who was in charge of serving the subpoenas for the Rapp-Coudert Committee. [They] had someone there who gave the information as to who was going to be subpoenaed. As a result, I was able to call in the teachers who would be subpoenaed to prepare them for the shock of the subpoena, to go over their stories, to go over whether they would or would not testify, as to whether they would or would not be dismissed, how to protect the Communist Party, and so forth and so on."[731] Pretty slick and pretty deep. This woman's action surely constituted a crime.

As for "Chester," who was identified in Bella's memoirs merely by that name and by his role as "in charge of Communist Party intelligence," his Party name was "Chester Bernard," and was most likely Bernard Schuster, a crucial CPUSA liaison to the KGB. Bella said that "Chester" received reports from secret communist agents in other left-wing organizations and government agencies and collected money from various businesses with ties to CPUSA. The Venona decryptions confirm Bernard Schuster's critical role in Soviet espionage in America.[732]

As for the pilfered information from the unidentified blonde mole who gave Bella slips of paper which bore the names of those witnesses subpoenaed by the Rapp-Coudert Committee, Bella took that advance information to the Teachers Union members who were to be called and warned them. "If we wanted to gain time, the person was told to send word he was sick, even enter a hospital if necessary," said Bella later. "If it were feasible, he was to move. If not, we assigned a lawyer or a Union representative to go with the person to the hearing. Most of the teachers were instructed not to answer questions and to take a possible contempt citation. Some were instructed to resign from their jobs." Why resign? In order to protect the Party, the movement, the Comintern, the Soviet motherland: "Because we feared the Committee would publish the facts about their international connections. If the teachers told the truth, they might involve other Party contacts."[733]

What the Marxists running the Teachers Union organized was a classic disinformation campaign, redirecting the eyes of the public to other issues—anything but the truth about the communist conspiracy maneuvering behind the scenes. Telegrams were sent to the Board of Higher Education, for example, protesting against the "persecution" of instructors, and opposing any moves to cut the education budget. The union used parents, students, and the general public in emotional propaganda. The Committee to Defend the Public Schools published a propaganda sheet slickly called the "Education Defense Bulletin," which was hostile toward the Rapp-Coudert Committee, accused it of being un-democratic, an adversary of free public education, and opposed to civil liberties and academic freedom. The usual platitudes of "tolerance" and "democracy" were sprinkled throughout.[734]

The Party pushed this line in all of its publications and to friendly liberal sources in the wider press. Headlines touted "academic freedom" and "constitutional rights," characteristic features of the United States that, of course, were not practiced in the Soviet Union.

Many liberal newspapers that sympathized with the teachers were particularly susceptible to the propaganda dished by Bella and the

Party. For example, the *New York Times* suggested that the Rapp-Coudert Committee and the Board of Education were suppressing graft and corruption in the four municipal colleges[735] and that the leaders of the committee were seeking publicity.[736] It ran headlines such as "Teachers Assail Inquiry. Twin Jobs Put Doubt on Committee's Purposes."[737]

Naturally, no headlines came from Moscow, Stalin, or the Comintern. The fact that Jack Stachel, a member of the US Politburo and chairman of agitation, publication, and education, was assisting Bella Dodd's Committee to Defend the Public Schools further illustrated a top-down operation greenlighted from Moscow. And the comrades zeroed in on Frederic Coudert himself as a special target of their rage and disinformation. Bella noted: "From the Communist Party and from the men who represented the Soviet interests in this country we got the go-ahead signal to make Coudert their target."[738]

Predictably, this meant that Coudert and his legislative allies were smeared—tactics right from the Party playbook. The Committee to Defend the Public Schools used every weapon at the Party's disposal: smearing, name-calling, careful combing each investigator's history and background. They were accused of racism, anti-Semitism, and whatever other mud the comrades could sling.

What they did to Coudert was especially unjust, given that the state senator had long been an ally of the teachers and sponsored the State Tenure Law which, among other things, protected faculty and staff at state and municipal schools from arbitrary dismissal. Coudert was a friend of teachers. But of course, he was not a friend of communists. Knowing that communists had hijacked the Teachers Union for their own purposes, he sought to help the teachers by exposing the communists. And so, for communists, Coudert was an enemy; they would frame up Coudert as a monster to the teachers at large. The Party made Coudert the target. Said Bella, he was the "one person on whom to turn our combined fury."[739]

Bella targeted Coudert in comments to teachers and remarks in publications like *New York Teacher*, where she said the most natural result of the Rapp-Coudert hearings was the introduction of the Slopes Bill, which would prohibit "state aid to any schools which authorize or permit teaching of doctrines or principles of government subversive of or contrary to the United States or State Constitution," adding that in the Assembly, "the faggots will be gathered fast for the book-burning which will ensue," and that no textbook with liberal ideas will be safe with these "witch-hunters."[740]

Senator Coudert was cast as the head of the serpent. "Some angle is found to explain the evil motives of those who are conducting the investigation," recalled Bella, "perhaps to show that the investigation is itself a blind for some ulterior motive and that the result will deprive people of certain rights. In the teacher fight we steadfastly kept before the public the idea that the investigation was intended to rob the public schools of financial support and to promote religious and racial bigotry."[741]

Could this work? Could the general public be so easily misled and duped? Absolutely. These campaigns almost always worked, thanks to the comrades' sustained and unwavering commitment and viciousness and the sheer gullibility of a sadly large portion of the general public. Bella remembered:

> Little by little we won the campaign, at least in the opinion of many people; and we distracted the attention of the public from the specific work of the Committee. Support for the teachers, which at first had come only from the Communist Party, increased and included liberals, left trade unions, national group organizations, religious organizations, then political parties of the left, then left-wing Democrats, then so-called Progressive Republicans. All the support, however, was for tangential issues and not the basic issue. It did not matter to us so long as they marched at our side. Their reasons were unimportant to us.[742]

The important thing to the closet communist organizers was to advance international Marxism-Leninism. The marchers merely needed to march; the less they understood about reality and the truth, the better. They were what Lenin called useful idiots.

Bella Throws Her Punches

Bella Dodd had an intense and comprehensive role throughout this battle, as legal counsel, as witness, as organizer, as spokesperson, as propagandist.

As part of the propaganda effort, a pamphlet titled "Winter Soldiers, the Story of a Conspiracy Against the Schools" was published with an introduction by Bella, a foreword by Franz Boas, and illustrations by leading artists such as Rockwell Kent, a fellow traveler. It was classic communist mendacity. The reality was that there was a conspiracy against the schools, but it was by communists, not by the Rapp-Coudert Committee seeking to expose the communist conspiracy and help the schools. The pamphlet even boldly and laughably accused the committee of indoctrinating the youth, rather than communists doing so. The pamphlet made an emotional appeal to parents and the general public castigating the Rapp-Coudert Committee for intending to "curtail schooling and to indoctrinate the young with the idea that all is well and that every attempt to adjust the old ways to new needs is subversive and will lead to disaster."[743]

Over ten thousand copies were printed, with proceeds going to the Defense Committee—that is, the Party's secret communist front group.[744] Other pamphlets soon flowed from the Defense Committee, with provocative titles such as "New York Schools Are Invaded" (not by communists, of course) and "A Shield for Pro-Fascists."[745] As part of their campaign, the Teachers Union organized yet another front, this one called "Friends of Free Public Schools," to enlist people other than teachers into the struggle and "Save Our Schools." The publicity was run by the Communist Party, with Bella orchestrating the entire effort.[746]

Meanwhile, Bella and the Party stonewalled the legal process. It was in October 1940 that the Rapp-Coudert Committee had issued the subpoena *duces tecum* to the union for the lists. In response, Bella and the union issued a legal challenge, which was denied. The stonewalling continued. Finally, the union appealed to the New York Court of Appeals, which ruled unanimously on January 23, 1941 in favor of the Rapp-Coudert Committee. The union and Bella claimed constitutional privilege.

Particularly notable was the information that the Rapp-Coudert Committee had in making the urgency of its case. The committee revealed that it had evidence that between 800 and 850 members of the Party in the Teachers Union were communists—a shocking and yet impressively accurate estimate (albeit an underestimate). The concern of the committee was never solely whether someone was a communist teacher but the extent to which these organizations influenced the conduct of the public instructional system.

Sparks flew when Bella Dodd, legal counsel, was called before the Rapp-Coudert Committee to testify. The hearing was held in New York City at 165 Broadway, on February 20, 1941. Bella later honestly admitted, "On the committee were men I could not dislike, mild, fair men such as Robert Morris, Philip Haberman of the Anti-Defamation League, and Charles S. Whitman, son of the former governor of New York."[747] But that did not matter in February 1941. This was war, and Bella was ready for battle. When confronted by the committee, Bella displayed her Bolshevik combativeness. Here is a hearing transcript of one confrontation between Bella, Haberman, and Assemblyman Chester A. Backus:

> Philip Haberman: Are those records in your possession?
> Dodd: They are in my possession, and my legal custody.

Philip Haberman: Mr. Backus, I ask that you direct the witness to produce the records.

Backus: Yes, I direct you to produce them, Dr. Dodd.

Dodd: Well, Mr. Backus and Mr. Hartman and Mr. Slocum, I am advised by counsel that production of those records, lists, and other items specified in the subpoena, would violate my Constitutional rights and the Constitutional rights of the union. For that reason I am not at this time producing them.[748]

Philip Haberman: Let me put a very specific question: Insofar as my question asks you to state whether you have had anything to do with the formulation of the policy that resulted in the introduction of that resolution [not handing over the union membership lists], your answer must be either yes, no, or I don't remember.

Dodd: I don't remember. You have helped me out a great deal.

Mr. Backus again directed Dodd to hand over the lists.

Dodd: Mr. Backus, as much as I regret in any way not doing what you advise me to do, I have been advised by counsel that the production of these, the compulsory production of these records, as called for by these two subpoenas, would violate my Constitutional rights and the Constitutional rights of the union. For that reason, I do not at this time present them. Well, one can summarize in different ways. My answer is not that I refuse. My answer is, I think you are asking me something which is unconstitutional. I think you are asking something which you have no right to ask me.[749]

As usual, here was an American Bolshevik dedicated to Stalin's Soviet Union and a "Soviet America" conveniently wrapping herself in the comfortable protection of the US Constitution, which would be the first document shredded if America was taken over by the Comintern. Bella and her minions were suddenly the self-appointed champions of freedom: disciples not of Moscow, 1917, but of Philadelphia, 1776.

Bella blasted the committee's attempt to "destroy public education and academic freedom."[750]

The Rapp-Coudert Committee and the union bargained back and forth, and eventually, the committee said it would accept only the minutes of the union. Finally, on January 27, the "union voted to turn over the list 'under protest.'" Bella attached a stinging statement of protest upon handing over the lists, denouncing the committee's "totalitarian subpoenas."[751]

Yes, the comrades were alleging "totalitarian" behavior not from Stalin's Soviet Union that they were pledged to but from the legislative committee seeking to expose them.

Summary of Findings of the Rapp-Coudert Committee

The Rapp-Coudert Committee interviewed or called as witnesses over nine hundred people during the course of the investigation in a series of open and closed hearings, mostly closed. Of these, only seventy-six individuals appeared in public hearings. The text of the private hearings was never made public. The committee never called students in public testimony and never publicized the name of any person unless it had identified him as a communist by at least two persons. Sixty-nine persons were publicly named as communists, although the committee indicated that it had information on another 434.[752]

The Rapp-Coudert Committee discovered that the bloated New York City Board of Education employed an instructional staff of over eleven thousand, while an additional three thousand taught in the city's municipal colleges. Out of these fourteen thousand, the committee identified one thousand communist teachers. Thus, of these one thousand, the Rapp-Coudert investigation exposed what was believed to be the single largest block of communist teachers in the country.[753] The majority of those joining the Communist Party as members or spies came from the Northeast and from Ivy League colleges.

Among the identified Party members, eight teachers were dismissed.[754] Morris Schappes,[755] an English teacher at City University of New York (CCNY) and the "acknowledged Party leader of the CCNY unit," was fired for refusing to cooperate with the Rapp-Coudert Committee and was convicted of perjury.[756] Isidore Begun, dismissed by the Teachers Union previously, was fired. Dale Zysman was also dismissed.

Considering Bella Dodd's estimate that there were 1,000 to 1,500 teachers in the union who were communists, as well as FBI estimates that there were approximately 30,000 Communist Party members in the New York City area in the 1940s, this was only a small portion of the total number of Marxist-Leninists operating in the Big Apple. Out of the 69, none, of course, was tortured or executed. All were allowed counsel. This was, after all, America, not the USSR.

And yet, these secret supporters of Stalin, the master of the show trial, sought to frame the Rapp-Coudert Committee as a show trial.

The Real Show Trials: the Moscow Trials

The parallel to the Moscow Trials is no minor point of comparison. It is worth underscoring, if only briefly, to illustrate the outrageousness of American communists casting elected New York legislators and their investigations as totalitarian.

Occurring just prior (1936–38) to the Rapp-Coudert hearings was a terrible series of infamous show trials held on the stage of the Soviet Motherland, produced and directed by Stalin himself. The trials were part of the purge that Stalin used to terrorize his country and assassinate real or potential rivals. Robert Conquest, the great historian of Russian terror, estimates that while the exact number may never be known, "the whole range of the Soviet regime's terrors can hardly be lower than fifteen million."[757] Of those on "trial," most were executed.

While the Moscow Trials alerted some American communists to the reality of Stalin's deadly tactics, many educators, progressives, and fellow travelers remained blind. Some signed a "Statement of American

Progressives on the Moscow Trials," which gave the correct "Party line" on the trials, including Morris Schappes, Margaret Schlauch, Louis Budenz, Corliss Lamont, and the "progressive" Jerome Davis. The statement justified the trials (and, therefore, the accompanying torture) as "the prevention of treason and the eradication of spies and wreckers," emphasizing that "American liberals must not permit their outlook on these questions to be confused, nor allow their recognition of the place of the Soviet Union in the international fight of democracy against fascism to be destroyed. We call upon them to support the efforts of the Soviet Union to free itself from insidious internal dangers, and to rally support for the international fight against fascism—the principal menace to peace and democracy."[758] This was one year before the Hitler-Stalin pact.

This statement was signed by many members of the Teachers Union, who referred to themselves not as communists but as "progressives." These members of the Teachers Union, which stoically claimed to stand for "democracy," "progress," and "intellectual freedom," justified the torture and executions of those who veered from Stalin's line. They had excused the killing of millions in the Ukraine for "progress." They now justified the Moscow Trials in an effort to cleanse the Party of traitors and "betrayers of the revolution."

This hypocrisy took place just prior to the Rapp-Coudert hearings.

Yet, in spite of what was known of the Moscow trials, the Rapp-Coudert hearings were portrayed by Bella and her communist friends and liberal fellow travelers with the usual epithets: "inquisition," "witch hunt," "Salem trials," "persecutions." The request for the union list was described as providing "a blacklist for the enemies of teachers."[759] The likes of Morris Schappes protested the placing of "teachers in handcuffs," and accused the Board of Education of acting against intellectual freedom.[760] When Schappes was in the Tombs prison, Bella and other teachers staged a "funeral" for academic freedom in Foley Square of New York City. Bella, chairman of the Shappes Defense Committee (yet another front group) and queen of agitprop, cried:

"An honest man is in that tomb. What crime has he committed? The crime of wanting racial and religious equality, of working for better educational conditions."[761]

Bella admitted later that the purpose of the march was to gain wider "public support."[762] But for now, there was no limit to the ridiculous levels of hyperbole by her and her comrades: Poor Morris Schappes— punished for fighting for "racial and religious equality."

Looking Back at the "School for Democracy"

Reflecting on her work in education and the Teachers Union, Bella said it "helped the Party gain in power in the field of American educa- tion." She had been "always ready to help in the struggle for admission to the academic world of the intellectuals." But she later regretted that this was "not education but propaganda."[763]

Bella and her band of Marxist and "progressive" intellectuals set out to rectify any tactical losses from the Rapp-Coudert fallout by establishing schools of their own. The Teachers Union assumed the obligation of helping the displaced professors and teachers who lost their jobs due to the Rapp-Coudert saga. She estimated that "there were about 50 teachers and professors who lost their jobs as a result of the fight." She and the Teachers Union established the School for Democracy. The dismissed teachers taught there.[764]

The School for Democracy was one of at least two dozen similar schools created throughout the country. Established in lower New York City, Dr. Howard Selsam was the director. Selsam was a hardcore Marxist, founder and organizer of the Karl Marx Society at Brooklyn College, where he taught. Attorney General Herbert Brownell, in his 1955 Office of Attorney General report looking into the School for Democracy, which took formal testimony from Selsam, stated: "Dr. Selsam testified, in substance, that Marxism-Leninism, the teaching of which is admittedly a prime, immediate function of the school, is syn- onymous with Communism; that Marxism-Leninism [is] contained authoritatively, in the so-called Marxist-Leninist Classics . . . and that

a follower thereof must accept the discipline of the Communist Party
. . . and that in so accepting Party discipline one must abide by and
adhere to decisions, positions, and interpretations of the Party."[765]

The school was largely staffed by communists and was Party controlled. They were clever enough to advertise it not as a school to
propagate communist ideas but as a school to propagate "democratic
and progressive ideas" with a broad public relations approach. Bella
was the organizer and the moving force behind it, and the school was
deemed a success.[766]

The School of Democracy's course catalogue for the 1941 fall
semester portrayed it as an educational center "designed to meet the
needs of adults for a courageous and forthright examination of society. Its teachers have been tempered in the struggle to maintain and
extend academic freedom. They have a passion for the truth. They have
learned democracy in the struggle to maintain it, and acknowledged
that it was under the auspices of the Committee for Defense of Public
Education."[767] Its offerings for January 1942 pushed the Party line that
the "School for Democracy believes it can help equip a democratic
people with the weapons to achieve unity, defeat fascism, and build a
more democratic society."[768]

Once again, the mantra was democracy.

Among the teachers at the School for Democracy were Morris
Schappes and David Goldway, who had been dismissed from the
Teachers Union before the Rapp-Coudert hearings, as well as Philip
Foner, dismissed by the Board of Education, and Margaret Schlauch.[769]

Bella was a member of the faculty and taught courses with names
like "How the American Government Works" and "Legislation, Lobbying, and the People's Program" (January 1942 semester). A bulletin
describing the latter course stated, "This course will consist of lectures and discussion on the ways of formulating a legislative program,
the method of following a bill through the legislature and the techniques of getting public support and mass pressure. Attention will be
focused on the leading pressure groups: organized labor, civil service,

education, welfare, consumer groups, farmers, religious groups, patriotic organizations, taxpayers' federations."[770]

One wonders if these courses on legislation and "how government works" included tutorials on withholding and destroying evidence and ordering witnesses to perjure themselves before legislative committees.

The Party already operated its highly touted "Workers School" at Party headquarters in New York, a school infamous for its thorough communist indoctrination. Now, it had created another school in New York. Bella had discussed the idea with Earl Browder and other Party apparatchiks. Browder wanted to establish a school that would have broader appeal to the masses. Bella and Browder felt that the Party's New York Workers School had goals that had become too narrow and sectarian. Thus it was decided to merge the School for Democracy and the Workers School into a bigger, broader, and more effective center of Marxist-Leninist education.[771]

Alexander Trachtenberg himself was put in charge of a committee to merge the Workers School and the School for Democracy. "An astute Communist, a charter member of the Party and before that a revolutionary socialist," noted Bella, "Trachtenberg was and is now one of the financial big wheels of the movement. He was also chief of the firm of International Publishers, which had a monopoly on the publication of communist books and pamphlets and on the distribution of Soviet books and pamphlets."[772]

Comrade Trachtenberg was ideal for this new American-Bolshevik school. He even supplied the (Soviet) funding for the building. Browder suggested the new school be named for Thomas Jefferson, champion of democracy.[773] Stated Bella:

> He [Trachtenberg] bought a beautiful building on the corner of Sixteenth Street and Sixth Avenue, a stone's throw from St. Francis Xavier School, to house the new Marxist School. Plans were already on foot for a string of Marxist Adult Education schools which would have a patriotic look. The patriots of the

American Revolution and of the Civil War were to be given a new sort of honor—a Marxist status. The new school in New York was named the Jefferson School of Social Research. In Chicago the school was named the Abraham Lincoln School, in Boston the John Adams School, and in New Rochelle, the Thomas Paine School.[774]

The American Communist Party continued to portray itself as the true inheritor of the American Revolution. Its members were hoisted up as the real sons and daughters of Jefferson, Adams, and Paine.[775]

In recalling this educational effort in her memoirs, Bella again, as she often did, recounted Trachtenberg's slick thinking about exploiting these democratic labels to hoodwink the wider masses: "Trachtenberg once said to me that when communism came to America it would come under the label of 'progressive democracy.' 'It will come,' he added, 'in labels acceptable to the American people.'"

The new Jefferson School for Democracy would fit perfectly in the expanding Soviet America. In 1944, it opened its doors. As Bella later said, these schools were to play a part in the new revolution to destroy a great nation.[776] They were part of a vast and ever-widening field of infiltration.

CHAPTER 13

BELLA AND COMMUNISTS TARGET AND INFILTRATE THE CATHOLIC CHURCH

B ella Dodd had become a master infiltrator for the Communist Party. As a concealed communist organizer for teachers' unions in New York state from 1936 to 1938, even before she was a formal Party member, she was quickly achieving head-spinning numbers: "At its peak the Union boasted ten thousand members, and in it the Communist Party had a fraction of close to a thousand," said Bella. "Among them were Moscow-trained teachers and men and women who had attended the sixth World Congress of the Comintern."[777]

In mere years, she and the Party placed a thousand communists in the teachers' union in one state, tantamount to 10 percent of all union members—some of them direct Moscow-trained disciples of the Soviet Comintern. Those members held firm like a rock, standing steady even as many other members of the union fled. Bella said that by 1941 the communist element remained virtually unshaken, with about one thousand of the four thousand remaining union members still being communists—a striking one-quarter of all union members.[778]

These communists, working in unison and concealing their ideological sympathies, had control of the union. In fact, as early as 1936, according to Bella, "the Communists had control."[779]

Nationwide, Bella later admitted that she "placed 1,300 teachers and 1,500 principals in the education system from grade school to university levels."[780] New York was the epicenter.

The key was to control the leadership. Bella said that the executive committee of the Teachers Union "always, from the time that I knew it, had a majority of Communists. As a matter of a fact, it was deplorably large. We had as many as 80 or 90 percent of the executive board were Communists." This ensured, said Bella, that "the teacher who was non-Communist didn't have a chance really of expressing her opinion or of really being heard."[781]

She emphasized that people never ceased to be impressed by the small number of communists needed to control an organization—something attested to in sworn testimony by numerous ex-communists, such as Ben Gitlow, Manning Johnson, and others.[782] In the vicinity of New York, they might represent a true majority, but that "does not explain their influence in a great many other quarters which can be often controlled effectively with as few as 10 to 30 percent of total membership, and the explanation is to be found, it seems to me, in a close examination of their ways."

Party leaders knew this very well. Manning Johnson explained to Congress in July 1953 testimony: "It is an axiom in Communist organization strategy that if an infiltrated body has 1 percent Communist Party members and 9 percent Communist Party sympathizers, with well-rehearsed plans of action, they can effectively control the remaining 90 percent."[783]

And particularly jarring, Johnson spoke to the infiltration of churches and seminaries in particular: "In the large sections of the religious field, due to the ideological poison which has been filtered in by Communists and pro-Communists through seminaries, the backlog of sympathizers and mental prisoners of socialistic ideology is greater than the 10 percent necessary for effective control."

All it took was merely 1 percent Communist Party members and 9 percent sympathizers. A trusting flock could, in the hands of a few deceitful shepherds, be led into spiritual harm.

It was that sort of especially insidious infiltration that Bella Dodd looked to next.

Seminaries as the Neck of a Funnel

Communists in America and abroad vigorously sought to penetrate churches and seminaries. Here at home, Manning Johnson testified: "The plan was to make the seminaries the neck of a funnel through which thousands of potential clergymen would issue forth, carrying with them, in varying degrees, an ideology and slant which would aid in neutralizing the anti-Communist character of the church and also to use the clergy to spearhead important Communist projects."[784]

Communists thus created cells and "small forces" in seminaries. As Johnson noted, these in turn were quickly augmented by new recruits promoted up and "siphoned into the divinity institutions" and "educational institutions." This was an actual "plan" to reorient the seminaries to generate potentially "thousands" of pro-communist clergymen. Johnson cynically observed, "Through Reds in religion, we have a true living example of the old saying: 'The Devil doth quote the Scripture.'"

The devil does indeed. He quoted it to Jesus. His atheist minions in the Marxist movement would quote it to Christians.

How successful was this effort?

"This policy was successful beyond even Communist expectations," asserted Johnson. "The combination of Communist clergymen, clergymen with a pro-Communist ideology, plus thousands of clergymen who were sold the principle of considering Communist causes as progressive, within 20 years, furnished the Soviet apparatus with a machine which was used as a religious cover for the overall Communist operation ranging from immediate demands to actually furnishing aid in espionage and outright treason."

This had been going on for decades. Twenty years prior to Johnson's testimony, Earl Browder, general secretary of CPUSA, openly boasted to students at Union Theological Seminary on February 15, 1935: "You may be interested in knowing that we have preachers, preachers active in churches, who are members of the Communist Party."[785] That was an astonishing concession. Bear in mind that Communist Party members were expected to be atheists. These Party members who were actual preachers were bearing a significant false witness.

Manning Johnson and Earl Browder were not the only ones who testified to this. So did Louis Budenz, Ben Gitlow, Herb Philbrick, and others—each of which will be quoted in this chapter. To be clear, these men testified to the infiltration of Protestant churches in America. There was a stunning degree of penetration of the mainline denominations, particularly the Episcopal Church and the United Methodist Church.[786] Abroad, of course, it was worse, especially the sabotaging of the Russian Orthodox Church in the USSR and all the churches behind the Iron Curtain.

What about the Catholic Church in America? We know there was an open effort to influence the Catholic Church through slick efforts like Earl Browder's infamous "outstretched hand" in the 1930s. This was very public and well-known. But was there ever a clandestine effort to infiltrate Catholic seminaries?

That is where Bella Dodd and her story are especially intriguing.

Infiltrating the Catholic Church

According to Bella Dodd, there were different ploys used at various times by the Communist Party to influence and undermine the Catholic Church, including (1) direct attacks through militant atheism and persecution, (2) the Earl Browder tactic of the "Outstretched Hand,"(3) infiltration of Catholic lay organizations, (4) establishment of "Catholic" front groups, and (5) infiltration (alleged) of seminaries. Some Catholics have gone further, arguing that the Vatican was infiltrated with spies, especially during the Second Vatican Council, by pointing to the Marxist heresy of liberation theology, among other outrages. Today, some of these same Catholics cite (or attempt to cite) Bella Dodd. All of this and more will be explored in this chapter.

For the record, none of what unfolded would have surprised the Catholic Church. "This modern revolution, it may be said, has actually broken out or threatens everywhere," said Pope Pius XI in 1937, "and it exceeds in amplitude and violence anything yet experienced in the preceding persecutions launched against the Church. . . . [It] aims at upsetting the social order and at undermining the very foundations of Christian civilization."

Direct Attacks through Militant Atheism

The Venerable Fulton J. Sheen summarized the truth about communism and atheism, noting that they are intrinsically related and "one cannot be a good communist without being an atheist, and every atheist is a potential communist."[787] Bella herself spoke about this: "There is no doubt that the Marxist-Leninist principles are completely materialistic and, therefore, against anything which has to do with religion."[788]

The Party's history was violently against religion. Lenin emphasized that atheism was "an integral part of Marxism."[789] He said that "all worship of a divinity is a necrophilia." Comparing religion to venereal disease, Lenin sneered that "any religious idea, any idea of any god at all, any flirtation even with a god, is the most inexpressible foulness . . . the most shameful 'infection.'"[790]

Nikolai Bukharin, founding editor of *Pravda* and one of Lenin's and Stalin's leading lieutenants, stated: "Religion and communism are incompatible, both theoretically and practically. . . . Communism is incompatible with religious faith." He spoke for Marx: "'Religion is the opium of the people,' said Karl Marx. It is the task of the Communist

Party to make this truth comprehensible to the widest possible circles of the laboring masses."[791]

A Communist Party must, therefore, carry on propaganda in favor of atheism. The 1929 platform of the Comintern Sixth Congress instructed communists worldwide, including in the United States: "One of the most important tasks of the cultural revolution affecting the wide masses is the task of systematically and unswervingly combatting religion—the opium of the people. The proletarian government must withdraw all State support from the Church." That proletarian state "carries on anti-religious propaganda with all the means at its command and reconstructs the whole of its educational work, on the basis of scientific materialism."[792]

William Z. Foster, national chairman of CPUSA, proudly boasted that in the "U.S.S.R., as part of the general cultural revolution, religion is being liquidated."[793] In America, echoes of atheism were present both from communists and socialists during the 1920s, the 1930s, and subsequent years. For example, Walter Reuther, a powerful establishment labor leader, addressed a Young People's Socialist League and was asked, "Do you believe in religion and God or in science as a religion?" His reply was astounding: "We do not believe in God, but that man is God."[794] Bella Dodd mentioned this in one of her interviews, saying: "This whole question of morality. The question of humanism as far as man is concerned and what he is, Man is God. That's the whole approach of the Soviet system and it's the approach that we are beginning to adopt. The God is Dead movement is by no means a college prank. It's a well considered cutting of the underpinnings of our civilization."[795]

Mary Van Kleeck, an acquaintance of Bella's when she was in the Party and often featured in the *Daily Worker*, echoed similar words. When speaking at a YWCA in 1937, Van Kleeck was asked what the churches' position was on the new changing social order. Her response: "The churches of tomorrow will be one of antichurch Christianity."[796]

That was the militantly atheistic new world and new Soviet America that homegrown communists were angling at.

Thorez and the Outstretched Hand—
Atheism but a Change in Strategy

Over the course of several decades, communists faced obstacles; namely, they were unable to destroy religion and faith through galloping horses and persecutions. Religion turned out to be a much more formidable foe, especially in the form of the Roman Catholic Church.

As late as 1932, the Kremlin lamented: "The Catholic Church, with the Pope in its van, is now an important bulwark of all counterrevolutionary organizations and forces." The Soviets claimed: "The Catholic Church aids and abets the fascists in their struggle against the revolutionary workers' movement, and it joins the chorus of all the other churches who are clamoring for war against the U.S.S.R."[797] In this, according to official communist propaganda, the Catholic Church did not stand alone. Other ecclesiastical organizations—Buddhists, Lutherans, Anglicans, Jews, Muslims, and others—helped capitalists and landowners exploit the masses and keep them steeped in delusion for a later heavenly reward. Or so the story went.[798]

In the early 1930s, communists began distancing themselves from their brutal tactics of liquidating Catholics because they proved incompatible with western democracies' laws against purges and gulags and mass killings and blowing up churches. Instead, the communists opted for a kinder, gentler approach by reaching out to Catholics.

The 1933 *Daily Worker* signaled the new strategy: Catholics made up one sixth of the country's population, and most of them were "workers like ourselves. When we work with Catholics we must use the progressive ideas of Christianity." Yes, "progressive ideas." Such as? The *Daily Worker* offered some tips: "For example, in our peace movement, if we were to point out that Jesus was the 'Prince of Peace' and that Catholics want peace on earth, don't you think they will listen?" The communist newspaper reported an example of its newfound success: "We recently recruited several young Catholics who still go to Mass on Sundays and have the closest ties with the Church. We must show the people the difference between the religious role and the political role the Church plays. We must study the Christian ideas, since most of the comrades know nothing of the Church ideas or its history."[799]

Of course, the goal was not for communists to become more Catholic but vice versa. Furthermore, Catholics needed to become communist and anti-Catholic, actively working against their Church. The *Daily Worker* took off its mask and admitted: "Most of all, we must build the League Against Catholics."[800]

In this approach, communists cloaked their rhetoric of class struggle in the language of the Gospels, illustrating Manning Johnson's warning that when it came to communists, "the Devil doth quote the Scripture." The pro-communist *Educational Vanguard* ran articles like, "Communism Puts Ideals of Christ into Practice." The article appealed to "progressive" Christians to create "a more brotherly society." The article righteously intoned that Christians "feel it is their religious duty to work for the removal of such an inhuman and ungodly social order" as that represented by capitalism.[801]

Fulton Sheen understood the signs of the times. Since communism was fundamentally "a religion to destroy a religion, or a politics which is a religion," noted Sheen, it had to create a new strategy other than force and persecution to deal with religion.[802] It had to suddenly reach out to religion in the guise of a loving brother.

And thus, we come to the gesture by Maurice Thorez, secretary-general of the French Communist Party and a leader in the "united front against fascism." Now, Thorez and his comrades eyed up a united front with Catholics.

Consistent with the united front policy, Thorez proclaimed in 1937 the policy of the "outstretched hand" (*la main tendue*), a term used to appeal to Roman Catholics.[803] This would stand in stark contrast to previous Communist Party policy. On April 17, 1936, Thorez announced the new tone in a radio broadcast: "People of France, a wind of distress is blowing over our beautiful country. We stretch out our hand to you, Catholic worker, employee, peasant; we stretch out our hand to you because you are our brother, and you, like us, are burdened with the same cares."[804]

The iconic clenched fist of the communists had morphed into a slippery outstretched hand to Catholics. CPUSA jumped at the approach. CPUSA followed the lead of the French Communist Party with praises for the Catholic men who had been fighters for the "economic and civil rights of our people." Earl Browder was fully on board, preparing in 1938 a mass "Message to Catholics,"[805] which became an instant headline in newspapers nationwide.[806] Browder quoted a cardinal, a bishop, priests, and a nun who expressed "progressive Catholic sentiments" and said that "Catholics understand us and our aims."[807] In his mendacity, he claimed that "only as a result of the rise of Soviet power, were Roman Catholics given equality and freedom of worship in Moscow."[808]

Browder eagerly noted to his American comrades that France's Maurice Thorez had made his "outstretched hand" effort to Catholics abroad. This had been especially fruitful, said Browder, in the "great trade union movement in France." CPUSA held out hopes that the same might transpire in the United States, particularly with Catholic workingmen and immigrants in industries from rail and steel to textiles and in groups like the CIO and AF of L, where millions of Catholics marched side by side (including in strikes) "with their brothers of all political shades and religious creeds." What happened in France could happen in America.[809]

Precisely that became a mass effort in America by CPUSA. The likes of Bella Dodd were enlisted into the cause, as was Louis Budenz, the communist editor of the *Daily Worker*, and a fellow former Catholic. He was elated about the new policy and thought Thorez's declaration was the "new proof of the healthy coming of age of the communist movement." On Christmas Day 1937, he penned a headline for the

Daily Worker: "Communists Hold Out Hand of Fellowship to All Enemies of War and Oppression."[810]

Bella and her comrades who read the *Daily Worker* saw that Thorez shrewdly called upon French Catholics to join in battle with communists "against their common enemies, fascism and war." Later in Bella's life, when she was on her way to a meeting with Fulton Sheen, she painfully remembered this slick effort. She recalled being startled by one of the Party's pamphlets: "And then before my mind's eye flashed the cover of a communist pamphlet on which was a communist extending a hand to a Catholic worker. The pamphlet was a reprint of a speech by the French Communist leader, Thorez, and it flattered workers by not attacking their religion. It skillfully undermined the hierarchy, in the pattern of the usual communist attempt to drive a wedge between the Catholic and his priest."[811]

Pope Pius XI could see through ruses like Thorez's and rejected them, stating: "It is unfortunately true that even today there exists a common enemy threatening everything all over the world, even the sanctuary of the family, the state, and society. That enemy is communism, which is trying to penetrate everywhere and, alas, has already penetrated so many places by violence, by plot, or by deceit, by going so far as to clothe its appearances with the best intentions."[812] He also noted how communism was more menacing when "as has been the case most recently, it adopts less violent attitudes and less profane appearances."[813]

This was one such attitude and appearance.

Discussions of this new outstretched hand followed in France, in Rome, in America. When questioned about the Church's persecution in communist countries, Thorez claimed that Catholics legally had freedom of religion in Russia. In a typical sham response, he quoted Articles 124 (which promised citizens the right of "conscience") and 136 of the Constitution of the USSR to prove that "coexistence of communists and Catholics . . . is possible in a democratic regime and quite obviously in that higher form of democracy, the Soviet regime."[814] After asserting that Stalin's regime represented a "higher form of democracy" and ensured freedom of religion and conscience, Thorez added that Jesus and Paul preached socialism, and he claimed that this could be observed in the "communist groups" of monasteries throughout Europe.[815]

The archbishop of Paris, after consulting with Pius XI, rejected the offer of cooperation.[816] Following their *modus operandi*, the *Daily Worker* editors twisted the archbishop's words, saying it was "the duty of the French Catholics to accept the 'outstretched hand' of the Communist Party for socially beneficial objectives."[817] Going one step farther, the *Daily Worker* claimed: "Pope Counsels French Catholics to Accept Communist 'Outstretched Hand' in Struggles." The Vatican vehemently denied this: "Collaboration? Our action is permeated with spirituality, materialism is the guide of your action. And this spiritual element which for us is the soul and the true goodness of all action, you repudiate. Is it possible then to collaborate? If this gesture of the outstretched hand expresses on your part the desire to know your Catholic brothers better in order to respect their convictions, their sentiments, and their works along with the religion that inspires them, the Church will not refuse to do this work of enlightenment."[818]

Communists had distorted and lied about the Vatican's position.

Meanwhile, this united-front policy continued as communists sought to infiltrate churches worldwide, reaching as far as Australia.[819] Manning Johnson confirmed that the term "outstretched hand," as used by the Party, was a scheme to infiltrate the churches. It was the extension of the hand of friendship and cooperation to the Church, "while in the other hand holding a dagger to drive through the heart of the Church. . . . If you cannot take over the churches by frontal attack, take them over by the use of deception and guile and trickery, and that is exactly what the communists practice in order to infiltrate and subvert the Church and prepare them for the day when they would come under the hierarchical and authoritarian control of Moscow."[820]

It was an olive branch in one hand and a dagger in the other.

By 1939, former CPUSA head William Z. Foster conceded that "a serious mistake of the American leftwing during many years was to wave aside religious sentiments among the masses. In recent years, however, the Communist Party, with its policy of 'the outstretched hand,' has done much to overcome the harmful leftwing narrowness of former years and to develop a more healthy cooperation with the religious masses of the people in building the democratic front."[821]

That was the passive, conciliatory approach that communists showed with one side of their face in western democracies, while on the other side, they continued to aggressively persecute churches in Eastern Europe. Quite shamelessly, the Party in America meanwhile spread propaganda about "religious freedom" in the Soviet Union, partly through Bella's New York Teachers Union. In the publication *New York Teachers News*, in a November 10, 1945 column titled "New Material for Classroom Use," a disinformation piece noted that a "deep source of misinformation about the Soviet Union has long been the question of religion. A fellow traveler, the Reverend William Howard Melish, refuted the idea that the Soviet government dominates the Church and that the Church is hostile to the Soviet government." The pro-Soviet Melish was in truth one of the most duplicitous ministers of the twentieth century. Of all the ministers that plagued the religious left, he stood as one the most pernicious.[822]

But that was not how Bella's Teachers Union described their comradely reverend in this union newsletter. The column continued its blatant mendacity: "Not only does the Church have complete freedom, but the Soviet government has taken measures to facilitate its material operation." The article said that Dr. Melish affirmed this grand measure of religious freedom for the Greek Orthodox Church and for "religion generally in the Soviet Union."[823]

If only America could accept brother Browder's outstretched hand, the Party assured American progressives, it might also experience the same splendid harmony that Stalin's Soviet Union felt between communism and Catholicism-Christianity.

Infiltration of Catholic Lay Organizations

Implicit to this "outstretched hand" campaign was for American communists and their allies to create as many concealed communist front groups as possible, including among Catholics.

A particularly revealing document exposing this effort is today located in declassified Soviet Comintern-CPUSA archives held at the Library of Congress. Prepared for the Comintern by American communists in 1937, it carried the title "Confidential report on work in religious and non-religious Catholic organizations." The reason for the outstretched hand, it explained, was that "a real race is on as to which force will win over the Catholic people in this country—the forces of reaction and fascism as represented by the Catholic church or the forces of progress and democracy." The report revealed that the Communist Party had sent agents into such Catholic organizations as the Holy Name Society. In one parish, the communists boasted, "We have a Party comrade who is secretary of the Holy Name branch in this parish, which is one of the largest branches in the city."[824]

The communists' strategy clearly was to attract Catholics. This confidential report revealed: "After the District Convention, it was decided in our Section to do some concentration work amongst the Catholic people and in Catholic religious and non-religious organizations. It was felt that if any results were obtained they would point the direction which the Party should take in its organizational work that would be of benefit and would also reveal new methods of work that would be of benefit to the Party generally." The report further stated that "it is very necessary that as many capable and qualified Party members as is possible become regular functioning members of the various Holy Name societies in the city." The report also mentioned a "Eucharistic League" on the West Side of New York: "The Party . . . will also have to carefully select available and qualified comrades to enter the Eucharistic League."[825]

The reality was that American communists, despite the sugary calls for olive branches and outstretched hands, were working against Catholicism and for Bolshevism at every turn. They held in contempt what Catholics held sacred. And they enlisted friendly priests wherever possible to help them.

Attacking Fatima—with Catholic Assistance

To that end, a fascinating example was on display in the communists' newspaper of record, the *Daily Worker*, in September 1952.

Warner Brothers had just produced and released a major Hollywood film, *The Miracle of Our Lady of Fatima*. It was wonderful news for Catholics. In it, Our Lady's words at Fatima to the three children can be heard, including Mary's request: "God wishes to establish in the world the devotion to My Immaculate Heart. If people do what I tell you, many souls will be saved." She then said: "If my requests are granted, Russia will be converted and there will be peace. If not, she will scatter her errors throughout the world, provoking wars and persecution of the Church."

The words heard by the three shepherd children in 1917, including the specific reference to Russia, were publicly revealed for the first time in 1942, when the first two secrets were made public with the consent of Pope Pius XII.[826] For Catholics, Fatima was the miracle of the century, no less than the most remarkable Church-approved apparition of the modern age. The Miracle of the Sun on October 13, 1917 was witnessed by some seventy thousand people in Portugal. But just as important was Our Lady of Fatima's messages which impacted Catholics everywhere. Of course, that was not how communists saw it.

In true Bolshevik style, the *Daily Worker* sharpened the knives and carved up the movie. The communist organ's review by writer David Platt was titled "'Miracle of Fatima' Film Aids Pentagon War Drive." Filled with sarcasm, the piece said that the "miracle" was the stuff of "Catholic storybooks." The "alleged" Miracle of the Sun was easy to explain: "The backward, superstitious and long suffering peasants . . . were hypnotically disposed to its appearance." The communist organ declared that the film "cynically and impiously manipulates the religious feelings of millions of devout Catholics in order to propagate the lie that Communism—inheritor of the entire scientific, cultural, and democratic development of humanity—is a menace to civilization and peace, an enemy of religion."[827]

Such was the contrast that the *Daily Worker* posed. There was the phoniness of this so-called "miracle" for the masses versus the "genuine world-shaking event"—the Bolshevik capture of Russia—where "for the first time a new type of social order was established born of reason, science, human planning; a harmonious society." Bolshevik Russia was a "society where everyone had the right to worship in any church he wanted and the right not to worship at all."

No Catholic would swallow this. And so, the communists at the *Daily Worker* searched for a priest to cite for their outrageous article besmirching the words of the mother of Christ at Fatima. They found one—a well-known Jesuit priest, Father Martindale. Or at the least, they exploited Father Martindale's writings, taking them out of context and using them to their propaganda advantage. The newspaper invoked Martindale's authority: "The Jesuit Priest C. C. Martindale, writing in 1950, admitted that in 1917, when the angel allegedly spoke to the three Portuguese children of Fatima, the heavenly messenger made no reference to Russia whatsoever. The lady from above spoke only of the danger of a calamitous new war if humanity didn't change its ways and turn its face to God. There was no accusation against any country, not even Germany or England."

The *Daily Worker* writer thus charged that there had been a "criminal manipulation of the miracle of Fatima," twisted by the Vatican's "strange announcement" in 1942 to bring Russia and communism into the Lady's message. This had been done by the pope "to increase hatred and prejudice toward the Soviet Union . . . as an afterthought a quarter of a century later." Here again, the *Daily Worker* went to the words of the Jesuit priest: "'It cannot be denied,' admitted Monsignor Martindale, that the sudden introduction of Russia into the miracle of Fatima, 'created so many difficulties—again of various sorts—and for so many people, as to cause them to doubt the authenticity of the whole story of Fatima.'"

Martindale, in reality, was speaking for himself and his concerns and doubts.[828] And now his doubts were being exploited to speak for the doubts of the *Daily Worker*. As for this new Warner Brothers movie, it was downright deceptive and diabolical—according to the communist newspaper: "The Warner Bros. movie compounds this crude and evil deception [of the Vatican] by putting even stronger words of hate against Russia and Communism in the mouth of 'Our Lady of Fatima.'"

Leave it to communists to find hate, evil, and deception not in communism but in Catholicism—and to deign to speak for the Blessed Mother.

The *Daily Worker* reviewer went on: "How politically convenient for clerical reaction that 'Our Lady of Fatima' was able to foresee the 'Russian threat to world peace' as far back as 1917. . . . How politically convenient to use the 'Fatima' miracle against a people's society that guarantees freedom, joy and the complete flowering of man's physical and moral well being."

Shame on Warner Brothers, railed the *Worker*, for assisting "this abominable political fraud" perpetuated by "reactionary clergy" in the Catholic Church. The film was serving not only the Vatican's lies but "Big Money's violent and irreligious crusade against the peace-loving Socialist and People's Democracies"—led by Stalin's Soviet Union, by Mao's Red China, and by Kim Il Sung in his hopes of creating a glorious Marxist-Leninist peninsula for the Korean people. The film was a dirty tool of warmongering capitalists, belligerently "released at this moment of extreme reaction to assist the Pentagon's relentless war drive." The communist newspaper effectively accused Warner

Bros. and the Church of weaponizing the Blessed Mother against poor, beleaguered, peace-loving—and religion-loving—Soviet communism.

And worst of all, insisted the *Daily Worker*, was the hypocrisy: "Marxism, contrary to what this irrational film says, does not demand the abolition of religion, with which it has nothing in common philosophically."[829]

The *Daily Worker* diatribe against Fatima wrapped up with this solemn recommendation to moviegoers interested in the film: "It should be opposed by all Americans and particularly by the churchgoers—Catholic, Protestant and Jewish—the majority of whom (according to the Gallup polls) want peace and peaceful co-existence with the Soviet Union."

In truth, the *Daily Worker* misspoke about the movie and about Fatima. The second secret of Fatima specifically referred to Russia: Our Lady of Fatima had told the Portuguese children in 1917 that to prevent a worse war, "I shall come to ask for the Consecration of Russia to my Immaculate Heart, and the Communion of reparation on the First Saturdays. If my requests are heeded, Russia will be converted, and there will be peace; if not, she will spread her errors throughout the world, causing wars and persecutions of the Church. The good will be martyred; the Holy Father will have much to suffer; various nations will be annihilated." But there was hope: "In the end, my Immaculate Heart will triumph. The Holy Father will consecrate Russia to me, and she shall be converted, and a period of peace will be granted to the world."[830]

As usual, communists were not advancing truth but peddling disinformation. They were vigorously looking for causes and front groups and front persons to undermine the Roman Catholic Church and its beliefs.

Establishment of Front Groups:
Catholic Committee for Human Rights

In pushing damaging misrepresentations like these, communists in America needed more front groups and front persons to work against the Catholic Church and for atheist Bolshevik Russia. They would create them.

Unlike in previous times when communists went to great lengths to hide their deceitful ways, their plans were now in the open. Looking back at the "outstretched hand" and communist efforts generally to create front groups, Bella Dodd, on September 9, 1952, told the Senate Internal Security Subcommittee: "At different times in the history of the Communist Party, they emphasized the fact that it was possible for you to be religious and, at the same time, Communist. But those were the periods in which they were trying to win over larger numbers of, let us say, Catholic trade-unionists, Catholic workers, and so forth and so on. Those were the periods which were called the periods of extending the hand of communism to the people in the religious groups."[831]

As Bella explained, Communist Party organizers, in sizing up Catholics, effectively said to one another: "These men have a blind spot. They believe in God, but we communists know that there is no God. But in order to get them to work with us, we will work with them on a minimum program." Bella then dropped a name of an actual organization: "As a matter of fact, even when you were in the Communist Party, the Communist Party from time to time established committees like the—there was a committee on Catholics for Human Rights, which consisted of Communists who had been Catholics, whose purpose it was to work with mass organizations which had a large number of Catholics. Substantially, Marxism-Leninism denies that there is any soul; that there is any after life; that there is any God. That is part and parcel of the entire theory."[832]

And yet, even as that was their theory, they sought to establish religious front groups. Bella here mentioned one such group.

Formally known as the Catholic Committee for Human Rights, the group was not entirely unknown to Congress. It had been flagged in major investigative reports by Congress, including the seminal 1944 work "Investigation of Un-American Propaganda Activities in the United States" by the House Special Committee on Un-American Activities. That 2,166-page catalogue, known as "Appendix IX," makes reference to the Catholic Committee for Human Rights.[833] Here in September 1952, Bella was certainly correct to say that the committee "consisted of communists who had been Catholics." Whether it was currently communist, or whether its primary purpose was indeed "to work with mass organizations which had a large number of Catholics," quickly became a matter of public interest after Bella's testimony.[834]

Bella was interviewed about the group by popular reporter Westbrook Pegler, who tracked her down and visited her to hear her claims. In an August 1953 column titled "Reds and Church," he said of his conversation with Bella: "The first purpose of our conversation was to enlarge by knowledge of a deliberate attempt of the communists to penetrate the Catholic community primarily in New York City. . . . The apparatus, as the communist jargon goes, for this penetration was the Catholic committee for civil rights" (original spelling by Pegler).[835]

Bella told Pegler that Harold King and Tom Davin, a teacher and a newspaper reporter, were known to her as card-carrying members of the Party who had taken part in the formation of the Catholic Committee for Human Rights. The man in charge of the formation of the committee was "one Bill Lawrence, who has since fallen into obscurity."[836]

Bella focused on the role of Emmanuel Chapman with the group. She told Pegler that "she was shocked when a communist approached her telling her that he was a brother of Emmanuel Chapman, a Catholic convert who was teaching the philosophy of beauty at Fordham

University, a Jesuit institution and that Emmanuel would 'help us to get Catholics' for the Catholic Committee for Human Rights."[837]

Chapman was definitely suspect. It was reported in the Catholic press that Dr. Emmanuel Chapman was a "fellow-traveling . . . professor."[838] The Catholic press noted the likes of Chapman in observing that "Communists are using prominent Catholics to 'lure the Catholic masses into Red projects . . . so successful have they been that the Catholic Church is genuinely worried.'"[839]

The group was originally set up in May 1939 as the Committee of Catholics to Fight Anti-Semitism—which indeed would have been a typical front group name, directing attention not to advocating communism but to the noble goals of fighting fascism and anti-Semitism (three months before the Hitler-Stalin Pact, ironically).[840] The group claimed it was created as a response to Pope Pius XI's statement in 1938 that "it is not possible for Christians to take part in anti-Semitism." The group was originally formed by supporters of the Catholic Worker Movement, with Emmanuel Chapman, professor at Fordham University, its first executive secretary. Certain prominent individuals in the group at one time had been communist sympathizers, though had since rejected communism.[841]

In August 1939, the group changed its name to the Committee of Catholics for Human Rights (CCHR) and the name of their publication to the *Voice for Human Rights*. According to executive secretary Emmanuel Chapman, "The original aim of the committee was to combat the growing error of racism by bringing before the public the positive Christian doctrines condemning such thought. Since those same doctrines which emphasize the brotherhood of man under the fatherhood of God apply to all races and peoples, we have felt that a broader application of them was imperative."[842]

Bella talked about the group not only to Pegler but also to Patrick F. Scanlon, the managing editor of *The Tablet*. *The Tablet* said of Bella's role: "As a Communist, she had the task, and it was not a difficult one, of infiltrating the outfit, and seeing that it helped Moscow's cause and did nothing to offend the Soviet."[843] Scanlon, in turn, reported that he received communication from an FBI agent who told him: "Between the card-carrying member of the Party and the dupe who participates in its machinations there is little to choose in the service rendered the Soviet cause. Study over the list of the Committee you have, and also the 'Voice,' whose blatancy would have made even the uneducated, as opposed to 'egg-heads,' suspicious, and note the names." Scanlon quoted the FBI agent also pointing to the staff of the left-wing Catholic publication *Commonweal* as being infiltrated: "The 'Commonweal' staff, you will observe, had the largest number of representatives on this Red-infiltrated and Soviet-serving organization."[844]

As for the Catholic Committee for Human Rights that Bella had called out, Scanlon had taken a look at the group's statements and observed: "Nothing was said about anti-Christianity or the persecution or Catholics and, although Nazis were condemned in every paragraph, not a murmur was uttered against Communism."[845] That was precisely the tone and method of communist front groups.

So, was this committee one of them? Was it guilty as charged?

What happened to the organization? It was investigated by Congress, though its leaders invoked the Fifth Amendment and refused to share details. Here is an exchange between the Catholic Committee for Human Rights' Harold King and the Senate Judiciary Subcommittee's chief counsel, Robert J. Morris, in April 1953:

> Mr. Morris: Mr. King, are you presently a member of the Communist Party?
>
> Mr. King: I decline to answer that for the reasons given before.
>
> Mr. Morris: Mr. King, have you been active in an organization called the Catholic Committee for Human Rights?
>
> Mr. King: I was a member of that committee.
>
> Mr. Morris: Do you know a man named Thomas Davin, D-a-v-i-n?

> Mr. King: I decline to answer that question for the reasons given before.
>
> Mr. Morris: Has Thomas Davin attended Communist meetings at your home, Mr. King?

Harold King refused to provide answers to these specifics, repeatedly invoking his right not to testify against himself. The jousting continued along those lines, with Morris asking questions and King giving no answers:

> Mr. Morris: Have you been assigned to do so-called Catholic work, within the Communist Party? . . . Did you know a man named Emanuel Chapman?
>
> Mr. King: I did know a man named Emanuel Chapman.
>
> Mr. Morris: You say you did know him? Did you say you did know Thomas Davin?
>
> Mr. King: I decline to answer, for the reasons given before.

The chairman of the committee, Senator William Jenner (R-Indiana), endeavored to explain to King that "This committee is not concerned with your political beliefs. We do not care about that at all. But what we would like to know is whether or not you are a member of the Communist Party and belong to a cell that is supposed to infiltrate into the Catholic Church."

To repeat: a cell to infiltrate the Roman Catholic Church.

And why was that crucial? In case King failed to understand, the chairman explained, "This is what we are interested in. . . . We know, as you know, that communism is dedicated to the overthrow of this country by force and violence. We know, as you know, that boys are dying this afternoon, fighting this thing—communism." [846]

That fighting was going on in Korea at that very moment. Some fifty thousand American boys died in Korea fighting communism.

At the end of the testimony, with King tight-lipped, Counselor Morris intervened to say that he wanted the record to show that the subcommittee had received closed session testimony "indicating that Mr. King was a member of the Communist Party and was a member of a cell designed to influence Catholic groups."

King declined to answer whether he was a member of the Communist Party and all other questions pertaining to any alleged prior or current Party membership. He protested that the subcommittee was invading his civil rights by asking him about his political beliefs. This prompted Senator Jenner to object: "Don't give us a sob story about civil rights. If you wanted to answer that question honestly, you could do so and walk proudly from this room as a free man."[847]

King instead walked out pleading his case as a victim. His progressive allies would eagerly portray him a victim of a McCarthyite "witch hunt." They would point to him as another tragic, martyred "liberal" whose civil rights had been attacked amid America's "crazed" fear of Red-under-every-bed communism.

Infiltration of Churches, Seminaries, Youth Groups, and More

This chapter opened with testimony from Manning Johnson. Consider further what Johnson said, and what others said—all of it primarily related to Protestant churches and seminaries—and then the special case of the Catholic Church.

As noted, Johnson told Congress in July 1953 that for communists, "the plan was to make the seminaries the neck of a funnel through which thousands of potential clergymen would issue forth." He watched all of this carefully, and swore to it: "The Communists have an advantage in religious organizations due to the fact that their forces within religious groups are well organized as a totalitarian group which, operating as a highly mobile force, works unceasingly toward a premeditated program," Johnson told Congress. "This gives this destructive element a great tactical advantage over all others in the religious organizations who deal with religion as individuals, operating ethics on the basis of an individual conscience before God."[848]

As noted, it did not take a lot of communists to establish control once an organization was secretly penetrated. "I know from my own experience in working in labor organizations, for example, that we had an organization with 10,000 members, and there were only about 60 or 70 Communists, and we controlled the organization," testified Johnson. "So with a small minority of ministers who work in an organized manner, they can always win over and subvert and dupe the majority who are disorganized and are individualistic."

And what kind of numbers was he talking about? By Manning Johnson's estimate, the number of trained forces by American communists operating in the religious realm reached into the thousands:

> In the early 1930s the Communists instructed thousands of their members to rejoin their ancestral religious groups and to operate in cells designed to take control of churches for Communist purposes. This method was not only propounded, but was executed with enormous success among large elements of American church life. Communists operating a double-pronged infiltration, both through elements of Communist-controlled clergy, and Communist-controlled laymen, managed to pervert and weaken entire stratas of religious life in the United States. Communists in churches and other religious organizations were instructed to utilize the age-old tradition of the sanctity of the church as a cover for their own dastardly deeds.

Likewise speaking to this method were others who testified under oath to Congress, including Ben Gitlow, Herb Philbrick, and more.

Ben Gitlow had been a major CPUSA figure. He had risen higher than anyone next to Earl Browder and William Z. Foster, twice running as the Party's candidate for vice president of the United States (1924 and 1928) and serving on the Executive Committee of the Soviet Comintern. After a long silence upon leaving the Party in 1929, Gitlow emerged to testify before Congress (first in 1939) and to write two major books, *I Confess* (1940) and *The Whole of Their Lives* (1948).[849]

Gitlow on July 7, 1953 (among other occasions) testified to the House Committee on Un-American Activities. Among his most shocking material was his information on how the American Communist Party and the Comintern penetrated the mainline Christian denominations, particularly the Episcopal Church and the United Methodist Church. Gitlow made clear that the worst agent for the Party and the Comintern was the Rev. Harry Ward, the ACLU co-founder, especially through his Methodist Federation for Social Action. The material from Gitlow on Ward and his organization was stunning. His testimony traversed almost seventy pages in the official on-the-record transcript, almost a third of which dealt with Ward and the Methodist Federation for Social Action. Every page of it deserves to be read, and much of it has been summarized elsewhere in a recent treatment.[850]

For our purposes, it needs to be underscored that Gitlow spoke at length to the "way that the members of the Communist Party could infiltrate church organizations for the purpose of conducting their propaganda among them, for enlisting their support for Soviet Russia and for the various campaigns in which the Communists were interested." Gitlow spoke to how: "The Russian Communists were the first to exploit ministers of the United States and through them, the church organizations, for the purpose of spreading propaganda in favor of Communist Russia and for the building up of a pro-Soviet sentiment among church people in America and among Americans generally." Gitlow listed page after page of names and examples. He also spoke to the united-front tactic: "The united-front tactic enabled the Communists to greatly increase the effectiveness of their infiltration activities. The united-front tactic was first directed toward the development of pro-Soviet sentiment and support of the Soviets; second, to build up support for the Communists in the trade unions and to create the organizations and conditions for their capture by the Communists; and third, to spread Communist propaganda, incite discontent among the people, undermine the loyalty of the American people and to divide them on religion, national, racial, and economic lines."

The congressional chief counsel, Robert Kunzig, asked Gitlow explicitly what the policy of the united front had to do with the infiltration of religion. Gitlow answered: "The united-front policy enabled the Communists to widely expand their infiltration activities on the religious field because instead of using the Communist Party directly in enlisting the support of the clergymen and laymen who were pro-Soviet and supported the Communist Party and its activities, the Communist Party could enlist them through the front organizations, and on the specific issues of the united front. It was, for the Communists, for men and women operating in a field hostile to communism, to operate in the name of a front organization instead of in the name of the Communist Party."

Following this was a very revealing exchange between Kunzig and Gitlow. The counselor focused directly on the crucial question at hand:

> *Mr. Kunzig.* When did the Communist infiltration of religion become a major policy of the Communist Party of the United States?
>
> *Mr. Gitlow.* It certainly did. On August 20, 1935, with a full delegation of the Communist Party of the United States present, a resolution was adopted unanimously dealing with the preparation of the imperialists for a new world war.

Gitlow said that the resolution was passed by the Seventh World Congress of the Communist International and "proves that Communist infiltration of the religious field was decided upon in Moscow as a major policy. Those who declare that such infiltration of religion, especially the Christian churches, is a figment of the imagination, either do so to hide the astounding facts about such infiltration or because they are too stupid to see or realize what is going on." This was a very specific event, a resolution with an exact date, named by Gitlow, as well as the place—Moscow. As this book shows, the date fits with the time period cited by Fulton Sheen, Bella Dodd, and others.

Kunzig then asked Gitlow if communists in America had played a part in formulating the policy of the Comintern for the "infiltration of the religious field." Gitlow answered in the affirmative: "The American Communists played quite an important part." Gitlow provided documentation to the congressmen, including a report made directly to Comintern officials in Moscow by Gil Green, head of the Young Communist League of the United States and New York state chairman of the Communist Party.[851]

Kunzig took Gitlow back a little further, asking: "Did the Communist infiltration of religion, on an intensified scale, begin in the United States before the decisions of the Seventh World Congress of the Comintern in 1935?" Kunzig was no doubt aware of prior activities. Gitlow again answered in the affirmative: "It actually was in full swing in the United States in 1934. The Seventh World Conference of the Comintern only reiterated and greatly stressed, as I have already indicated, what had always been the policy of the world Communist movement."

Much more could be quoted from Gitlow's testimony, but clearly, he had testified to a mass effort by communists to infiltrate the churches.

One added testimony, here summarized briefly, was that of Herb Philbrick, who, along with Bella Dodd and many other teachers, was called to testify to the Senate Judiciary Committee in March-April 1953 on subversive influence by communists in the educational process. Most of those called were current or recent communists who hid behind appeals to the First and Fifth Amendments and "academic freedom," whereas Philbrick (like Dodd) spoke openly and honestly. That was because Philbrick was a famous case—a household name—of a private citizen who cooperated with the FBI to infiltrate the Communist Party. He wrote about his experiences in his bestselling memoir *I Led 3 Lives*, which became the basis for a popular television series by the same name.

Philbrick testified on April 7, 1953. As with Gitlow and Manning Johnson, the entire testimony deserves to be read, but here we will note just a few of his remarks on religious infiltration.[852]

As a born and raised Baptist, Philbrick was asked by the Party to penetrate Baptist churches and youth groups. He witnessed numerous cases in his Boston area alone of the Party infiltrating churches. In one high-level Party group in Boston, he recalled "a very dismal fact, that actually the Communist Party had in its pro group section between 7 to 8 individuals, hardened, disciplined, steeled party members posing as ministers of the gospel." All had been "Communists prior to their becoming ministers."[853]

Shockingly, these were Communist Party members so committed to atheistic Marxism-Leninism that they were willing to become fake ministers in order to delude the people in the pews. They had gone through seminary.

Philbrick played a special role with religious youth. "I had many contacts in the religious field," he told the Senate. "I was widely known as a church youth leader. I had many contacts as far as the Communist Party was concerned with church youth leaders and with adult leaders of the Christian youth movement in the New England area." It was important for him to always conceal his communist affiliation because the Christians that he attempted to manipulate for the Party "would not have paid their dues to Herb Philbrick, the Communist Party member, but they did pay their dues to Herb Philbrick, the Baptist youth leader."[854]

This also allowed the Baptist-communist to reach Catholic youth. "So thoroughly respectable was my front," Philbrick recalled, "that at one big Communist-sponsored rally—without the Communist label, of course—I was able to obtain the services of a snappy Catholic Youth Organization band."[855]

Ironically, the communists were not always adverse to religion, or even the Bible. Consider the advice and instructions that Philbrick was given when handed his Communist Party membership card: "If you are questioned or if you are charged to be a member of the Communist Party, you will swear on a stack of Bibles that high [hand gesture] that you are not and never have been a member of this organization."[856]

So, communists were willing to invoke the Bible—in order to lie on it.

"To Deceive and Corrupt from Within"

The previous section included sworn testimonies of men under oath to Congress speaking to the issue of infiltration of churches. Thus, these statements carry significant weight. Congress itself would make several crucial observations in a 1948 report, stating: "In all their plans and actions, the Communists mark down religion as Enemy No. 1. Where they dominate, they attack it head on. Where they do not dominate, they try to deceive and corrupt from within just as they do in government, in education, in labor unions, and throughout a nation's life in general."[857] The report attested:

> The Communist Party of the United States assigns members to join churches and church organizations, in order to take control where possible, and in any case to influence thought and action toward Communist ends.
>
> It forms "front organizations," designed to attract "fellow travelers" with religious interests.
>
> It tries to get prominent religious leaders to support Communist policies, disguised as welfare work for minorities or oppressed groups. In the words of Earl Browder, former head of the Communist Party of the U.S.A.: ". . . By going among the religious masses, we are for the first time able to bring our anti-religious ideas to them."

That, of course, was exactly what Browder sought to do with Catholics via his outstretched hand.

The report further noted there were "unfortunately, yes" clergymen who were members of the Communist Party, and "the Party requires Communists to keep their membership secret." (As noted earlier, Browder had spoken of these member-clergymen to Union Theological Seminary students in February 1935, and Herb Philbrick testified to it in April 1953.) Further, said the report, young communists "are ordered" by the Party to join youth groups (Herb Philbrick was an example of that) in order "to win over youth to Communism and atheism, and to turn their groups into tools of the Communist Party." This was not done openly but secretly: "Communist youth, like Communist adults, work under cover. They won't admit being Communists if you ask them unless and until their Party officers direct them to do so."

The report also called out church front groups, such as the Rev. Harry Ward's Methodist Federation for Social Action, which it correctly called "a tool of the Communist Party, denounced by numerous loyal American Methodists. It claims to speak for 17 Methodist Bishops and 4,000 clerics and laymen. Not an official church organization . . . it is trying to use the prestige of the Methodist Church to promote the line of the Communist Party."[858]

Of course, the Methodist Church was just one among many targets.

Infiltrating the Catholic Church

Again, it must be clearly understood that men like Manning Johnson and Herb Philbrick were speaking to the case of Protestant churches, to non-Catholic churches. As Congress itself stated in its 1948 report, however, invoking the likes of Earl Browder (who had a special target drawn on the Catholic Church), this was a united effort of corruption by communists aimed at all churches and church organizations throughout the United States. Alas, the Catholic Church was not outside the crosshairs.[859]

In that respect, the testimony of Louis Budenz is especially important.

Budenz was a top American communist in the 1930s. He would also become a leading ex-communist and significant convert to the Catholic Church. It was Fulton Sheen who brought Louis Budenz into the Catholic Church with his wife and three daughters. Quite uproariously, the priest managed to bring Budenz back into the fold while the *Daily Worker* editor's name was still on the newspaper's masthead.[860]

By the mid-1940s, Budenz was ready to offer some serious public penance for his past sins with communism. This included his important testimony before Congress on November 22, 1946. He spoke to what he called "the present tactics of the Communists in regard to the Catholics." He had come to Washington that day in part to call attention to those tactics. Budenz stated quite dramatically:

> I mentioned also the question of the Catholic Church, and I raise that because today it is a question that is of concern to every American, and it's part of the tactics of Communists as I learned them. I was one of those who were fooled into believing that in America there could be cooperation between the Communists and the Catholics.
>
> I found that was considered undesirable from the Communist viewpoint, but beyond that I learned toward my latter days in the Communist Party from material I read in the *New Times*, which is now the name of the Communist International magazine, that the Communists everywhere plan to wage war on the Catholic Church as the base for obliterating all religion.[861]

That is an alarming statement from a leading ex-communist, one that bears repeating: "The Communists everywhere plan to wage war on the Catholic Church as the base for obliterating all religion." The outstretched hand of brother Browder had been a Trojan horse in that attack. Budenz was part of that effort. So much so that Budenz ended up in direct public debate (via the printed word) with none other than Fulton Sheen on the subject.[862] Sheen's responses were so persuasive that they won over Budenz—all the way across the Tiber.

Evidence that those who stretched out their hands in a gesture of friendship to the Catholic Church had their fingers crossed behind their backs surfaced when Sheen, then auxiliary bishop of New York, revealed in an April 27, 1952, speech delivered at Saint Susanna Church in Rome that, in 1936, communists were given instructions to infiltrate religious communities in order to destroy them from the inside. That Sheen statement in Rome made its way onto the front page of the *New York Times* under the headline "Sheen in Rome Says Red Agents Tried to Infiltrate the Priesthood."[863] The brief article (which was actually an Associated Press report) stated:

> Rome, April 27—American Communists were under secret orders in 1936 to infiltrate the Roman Catholic priesthood, Bishop Fulton J. Sheen said today.
>
> The 57-year-old Auxiliary Bishop of New York, speaking before an overflowing congregation in the American Catholic Church of Santa Susanna, said:
>
> "In 1936 the [Communist] wolves went into the forces which control public opinion. There was hardly a prominent newspaper commentator who did not have a Communist secretary, although he or she did not necessarily know it.
>
> "This was the beginning of the planting of forces of evil communism within the religious communities to destroy them from within. A call for volunteers to enter religious orders and make the great sacrifices of the life of a seminarian was made at a secret Red meeting in a large [American] city."

Sheen's bombshell address in the Eternal City was the first and only time he publicly spoke of such an infiltration. He did not divulge the source for his information. It is no coincidence, however, that his revelation came immediately after leaving America for Europe just after he baptized and heard the confession of Bella Dodd three weeks earlier on April 7, 1952, and after months of giving her personal instruction in entering the Church, which no doubt in Bella's case involved many occasions of her pouring out her heart.[864]

So, maybe Sheen heard it directly from Bella.[865] Note the date and place that Sheen cited: "secret orders in 1936" and a "large [American] city." That was precisely when Bella Dodd was organizing and inserting a thousand communist teachers into teachers' unions in New York City. In fact, Bella was tasked with organizing the teachers' contingent that marched in New York's huge May Day parade that year, where she commandeered a mass of five hundred marching teachers who were secretly communists.[866]

That was a busy year for Bella Dodd, as this book has shown repeatedly—it is the year that pops up often in Bella's maniacal life of activism. In 1936, the Party ordered her to organize committees of striking seamen against ship owners. Thus, she was organizing not only teachers but seamen, as well as doing trade union work for the old AF of L. She had her hand in more than merely the teachers' front.[867]

Importantly, the year 1936 also squares perfectly with what we know of Albert Vassart's effort that very same year.

Albert Vassart was a leader of the French Communist Party and its official representative to the Soviet Comintern. In April 1934, he had been summoned to Moscow, where he was given orders to create a French popular front—*Le Populaire*—between the French Communist Party, the French Socialist Party, and a wider united coalition of leftist groups. Like Ben Gitlow and Manning Johnson and Louis Budenz and Bella and others, he later broke from the French Communist Party and testified to his past work.

Vassart's effort was known to senators in the United States. A major 1960 study on Soviet propaganda by the Senate Judiciary Committee noted that Vassart later admitted to an infiltration of seminaries. "Contrary to what might be expected," the report stated, "churches are also highly infiltrated." The report pointed to seminaries and even to religious orders, naming a specific Moscow edict: "In 1955, a former member of the French Communist Party, Albert Vassart, revealed that in 1936 Moscow had sent out an order to have sure and carefully selected members of the Communist Youth enter seminaries and become priests. Others infiltrated the religious communities, particularly the Dominicans."[868]

Unfortunately, the report gave no further details, even as it lamented: "Infiltration of all churches is one of the major tasks of the Soviet propaganda apparatus."[869]

The year pinpointed by Vassart, 1936, fits with what Sheen said in Rome and with the very height of Bella's organizing and activism.

Bella on Directing Communists to Catholic Seminaries

After she left the Communist Party, Bella Dodd reportedly confessed that she herself was one of the comrades who participated in this infiltration scheme, seeking to help place communists directly into United States seminaries. Her reported claim of directing "over a thousand communist men" (sometimes reported as 1,100 or 1,200) to Catholic seminaries specifically has been one of the most sensational and controversial claims in the recent history of the Catholic Church. Many of those reading this book might have come to it for information on precisely that claim.

Where and when did Bella Dodd actually say this?

There are numerous sources that quote Bella and her numbers, many of them plainly not reliable and citing no firm evidence. Others are more credible. To cite just one example of a more credible source, in a 2015 article in the *Catholic Herald*, Father Andrew Apostoli, the late vice postulator for the canonization cause of Fulton Sheen, stated: "Joseph Stalin's plan at the time was to encourage unholy priests to support unworthy men to enter the seminary to bring the Church down from within. The communists were worried about the international influence of the Church and saw it as a threat. Bella herself had recruited approximately 1,100 men into the seminaries."[870]

This chapter could be filled with quotes like these, but it will instead focus on actual eyewitness testimonies to Bella's statements. The most authoritative are from Alice and Dietrich von Hildebrand, Johnine and Paul Leininger, and Sherry Finn.

Von Hildebrand's Eyewitness Testimony

One of us (Mary Nicholas) interviewed the respected Catholic writer and philosopher Dr. Alice von Hildebrand on this precise question. Alice was born in March 1923 and went on to live a long life, dying in January 2022 at age ninety-eight. In 1940, she came to the United States from Belgium, early in World War II, escaping the Nazis. It was in America that she met Dietrich von Hildebrand, the renowned Catholic scholar and theologian and fellow fugitive from Hitler. He was a leading prominent theologian who spoke out against the Fuhrer.

Dietrich, thirty-four years older than Alice, met her at Fordham University, where she was a student and he was a professor. They married in 1959, after the death of Dietrich's first wife. Dietrich died in 1977. Alice became a renowned voice in her own right, frequently appearing in Catholic media, particularly on EWTN radio and television, where she hosted several series and participated in various documentaries.

Alice was a personal friend of Bella. Both she and Dietrich talked with Bella about the infiltration of seminaries. Alice says that Bella told her that the number of men she recruited was "approximately 1,200." Mary Nicholas asked Alice about their conversation and relationship.

"My contact with Bella Dodd was one of these friendships that grew very fast," Alice told Mary. She remembered of her and her husband and Bella: "We met her in the fall of 1965 and she died in April 1969."[871] Though she and Dietrich did not see Bella often, when they did, there was a bond among them, one that Alice said was "very warm." Part of that bond related to her upbringing in Italy: "She was born in Italy and my husband was born in Italy," noted Alice. "She was very Italian. You would immediately identify her as Italian."[872]

Among her physical characteristics, Alice pointed to two quite visible things that immediately struck her about Bella: "She had this slight limp. She was tortured by this criminal situation."

The "criminal situation" was her work with communists, including their actions against her beloved Church. Said Alice of Bella: "She said to Fulton Sheen, 'I want to enter the most severe penitential order that exists to pay for my sins.' He said, 'No. I command you to give lectures on communism because these people are blind. They are totally blind to the dangers of communism.'"

That was a command that the pope himself, Pius XI, had given to Sheen: speak openly and always about the dangers of communism.[873]

Alice continued, with some remarkable revelations: "She was in close contact with four cardinals who were in the Vatican who were working for the Communist Party." Knowing that this shocked Mary Nicholas when Alice told her, Alice hastened to add: "It goes to show you. You are too young. My husband had received extraordinary gifts from God. And one of them was his clear sightedness. That is to say he could see immediately the danger with Hitler." He saw it, of course, when others did not. "France was blind. Holland was blind. They all said it was not so bad. I have found my destiny to waken people's eyes to the dangers of Nazism and communism." That had been her husband's destiny and hers as well. That was especially so after World War II, when it was clear to both Alice and Dietrich that "communism is a greater danger because Nazism is defeated."

And then, Alice told this to Mary Nicholas about Bella and the infiltration of the Church: "The only thing that I know about Bella Dodd that I could swear to—it was after Vatican II. My husband said: 'There is something going on in the Church. I fear that the Church is being infiltrated.' Then Bella said, 'You fear it. I know it.' Then my husband jumped up in his chair and said, 'What do you mean?' And she said, 'When I was a full-fledged Communist I was in close contact with four cardinals in the Vatican working for us, and who remain active today.' That was in 1967."

Dietrich then asked Bella: "Who are they? It is crucial that I know it." But Bella did not divulge names. Alice explained to Mary that it was her understanding that "Bishop Sheen would not allow her [to name names] for fear of causing a scandal [in the Church] or problems." Nonetheless, said Alice in this October 2013 interview, "I am convinced. Absolutely convinced that they are still there."

Bella would not give details, and Dietrich would go to his grave in 1977 never knowing. As for Alice, she spoke about this to others, and would go on the record in interviews testifying to what Bella told her. In a 2001 print interview, she stated: "It is a matter of public record, for instance, that Bella Dodd, the ex-Communist who reconverted to the Church, openly spoke of the Communist Party's deliberate infiltration of agents into the seminaries. She told my husband and me that when she was an active party member, she had dealt with no fewer than four cardinals within the Vatican 'who were working for us.'"[874] That is exactly what Alice told Mary Nicholas.

Fortunately, some of Alice's interviews were videotaped and are now available on the internet. One interview, preserved on camera for posterity by *Church Militant's* Michael Voris, was posted by Voris on YouTube on January 29, 2016.[875] There, Alice stated: "The Church has been infiltrated. I repeat these words: *the Church has been infiltrated.*" She told Voris: "Bella Dodd gave a talk in Orange, California, in which she declared publicly—I repeat, *publicly*—that in the course of the 20 years of activities for the communists she recruited some 1,100 young men, neither faith nor morals, that entered seminaries. And they were so superbly trained."

In this case, Alice had gone further, speaking of not only what Bella told her and her husband directly but of an occasion when Bella spoke publicly to a large audience about the infiltration, letting loose a tantalizing admission. Fortunately, there were witnesses, still alive. But before examining the testimony of those witnesses, first consider one more statement from Alice, one that was written and comprehensive:

In April 2003, Alice von Hildebrand published a letter to the editor in *Crisis Magazine*, where she took issue with a December 2002 piece by author Sandra Miesel on "Catholic conspiracy theories," which contended that "Dodd implausibly claimed to have sent a thousand young men into American seminaries." Von Hildebrand vehemently objected to Miesel's dismissal:

> It is clear from the content of her article that Miesel never met Dodd personally. I knew her and can call her a friend. After dedicating 21 years of her life to the Enemy, she was so shattered when her eyes opened that she wanted to devote the years left to her to penance and to join the most severe penitential order. She turned for advice and help to Bishop Fulton Sheen. She opened her heart to him, went to confession, and put herself under his guidance. He became her spiritual director and gave her the order to remain in the world and open the eyes of Americans to the deadly poison of Communism, its atheism, its hatred of God and the Church. She lectured extensively. It was at one of her talks that my husband and I made her acquaintance. We immediately perceived that she was an exceptional person: her intelligence, her sincerity, her humility, and her desire to make good for the harm that she had done.
>
> Dodd visited us in New Rochelle, New York. I recall that one day my husband—who had become increasingly worried about what was dubbed "the spirit of Vatican II"—said to her, "Bella, at times I wonder whether the Church has not been infiltrated." I can solemnly testify that she answered, "Dear professor, you fear it; I know it. When I was a fanatic Communist, I was in close contact with four cardinals in the Vatican working for us. They are still very active today." My husband jumped in his seat and said, "My nephew is German ambassador at the Holy See. Who are they?" Bella Dodd refused to answer: Bishop Sheen had not allowed her to reveal their names.
>
> As long as Bella Dodd lived, she remained in close contact with Bishop Sheen. He knew what she was revealing in her numerous lectures and never tried to curb her or to challenge

what she was saying, but he did not allow her to reveal names. The Roman Catholic Church rightly fears scandals.

While speaking in Orange County, California, Bella told a packed auditorium that in the 1930s Stalin ordered his subordinates to try to infiltrate Catholic seminaries. Dodd was appointed to faithfully follow this directive, and given her extraordinary charism to persuade people, she claimed publicly that she alone was responsible for the infiltration of hundreds of Judases in Catholic seminaries: "Young men who had neither faith nor morals" was the way she put it.

That written statement from Alice von Hildebrand is significant because it confirms in writing, with consistency, what she said in various interviews, including for this book. It is also consistent with what she stated in her 2014 memoirs—another occasion in which Alice went on the record in writing.[876]

Leininger Eyewitness Testimony

That brings us to Alice von Hildebrand's reference to a speech in Orange County, California. Two witnesses to that talk, who found Bella's statement on infiltration so significant that they came forward to affirm it in an official affidavit four decades later, were Johnine and Paul Leininger. They had their affidavit certified by a notary public in Lavaca County, Texas, on March 28, 2002. Written in Johnine's first-person narration, but signed by both Leiningers, the affidavit attested: "At a large public meeting in Orange County, California in the 1960's, I was present in an auditorium filled to capacity with 600 to 800 people who had come to hear a former Communist Party official give an expose of the infiltration of the Communist Party into every facet of American life."

That official was Bella Dodd. The Leiningers related examples of the penetration that Dodd detailed in various elements of labor, including teachers' unions. The Leiningers also attested to what Dodd had said about an infiltration of seminaries: "In the late 1920's and 1930's, directives were sent from Moscow to all Communist Party organizations. In order to destroy the Catholic Church from within, party members were to be planted in seminaries and within diocesan organizations. Dr. Dodd said, 'I, MYSELF, PUT SOME 1,200 MEN IN CATHOLIC SEMINARIES.'"

The Leininger statement used capital letters at that spot to emphasize the significance of that particular claim. They knew how momentous it was. The affidavit continued: "Dr. Dodd also detailed the influence being implemented in the Vatican itself by Cardinals who were members of the Communist Party. She said she knew the truth of her statement because 'I KNOW WHO MY CONTACTS WERE!'"

That was the same thing that Bella had told Alice and Dietrich von Hildebrand.

The Leiningers said that Dodd shared this information because she had returned to her Catholic faith and was "truly repentant of the damage she had caused," including to "her Church and the American way of life."

The Leiningers added that they often quoted and passed along Dodd's testimony, "especially when public scandal and dissent by high Church officials caused irreparable harm to the Body of Christ. This dissent was more open and obvious beginning in the 1960's. Massive infiltration within seminaries and teaching and formation programs appear to be the only explanation." They stated: "It became obvious that the Roman Catholic Church had been the victim of a massive Communist/Masonic infiltration. . . . Today we are witnessing the results of a well organized, diabolical plan whose blue print was laid over 70 years ago and patiently implemented. The Communist goal of destroying the American way of life could only be accomplished if her most formidable opposition—the Roman Catholic Church—was infiltrated, compromised and ultimately destroyed."

This March 2002 Leininger affidavit is one of the best eyewitness forms of evidence to what Bella is said to have claimed. Speaking to its authenticity is Catholic scholar Kevin Symonds. Symonds is a meticulous researcher who has published important articles and books, especially on Fatima, with a reputation for a very healthy skepticism, double checking and even debunking spurious claims by people in the Church, including popular Catholic authors.[877] Symonds has applied his skills and caution to precisely the claims of Church infiltration, which he has analyzed in podcasts and writings, including a lengthy and incisive December 2021 piece, "Rethinking Bella Dodd and Infiltration of the Catholic Priesthood," for the Catholic journal *Homiletic & Pastoral Review*.

Both of the authors for this book have worked with Kevin Symonds on this issue. Particularly noteworthy, Symonds personally knew the Leiningers and knew the importance of getting their eyewitness on the record. For the purposes of documentation for this book, Symonds stated to Paul Kengor in a February 23, 2022 email:

> On February 22, 2022, I received an E-mail from Dr. Paul Kengor of Grove City College. He wished to speak with me about my recent essay *Rethinking Bella Dodd and Infiltration of Catholic Priesthood* (Homiletic & Pastoral Review, December 24, 2021). We struck up correspondence, during which Dr. Kengor asked if I had confirmed the 2002 affidavit of Paul and Johnine Leininger. This affidavit stated that Dr. Bella Dodd gave a talk in Orange County, CA for which the Leiningers were present. They claimed in their affidavit that they heard from Dr. Dodd about the Communistic infiltration of Catholic seminaries. I can confirm and attest to having received a copy of this affidavit *directly from Johnine Leininger herself* on 30 June, 2015 in Victoria, TX. I can further confirm and attest that Johnine appeared to stand by her sworn statements and was encouraging me to give the physical copy of the affidavit to Dr. Mary Nicholas who was then researching Dr. Dodd for a book. On 2 July, 2015, before sending the affidavit to Dr. Nicholas, I took photos of it

and retained these photos in my personal records. The affidavit was referenced in my aforementioned essay, as well as displayed in my video (YouTube, 2021) about Bella Dodd.

-Kevin J. Symonds, M.A.

February 23, 2022 A.D.

Kevin played this role because of his personal relationship with the Leiningers. He stated in a separate email (to Paul Kengor) on February 23, 2022:

> Dr. Nicholas . . . was in communication with Johnine. In 2015, I was living in Waco, Texas. Dr. Nicholas, who was then in the research stage for her book, asked me if I would be able to pick up a packet of information from Johnine. I've known the Leiningers since 2007 when I lived in Victoria, TX teaching at the local Catholic high school (St. Joseph's). We had mutual friends (Paul and Marjorie Tasin) and attended the Extraordinary Form. I had been meaning to get back to Victoria for a visit, so Dr. Nicholas' request gave me every reason to do so. Additionally, at that time there was a video on YouTube with an audio recording purporting to be a Bella Dodd lecture. Dr. Nicholas wanted to know if it was truly Bella.
>
> I drove down to Victoria and stayed with the Tasins for several days. During which time, on 30 June, I met with Johnine to pick up the packet and visit for a bit. During the all-too-brief visit, I played the video for Johnine through my car's speaker system. She listened in and then stood up and said, "Yup, that's my friend. That's Bella Dodd."
>
> After returning home, but before mailing out Johnine's packet, I took photos of everything on 2 July. That's how I ended up with the cleaner copy of the affidavit that I used for my video on Bella Dodd.
>
> Enclosed is a picture of Johnine from our visit.

Here we see on display the aforementioned meticulousness of Kevin Symonds, a crucial carefulness applied to Bella Dodd's claims—a level of scrutiny too often lacking by those who jump at alleged statements of Bella without knowing their provenance. Symonds has helped us confirm two eyewitnesses to Bella Dodd claiming an infiltration of Catholic seminaries.

Eyewitness Testimony of Sherry Finn

A living eyewitness to Bella Dodd's statement about infiltration is Sherry Finn of Redondo Beach, California.

In March 1963, Sherry and her husband, John, moved to Richardson, Texas, a city between Dallas and Plano, and stayed there until July 1966, when they relocated to San Diego. They knew of Bella Dodd as a famous person who, by that point, was lecturing at the University of Plano. Sherry's husband, John, was the program chairman for the Richardson Republican Men's Club.

One evening (Sherry does not recall the exact date but believes it would have been in 1964 or 1965), Sherry and John joined two friends at their home as they hosted Bella Dodd for dinner.[878] Sherry and John joined the three after they had dinner.

Sherry remembers Bella Dodd being entertaining and "very engaging." She also remembers—in fact, has never forgotten—Bella speaking of a large infiltration of the Catholic Church by communists. "I remember the huge number of a thousand who had infiltrated the Catholic Church—some to the very top levels of the Church," recalled Sherry in a June 17, 2022 interview for this book. "I remember her saying a number that was around a thousand. When I hear people today say that Bella Dodd said a thousand or eleven hundred, it clicks with me. It could have been either of those two numbers. When she said it, I thought to myself, 'Oh, my gosh!'"

Sherry does not recall if Bella at that moment had specified seminaries, but she does recall her acknowledging a large number of men, around a thousand, who had infiltrated the Church, some of them reaching the highest levels.

Sherry, who today is eighty-two years old, has never forgotten this.

Who Were They? Where Are They?

Okay, who were these men that infiltrated the seminaries? And where are they now?

To be sure, if these thousand or so communist men recruited to penetrate the priesthood really existed, one would expect that at least some of them over time might have come forth to tell their story, especially those who changed or repented. Among this group, did some stay and remain communists? Did some become disgruntled and frustrated and leave the priesthood? Did many spend their remaining years in silence, perhaps ashamed by their deceitful behavior? Of course, many might have stayed and became committed left-wing priests who were highly political and ideological, adopting positions that were pro-communist and falling in line with ideologies like Marxist liberation theology.

Who are they? Where are they? What became of them?

That is indeed an enigma, one that will prompt many incredulous observers to dismiss the entire thing as "conspiracy nonsense." No doubt, the lack of such testimonies gives pause.

We might also speculate that many of these men left the seminary quickly once inserted or were let go as it became clear to superiors that their hearts and minds and souls were not committed or prepared for a life in the priesthood. The preparation in seminary is very rigorous. Their time could have been predictably short-lived. Most men not suited for the priesthood often show just that to their superiors, who do not promote them to the next level. No matter how committed the devious young communist, the path to priesthood is a long haul that involves thorough and intense self-sacrifice. Many an infiltrator likely did not follow through all the way to the long, long end of being ordained. One imagines that of the thousand or so communist men, the vast majority would have never made it through. Many might have even been exposed and expelled.

Unfortunately, we do not have the answers.

This speculation may also help shed light on an interesting statement by Bella Dodd only recently found. Mary Nicholas secured the audio of a September 1, 1961 speech that Bella Dodd gave in Detroit. During that long and remarkable address,[879] Bella was asked during the Q&A that followed, "Have you ever met communists among the clergy, and, if so, were these people ever exposed?" Courtesy of Kevin Symonds, here is a verbatim transcript of how Bella answered, including her hesitations:

> I never met a Ca-, uh, Communist, uh, who was, uh, a member of the Catholic clergy. Now I say that, not because I'm a Catholic. Because I was familiar with a number of the young ministers in the Protestant, uh, among the Protestant clergy. God bless some of them. They wanted so much to do good. The Communist Party used to raise money to send them to seminaries, which would last maybe for one year, two years. And, uh, then they'd come back and preach the social doctrine. Now, I never had met anyone in the Ca-, uh, among the Catholic clergy. That doesn't mean that they may not be [Communist]! My feeling is that, uh, the long years of [slight pause] preparation required for the Catholic clergy may deter, uh, the Communist Party line as to putting people in.[880]

Kevin Symonds published excerpts from the speech and analyzed it in his article, including every word and pause in that passage. That specific passage brought some doubters. Both of the authors for this book, as well as Kevin Symonds, received email inquiries asking if Bella's answer does not cast doubt as to whether she ever made the alleged claims about communist infiltration.[881] We do not think so. Consider the balance of evidence for and against:

As laid out at length above, there are witnesses to Bella making those claims, including the von Hildebrands, the Leiningers, and Sherry Finn. But more important, look closely at Bella's answer in this Q&A in Detroit in September 1961: She neither denied nor said anything about recruiting communists for the priesthood; she only said that she had not met any communists among members of the actual (ordained) Catholic clergy. Although Bella may have easily recruited these undercover seminarians, she may have never encountered them again. Note, too, an important acknowledgment in her answer, one that we alluded to above: "the long years of preparation for the Catholic clergy may *deter* [our emphasis]" the Party member from entering the priesthood permanently. Bella rightly posed this in contrast to Protestant seminaries, where the preparation is far shorter, "maybe for one year, two years."

And besides, why would Bella have later met her recruits? Think about it: For starters, she might have never actually met them in the first place, instead having had a middle-man task of gathering names and forwarding them. For the perhaps minority of them who might have made it through seminary, they later would have avoided Bella Dodd like the plague, given that she had become the most public and vocal Catholic ex-communist in America. In that role, she was notorious for naming names constantly (albeit not of clergy) to the FBI and congressional committees. To the Party, Bella Dodd had become a despised "stool pigeon" and "Judas betrayer." The excellent ex-communist historian Ron Radosh, who knows the movement as well as anyone, noted that when it came to communist teachers in New York, no one ever named names like Bella Dodd did: "We know she gave the Senate Internal Security Subcommittee the names of at least 100 teachers and undoubtedly handed over many more."[882]

Again, any such recruits-turned-ordained-clergy would have avoided Bella Dodd like the plague.

But even then, these infiltrators need not fear being named, which returns us to a crucial point about Bella Dodd's statements (or lack thereof); namely, Fulton Sheen, Bella's priest and confessor, told her not to name names. To repeat: Bella Dodd was told by her priest, Fulton Sheen himself, not to name names. Sheen thought it would only do more harm than good for the Church. Under his guidance, if not obedience, she listened. She never mentioned any clergy names. One of the authors of this book was told this directly by Alice von Hildebrand, who had been told directly by Bella herself.

Despite years of extensive research on Bella Dodd's writings or writings about her, we discovered that she rarely publicly talked about the infiltration. The only speech where we could find her doing so was in Orange County, witnessed by the Leiningers. Her statement in Detroit clearly showed hesitancy if not ambiguity. Otherwise, she kept quiet in public.

Remember, too, that Bella Dodd was a lawyer, and she was keenly aware of threats of libel. In fact, during a public speech about the same time, in Omaha, Nebraska on May 14, 1962, when speaking about a certain publisher, she stated: "I'm not going to mention the man's name publicly because I'm a lawyer and I don't want to get sued in a libel suit. Because even though I'm telling the truth, a libel suit is an expensive thing to defend. If you want his name privately, nobody around, I'll tell you his name."

Yes, perhaps privately—like with the von Hildebrands.

Given that well-advised caution, it is hard to imagine Bella Dodd in a huge public forum rattling off the names of dozens to hundreds if not a thousand recruited communist clergymen—assuming that she was even still in possession of those names. In fact, given the way that the Communist Party operated, she almost certainly would have turned over any such list of names (there were no photocopiers or phones to take pictures with). The Party was notoriously secretive about concealing names, membership numbers, and everything, and likely would have shredded or burned the lists.[883] Recall how Bella herself, as legal counsel for the Party during the Rapp-Coudert Committee, had gone so far as to burn lists of Teachers Union college teachers—that is, destroying evidence, a crime.

As for other instances, Bella made no assertions about infiltration in her public testimonies to Congress (though it is possible she talked about it secretly in closed session), despite recklessly sloppy "citations" by people on the internet who clearly have not paused to square the alleged quotes with the actual printed text of the testimonies. Perhaps the closest she came to a relevant statement in open testimony came in response to a question from Senator Homer Ferguson on September 9, 1952. In her testimony, Bella addressed the infiltration of "mass organizations which had a large number of Catholics," such as the Catholic Committee for Human Rights, when she said briefly, "This whole question of using ministers or using men of religion to help in many of their [communists'] causes is just in order to win over more people who are entrenched in the religious life."[884] But that was a mere admission of the usefulness of tapping ministers rather than a statement on her recruiting Catholic clergy for the Party.

Words from Bella about infiltrating seminaries are also non-existent in her memoir, *School of Darkness*, again despite internet "citations" and memes suggesting so. But again, such information would not be expected to be in her memoirs if Fulton Sheen had forbidden her to publicly share details.

Notably, Bella did briefly mention infiltration elsewhere in the Detroit speech, in fact in her very next statement during the Q&A. She shared an exchange she had with Father Keller of The Christophers, who she asked: "You're forming The Christophers organization. Why don't you establish a national organization so everybody can join?" As noted earlier, Keller looked her in the eye and said, "Bella, you should know better. In three months, they would infiltrate it, and either they would paralyze it or smear it, make it impossible for us to do anything." Bella unhesitatingly agreed with Father Keller, noting that communists were "the best infiltrators that God ever created."[885]

That was a clear affirmation of infiltration in that same Detroit speech, though again without elaboration by a Bella who was clearly being careful with what she said publicly about infiltration and her Church.

Was a Thousand Communist Men Possible?

The Bella claim gives sober-minded observers pause because of the sheer volume of numbers posed. Over a thousand men sounds like a huge number, utterly impossible to secure. But was it?

Actually, such a number was hardly out of bounds given what Bella was accustomed to as a communist organizer for teachers' unions in New York state from 1936 to 1938. Remember that Bella placed over a thousand communist teachers in a union of less than ten thousand. Such a target among the priesthood would have seemed easier. Consider:

According to the *Official Catholic Directory*, in 1936, there were 30,250 Catholic priests in the United States: 20,836 diocesan clergy and 9,414 priests in religious orders. This was the start of an upswing in vocations that would eventually reach a peak number of 59,892 priests by 1967. As for seminarians, in 1936, there were 23,579 students in Catholic seminaries, which likewise would more than double by 1965 (before plunging after the Second Vatican Council).[886]

As noted by Dr. Paul Sullins, a priest and sociologist at the Catholic University of America: "Given an eight-year formation track, then, about 3,000 men would enter seminary each year; about 2/3 would drop out before ordination." Sullins notes that Dodd's claim "is thus plausible by the numbers, especially if she meant 'by 1936' or 'since 1936' or 'around 1936,' not that all 1100 entered seminary in 1936." Sullins also notes that 1936 was an unusually high year for number of seminarians, higher than any year until 1948.[887]

As daunting as Bella's one thousand (or so) figure might initially appear, upon closer inspection, it may have seemed a cinch given what

Bella was accustomed to. She had secured 10 percent communist infiltration of the Teachers Union. Seeking out a thousand priests among a mass of fifty thousand or so priests and seminarians probably seemed like a breeze to Bella.

Those large numbers aside, what is most important to remember is that organizers like Bella Dodd (and Manning Johnson, Ben Gitlow, and others) understood that to corrupt an organization, the Party did not need over a thousand infiltrators; it needed as little as a hundred, a few dozen, even a handful. Bella said just that to the US Senate Subcommittee on September 9, 1952, one of several such occasions where she emphasized the importance of "strategically placed" comrades:

> As a matter of fact, you have over a million teachers in America, and, by and large, your schools are not manned by Communists. The Communist influence is important only where it is strategically placed, and no Communist is ever satisfied with remaining in a position of inferiority. He seeks a strategic position.
>
> If you had Communists in these schools of education, that is a very strategic position because not only are they affecting the philosophy of education but they are also teaching other teachers, who, in turn, are teaching the pupils.
>
> If you have one Communist teacher in the school of education, and he teaches, let's say, 300 teachers, who then go out all over the United States, that is a strategic position.[888]

In that case, Bella was talking about teachers. But as her Protestant comrades noted, the same tactics applied to ministers as well. You did not need 1,200 clergymen. Strategically placed and well trained, less than a hundred could cause massive damage.

In short, the goal was to target, infiltrate, and corrupt the Catholic Church—through the priesthood, front groups, the "outstretched hand," or by any available means. In this endeavor, communists were hell-bent on success.

CHAPTER 14

MARXIST INFLUENCE INSIDE THE CHURCH

Regardless of Bella Dodd's specific role or claims, it seems hard to deny that a Marxist influence took place inside the Catholic Church, whether she helped to create one or through other individuals and processes.

As for seminaries specifically, did other Catholics notice an infiltration at the time? Yes.

A case in point was Blessed Solanus Casey, a popular twentieth-century priest on a path to potential sainthood. Casey (1870–1957) was the first man born in the United States to be declared "Venerable" by the Catholic Church—namely, by Pope John Paul II in July 1995. A gentle soul renowned for holiness, kindness, and virtue, he has been credited with many gifts and even reported cases of miraculous healings. The Capuchin-Franciscan friar was born to Irish-Catholic parents who raised him in Wisconsin. He would spend stints in novitiates, monasteries, and churches in Indiana (Huntington), Michigan (Detroit), New York (Brooklyn, Manhattan, Yonkers), and Wisconsin. He died on July 31, 1957.[889]

Casey encountered communist infiltration into seminaries. Fortunately, documentation exists registering his concerns. For instance, in a January 15, 1955 letter to a Dominican sister in Grand Rapids, Michigan (Sister M. Bernice), Casey wrote clearly and unequivocally:

> There is such a thing as "red communism" stealing into convents and monasteries. Very clever young men have been known to

offer themselves as candidates for the Order who have turned out after months, sometimes after years, to have been nothing more than secret promoters of unrest and red communism. Such candidates, I have heard of and in one case at least have known to show themselves very clever and experienced and naturally older than real promising candidates. They are in their late 20's or even middle 30's and, of course, are not fervent at all, even though they keep the rule fairly to the letter.

Of course, to suspect anyone deliberately without a conscience [sic] observance and prayer, is a dangerous course. Nevertheless, self-preservation and "charity begins at home" where right order and charity always must begin. Superiors especially are expected to be on the alert concerning any subject who persists in refusing to speak to, or associate with any other member of the religious family.[890]

We see here in this letter from Casey attestation that infiltration existed, that indeed some of these candidates for the priesthood were suspect, given their obvious lack of fervent faith, and that superiors were on the alert. If we can observe this now, in the 2020s, from a letter in 1955, imagine how many superiors and men like Casey (and Fulton Sheen) were observing it or looking for it in real time.

The Marxist influence inside the Catholic Church had many manifestations.

Prior to the Second Vatican Council, there was (at least) one Soviet mole in the Vatican who was close to Cardinal Montini, the future Pope Paul VI. We know this because he was corresponding with various Soviet agencies. Eventually, the Vatican mole was discovered: Alighiero Tondi, a Jesuit. Tondi was an agent working for Stalin whose mission was to keep Moscow informed about initiatives such as the sending of priests into the Soviet Union. Pope Pius XII, like Pius XI, had been sending priests clandestinely into Russia to give comfort to

Catholics behind the Iron Curtain. Many were systematically arrested, tortured, and either executed or sent to the gulag.[891]

Venerable Fulton Sheen, who happened to be in Rome preaching at the time, said the Tondi case worried him, as it paralleled the communist attempt to infiltrate US seminaries starting in 1936.[892] In fact, the April 1952 front-page *New York Times* piece on Sheen's speech at Saint Susanna church stated in the next-to-last paragraph: "Although he did not mention him by name, Bishop Sheen strongly indicated in his sermon that the case of Alighiero Tondi, 44, Italian Jesuit priest who has just 'embraced the Communist idea,' parallels American Communist infiltration. Communist propagandists have been stressing the defection of Tondi strongly."

Also in the *New York Times* of April 28, 1952 was a shorter accompanying article titled "Sheen Leaves for Paris: Sheen Says Reds Had Church Spies," reported by United Press. It was also on page one of the newspaper. It noted that Father Tondi "had left the [Jesuit] order and has become a Communist. Such actions involve automatic excommunication." The piece noted that Tondi "had been a Jesuit for sixteen years" prior to "his conversion to communism," which he outlined in a lengthy article in the pro-communist Italian newspaper *Il Paese*.

These were not the first pieces in the *Times* on Tondi. Two days earlier, in the April 26, 1952 edition (on page twenty), the *Times* ran a piece titled "Jesuit Joins Communists, Calls Church 'Outdated.'" It noted that Tondi was vice-director of the Institute of Higher Religious Culture, attached to the Pontifical Gregorian University in Rome. He had gone missing and telephoned the school to inform staff that he was not coming back. The police found him at the apartment of a "woman known to entertain Communist leaders."[893]

The Tondi case was well-known. *Life* magazine covered it in its May 26, 1952 issue. The piece was titled "A Jesuit Goes Communist."

The press had it right. Tondi had indeed become a communist and left the order after sixteen years. He seems to have been a mole for the Kremlin inside the Vatican, though whether he began that way as an atheistic, pro-communist plant and infiltrator is something we do not know. He turned on the Vatican, yes, and sided with and supplied Moscow.

Father Robert Graham, a Jesuit, a historian, and an expert on espionage, once documented the phenomenon of the Church's enemies working as spies. "During the 1930s," writes Graham, speaking of precisely the period that Bella and Sheen and others identified, "Bolshevik agents were active in Rome and several unpleasant events ensued leaving their scars. This activity did not cease even in 1941 when Soviet diplomats had to leave Italy."[894]

These events were not unique. A highly regarded historian who has given special attention to the subject is John Koehler, the former AP reporter who wrote *Spies in the Vatican: The Soviet Union's Cold War Against the Catholic Church*. Koehler focused in particular on the notorious East German Stasi and declassified material from its files. The Stasi (i.e., the Ministry for State Security) was the infamous secret police of the East German communist regime from 1945 through the end of the Cold War.

Koehler examined how priests and possibly even bishops and cardinals were coopted. Koehler includes chapters with names like "Spies Penetrate the Papal Sanctum" and "A Potpourri of Spies." His best material dug into Stasi Department XX/4, which was also tasked with surveillance of the Catholic Church in East Germany, and the role of the infamous Markus Wolf and his HVA (*Hauptverwaltung Aufklaerung*), which was second only to the KGB as the Communist Bloc's most formidable espionage service. Wolf was one of the leading spymasters of the Cold War.[895] Koehler offers groundbreaking research on cases such as the controversial German Monsignor Paul Dissemond, long reasonably suspected as having been an unofficial collaborator and Stasi informer, though he would always plead innocence.[896]

Another recent book by a respected scholar is the work by Elisabeth Braw, *God's Spies: The Stasi's Cold War Espionage Operation Inside the Church*. Like Koehler, her concentration is the former East

Germany. Braw shows the disturbing lengths taken by the Stasi to control churches in East Germany, focusing intently on the Lutheran Church, where the Stasi made great inroads.[897]

Braw's book highlights four specific "pastor agents" and the recruiting work of a Stasi official named Joachim Wiegand (still living and interviewed by Braw), who headed up the Stasi's so-called "Church Department," formally known as Department XX/4. These pastor agents, states Braw, were "very active," engaging in regular clandestine meetings with Stasi contacts and "extensive cooperation over many years," agreeing to "spy on their fellow human beings," including their own congregants. As Braw notes, these pastors "betrayed and sold out their friends and acquaintances."[898]

Braw focuses on Protestant ministers, but the Stasi and other secret police behind the Iron Curtain also targeted the Catholic Church. These efforts were especially vigorous by secret police in heavily Catholic countries, such as the insidious SB (Ministry of Public Security) in Poland, which was responsible for surveillance of all religious groups.

The SB took a special interest in the Second Vatican Council. In fact, SB officials devoted extensive coverage to a series of Second Vatican Council meetings from October 1 to 21, 1963. We know this because Stasi files today include a top-secret twenty-seven-page report on the Vatican Council from the SB that was received by the KGB's Fifth Directorate at 12 Ulitsa Lubyanskaya in Moscow, KGB headquarters. It came directly from the Polish security service. It was concluded that the operation that netted the report was carried out by a Polish priest.[899]

The Fifth Directorate organized many of these efforts from Lubyanka, KGB headquarters. The man who spearheaded the Fifth Directorate was the odious Yuri Andropov, who would give permission to the Soviet GRU to assassinate Pope John Paul II on May 13, 1981.[900] One of the most audacious moves in the long, dark, bloody history of the Kremlin.

When Andropov took the reins at KGB headquarters in May 1967, he ordered a systematic reorganization of its directorates and duties. This included heightened surveillance and control of religious groups, which were already heavily monitored and repressed. That responsibility became the duty of the newly created Fifth Directorate. Among the religious entities of utmost special interest to Andropov was the Vatican. In 1969, he ordered an intensification of espionage operations against the Holy See.

That specific espionage operation was John Koehler's central focus in *Spies in the Vatican*. "Besides the prime target, the pope, he [Andropov] was particularly interested in the activities of Archbishop Agostino Casaroli," wrote Koehler. That is no surprise. Cardinal Casaroli became the Vatican's principal Kremlin accommodationist, managing the Holy See's policy of *Ostpolitik*, which warmly embraced Eastern Europe's worst communist despots in the hopes of getting along and convincing them to cool down.[901]

Did they cool down? How rigorous was Andropov's order to expand espionage operations against the Holy See? Koehler stated: "Eventually, every department of the Church had been infiltrated."[902] They even tried to kill the pope.

To repeat: Every department of the Roman Catholic Church had been infiltrated. To be sure, Koehler here is not writing of, say, American Catholic seminaries specifically. His book has no information on that subject. But there was indisputably a mass attempt of Catholic Church infiltration by the KGB and by its affiliated secret police agencies throughout Europe.

As for Casaroli, Moscow was particularly interested in his activities as its friendly secretary of state at the Vatican. As a result, spies were planted in the cardinal's office. Illustrating their ingenuity, the East Bloc intelligence services used Cardinal Casaroli's housekeepers. One of them, Irene Trollerova, a native of Czechoslovakia, was married to Marco Torreta, a nephew of the cardinal. According to a 1990 statement by SISDE, the Italian Security Service, both were moles for the

KGB. Irene had a Czech ceramic art statue of the Virgin Mary about ten inches high. They presented the statue to Cardinal Casaroli, who accepted it gratefully, and it was placed in an armoire in the dining room outside the cardinal's office. Inside was a "bug," a tiny but powerful transmitter monitored by the couple's handlers from the Soviet embassy in Rome.[903]

There was also the case of Brother Brammertz, a Benedictine monk from St. Matthias Abbey in Trier, birthplace of Karl Marx, near the Luxembourg border. The monk first registered as an agent with the HVA, the German foreign intelligence agency, in 1953. His code name was "Lichtblick." Born a Catholic in Aachen, he entered St. Matthias Abbey in 1934 and was ordained in 1939. Drafted into World War II, he served as a medic and was held in a Soviet field hospital for a short time. He wound up in Berlin, where he renewed contacts with the Soviets.[904] According to a top German researcher on communism and the Catholic Church, Brammertz was sent to Rome in 1975, where he worked as a writer and translator of the Vatican newspaper *L'Osservatore Romano*.[905] HVA chief Markus Wolf described Brammertz as "one of the most brilliant monks, member of a Scientific Commission and very close to Cardinal Casaroli."[906]

Penetration of the Second Vatican Council (1962–65)

Amidst the conflict and infiltration of the Church, Pope John XXIII convened a historic ecumenical council. As part of his design for the council, John XXIII wanted to convince Nikita Khrushchev to send two Russian Orthodox clerics from the USSR to attend the council in Rome as observers. In 1962, Pope John XXIII arranged a meeting at Metz, France, between Cardinal Eugene Tisserant and the Russian Orthodox Patriarch Boris Nikodim.[907]

Msgr. Georges Roche, former secretary of Cardinal Tisserant, spoke publicly of the Metz agreement and confirmed the existence of the agreement between Moscow and Rome, adding that the initiative for the talks was "taken by John XXIII personally, at the suggestion of

Cardinal Montini, and that Tisserant 'received explicit orders, both as to the signing of the accord and to ensuring that it was fully observed throughout the council." As part of the Metz agreement, according to one historian, the pope would ensure two things: that his forthcoming council would issue no condemnation of Soviet communism or Marxism generally and that the Holy See would in the future abstain from official condemnations.[908]

One must view this within the context of religion in the Soviet state, which, of course, was a disturbing portrait. The Soviets viewed religion purely within a political and ideological framework, and a decidedly hostile one. Decisions regarding religion and also for attending the Second Vatican Council were made by the Politburo and the Central Committee of the CPSU (Communist Party of the Soviet Union). CROCA (Council for Russian Orthodox Affairs) and the CRCA (Council for Religious Cult Affairs) would also discuss the invitation and submit their recommendations to the Politburo, with CROCA being the more important determinant.[909]

The head of CROCA at the time was G. G. Karpov, who came from the NKVD and had written that "one of the duties of CROCA is to assure a normalization of the relations between Church and State and to use the Church for our state's sake."[910] While Khrushchev was waging his de-Stalinization campaign, one of the areas of struggle was religion. He escalated the attack on religion after Stalin had lessened the assault during World War II. Khrushchev's aggressive stance was formalized in a resolution of the Central Committee of the CPSU on October 4, 1958, to all organizations of the Party to "begin an attack against what remained of religion within Soviet society."[911]

Given this resolution, something truly intriguing happened just four months before it was issued.[912] On June 6, 1958, Sister Lúcia dos Santos, the last surviving visionary of Fátima, wrote to Pope Pius XII about the famous third part of the Secret of Fátima. Her handwritten text is preserved at the Vatican. Sister Lúcia wrote the following to the Holy Father: "Your Holiness is aware of the existence of the so-called secret of Fátima, enclosed in a sealed envelope that can be opened after the beginning of the year 1960. Although I cannot talk [about] the text contained therein, because the time is approaching, I must say that, in the 60s, communism will reach its high point, which can be diminished in intensity and duration, and which must be followed by the triumph of the Immaculate Heart of Mary and the Reign of Christ."[913]

This remark about the apparent connection between the third part of the Secret with the rise of communism in the 1960s harmonizes with Nikita Khrushchev's desire to escalate the attack on religion. It thus seems that Pius XII had a supernatural warning of coming trials. Sisiter Lúcia further wrote in her letter that the remedy to this problem was to "intensify all the apostolic works" (*intensifiquem todos os trabalhos apostólicos*) of the Church and that she be allowed to explain the Message of Fátima so as to help avoid errors and false doctrines.[914]

Now, during the preparatory phase of the council, as bishops' recommendations began arriving in Rome, communism appeared as the "most [common] error to condemn."[915] A full 378 bishops requested that the council deal with atheism and particularly communism. Archbishop Ngo-Dinh-Thuc of Hue, Vietnam, called it the "problem of problems" and added: "We are all stupefied by the silence of the Catholic world with regard to the agony of the most unfortunate Laotian people and the passion that the Vietnamese people are going through, while in the meantime one hears everywhere the voice of the communists and of their accomplices who live in the democratic nations, of which some are Catholic, who prefer to howl with the wolves: the voice, I say, of those who condemn the victims and glorify the executioners."[916]

It was only in 2017 that the documents written by the bishops and others gathered in Rome in the preparatory phase of the council were translated into English and publicized by Matthew C. Hoffman. They constituted a global offensive for defeating communism. These preparatory schemas of the Second Vatican Council had proposed declarations to address the menace of communism and to prescribe a specific program to oppose it and "shatter its audacity." These were initially approved by the "General Session" in February 1962. The first and lengthiest of the three was titled "On the Care of Souls with Regard to Christians Infected with Communism." The second document, which was also approved that February, was titled "On the Care of Souls and Communism." The third document, approved in April 1962, was titled "On the Apostolate of the Laity in Environments Imbued with Materialism, Particularly Marxism.'"[917] One particularly poignant recommendation was this one: "Catholics who, infected by 'progressive' doctrines and zealous for revolution, or because of a false so-called 'idealism,' or a wavering judgment, or an erroneous notion of charity, or because of fear of Soviet power and a foolish shame of the judgment of man, impede action against atheistic communism, should be publicly silenced by ecclesiastical authority. Priests delinquent in this regard are to be severely admonished, and, if the case so merits, inflicted with penalties."[918]

Unfortunately, many of those present at the council were clerics infected with "progressive" doctrines, as seen in the later demonstrations in favor of liberation theology by left-wing Jesuits.[919] In spite of the desire of the bishops and pleas of the clergy from persecuted countries, Cardinal Tisserant demanded that the very word "communism" be removed from the drafts. He wanted no denunciations of the persecutions in communist countries.[920] History now bears out that the word "communism" does not appear even once in the final publicly published documents of the council.[921] Yet, at the time of the Second Vatican Council, the Catholic faith faced its greatest threat from communism.

According to Italian scholar Professor Roberto de Mattei, during the first session of the council, Cardinal Tisserant, who "presided over the mixed sub-commission responsible for the schema *De Cura Animorum*, insisted that the word *communismus* be removed from the draft and, according to Giovanni Turbanti, intervened also for deletion of the paragraphs denouncing the persecutions in communist countries."[922]

The agreement between the Vatican and the Kremlin not to condemn communism became known as the Pact of Metz or the Vatican-Moscow agreement. At the council, it was only a select few who were aware of the agreement between Moscow and the Vatican. Dramatic events and discussions had taken place in the council with respect to communism from December 1964 to December 1965. While the council was discussing Schema XIII, which became *Gaudium et Spes*, Bishop Haubtman from France, former chaplain of the ACO (*Action Catholique Ouvrière*), was coordinating its reworking and requested the assistance of Fr. Giulio Girardi, a Salesian. In February 1965, the reworded text of Girardi, who was later expelled from the Salesians and became an advocate for liberation theology, was preferred to that of Archbishop Wojtyła, later Pope John Paul II. Girardi's text presented a "more positive approach" to what was called "Marxist humanism," something he incorporated in his books, *Teología de la liberación y refundación de la esperanza, Fe en la revolucion/ revolucion en la cultura,* and *Marxismo y cristianismo.*

Bishop Haubtman presented Girardi's reworded document to Pope Paul VI on February 16, 1965, who said the document was "sensitive and strictly necessary."[923] A condemnation of communism was missing. The new text was discussed in the council hall between September 1965 and October 1965. Those who composed the document said any discussion of communism would go against the pastoral character of the council's desire for "dialogue." Numerous council fathers were dissatisfied with the schema. Nonetheless, states one historian, "the agreement had a powerful, albeit silent, effect on the course of the council when the requests for a renewal of the condemnation of communism were rejected in order to observe this agreement and say nothing about it."[924]

Various viewpoints were discussed regarding a mention of communism, including the comment by Cardinal König that the roots of atheism must be sought in Christianity because Christians do not have a right notion of God and a precise image of man. Father Pedro Arrupe, then the new superior general of the Jesuits, said the Church after two millennia had not yet learned how to defend her message.[925]

Many bishops, cardinals, and patriarchs expressed their opinions, some favoring a condemnation and others objecting. Bishop Hnilica of Czechoslovakia, who had been consecrated a bishop clandestinely behind the Iron Curtain, lamented that the Church is suffering "under the oppression of militant atheism, but this cannot be deduced from the schema, which nevertheless claims to speak about the Church in today's world. History will justly accuse us of cowardice or blindness on account of this silence."[926] Hnilica was not speaking in the abstract; he had been in a concentration camp with hundreds of priests and religious. "I speak from my direct experience," said Hnilica, "and from that of priests and religious whom I have known in prison and with whom I have borne the burdens and dangers of the Church."[927]

Bishop Elko of Pittsburgh agreed that it was necessary to mention this plague of modern society and to condemn it.[928] Bishop Rusnak of Toronto said it "would be a scandal and an act of cowardice if a council of the twentieth century neglected to denounce before public opinion the errors and lies of communism."[929] On September 29, 1965, Cardinal Slipyj of Ukraine in the USSR observed that many speakers "seem unaware of the existence in the East of countries where it has set up a system and all sorts of methods are adopted to eradicate the Catholic Church and every other religion. And this is no secret to anyone."[930] Cardinal Baffi uttered the memorable words that such a silence on communism would be a collective sin and a council that fails to deal with it "may seem to be a failed council."[931]

The discussion of the draft of the constitution known as *Gaudium et spes* was concluded on October 7, 1965. The following day, October 8, Bishop Felici let the council fathers know that objections to the schema could be presented through the following day. In response, the *Coetus Internationalis Patrum*, an influential group of the "conservative" or "traditionalist" minority at the Second Vatican Council, prepared a petition requesting that a paragraph on communism be added after section 19 of the schema on "The Church in the Modern World," which dealt with atheism. The group asked: "Is there any other problem that is more pastoral than the problem of preventing the faithful from becoming atheists through communism?"[932] The proposed amendment addressed this unique form of atheism that "has exerted the greatest influence to the detriment of the Christian faithful, and of the followers of any religion, and therefore worries the pastors of the Church"—namely, "the one that spreads widely under the name of Marxist socialism or communism."[933]

As many as 334 council fathers replied to the invitation of the *Coetus Internationalis*, writing their petitions on separate pages, duly signed. These petitions were delivered personally by Bishop Sigaud and Archbishop Lefebvre to the secretary general of the council on Via Serristori 10 at noon on October 9, 1965, the last day for amendments to be submitted. Thus, the authors followed protocol and directions. An additional seventy-one new petitions supporting the inclusion were delivered and were presented to the secretary general. There were, then, a total of 435 council fathers who voiced their recommendation for the inclusion of a specific statement against communism.

It was then that a mysterious event occurred.

On October 11, 1965, the petition came into the hands of Monsignor Achille Glorieux, secretary of the mixed commission responsible for the preparation and revision of the schema on "The Church in the Modern World," as well as the Rome correspondent for the French daily *La Croix*. On November 15, 1965, Ralph Wiltgen, a journalist and eyewitness, sent out a news release explaining that the four hundred-plus signed interventions had disappeared, and therefore the International Group of Fathers was making a new try at "having its voice heard by submitting a qualification, that morning, nearly identical to the intervention."[934]

Wiltgen wrote that he was told by Archbishop Sigaud that approximately 450 fathers had signed petitions at the request of the *Coetus Internationalis*. Three of the largest Italian newspapers ran front-page stories on Wiltgen's press release. Approximately one month later, on Saturday, November 13, 1965, the revised text was presented to the council fathers—with no mention of communism. The council fathers who had written their petitions were dumbstruck.

Wiltgen confirmed from four different sources that Monsignor Glorieux of Lille, France, did not pass the petition to the commission. On November 23, 1965, Wiltgen sent out a press release describing Monsignor Glorieux's role in the mystery and personally delivered it to the Vatican Press Office, where it came to the attention of the Vatican authorities. The morning newspapers carried stories on Monsignor Glorieux, who had acted as a "red light" for the interventions on communism.

That morning, Pope Paul VI asked that a footnote be added to the schema on the Church's teaching on communism. We find in *Gaudium et spes* the response to the pontiff's request: "In her loyal devotion to God and men, the Church has already repudiated (16) and cannot cease repudiating, sorrowfully but as firmly as possible, those poisonous doctrines and actions which contradict reason and the common experience of humanity, and dethrone man from his native excellence." This is followed by a notation to a footnote: "16. Cf. Pius XI, encyclical letter Divini Redemptoris, March 19, 1937: AAS 29 (1937), pp. 65-106; Pius XII, encyclical letter Ad Apostolorum Principis, June 29, 1958: AAS 50 (1958) pp. 601-614; John XXIII, encyclical letter Mater et Magistra May 15, 1961: AAS 53 (1961), pp. 451-453; Paul VI, Ecclesiam Suam, Aug. 6, 1964: AAS 56 (1964), pp. 651-653."[935]

That was the extent of the council's condemnation of communism: a footnote.

This scandal can be summed up in one particular sentence in Wiltgen's book on the Second Vatican Council. It concerns Josef Cardinal Beran, formerly exiled archbishop of Prague, who had been imprisoned at Dachau, and whose cause for canonization is being considered. Beran was exiled to Rome in 1965. Wiltgen wrote that Beran "residing in Rome, received a Czechoslovakian newspaper clipping which boasted that communists had succeeded in infiltrating every commission at the Vatican Council."[936]

That is an alarming assertion: every commission at the Second Vatican Council—infiltrated. Is that an overstatement? Possibly. But clearly something had gone seriously wrong. To quote the later words of Pope Paul VI, the "smoke of Satan" had entered the Church.

Second Vatican Council and Post Council Timeline: Seminary Cadres?

With the backdrop of the Second Vatican Council, let us return to the infiltration of seminaries.

Bishop Sheen noted that the infiltration of seminaries began in 1936. At that time, the average age of a man entering the seminary was between eighteen to twenty years old, with priestly ordinations around twenty-three to twenty-seven years old. Thus, people who had entered the seminary in 1936 would have been ordained in 1941–43. That would make them approximately forty-five to sixty years old at the time of the council (1962–65) and would put some priests, monsignors, bishops, and cardinals in a position to influence and participate in procedures during the Second Vatican Council. And recall that Bella, in 1967, two years after the council, said there were four cardinals in the Vatican who remained active. She never named them, as Sheen had reportedly forbidden her to do so.

Nonetheless, if Bella's charges were accurate, it would not be unreasonable to suspect that there could have been cardinals, bishops, and others at the council who were working for the Kremlin or harbored communist sympathies, aside from any official KGB representatives.

Beyond the council itself, there was the new "spirit" of the Second Vatican Council, whereby a whole generation of Church liberals in the clergy and elsewhere heralded a momentous epoch to bring vast "progressive" change to the Church and bring it in accord with the spirit of the age and modern culture. That included a Church culture of dissent, liberalism, left-wing activism, and even moral corruption.

We know from the later dissent against *Humanae Vitae* in 1968, only three years after the Second Vatican Council, that some of these dissenters attended it. To (needlessly) cite merely one example, Gregory Baum was a peritus (expert) accompanying the Canadian bishops to the Second Vatican Council.[937] He was a prominent dissident on contraception at the third session of the council. Later, he was instrumental in advising the Canadian bishops to issue the infamous Winnipeg Statement, which rejected the 1968 dogmatic statement *Humanae Vitae*.[938]

In the 1960s, Baum went to the New School for Social Theory in New York. Even Wikipedia acknowledges his leftist sympathies, which included creating a "dialogue" between classical sociology (Marx, Tocqueville, Durkheim, Weber, etc.) and Christian theology. In the 1970s, he welcomed the insights of the Theology of Liberation. Wikipedia concedes, "In the 1980s and 1990s, Baum continued his study into ideology critique by integrating the work of the Frankfurt School of Critical Theory. He connected the Frankfurt School's concept of 'the end of innocent critique' with Liberation theology's 'preferential option for the poor.'"[939] Baum's *Religion and Alienation* carried a clear indebtedness to Marx and Freud (recall that the Frankfurt School sought a unified theory of Marxism and Freudianism) as well as the various liberation theologies gathering speed in the developing world.

In later years, Baum aggressively advocated for same-sex marriage and only later admitted his secret homosexual lifestyle, saying he had kept his behaviors secret so that he could be part of changing the Church. In his autobiography, he wrote openly of his "gay journey." In fact, Baum had been very bold on these subjects long before the culture went over the cliff in the twenty-first century. In the February 15, 1974 issue of the left-wing *Commonweal*, Baum wrote a piece titled

"Catholic Homosexuals" in which he attempted to make a moral-ethical defense of homosexual relationships.[940]

Monsignor Vincent Foy, a well-known Canadian priest who died at the age of 101 in March 2017, documented Baum's destruction in the Church.[941]

To be sure, this new "spirit" of the Second Vatican Council fell on fertile soil already seeded by many left-wing Catholics. For instance, an intriguing case among American priests, one that has escaped historical notice, was Monsignor John A. Ryan.

Ryan was an iconic figure in the American Catholic Church of his time, a noted moral theologian, advocate of social justice, and one of the most influential "reformers" of the Progressive and New Deal eras. A contemporary of Bella Dodd, Ryan aggressively peddled socialism. From 1922 to 1940, he directed the Social Action Department of the National Catholic Welfare Conference, which was the forerunner of the USCCB, and taught at the National Catholic School of Social Services. As noted by John Coleman, Ryan "believed in socialism and was a strong supporter of Roosevelt." His nickname was the "Right Reverend New Dealer," and he became known as "the padre of the New Deal."[942] The left-wing Catholic publication *Commonweal* heralds Ryan as a pioneering "social justice warrior," who pursued nothing short of a "revolution in social and economic justice."[943]

A devout follower of the leading Fabian Socialist Sidney Webb, Monsignor Ryan authored "Socialism: Promise or Menace." Fabian Socialists used his National Catholic Welfare Council to penetrate and permeate Catholic churches across America. To the likes of Ryan, the New Deal was a big step toward the larger goal of more and more government involvement, management, and ownership. In keeping with the goals of Fabian socialists and their approach of evolution rather than revolution (revolution was the Bolshevik approach), they took what they could when they could.

Monsignor Ryan is just one example of too many clergy who were duped into socialism and spread her errors in the pews. For those of his thinking, the new "spirit" of the council was wind behind their socialist sails. For any radical left-wing priest who slipped through seminary in Bella's day, and perhaps even with the aiding and abetting of her and her Party, the likes of Monsignor Ryan would have been sought out as sympathetic allies to their cause.

Liberation Theology

There was also the rot of Marxist thought known as liberation theology, which left a trail of destruction and whose priests sometimes even advocated for armed Marxist insurrections throughout Latin America. Its Marxist influence is obvious on its face, though it runs deeper than most people even realize.

Lt. Gen. Ion Mihai Pacepa, the leading Romanian spy chief who defected to the West in the late 1970s—the highest-ranking military official ever to defect from the Communist Bloc—went so far as to claim that liberation theology was created by the KGB. "The movement was born in the KGB," stated Pacepa unequivocally, "and it had a KGB-invented name: Liberation Theology." Pacepa gave specific details: "The birth of Liberation Theology was the intent of a 1960 super-secret 'Party-State Dezinformatsiya [Disinformation] Program' approved by Aleksandr Shelepin, the chairman of the KGB, and by Politburo member Aleksey Kirichenko, who coordinated the Communist Party's international policies. This program demanded that the KGB take secret control of the World Council of Churches (WCC), based in Geneva, Switzerland, and use it as cover for converting Liberation Theology into a South American revolutionary tool."[944]

Pacepa said that he personally learned the "fine points of the KGB involvement with Liberation Theology from Soviet General Aleksandr Sakharovsky, communist Romania's chief razvedka (foreign intelligence) adviser—and my de facto boss, until 1956, when he became head of the Soviet espionage service, the PGU1, a position he held for an unprecedented record of 15 years."[945]

On October 26, 1959, Sakharovsky and his boss, Nikita Khrushchev, came to Pacepa's Romania for what they termed "Khrushchev's six-day vacation." It was not really a vacation. Stated Pacepa: "Khrushchev wanted to go down in history as the Soviet leader who had exported communism to the American continent. In 1959 he had been able to install the Castro brothers in Havana, and soon my former intelligence service became involved in helping Cuba's new communist rulers to export revolution throughout South America."[946] In the 1950s and 1960s, millions of Latin Americans were poor, religious peasants who accepted the status quo, and Khrushchev was confident they could be converted to communism through the "judicious manipulation of religion."[947] The key was a kind of twisting of communism that could be forcibly reconciled with (or so it seemed) their Catholic faith.

As preparation for this plan, in 1968, the KGB was able to maneuver a group of leftist South American bishops into holding a conference in Medellin, Colombia, to "eliminate poverty" in Latin America. According to Pacepa, the undeclared goal was to "legitimize liberation theology and to incite Latin America's poor to rebel against the institutionalized violence of poverty generated by the United States."[948]

Pacepa continued, "This program demanded that the KGB take secret control of the World Council of Churches (WCC), based in Geneva, Switzerland, and use it as cover for converting Liberation Theology into a South American revolutionary tool. The WCC was the largest international ecumenical organization after the Vatican, representing some 550 million Christians of various denominations throughout 120 countries."[949]

Pacepa, who wrote the book *Disinformation*,[950] maintained that liberation theology was nothing short of a KGB plot. Not unlike Bella Dodd, he would harbor great regrets for his past, ultimately converting to the Catholic Church and thereafter seeking penance for his previous sins on behalf of communism.[951]

Roberto de Mattei, the renowned Italian-Catholic historian, called liberation theology the "most radical expression of the politicization of the Catholic world."[952] Malachi Martin, who wrote a bestselling book on the Jesuits, noted that so many "powerful religious orders of the Roman Church," from the Jesuits to the Maryknollers, "committed themselves to Liberation Theology."[953] As Martin laid out, the Jesuits in particular, but others as well, were busy in South America peddling liberation theology "based on Marxist revolutionary principles and aimed at establishing a communist system of government."[954]

This, of course, was well-known and strongly condemned by the likes of Pope John Paul II and Cardinal Joseph Ratzinger, who, as prefect of the Sacred Congregation for the Doctrine of the Faith (CDF), addressed this new heresy (which he labeled a singular heresy). When he was prefect of the CDF under John Paul II, Ratzinger issued two documents on liberation theology. The first, *Instruction On Certain Aspects of the "Theology Of Liberation" (Libertatis Nuntius*, issued in 1984), addressed "developments of that current of thought which, under the name 'theology of liberation,' proposes a novel interpretation of both the content of faith and of Christian existence which seriously departs from the faith of the Church and, in fact, actually constitutes a practical negation." The statement condemned the "corruption" caused by these "concepts uncritically borrowed from Marxist ideology."[955] The second instruction, *Libertatis Conscientia*, issued in 1986, sought to "highlight the main elements of the Christian doctrine on freedom and liberation" as a corrective to the errors of liberation theology. The CDF found it necessary to draw attention to "deviations, or risks of deviation, damaging to the faith and to Christian living." Liberation theology was one such concept that ran "contrary to the Gospel."[956]

Thus, we have a Marxist heresy, condemned by the two men who would succeed the Second Vatican Council's popes, formally entering the Church in the late 1960s, just as Bella Dodd was passing on, and just after the close of the Second Vatican Council. Clearly, Marxist influences had seeped into the Church. That was what communists had always wanted.

CHAPTER 15

QUESTIONS BEGIN: BELLA DOUBTS HER COMMUNIST FAITH

As these chapters have shown, communism was all about conflict. It was rooted in and spread conflict.

As for Bella Dodd, her struggles with the Communist Party began almost immediately once she openly joined the Party in 1943 and gave her entire self to the cause. She effectively already had done so years prior to joining. She later recalled a moment late one evening in 1938 when she was running for New York State Assembly on the American Labor Party ticket, representing an area in Greenwich Village. She found herself "winding up a street-corner meeting at Seventh Avenue and Fourteenth Street, and saw David Dubinsky and George Meany go by. They stopped, listened for a few minutes, smiled, and walked on." Suddenly, she said, for the first time, she felt a sense of "utter futility" over the endless activity in which the communists were involving her.[957]

But now, upon formally joining the Party, the commitment was even higher. Party members, after all, swore an oath: "I pledge myself to rally the masses to defend the Soviet Union, the land of victorious socialism. I pledge myself to remain at all times a vigilant and firm defender of the Leninist line of the party, the only line that insures the triumph of Soviet Power in the United States."[958]

Yes, at all times.

This was also a time when she was meeting new friends and had a new roommate. Many of those friends, not surprisingly, were from the movement. At night, when Bella came home, the apartment was often swelling with people from civil service unions and the Maritime Union and every other organization friendly to the Party.

One evening at the apartment, she met Paddy Whalen, known as "Red," who had been raised Catholic but left the Church, became a member of the International Workers of the World (IWW), and worked with the Communist Party. Bella proudly announced her decision to become an open communist. His words struck her: "Are you sure that is what you want?" he asked. "You see, I don't think they have the answer. I simply can't make myself believe that we are only clods of earth and that when we die, we die and that's all." Paddy went on: "I've seen bad conditions in lots of places, on ships, in jails, and in foreign ports in China and India and Africa and South America. I've fought against these conditions. There's no doubt that out of it, revolution may come—the way the Communists want it to—but what will come after that? I hate to think about it. But I'm pretty sure they haven't got the answer."[959]

Bella was startled to hear this response from "Red," who had stubbornly fought for labor his whole life. She sensed an "uneasy feeling that sometimes came over me, even though I tried to ignore it. It was as if this man's words were the echo of my own unformulated fears."[960]

There were several such incidents, each small in itself, but they made Bella think about the Party in a new light. They began to instill doubts.

"Something Was Wrong"

The Communist Party convention of 1944 was held at Riverside Plaza, a hotel on West Seventy-Second Street in New York City. Surprisingly, the American Communist Party dissolved its name. By another resolution, the delegates re-established it under the name of the Communist Political Association, with the same leaders, same organization, same friends. Bella Dodd was elected as a member of the National

Committee of the Communist Political Association, which brought her into top leadership. (The name soon enough would change again; these were mere tactics.) Bella could not understand why this drastic action took place.[961]

As was typical of how the Party functioned, however, you did not question. That was not permitted. You simply obeyed.

Bella's doubts grew: "After I had joined the Party apparatus officially, after I had become an employee of the Communist Party on the inside, almost from the very beginning I recognized that something was wrong, that this wasn't the thing which I had dreamed about, worked for, and which I believed in. That was 1944."[962]

That same year, the Party assigned Bella to handle its election campaigns for New York State. She was taken aback to come into contact with communist candidates who concealed their true beliefs and ran and were elected on Republican, Democratic, and Labor tickets. These people elected on these tickets were members of the Communist Party or subjected themselves to communist discipline. But they concealed it. This shocked her. She thought, "One should be that which one pretends one is."[963]

It was quickly thereafter, said Bella, that "the little sparks of my conscience caught fire. I began to realize and to feel uneasy at the contradictions between what the Communists preached and what they did."[964] In the post-war period of 1945–46, she realized that she was now suddenly "face to face with something which I had not bargained for. I was face to face with brutality, cynicism, and with an organization which said one thing and did another. . . . It was only when I got within the sacred precincts of the Party that I actually saw the things which are abhorrent not only to decent people, but to anyone who has any feelings for his fellow man."[965]

Deeper philosophical and theological questions persisted. Bella began to question the answers communists were giving to the problems of the world. Repeatedly, she asked herself, "What is man's goal?" She questioned whether it was "merely his physical development, and whether his goal would be reached when man is well fed, well clothed, and well housed. Who of us has not seen the neurotic misery of people who have all the material security which they need? I found myself repeating, 'Man does not live by bread alone.'"[966]

Another incident that had made Bella uneasy was a strike she led on the waterfront, which lasted for weeks upon weeks. She went to see the chairman of the Communist Party himself, William Z. "Bill" Foster, and said to him, "Bill, why don't we settle this? The men are losing money, their families more." In a jaw-dropping response, he said to Bella: "Dodd, don't be so sentimental. We've got to train these people so that they are able to kill." That was a shock: "I hadn't quite realized what I had entered. I fell back on my heels."[967]

She was seeing what brutes these communists really were, despite their flowery talk of loving the common man. Her experiences on the National Committee revealed this repeatedly. Bella later recalled:

> My work on that committee of thirteen was an experience I shall never forget. Bill Foster was technically chairman. His constant attendant was Robert Thompson. [Ben] Davis of the Philadelphia A.F. of L. food workers' union and Ben Gold of the CIO Furriers were the ranking members. The procedure was fascinating and fantastic. It was the nearest thing to purge trials I have ever seen.
>
> One by one the leaders appeared before this committee. We were silent and waited for them to speak. Men showed remorse for having offended or betrayed the working class. They tried desperately to prove that they themselves were of that working class, and had no bourgeois background, and were unspoiled by bourgeois education. They talked of Browder as if he were a sort of bourgeois Satan who had lured them into error because of lack of understanding due to their inadequate communist education. Now they grieved over their mistakes and unctuously pledged that they would study Marx-Lenin-Stalin faithfully, and never betray the working class again. One by one they came before the

committee and I began to feel like one of Robespierre's committees in the French Revolution.[968]

Very much like Robespierre's Jacobins, they were eating their own. They were turning to violence. It was an internal purge. Bella watched it.

There was another incident, this time in 1946, which pierced Bella's armor. Congressman Vito Marcantonio, the political voice of the Communist Party, was running against Joseph Scottoriggio, a strong Republican candidate. Scottoriggio was assaulted by four men on the way to the polls and hospitalized with a fractured skull. Bella, who was in charge of the upper Tenth District on the Upper East Side, was called in for questioning when Scottoriggio died of his wounds. Someone in the district attorney's office asked her why she became a communist. She began giving her regular Party line answer: "Because only the communists seemed to care about what was happening to people in 1932 and 1933."[969]

But while she was speaking, Bella realized that she "no longer had the old faith in the cause," nor "the same deep conviction about the Party's championship of the poor and dispossessed. I knew now that its activities were conceived in duplicity and ended in betrayal."[970] She had witnessed too much of the ugly truth.

Bella recalled sitting at "Party meetings for hours, watching men play a cunning game for power. I suffered each time we broke faith with the people, each time we said one thing and did another. I squirmed at the cynicism which was apparent everywhere, and I was revolted by the lies and half-truths which increasingly formed the basis of our propaganda."[971]

"No One Gets Out"—Confrontation and Showdown with the Party

Trouble continued to brew for Bella. By 1947, she was disillusioned and longed for a life beyond her total allegiance to the Party. She was pulling away, which would make the Party very suspicious of Bella Dodd. And as she knew, once the Communist Party had suspicions of you, it would begin closing in around you. It would start readying itself to destroy you. Those who left the Party became the worst of heretics; they were pariahs. They had to be destroyed.

"During the latter months of 1947 my world was shifting all about me," Bella later wrote in *School of Darkness*. "The certitude which I had so long known in the Communist Party was now gone. I was ill in mind and often in body, too, for I had a constant and terrible fear that every effort was being made to destroy me." She had seen how the savagery operated: "I had watched the pitiless and methodical destruction of others. I did not have the will to fight back, nor did I want to involve the innocent. At that period little dissident groups were forming and they criticized the Party, both from the right and the left. Each had its own leader. Each vowed devotion to the Party and each charged that the leadership of the Party in the United States had gone off the Marxist-Leninist track." Of course, this was not permitted. "I had noted the futility of such attempts before and, although I never refused to see anyone who sought me, I did refuse to become involved with them."[972]

Could Bella pull away? No, not easily. "I knew well that no group could be organized without being under the surveillance of Chester, the smooth, dapper director of the Party's secret service. His men were everywhere." Bella was being watched. Old friends like "Chester," a shady ally in her previous battles for the Party to destroy anti-communists, were on her trail. Her "non-person" status was growing among the Party's henchmen and henchwomen. She recalled: "I turned to my law practice and sought to forget my fears by immersing myself in work, but inwardly I was so disturbed that my work suffered. I did not know how and when the ax would fall. I knew my office was still under constant surveillance and I had no way of stopping it. Certain agents from communist headquarters made a practice of visiting me at regular intervals trying to get me to take part in some meaningless activity. I knew well that was not the reason they came."[973]

They were there to keep tabs on her.

Through the spring of 1948, Bella had withdrawn from organized activities and stopped attending Party meetings. She tried to build up her law practice and a private life for herself. But she was living in a nightmare, and morning never broke. She searched her soul. Half praying, she would ask herself each day: "How did I get into this blind alley?"[974]

They were already angling for avenues to smear her, suspecting that Bella had broken away. "I outwitted a number of well-laid plans to injure me," she said later. "I learned during those months that some of the agents of the International Communist movement look and talk like your next-door neighbor. While I still saw many rank-and-file Communists, I avoided contact with the rest when I could." She "hoped against hope that I would be permitted to drift away from the Party."[975] Many Party members had broken away, but not many had reached a position of importance in the Party like Bella had. She had done too much; she knew too much.

Though she had withdrawn from most Party activity by then, she did continue as the exceptionally productive Party contact for the Party teachers' groups. But now, even that changed: "I was replaced even there and by a man who knew nothing at all about education."[976]

And yet, even as she had quit attending Party meetings, she did receive a notice to go to the state convention held that year in Webster Hall on the East Side. But why? When she got there, she could feel the suspicions: "There I found I was a marked person, that people were afraid to be seen sitting with me." After some hesitation, she finally sat down at a table beside David Goldway, who had always been a friend. But this time, "He greeted me only with his eyes and with a short nod of the head. His lips were a thin line. He did not smile or speak."[977]

She heard loud voices, then Robert Thompson, a militant young Party functionary named by Eugene Dennis as leader of the New York district, marched in with Ben Davis, a communist councilman from Harlem, at his heels, followed by some young people. These were the Party's fiery cadres. It reminded Bella of her visit to Munich in the 1930s when she saw the "same intense look on young faces" devoted to their leader, Hitler. This would be the last Party meeting she attended.

Bella had run-ins with Thompson before, some of which had helped spark her disillusionment. The "discipline committee" had brought charges of "white chauvinism" against her twice in 1946. One of her acts of rebellion against groupthink occurred during a meeting when she blocked the Party's plan to support a union leader charged with stealing funds, which resulted in "rough treatment from the comrades." The explosive Robert Thompson leaned over his desk and started shouting at Bella. Her temper flared up. She stood, knocking over a chair, and said icily, "You think like pigs," and stormed out.[978]

Like clockwork, the next day, Bill Norman, the Party's state secretary, summoned her to his office. And there, for the first time, she dared to say to a Party leader that she wanted out: "He talked to me in his quiet and reasonable way and I told him frankly that I wanted to get out of the Party. His expression changed. He fixed his eyes on me and said, almost harshly, 'Dodd, no one gets out of the Party. You die or you are thrown out. But no one gets out.' Then he became his mild self again."[979]

Bella recalled that moment in her 1954 memoir, *School of Darkness*. A decade later, in a 1961 speech in Detroit, she said more:

> And Bill Norman, who was then secretary, he looked at me. He said, "Dodd, nobody gets out of his party. You die, you disappear, or we get rid of you. Nobody gets out." But somewhere within me that somebody was praying for me, or some residue of that American spirit, which I had imbibed in my early days and high school and college with me. I threw my keys across [Norman's] desk and I said, "I don't care what you do. I'm not going to work for you anymore." And I slammed the door and walked

out scared to my very inner being. Trembling and shaking as I'd never shaken before.[980]

Was there anyone or anything to help her? She felt alone. But maybe there was someone praying for her. She would need it because her troubles would only intensify.

Bella had experienced scary situations before, where she felt personally at risk. She once distributed leaflets at the tough waterfront. And she once visited the bad sections of Harlem campaigning for pro-communist Congressman Vito Marcantonio. But she had "never been frightened. Now, suddenly, I was scared."[981]

In 1948, Bella was summoned by the discipline committee before the National Convention. It ordered her to appear on "the ninth floor." This was a very familiar spot to communists.[982] The tawdry 35 East Twelfth Street building near Union Square was the command center of the US Communist Party, also known as the "American Kremlin." Fittingly, she described the headquarters as unbelievably drab, with pictures of Lenin, Marx, and Stalin on the walls. Any attempt to beautify it was belittled as "bourgeois pretentiousness."[983]

Reacting to the summons, conflicting thoughts crossed her mind. "But," she would object to herself, "I am an American citizen with the right to be free of coercion." And thus, "I did not have to go to Twelfth Street and ride the dingy elevator to the ninth floor. I did not have to face the tight-lipped faces of the men and women who kept the gates and doors locked against intrusion, nor meet their eyes, scornful now because they knew I was persona non grata. I did not have to go, but like an automaton I went."[984] She was struggling within the depths of her soul.

When she arrived, she almost laughed. There were three old men: Alexander Trachtenberg with his walrus mustache; Pop Mindel, the hero of the communist training schools; and Jim Ford, a "Negro leader and perennial vice-presidential candidate," whose look at her was "distant and morose." She had been friendly with all three and never had any disputes with them. Trachtenberg had been the Party's "cultural commissar."[985] Bella once had breakfast with him, which was when he confided those words she repeated so often in the years ahead: "Bella, when the thing comes in this country—and by 'the thing' he meant control of the people—it will not come under the label of Communism, it may not even come under the label of Socialism. When the thing comes, it will come under labels acceptable to Americans. It will come under 'progressive,' it will come under 'liberal,' it will come under this kind, that kind."[986]

At this tense disciplinary meeting, Bella began by nervously asking: "Will this take long?" The austere Trachtenberg, head of the GPU in the United States, the notorious Soviet military police, confronted her: "We want to ask you a few questions," said an accusatory Trachtenberg in his thick German accent. "We hear you attacked the Cominform."[987] The Cominform was the rebranded name for the Comintern after World War II. Bella had questioned whether the new Cominform was a good idea, but no Party member was permitted to question anything that the Kremlin did.

"I've been ill, Comrade Trachtenberg," Bella said in her defense. "I guess I'm all right now." Said Trachtenberg: "But you are all right now?" Bella replied, "Yes, I guess I'm all right now." He pushed: "We want to ask you a few questions." A very rattled Bella began to nervously plead to herself in silence: "Dear God, dear God."[988]

Then came the matter of Bella's confrontation with the vicious Robert Thompson, who, being her superior in the Party hierarchy, was not to be questioned. Said Trachtenberg: "We hear you do not like Thompson." Bella replied, "Really, Comrade Trachtenberg, whether I like Thompson or not has nothing to do with the case." Bella accused Thompson of being a menace, endangering the lives of American workers.[989]

But this was about more than Thompson. Trachtenberg then asked Bella why she was not active in membership any longer and why her activity was at a standstill. She again appealed to her "illness," which, for the Party, was often the only acceptable reason. After all, only someone who was ill would doubt the rightness of the Party. "I am still not quite well, Comrade Trachtenberg," explained Bella. "And I have personal problems. Let me alone until I can find myself again." She asked to go. Then, from Trachtenberg, like words slipping from the edge of a razor blade: "You will hear from us again."[990]

Trachtenberg was speaking to an accomplished attorney, lobbyist, and professor, who was also a member of the National Committee of the Communist Party. She was described by some as the most important female communist in the United States at the time, the legislative representative of the Communist Party.[991] But, like all members of the Communist Party, Bella was under discipline committee. A semi-military or "Bolshevik" discipline was something each Party member agreed to.[992] It was, above all, the ability to "execute orders faithfully from above."[993] And "above" still meant Josef Vissarionovich Dzhugashvili, or Stalin. That was Trachtenberg's boss.

When a person was accepted as a "card-carrying" member of the Party, he signed an oath: "The undersigned, after having read the constitution and program of the Communist Party, declares his adherence to the principles and tactics of the Party and the Communist International; agrees to submit to the discipline of the Party as stated in its constitution and pledges to engage actively in its work."[994] Totalitarian philosophy required totalitarian obedience.

As a member of the National Committee, Bella Dodd met four times a year to learn of any changes or new interpretations in the Party line laid down by Moscow. The national leader of the Party presented a report over several hours in which the line was defined. Then each member of the National Committee rose and expressed his agreement with the report, explained "how he would carry it out, what forces" he could bring to play, and "what organizations he could infiltrate."[995]

This was not something that someone like Bella Dodd was permitted to break from. The Party owned her.

Expulsion from the Party

The Party realized, however, that Bella Dodd had broken ranks. She could no longer be trusted. She must now be expelled from the Party, even destroyed.

On May 6, 1949, a youth leader of the Communist Party arrived at Bella's house. Refusing her offer of coffee, he handed her the written charges and ordered her to appear the next day for a "trial" near her house in Harlem.[996] And so, Bella again obediently climbed the stairs to the "drab, dirty meeting room with its smell of stale cigarettes." Petty employees waited, "those at the lowest rung of the bureaucracy," she thought, including three women who had "faces hard and full of hate."[997] They were Party faces. Humorless. Rigid. Faces ready to determine the destinies of human beings. A young Puerto Rican woman began shouting her hatred at her.[998] This, she said, was an odd kind of trial: "The Commission before me had already made up its mind."[999]

Of course, this was a typical communist "trial." It was a show trial. For communists, this was not odd at all. This was standard procedure.

Bella, the attorney, once the Party's and Teachers Union's star legal counsel, including in epic battles like the fight against the Rapp-Coudert Committee, asked whether she could produce witnesses. The answer was a firm no.

Recall from chapter one of this book that the issue had involved a landlord, a friend of Bella, an immigrant woman named Frances Dzerlin who could not pay a fine and who Bella had befriended and offered to help. All of which the Party in its typical nasty mendacity had somehow twisted to frame Bella to the media as (in the words of the Associated Press reporter) "anti-Negro, anti-Puerto Rican, anti-Semitic, anti-labor, and the defender of a landlord."[1000]

Of course, this was all trumped-up nonsense. Just like in the Soviet Union, when the Party purged dissenters, a manufactured crime was created. This was the crime used against Bella Dodd. She would later sum up her "crime" and the charges against her:

The incident which was used as the excuse for my formal expulsion from the Party was of no importance in itself. The way in which it was handled was symptomatic of Party methods. On Lexington Avenue, a few doors from my home, lived a Czechoslovakian woman with whom I sometimes talked. She lived in a small three-story building where she served as janitor from 1941 to 1947. Her husband was permanently incapacitated and she was the sole support of the family. Acting as a janitor and working as a domestic several days a week, she managed to keep her family together.

In 1947 the owner of the building decided to sell it. The woman, afraid she would lose both her apartment and her job, made up her mind to buy it, and borrowed the money to do so. Thus she became technically a landlord; but her daily life remained the same; she was still the janitor. However, as owner of the house she had become involved with her tenants and in quick succession three judgments were entered against her. Her husband quarreled and left her. The attorney for the plaintiffs, eager to collect his fees, asked warrants for her arrest.[1001]

At that point, the woman, Frances Dzerlin, came to Bella for help. As someone who sincerely believed in helping the working man, or woman, and the genuinely oppressed, Bella agreed to represent her. And she represented her very well. In the end, the court granted Bella's plea, the tenants were paid, and the woman escaped time in prison.

One would think that this was precisely the kind of championing of the Proletariat that communists would hail. But in truth, the Party needed a story to twist so it could twist a knife into Bella Dodd. The Party creatively flipped the thing into a matter of a Communist Party member unacceptably siding with a "landlord." Said Bella later:

One thing was clear: only technically could she have been called a landlord. But the communist leadership heard with delight that Bella Dodd had appeared as "attorney for a landlord." At last they had the excuse for getting me politically, the excuse for which they had been looking. Of course they could have simply expelled me but this would involve discussion of policies. They were looking for an excuse to expel me on charges that would besmirch my character, drive my friends away, and stop discussion instead of starting it. What better than to expel me for the crime of becoming a "hireling of the landlords?"

They must have realized that such an argument would scarcely be cogent to outsiders. Even to many of the Party it was weak. They must add something really unforgivable to make me an outcast in the eyes of the simple people of the Party.[1002]

The charge of defending a landlord was a sore point to communists. In one of her addresses, Bella noted that for the Bolsheviks and their "socialist state of peasants and workers," they earned their "power by killing off the landlords and the bosses."[1003] Now they would use the landlord charge to kill off Bella, at least as much as they could in a country like America. They would assassinate her character.

Hence, the smears began. Bella's old comrades spread a story that during her court appearances representing the poor woman, Bella had made remarks against Puerto Rican tenants; in Bella's words, "that I had slandered them, and showed myself a racist, almost a fascist. And last of all, a charge of anti-Negro, anti-Semitism, and anti-working class was thrown in for good measure."

That was about when, on May 6, the youth leader from the Communist Party came to Bella's house. She asked him in and offered him a cup of coffee, both of which he refused. The show trial of Bella Dodd had begun.

And so, during her "trial" before her erstwhile comrades, Bella asked if she might bring the woman involved in the case who she had represented to defend her. The answer was no. Would someone come to her house and speak with her and the tenants? Again, "No, no." Then she asked if she might bring a communist lawyer who at least understood the legal technicalities she was faced with in trying this simple case. There was a final no.

From the beginning, she realized that these indoctrinated souls were hostile and would continue to be so despite arguments and proofs. They were disciplined Bolsheviks. A Finnish woman announced that Bella would be informed of the result and dismissed her from the proceedings. Mercifully, of course, this was not the Lubyanka, the infamous prison in Moscow where enemies of the state were executed, and Bella was not a Nikolai Rubashov. This was America. But the template was the same: a phony trial, like the Moscow show trials, with the verdict pre-ordained, and unspoken threats.

Bella now suddenly realized the superiority of the United States over the USSR when it came to judicial systems. This was the very United States that Bella as a Party member had fought to convert into a "Soviet America."

Either way, she was doomed. During a meeting of Party officials in their "law" offices at 100 Fifth Avenue, in the offices of Unger, Fleischer, and Freedman (Abe Unger had been a Party ally of Bella), Bill Norman informed the coordinating committee that it was "decided that Bella Dodd will be expelled."[1004]

"Masterpiece of Liquidation"

After her dismissal, the emptiness of Bella's life overcame her. She had devoted twenty years to the Party, prostituting herself to an imaginary Proletariat. At the end, she was left staring at a few "shabby men and women," inconsequential "Party functionaries drained of all mercy," with "no humanity in their eyes." Examining the situation, she said: "Had they been armed, I know they would have pulled the trigger on me."[1005]

They would have if they could have. They could in the Soviet Union. But even without a bullet to the head, she was treated cruelly, almost violently, or so it felt. "It was inevitable that the communists should expel me with violence and cruelty," she said later. "The resolution of expulsion was a masterpiece of 'liquidation.' As I read it today, I can almost hear the whiz of the bullet which they might have used if they had had power."[1006]

This was not the Church of mercy that Maria Assunta Isabella had experienced in Italy. This was the church of communism, where there was no mercy, only violence and cruelty.

She thought of others who had been through a similar ordeal and those who would go through this terror. She shivered at "the thought of harsh, dehumanized people like these, filled with only the emotion of hate, robots of a system which was heralded as a new world." And she shivered "at the sorrow for those who would be taken down the long road whose end I saw, now, was a dead end."[1007]

After she was expelled, Bella suffered morally, physically, and financially.

Bella discussed her feelings about the expulsion a few months later in an interview with Louis Schaeffer of the *New Leader*, who had known Bella as "genial," energetic, and an "effective speaker." He told Bella not to feel so bad—this malevolent treatment had happened to many others. Still, that was little consolation. "Maybe I'll get used to it with time," she said, but she thought of herself as a "divorced woman who has just lost her husband because he is a scoundrel, but nevertheless doesn't want anyone else to berate him."[1008]

Among all the slanders of her, she said that the charge of anti-Semitism especially stung. Her closest friends were Jews prior to her joining the Party and even in the Party. "In all the other charges, I can find some shred of explanation for the attitude of the State Committee," she told Schaeffer. "But no matter how hard I think about that accusation, I cannot recall the slightest occasion which would give them the right to make it . . . unless it's because the witnesses at my wedding were two of my best Jewish friends."[1009]

She need not be defensive. The charge of anti-Semitism was as ludicrous as it was vicious. No one who knew her took it seriously. But of course, those who did not know her might take it seriously. That was why the Party apparatchiks slung it. It would take her years to crawl out of the mud and slime.

During later congressional testimony, Bella said it took her five years to disentangle herself from the Party. She told Robert Kunzig, counsel for the House Un-American Activities Committee: "It took me five years to get out of the Communist Party completely. . . . During that time, I would rather not talk about it. My life was one of misery. I was hounded, publicized, and given the treatment that everybody gets who becomes a deserter to their cause." She was followed, had the windows of her house and office broken, had her clients taken away: "They tried to make it impossible for me to make a living. They did everything they could."[1010]

But regardless, Bella was out. She was liberated: "The resolution of expulsion sealed the end of my slavery to Communist thought." She could now begin finding her way back home.[1011]

Fortunately, there was something and someone who wanted to rescue Bella Dodd. It was the Church of her youth and a special priest who took special interest in her.

CHAPTER 16

MEETING SHEEN: RECOVERY AND RECONCILIATION

In her June 1953 public testimony, Bella Dodd informed counselor Robert Kunzig and the congressmen on his committee, "I only got out of the Communist Party completely, emotionally, when I found my way back to my own church."[1012]

In the late 1940s and early 1950s, Bella's life was in chaos—a battleground of devastation and wreckage. Inch by inch, she withdrew from the Communist Party and reached for something better, something higher. It was God who was reaching for her. "God extended His hand repeatedly to me," she said later, "but so blind was I that I ignored Him and went on in the pattern of my own desperation, caring not whether I lived or died, afraid to face each coming day, with no will to strike back at those who struck or degraded me. My mind was unable to give me the answers. I was left adrift like a ship without a rudder."[1013]

Instead, Bella first sought a hole "to crawl into."[1014] She was a fugitive from the Party, and her soul a fugitive from God. She faced nervous exhaustion. She found herself "besmirched, smeared, and terrorized."[1015] From 1948 to 1952, she was in a vacuum, her soul feeling as empty as her apartment: "In those days I moved from one hotel to another, from one furnished room to another because I lost my home in all this thing and I kept moving because, as I moved the same faces would appear. . . . How did I find my way back?"[1016]

Finding Her True Home

In the fall of 1950, Bella went to Washington as a private attorney to argue an immigration appeal. While walking down Pennsylvania Avenue toward the Capitol, she ran into her old friend, Congressman Christopher McGrath, who represented her old East Bronx neighborhood. When they were inside his private office, he said abruptly: "You look harassed and disturbed, Bella. Isn't there something I can do for you?" She had a lump in her throat.[1017]

McGrath asked her if she wanted FBI protection. Though afraid, she refused. "I don't want any more police protection. I've got them following me all the time, I'm forced to change my room, my hotels, and so forth, and so on; it's just not a good idea." At this time, Bella was being followed by both the FBI and the KGB.[1018]

McGrath did not press the issue. Instead, he said, "I know you are facing danger, but if you won't have protection, I can only pray for your safety." Then he added, "Well, would you see a priest?" And suddenly within her, Bella shouted "Yes!" She feared, however, that she did not know what she would say to a priest.[1019]

The years of communist atheism had hardened Bella to that very prospect of talking to a priest, but now she felt it was something she could no longer resist. "Yes, I would," she said with an intensity that surprised herself. McGrath responded: "Perhaps we can reach Monsignor Sheen at Catholic University." Working with his secretary, Rose, McGrath arranged for Bella to meet Fulton Sheen.[1020]

Things were about to change, dramatically.

Meeting Sheen

Sheen agreed to see Bella that evening at his home in Chevy Chase. Only two years earlier, Sheen's powerful book *Communism and the Conscience of the West* was published. It was as if Sheen had been studying Bella from afar. His writings on communism were second to none, especially among Catholics. And at last, Sheen would have the chance to meet a soul whose conversion he likely had been praying for and whose ideology was a clear threat to his flock.

On her way there, Bella already felt the "tiny flame of longing for faith within me." It seemed to grow as she drove closer to Sheen.

Even then, she wanted to look for an "easy exit" as the famous priest walked into the room, "his silver cross gleaming, a warm smile in his eyes." She said later, "He came out very much as he does on the television screen."

It must have seemed intimidating at first, but her reservations quickly vanished as Sheen held out his hand: "Doctor, I'm glad you've come."[1021] She would forever fondly remember those warm words. As she later recalled appreciatively, perhaps remembering how her communist "friends" would have received and berated her: "He didn't say, 'you old Bolshevik, you old bag.' He said, 'Doctor, I'm so glad you came.'"[1022] He then observed: "Dr. Dodd, you look unhappy." She said: "Why do you say that?" Sheen replied: "Oh, I suppose, in some way, we priests are like doctors who can diagnose a patient by looking at him."[1023]

She began to cry as he put his hand on her shoulder. He comforted her. Unlike the American Bolsheviks who descended on Bella in show trials without mercy, Fulton Sheen was all mercy. Bella recalled: "He kept saying, 'There, there, it won't be long now.' . . . He only let me cry, and then, without realizing it, I found that we were both on our knees before the Blessed Mother in the little chapel."[1024]

As the conversation seemed to slow to a halt, Sheen had led her gently into that small chapel, where both bowed before a statue of Our Lady. Like a little girl again, Maria Assunta Isabella felt a peace, stillness, calm.

This was certainly a turning point in the life of Bella Dodd. She was to remain deeply devoted to the Blessed Mother for the rest of her life and keep a statue of her in her office. Later, she could not recall how long she and Sheen had remained there, but "for the first time in my life, I knew peace, which I hadn't known for many years.

When I got up from my knees . . . my tears were dry." Sheen then said to her: "Bella, if you want to protect the people whom you say that you love, the people of this country, and all the human beings of the world, then to do the right things, you must know something about Christianity. Your parents were peasants, but you, an educated woman, have to know."[1025]

When they left the chapel, Sheen gave Dodd a rosary. "I will be going to New York next winter," he told her. "Come to me and I'll give you instructions in the Faith." On her way to the airport, she marveled at "how much he understood." With an unexpected sense of serenity, she held that rosary tightly all the way to New York and thereafter carried in her pocket always.[1026]

But Bella put off her visit to Monsignor Sheen. By winter, she had again retreated into darkness. She wandered into some New York City churches, which she said were the only places where the churning inside her stopped and where fear left her. She spent Christmas Eve with Clotilda and Jim McClure, who had previously lived at her house on Lexington Avenue. They read from the Bible, ate a simple supper, and then Jim walked her to the bus stop. She said she has no recollection of leaving the bus that evening, but she found herself in Saint Francis of Assisi Church on New York's West Side. The choir sang Christmas hymns, and she realized that these were "the masses I had sought through the years, the people I loved and wanted to serve, people of all races and ages. Here was a brotherhood of man with meaning."[1027]

The Midnight Mass was packed. She wedged her way in. She prayed over and over, "God help me. God help me." When Mass ended, she walked the streets alone for hours, but she felt different; she felt a "warm glow of hope." "I knew I was traveling closer and closer to home," she wrote later, "guided by the Star."[1028]

She was on a different walk now. She would never again return to the School of Darkness.

Lighting a Candle

In early 1951, Bella went to the Board of Education to see Dr. Jacob Greenberg, superintendent in charge of personnel. Waiting for him, she struck up a conversation with Mary Riley, his assistant.

Bella remarked to Riley that she had been having a lot of trouble. Riley said, "That's putting it mildly." Riley said that she and Dr. Greenberg did not like communism but always admired those like Bella who help human beings. A few days later, Bella received a package from Mary Riley that contained books about Catholic missions, Interracial Councils, and a volume by Father Keller, *You Can Change the World.* These were not the stirrings of hate she encountered in Marxist-Leninist literature but the flames of love.

Bella could not put the book down, and she kept thinking of the truth of Father Keller's statement that "there can be no social regeneration without a personal regeneration." She was awakening from a long sleep. Not long after, she ran into Judge Louis Pagnucco, who had interrogated her in the Scottoriggio investigation. They talked about individual responsibility for actions, and Father Keller's words came up. The judge asked if she would like to meet Keller. She agreed.[1029]

The next day, Bella and the judge met at the office of Godfrey Schmidt, a tough Catholic attorney who would later represent her in the House Un-American Activities Committee hearings. Godfrey Schmidt taught at Fordham Law School. Bella remembered the Party's campaign of hate against him earlier, when they framed him as a Nazi, calling him "Herr Doktor Schmidt." Father Keller entered, and she thought how different this group was from the little communist groups she had attended. There was no fear and no hatred.[1030]

She had new friends—friends who were better people. They were bringing her closer to what mattered, and to the faith of Jesus.

Gradually, Bella began to pray each morning and go to daily Mass at the Church of Our Lady of Guadalupe on West Seventeenth Street, arriving on time to hear the brothers sing Matins before Mass. She sat in a rear pew as a spectator. She told herself she was not ready yet for full communion with the Church. But she was taking major steps forward.

She met the group of religious men, The Christophers, whose motto is "It's better to light a candle than to curse the darkness," a darkness that Bella was trying to escape by rekindling the light of her Catholic faith. She began reading, including Augustine's *City of God*, and also Aquinas. "Like one who had been starved," she grabbed "books which the Communists and the sophisticated secular world marked taboo or sneered at." She found *City of God* "infinitely more life-giving than the defiant modern professors who wrote *The City of Man*. I found St. Thomas Aquinas and I laughed to remember that all I had learned of St. Thomas was that he was a scholastic philosopher who believed in the deductive method of thinking. Now, as the great storehouse of his wisdom was opened to me, I felt rich beyond all words."[1031]

One day, at lunch, she explained to Godfrey Schmidt that she must learn more about the faith. He knew that. As they walked down Park Avenue, he took her into a bookshop and bought her a prayer book. The next day, he called her to say that the newly ordained Bishop Fulton Sheen was back in town and had agreed to see her again.[1032]

That invitation, said Bella, "was like a joyful summons from an old friend."[1033]

Easter 1952: Received by Sheen

With Godfrey Schmidt, Bella walked to East Thirty-Eighth Street, to the offices of the Society for the Propagation of the Faith, and rang the bell. Bishop Sheen himself opened the door. "I saw the silver cross on his chest," said Bella, "the smile in his eyes, but this time I heard a 'welcome home' in his greeting. And so I began to receive instructions in the Faith."[1034]

It was 1951, and Bella thus began to receive weekly instruction from Fulton Sheen, taken by his kindness, his knowledge, his keen logic and

reasoning, his patient telling of the love of God for man, of man's longing for God, of the words of Christ, and of the founding of Christ's
Church. She followed each session by reading long into each night.

By Easter of 1952, with a year of intense instruction, Sheen felt that
Bella Dodd was ready. Reasonably certain that she had been baptized
as an infant in her little native town in Italy, she received a conditional
baptism. On April 7, 1952, the anniversary of her mother's birthday
and the Monday of Holy Week, Bella Dodd was baptized by Sheen in
the baptismal font of St. Patrick's Cathedral. Afterward, Sheen heard
her first confession and gave her absolution. At Mass the next morning, he gave her Holy Communion.

Bella recalled her excitement: "With my heart pounding as one
pursued, I hastened up the steps of St. Patrick's Cathedral on Monday, April 7, 1952. Inside the open doors were a few friends who 'for
the love of God and in the way of charity' had cleared the path. . . .
Believing in the mercy of God with my whole being, I walked freely
into the baptismal font."[1035]

"It was as if I had been ill for a long time," she would later recount,
"and had awakened refreshed after the fever had gone. . . . I seemed to
have acquired a new heart and a new conscience."[1036]

Prior to that moment, Bella Dodd had lost her home, her family,
most of her friends, and much of her law practice. She was driven
to part-time jobs, such as babysitter, cashier, and dishwasher.[1037] The
Party smeared her and sought to ruin her. It literally spat on her; she
remembered the day the rabid young American Bolshevik, Gil Green,
spat in her face on Fifth Avenue.[1038]

But she persevered. Despite it all, Bella was a Catholic again, baptized, reconciled, and having received Holy Communion for the first
time in twenty-five years. "A new life had begun for me," she said.
"I had come to this life over a long, long road."[1039] She was "happier
now than ever before. . . . An order and peace of mind returned to
my life."[1040]

Now, Bella Dodd would begin the final stretch of her life just as Bishop Sheen would begin his initial stretch as a shepherd of the Church. She found redemption and reconciliation, and now she would begin making amends as a witness to what communism had done and what her Church could do.

Chapter 17

Courageous Witness

Bella Dodd would now seek to make reparation for her past choices, especially advancing a diabolical ideology. She said in anguish to Fulton Sheen, "Monsignor, I have committed such grave sins. It is my greatest wish to enter the most severe order to do penance." Sheen directed her otherwise: "No. I give you this mission: to give lectures on communism because these people are blind. They are totally blind to the dangers of communism. . . . This is the penance I give you."[1041]

The words in this book bear witness to Bella making good on that vow to Sheen. Every time she spoke to audiences, to the media, to the FBI, to Congress, she was fulfilling her penance. You could see the turmoil, the courage, the fight in her face. When asked how he would describe Bella Dodd, Robert H. Goldsborough, staff investigator for the House Committee on Un-American Activities under Congressman Francis Walter from Pennsylvania, said, "very soulful. She looked like she had the weight of the world on her shoulders. You could see, pouring out of her eyes, the sorrow of being part of the atheistic conspiracy against God."[1042]

Initially, Bella was reluctant to be a witness, as most ex-communists were. For her, there were multiple reasons for her reticence. Some of the people she would be testifying about had been her friends, and she did not want to hurt them. Also, Bella feared she was being followed not only by the FBI but by Russian secret police—that is, Trachtenberg's unit.

None of that was paranoia on Bella's part. She was being watched by friends and foes alike. The Party and Trachtenberg certainly had watched her every step, and so did the FBI, especially in the days when she had served the Party.

The FBI had her in its sights. Here is a sample from an August 6, 1948, surveillance report, which can be found in her newly released FBI file:

> Washington T-3, a reliable informant, provided information early in 1945 that JAMES L. BRANCA was to meet BELLA V. DODD, a national functionary of the Communist Political Association, on the evening of February 1, 1945 at Union Station in Washington, D. C. Washington T-4 advised that BRANCA was Chairman of the local branch of the Communist Political Association. He was observed by Special Agents Logan J. Lane and Richard L. Levy to meet DODD as planned and they were also observed to drive away from Union Station in a 1936 Plymouth Sedan bearing District of Columbia license tags No. 203-086.

The report continued with details. Replete with cryptic code-named informants and FBI special agents, it captures the real life cloak-and-dagger undercover world of American communism that Bella Dodd had lived day to day.

By the time she met Sheen, that life undercover serving the Soviets was behind her. Still, the FBI wanted to talk to her now as much as ever, as did Congress. They wanted to know what she knew.

All of this took its toll on Bella Dodd, emotionally and financially. "To be a witness against the communists," noted Bella, "you must not only suffer the attacks of opposing lawyers, but you may find yourself tied up in litigation for years. Besides that, you are subject to attack by anti-anti-communists."[1043] She had to endure "those who could not muster the charity to forgive her for having been a communist," as well as Party members who both feared and hated her for her defection. "The terrible thing afterward was that nobody trusted you," she said in

November 1968, nearing the end of her life. "People on the other side hated you and your own people just said, 'Once a Communist, always a communist.'"[1044] She told an audience: "I went back to my own Church, my mother and father had become Catholic, but I can assure you that even among Catholics—most of them received me warmly—but even among Catholics I have found people who have said, 'I don't believe she's a Catholic; I believe she's still a communist.'"[1045]

Bella said that after she saw Bishop Sheen, she was puzzled as to whether she should testify before the Senate or before the House Committee on Un-American Activities. One day she went to Sheen and said, "Look, I'm being pushed by the FBI, I'm being pushed by the committees in Washington. What shall I do?" He said to her, "Bella, I'm not going to make that decision for you. You're going to make the decision yourself. But I'll help you by giving you three things which you ought to ask yourself." He advised her: "One, ask yourself, Do I have information which is essential for the safety of my country? Two: Will I be telling the truth? Three: Will I be doing it out of malice?" In answering those three questions, said Sheen, she would be able to make the right decision. Said Bella: "At the end of the week, I began testifying."[1046]

And it was in that capacity that Bella Dodd did her best and boldest work as witness *par excellence*. One such venue was the Senate hearings on "Subversive Influence in the Educational Process,"[1047] which this book has quoted repeatedly, and where the girl from Picerno was fearless. Most of the teacher comrades called to testify in those hearings were rude, sarcastic, and refused to share any information, hiding behind the Fifth Amendment of the US Constitution. Bella Dodd more than made up for their silent mockery of the committee. She was a *tour de force*. The Senate hearings opened with this introduction from Senator Homer Ferguson: "We are here today to take testimony relating to subversion in our educational process. The training of our youth today determines the security of the nation tomorrow. The nature of this inquiry will be national in scope and will seek to determine whether or not organized subversion is undermining our educational system. We shall endeavor to sketch a broad general picture, leaving the determination of individual cases to State and local authorities."[1048]

Bella was the first witness. Mr. William Morris was the subcommittee counsel, and Benjamin Mandel, who had left the Teachers Union and the Communist Party, was director of research. After being sworn in, Bella gave a summary of her positions with the Communist Party.[1049] Thus began some of the most important hearings ever in the United States documenting the subversion of education by communists in America. Without the witness of Bella Dodd, they would have been a failure. Her presence made them a great success.

Bella testified throughout the 1950s. And a decade later, her words were being considered even when she was not in the room. At a 1964 congressional hearing on school prayer, for instance, the committee quoted an article that Bella wrote for *Guideposts*, which was excerpted into the *Congressional Record*: "It is not surprising that those against God should aim their biggest weapons at our schools. Our school years are our most impressionable. Eliminating the concept of God from education leaves the student with no basis for determining right from wrong. Therefore, I feel that the argument presented by some political and religious leaders that the Court's decision put religion back where it belongs—in the church and the home is unrealistic. American youngsters need more—not less—emphasis on spiritual values in school."[1050]

If anyone knew about the undermining of spiritual values in schools, it was former communist Bella Dodd. She would not have said such things to Trachtenberg and Foster and Browder and boys in the 1930s. But now, making good on her penance, she was warning the world.

Teaching at St. John's University and Plano

Bella also returned to teaching, albeit with a quite different voice and message than at Hunter College, joining the faculty at St. John's

University from 1953 until 1961. The first two years, she taught history and sociology in the School of Education, where her content was nothing like the harmful nonsense she had experienced at Columbia University.

In 1953, she organized the Sixteenth Annual University Lecture Series and gave a talk on communism and the United Nations Charter.[1051] In the spring of the same year, she taught a course on "Communism in Theory and Practice," which was described as "a survey of Communist philosophy, economics, and politics." It analyzed the effect of communist theory on social, juridical, cultural, and labor aspects of society. It also examined communist substitutes offered for spiritual values and analyzed the "Communist position on ethics and religion."[1052]

At St. John's, Bella also taught "Strategy and Tactics of Communism," which exposed "the method by which the Communists won the revolution in Russia, China, and other satellite countries." It examined the tactics by which "the communists confuse, weaken and immobilize the leadership in non-communist countries so that they become ready for communism."[1053]

From 1955 to 1961, Bella also taught labor law at St. John's Law School. It speaks well of St. John's to have given her this platform. And she used it well.

For a brief time, Bella taught at the University of Plano in Texas. One of her students, Timothy Carlin, described her as a popular and dynamic teacher: "The first class I ever had with her was Political Science. I went into the classroom at 2:30 and was scheduled to be out at 5:30. There were 40 students in the room, and as soon as she began to teach, she had them right in the palm of her hand. . . . There's just no other teacher like her."[1054]

Bella went further. She wanted to start her own college, one that would "train young people to meet the emergencies of the present and to understand what that present really is. I don't believe people who have not been actively engaged in the Communist movement fully understand what they're up against. I want my students to understand and not be frightened by it."[1055]

This new university would be non-sectarian: all denominations would be welcomed, but it would be God-centered. The basic ethical approach would be the Ten Commandments. "It's not going to be a question of going to college for four years and having a good time," averred Bella. "My students are going to work physically and mentally. They're going to get tough training to meet the emergencies of the present and to enable them to carry on our civilization. There must be stiff understanding of the culture of Western Europe, an understanding and appreciation of it."[1056]

According to correspondence among her friends and advocates of the university, such as Rosalind Frame, G. Edward Coey, Jim Cardiello (a partner in her law firm), Percy Greaves, Jane Rogers, Catherine Babich, and Tim Carlin (a faithful former student)—all of whom became vigorous promoters and preservers of Bella's legacy—there was even some support from Rome. Frame had written that "Rome had asked Bella to set about the task of putting together an institution of higher learning built upon TRUTH." Frame said that Bella had "corresponded with the Vatican" in the hopes of getting "the Papal blessing for our endeavors and the necessary aid from His Holiness."[1057]

The college was to be named Veritas—that is, Latin for "Truth." Unfortunately, due to Bella's health and sudden death, that university never became a reality. And yet, Bella's death gave the cause new momentum. Her friends and advocates (led by Rosalind Frame, in particular)[1058] immediately began writing one another to see if the college could be carried through in her honor and even her name. "There should be a Veritas University in tribute to Bella," wrote Percy Greaves in a May 23, 1969 letter to Rosalind Frame.[1059] Some went so far as to suggest renaming it after Bella: In a May 28, 1969 letter to Frame, Ed Coey expressed his shock and grief over her death and implored, "Yes, Bella V. Dodd University must go on. It will."[1060]

But alas, it did not. The momentum was short-lived. Bella's college was not meant to be.

Political Candidate and Attorney

As she had in 1938 for the American Labor Party, Bella ran for political office several times after she left the Communist Party. She was a candidate for justice of the Supreme Court of New York on the conservative ticket both in 1965 and 1966. An ad read: "Bella V. Dodd for Justice of the Supreme Court of N.Y. Elect a Woman of Courage to Safeguard Your Right to Justice. Vote Row D."[1061] She did not win. Then, in 1968, she was a candidate for the Nineteenth Congressional District for Congress on the same ticket but also lost.[1062]

Bella returned to law. She started the law firm of Dodd, Cardiello, and Blair in New York City and handled criminal work, immigration, and some divorce cases. She was a member of the National Association of Women's Lawyers of the New York State Bar Association. In this new law practice, she found herself inevitably the champion of the "little people," observing, "There's no question about it, your primary motivations never really change."[1063]

As for the divorce cases that she accepted, her perspective was altogether different from her days in the Communist Party, where marriage was not sacred, and where the Bolsheviks had made divorce easy. "I handled divorces before I left the Communist Party," she noted in 1968, "but I handled them very differently from the way I do today. I still handle divorce because I am a lawyer, and the law permits people to have a divorce. But I do try in every possible way to bring people to an understanding of what the purpose of life is."[1064]

She had gained a Christian perspective on marriage rather than a destructive Party perspective.

Speaking of which, Bella's law firm represented the disadvantaged, though this time in a way that Jesus saw the disadvantaged rather than how Marx viewed them. She handled many cases that involved immigration and petty legal infractions. A reporter said that when Bella Dodd fought, she really fought, noting a recent case of a Polish sailor who jumped ship in Philadelphia and came to New York seeking asylum.[1065] Immigration authorities and the State Department ordered him deported. But Bella Dodd said no. She obtained a writ of *habeas corpus* and went up to the Polish vessel that evening. Climbing a rope ladder to the main deck, she served the papers and disembarked with the sailor, who was later granted asylum.

"I'm not only a lawyer in this instance," said Bella, "I'm an adviser and a guidance counselor. If you're a lawyer alone, in problems where you're dealing with human beings, you can become a machine, and making money becomes the only thing that's important. The thing that saves you from becoming a machine and not just a money-maker is a real involvement in the problems of your client."[1066]

In full bloom, Bella Dodd was a quintessential New Yorker, a fighter, someone you would want scrapping on your side.[1067] She said, "I don't know why I am a fighter. I guess I have always been interested in human beings. The sight of any injustice burns me up."[1068]

Bella also stayed involved with writing, though this time avoiding deceptive front publications and propaganda sheets. In her later years, she was editor of the *New York Independent*. She was also on the board of governors of the Independent Bar Association and chaired its editorial board.[1069] This was a far cry from her days as an editor for *The New Masses*.

Witness to Faith

As Bella Dodd's life unexpectedly began drawing to a close in her mid-sixties, it is worth reflecting on an eloquent statement she wrote in 1952 reflecting on her Catholic conversion that year. She wrote it at the request of the National Catholic Welfare Conference, and it was printed in various publications, including the *Brooklyn Tablet*. It was titled "My Testimony to the Faith." It is worth reading in full as a powerful witness to her newfound faith, her rebirth, and her escape from the hateful force of communism:

> For many years I gave public scandal as a notorious Communist. The time has come, I think, to make equally public my rebirth in the Faith of the Roman Catholic Church and my repudiation of Communism—a repudiation whose formulation began in my own mind and conscience, thanks to God's grace, several years ago. That repudiation came to a most wholesome and definite climax when, on April 7 of this year,[1070] I was baptized at St. Patrick's Cathedral by Bishop Fulton J. Sheen. Thus, after many years of wandering in the desert, I came full circle, returning to the Faith of my father and mother—contrite, sadder, and, I pray, wiser.
>
> For years, I filled my heart and mind with spiritless Communist dogma, frenetic zeal for Communist action and propaganda, and too frequent rejections of God's grace. These wasted years now stand like forbidding wreckages in my memory. Now, I must redeem them. From Communism I turn, humbly and gratefully, to that Household of the Faith of which the greatest of all converts, Saint Paul, wrote.
>
> My remorse for straying from the gracious precincts of that household is rendered less galling by the joy of my return and by the manner of Christ's unforgettable parable. Today I understand what "felix culpa" means.
>
> During the days of my most obdurate Communism, one thread tied me to Christianity: I never failed to read the New Testament—not because I was religious or believed it was inspired, but because I deemed it the most beautiful and compelling literature I had ever read.
>
> Now, as a believer, I know that that inspired Word, under the guardianship of the Church (its authentic interpreter), holds

more hope of redemption for mankind than all the writings of social dreamers or the accumulated rantings of revolutionaries.

In a valid sense, the only worthwhile revolution is that of the Gospel. By repentance, it gives men new hearts and new minds. By grace, it recreates them. It tells us that to be good is an effort inside the soul, where God's initiative is nearer to us than we are to ourselves. It is not something external, like politics, human law, or the messages of calculating reformers who would substitute man's providence for God's.

Centuries of history should have taught me, long before this year of my deferred maturity, that "in vain they build who build without God," that man stands utterly alone in the immense cosmos when only men without God share this fellowship. The most primal and damning lie ever invented by the dirty ingenuity of man or Satan is the lie that we can eventually be like God—and that, therefore, we do not need God.

All through recorded history, men, realizing their own piteous state, their narrow limitations, their sins, have sought redemption. The world's tragedy is that they have gone so often to false redeemers. As often as men have turned to Hitler, to Mussolini, to Stalin, to Mao and their unholy ilk, they have crawled back on their hands and knees, slobbering blood, mutilated, deformed slaves—no longer men characterized—with the dignity of persons and elevated to the destiny of children of God.

That is why there is more that is good and sacred in one little Francis of Assisi—who perhaps could not pass a modern high school examination—than to whole colleges of proudly learned professors who lack charity for God and man. It is a measure of our modern failure that we set more store on science and technologies and mechanisms than on sanctity; and that we have today as few humble servants of God and of men like Il Poverello.

> I have learned from bitter experience that you cannot serve man unless first you serve God in sincerity and truth, with the faith of little children.
>
> For those misguided and starved souls, my former comrades in the Communist conspiracy of hate, I have only my pity, my prayers, and God's lovely gift of charity—not hatred. Perhaps in God's good time, some of them—I hope all of them—may one day learn, as I have, that this is the victory which overcometh the world: our Faith.

Certainly, this was Bella's greatest piece of writing. It captured her unique journey so poignantly.

For years, she had filled her heart and mind with "spiritless Communist dogma" and a toxic "frenetic zeal" for Marxist-Leninist activism, agitation, and propaganda. Those wasted years of wreckage needed to be redeemed. The Household of the Faith and inspired Word of God, under its authentic interpreter and guardian, the Church, offered the opportunity for redemption. It was truly the only worthwhile revolution, one of love. And like the prodigal son in Saint Luke's Gospel, Bella was the prodigal daughter. No, she did not drown her life in sinful pleasures, but she once supported a cause that sought to destroy what is good and holy in this world. And it was Bella's spiritual father, Fulton Sheen, who came running toward her. As a shepherd of the Church, Fulton longed to bring his stray sheep, Bella, out of the school of darkness and into the school of Christ's light. For the Catholic Church cannot be defeated, because Christ said the "gates of hell shall not prevail against it" (Matt. 16:18).

Communism, on the other hand, was the god that failed, because, as her Church had stated, it was diabolical, a Satanic scourge. As Bella noted, the most damning lie of man or Satan is that we can eventually be like God. That was the lie of false redeemers like Marx and Engels and Lenin and Hitler and Mussolini and Stalin and Mao and indeed "their unholy ilk." There was indeed more good and sacred in one little Francis of Assisi than in all the "learned professors" of Columbia Teachers College.

And as for Bella's old comrades, "those misguided and starved souls" who served the "Communist conspiracy of hate," she really did possess only pity and prayers for them and willed their eternal salvation. Faith offered the world's only hope for victory. It did for her.

Final Years

Just as she had promised to Fulton Sheen, Bella worked tirelessly and courageously in her final years to speak out against communism so others would not fall into the same darkness. Deeply repentant, she wanted to repair some of the damage done. In November 1968, not long before her death, she noted that she had indeed "traveled throughout the country and went to every single meeting, no matter how small, whether it was a PTA meeting, a Boy Scout meeting, or a Young Catholic Workers meeting. Wherever I could bring the message, I went. I crossed and re-crossed the country."[1071] In a way, Bella's zeal to snatch souls from the clutches of Lucifer's fake church on earth, communism, was reminiscent of Saint Paul, who traveled on four missionary journeys "that they (Gentiles) may be converted from darkness to light, and from the power of Satan to God" (Acts 26:18). Ironically, Bella and Saint Paul had once labored to persecute Christians, but now, they were the ones being persecuted for living their faith.

Bella's claim of traveling countrywide attending every meeting was not an exaggeration. A review of her speaking engagements after her reversion to the faith reveals travels to Oklahoma, New York, Nebraska, California, Connecticut, Indiana, Washington, Michigan, and Texas, among other states. She was associated with the Cardinal Mindszenty Foundation and the Christian Anti-Communist Crusade. Press releases beginning in 1952 and ending right before her death in 1969 show her addressing the American Legion, the Carroll Club, the Newman Club, the Oriel Society, and many other private groups and colleges.

With her rediscovered faith, Bella devoted the rest of her life to opposing communism. She worked as an attorney, a teacher, a witness in congressional hearings, a speaker exposing the techniques and methods of communism, and a candidate for congressional office. She gave numerous interviews, spoke to FBI investigators, and wrote her compelling autobiography, so aptly titled *School of Darkness*.

A warrior to the end, Bella Dodd's final years were physically difficult. She suffered from many health issues. These were obvious before she had even turned sixty. They were noticed by friends, associates, and media. According to FBI files, John Lautner, former special agent of New York, contacted an FBI agent in February 1964 and gave details of Dodd's serious health situation, including a three-month hospitalization for pleurisy, diabetes, and a myocardial infarction.[1072] At that point, Bella was only fifty-nine years old.

Her financial condition was also precarious. *The Tablet* initiated a fund drive for her in January 1964.[1073] It said that a gathering to raise money would be held on February 9 at Thirteenth Street in New York City, with an admission of ten dollars. Organizing the effort was the Apostolic Layman's League and a group associated with the Russian Institute of Fordham University. There was also an appeal for funds printed in certain sympathetic newspapers, such as Utica's (Bella had spoken there) *Observer-Dispatch*.[1074]

Bella's condition never improved. By the last year of her life, 1968–69, she was in a wheelchair. A knee infection led to septicemia, and she was hospitalized for eleven months. Along with these illnesses, she had problems with her gallbladder.[1075]

In late April 1969, she was scheduled for gallbladder surgery at St. Vincent's Hospital in New York. Most friends expected that it would be fairly routine surgery, even given her poor health. Before going to the hospital, Bella continued her normal plans, including prospects for her Veritas University. Unfortunately, the surgery went bad, which was not a surprise given her underlying conditions.

Bella struggled, going into a coma. A priest was sought out. Providentially, she momentarily came out of the coma just as she was receiving a visit at the hospital from a priest who had become an old friend—none other Fulton Sheen. Bella's spiritual father had once again come for her. As he spoke to her, she opened her eyes. Bella mustered a slight nod of recognition and a smile as Sheen touched her forehead. Sheen had brought Bella into the Church. Now, he administered to her last rites. She was now ready to return to her true native land, heaven.[1076]

Bella Dodd died on April 29, 1969, succumbing to complications from gallbladder surgery. It was the feast day of Saint Catherine of Siena, patron saint of Italy, Bella's native land. Catherine was a stigmatist, a doctor of the Church, and a bold fighter who courageously bore witness to the faith, whether admonishing the masses or the popes. Catherine, too, fearlessly spoke truth to power. She never backed down.

Born in Picerno, Italy, in 1904, Bella Dodd died in New York City.[1077]

Bella's death happened so quickly and unexpectedly that most friends missed the funeral. A Requiem Mass was offered on May 3, 1969, in the Church of the Guardian Angel in Manhattan.[1078]

A Solemn High Mass was held a month later in the Church of the Blessed Sacrament on West Seventy-First Street, with the eulogy provided by Bella's friend Monsignor John J. Cleary. He eulogized her as a woman with a "heart open to all humanity." That heart had once misguidedly drove her "into the clutches of the Communist Party," but it had also driven her to "atone for this great error." Father Cleary said that her history "reads in many ways as that of Saint Paul. For like the apostle, she squandered her early life in the service of Satan, and like him, she spent her remaining years in repentant missionary work."[1079]

Satan had once walked with Bella Dodd. But she rejected him and left him forever behind to follow the Master of her youth. A Master whose name is Jesus and who commands love, not hate. A Master whose Church spreads truth, not errors.

Bella was buried at Gate of Heaven Cemetery in Hawthorne, New York, Westchester County, among the likes of Babe Ruth, Father Malachi Martin, Billy Martin, Mary Higgins Clark, and countless other souls who lived famous and not so famous lives.

Bella Dodd knew we were in a battle. She was a brave warrior in that fight, never backing down. And she found herself in mortal combat against more than just communists in New York City. This force of evil ran deeper and darker.

Bella was asked at one of her presentations, "If you could uncover, if you could unmask the leadership of this worldwide conspiracy, who would it be?" People leaned at the edges of their seats awaiting the answer, because they knew that this tough lady spoke from the depth of her heart with deep conviction as a survivor of vicious attacks and smears and as a reborn convert to Catholicism. She was driven by the need and the zeal to unmask this atheistic criminal conspiracy. She was asked if she could name, unmask the leader. She did not hesitate to say: "I would have to say and have to identify that person as Lucifer."[1080] And thus Bella had exposed the Father of lies, Lucifer, as the leader of communism. Yes, she had exposed the one who masquerades as an angel of light as the one who spreads hatred, atheism, murder, and much more. After all, it was Lucifer who traveled side by side with Bella, leading her to only misery and darkness. He was no guardian angel, but an accuser and a deceiver, who shackled Bella for years under his false religion.

In the clash between the devil and Bella Dodd, Lucifer had his small victories along the way, but in the end, Bella Dodd prevailed. She won, Bishop Sheen won, and her Church won.

And yet, that battle against the devil of communism is not over. Bella Dodd would hope and pray that her country and her Church can persevere again. She had that faith. Like her, they need to be willing to fight with courageous witness.

ACKNOWLEDGMENTS

From Mary Nicholas

I would like to thank the following for their time, comments, and encouragement: the late Alice von Hildebrand, Richard Payne, Cardinal Raymond Burke, Charles Donohue, Robert Goldsborough, Emily Moog, Caroline Beckenhaupt, Kevin Symonds, Nina Ives, Caroline Corley, Dr. Edgar Lucidi, Frank Vasile, Armelle Sigaud, Blythe E. Roveland-Brenton, Astrid Emel, Deb Pentecost, and the late Sr. M. Stanislaus.

I am also grateful to Tamiment Library at NYU, as well as the Columbia University Archives, Harvard University Library, St. John's University Archives, the Bar Association of the City of New York Library, the New York Public Library, the Rose Library of Emory University, the Kramer Collection at the University of Michigan, the Rauner Special Collections at Dartmouth University, and the Rosalind Kress Foundation, Dr. Louise Sherby and Julie Sorokus of Hunter College Library Division, Dr. David Noebel and the Christian Anti-Communism Crusade, Nikki Maounis and Nora Curry of Camden, Maine Public Library.

In a special way, this book is dedicated to my late mother, Barbara J. Nicholas, and my aunt, Elise French Johnston, who knew communism and fought against its penetration into the United States.

From Paul Kengor

If readers (and Mary) will indulge me, I feel the need to take more space than did the humble Mary. I want to explain how the book and my partnership with Mary came about.

I was contacted on September 4, 2018, by Mary. She was frustrated by the trouble she was having with her manuscript on Bella Dodd, especially in getting a publisher. She asked if I could help—if I would be the co-author.

I noted to Mary that I was overwhelmed with other book projects (nothing has changed in that regard), and I could not in good conscience add my name to a manuscript for which she had by far done most of the work. I did, however, offer to write the foreword and recommend the book to editor friends at various publishing houses. I even emailed those friends with the manuscript and my endorsement. They declined the book. In the meantime, Mary struggled and wondered if her exceptional work studying the life of Bella Dodd would ever see the light of day.

Things suddenly changed three years later. In February 2021, I was asked by Patrick O'Hearn, my editor at TAN Books, about the second book in my current two-book contract with TAN Books. We had left the subject open. What would I like to do for that second book?

As a nudge, Conor Gallagher, the CEO of TAN Books, told me that he would like to do more books with the theme of "The Devil and . . . ," following up on the considerable success with my 2020 book for TAN, *The Devil and Karl Marx*. I told Conor that while I was open to that, I knew of few historical cases where this uniquely disturbing label fit. Karl Marx was utterly unique, not only in his diabolical ideology, but in his fascination with and even writings on the devil. I did not see this as a franchise or brand, unlike my previous set of "God and . . ." books, which included *God and Ronald Reagan*, *God and George W. Bush*, and *God and Hillary Clinton*. I told Conor and Patrick that I did, however, know of one intriguing case that might constitute a worthy exception: Bella Dodd.

I had written about Bella in chapter eleven of *The Devil and Karl Marx*. I noted that she was one of the most famous converts of Fulton Sheen, with a wonderful conversion story at that—far more edifying than anything in the life of Karl Marx. Here was a woman who left the clutches of atheistic communism and openly acknowledged that she had wrestled the devil. She called Satan himself the head of the international "atheistic criminal conspiracy" that was communism.

Unlike Karl Marx, hers was a story of redemption, of someone who overcame the devil and even joined the Catholic Church. I related to Conor and Patrick that Bella's story had been shared only in her memoirs, *School of Darkness*, published nearly seventy years ago. This was a story begging to be written, long overdue. I noted that the only other serious looks at her story were my lone chapter and an unpublished biography by Mary Nicholas, a retired MD from Maine, who had done the most comprehensive research on Bella Dodd and knew everything about her.

And it was there, I told Conor and Patrick, that there was an opportunity for that second book. I related how Mary, in 2018, had asked me to join her as co-author. I couldn't do it then, but now the time was right, especially because of some interesting developments since then: First and most important, I had begun filing FOIA requests on Bella Dodd's FBI file years prior through my colleague Bill Marshall of Judicial Watch. Bill and I had never seen an FBI file classified for so long and with so many obstacles. The secrecy was quite striking. And yet, finally, we were going to be receiving, in mid-March of that year (2021), a batch of documents from the FBI file. I shared my excitement that I was hoping to get from that file (among other things) resolution regarding Bella Dodd's alleged role in helping to infiltrate Catholic seminaries.

I told Conor and Patrick that this could be a special book. I was willing to be a co-author with Mary Nicholas, although her name must be listed first.

Conor and Patrick and others at TAN Books jumped at the idea. When I thus reconnected with Mary, via a March 4, 2021 email that was a response to her original September 4, 2018 email to me, I told her about TAN's interest and asked her to "prayerfully consider." She responded just three hours later: "Hi Paul, this is amazing and the timing could not be better considering what is going on in the Church. God never ceases to amaze us, does He not? . . . Of course I am on board."

We had a deal. From there, the book took much more time and effort than I initially realized, but after much careful work, we put it together. It was truly a team effort, and Mary was a delight to work with. We hope we have not disappointed.

So, my thanks go to Mary Nicholas primarily, as well as everyone at TAN Books—Conor Gallagher, Patrick O'Hearn, Brian Kennelly, and anyone else involved. I am also grateful to my Grove City College student assistants who helped, especially Jaclyn Nichols, and also Hannah Bowser, Emily Burke, and Timothy Hughes. Especially helpful and generous with his time was Kevin Symonds, who carefully read and reviewed the chapter on infiltration and the one that followed on Marxist influence inside the Church. He was a major help. Kevin has a terrific mind and abilities. Most significant, Kevin interviewed Johnine Leininger for us and also discovered and tracked down Sherry Finn, who we providentially were able to interview at the last minute in the copy-editing stage of this book. We are very grateful to Sherry, too, and especially her impressive memory. We are sad to report that Johnine died just before this book went to copy editing. She passed away on May 25, 2022 at age eighty-eight. May she rest in peace.

Finally, I must thank Joe Savey, who I have never personally met and rarely emailed with, but who on October 13, 2014 (the anniversary of the Miracle of the Sun in Fatima) had the extraordinary insight or intuition or something Holy Spirit-led to send me an email with a searchable PDF of Bella Dodd's memoir, *School of Darkness*. Joe had read other works of mine dealing with communism and the Church. He must have somehow known I would be needing that PDF at some point. It was providential. That PDF kindled something. I have gone back to it countless times, especially in the writing of this book. It is open now as I finish.

Joe, I don't know where you are or whatever happened to you, but thank you.

Finally, my thanks as always to my wife and family for always giving me the time and support to write, and to the Father, Son, Holy Spirit, and all the angels and saints who gave their protection and intercession. More than a few prayers went up to a diverse group of intercessors, from Our Lady of Fatima to Venerable Fulton Sheen.

NOTES

[1] Bella Dodd stated this in her self-written chapter in O'Brien, *Roads to Rome*, 43, 46.

[2] Style guides differ on the usage of uppercase or lowercase for the word "communist/Communist." Some use exclusively uppercase, which is a bad choice. This book uses uppercase if describing a person who was a formal member of the Communist Party versus lowercase for someone who was a communist ideologically but not a Party member. The distinction is very important. The vast majority of ideological communists refused to go so far as to join the Communist Party and become uppercase "Communists" because doing so required them to take a formal loyalty oath to Stalin's USSR. Those Communists who did swear the oath took a huge step beyond those communists who refused to take the leap. Likewise, this book employs an uppercase "P" for "Communist Party," including when the word "Party" is alone. When quoting from other books and documents, however, we have honored the uppercase/lowercase usage by those original sources. Admittedly, this serves to confuse readers. We wish there was a consistency on these matters, but alas, there is not.

[3] This is stated by Robert Goldsborough, Jim Demers, and Tom Mehmel, and their "The Days of Bella Dodd," posted online at https://www.youtube.com/watch?v=Yyw-M8k9UEw, and it was confirmed by Mary Nicholas in conversation with Goldsborough. Goldsborough was a staff investigator for the House Committee on Un-American Activities under Congressman Francis Walters, a Democratic congressman from Pennsylvania. Goldsborough, president of the American Research Foundation, is author of several books.

[4] Dodd, *School of Darkness*, 67.

[5] Dodd in O'Brien, *Roads to Rome*, 43.

[6] Dodd, *School of Darkness*, 233.

[7] See the language of the 1937 encyclical by Pius XI, *Divini Redemptoris*.

[8] Wikipedia and other online sources misspell the "Assunta" part of Bella's name as "Asunta." The correct spelling is "Assunta." See Dodd, *School of Darkness*, 3.

[9] See Wagner, *Black Poets of the United States*, 435 and Berry, *Langston Hughes*, 296–97.

[10] "Hearings Regarding Communist Infiltration of Minority Groups-Part 2," House Committee on Un-American Activities, U.S. House of Representatives, July 1949. Testimony of Manning Johnson, 502.

11 Stalin, *Problems of Leninism*, 134–35.

12 Printed in "The Communist Party of the United States of America: What It Is, How It Works," Committee on the Judiciary, U.S. Senate, 84th Congress, 2nd Session, April 23, 1956 (Washington, DC: GPO, 1956), 2.

13 Leon Trotsky, "Speech to the Thirteenth Party Congress," May 26, 1924, published in Allen, *The Challenge of the Left Opposition*, 161.

14 See Kennan's seminal work on this subject: "The Sources of Soviet Conduct," published in *Foreign Affairs* in July 1947, under the pseudonym "X."

15 Ronald Reagan, "The President's News Conference," January 21, 1982.

16 Ronald Reagan, "Address to the National Association of Evangelicals," March 8, 1983.

17 Denning, *The Cultural Front*, 544.

18 Vladimir Lenin, *The State and Revolution*, written August–September 1917, published in Lenin's *Collected Works*, Volume 25, 381–492.

19 Chambers, *Witness*, 242, 264.

20 Dodd, *School of Darkness*, 150.

21 This entire speech by Bella Dodd, given in Utica on May 23, 1961, can be listened to online. It is posted on YouTube under the title, "Communist Leader, Dr. Bella Dodd, Confesses to Infiltrating the Church & USA," at https://www.youtube.com/watch?v=37HgRWTsGs0.

22 The Frankfurt School was established in Frankfurt, Germany. Its leaders include the likes of Theodor Adorno, Erich Fromm, Max Horkheimer, and (among others) Herbert Marcuse. Critical texts included *Escape from Freedom*, *The Mass Psychology of Fascism*, *The Authoritarian Personality*, *One Dimensional Man*, and *Eros and Civilization*.

23 Alfred Willi Rudi Dutschke (March 7, 1940 – December 24, 1979) was the most prominent spokesperson of the German student movement of the 1960s. He, in fact, advocated a "long march through the institutions of power." He took up this concept from his interpretation of Antonio Gramsci and the Frankfurt school of Critical Theory; accordingly, the quote is often wrongfully attributed to Gramsci.

24 See Malia in the preface to his edited volume of the *Communist Manifesto*; see also Kengor, *The Devil and Karl Marx*, 345–53.

25 Chambers, *Witness*, 33.

26 Meyer, *The Moulding of Communists*, 11.

27 Chambers, *Witness*, 12.

28 Chambers, 46.

29 The Soviet Comintern was a shorthand name for the Soviet Communist International, which was set up as the headquarters to fight the world revolution that Marx and Lenin envisioned. Loen Trotsky called it the "General Staff of the World Revolution."

30 USSR Academy of Sciences, *Maxim Gorky*.

31 See Lenin's classic piece, "'Left-Wing' Communism: An Infantile Disorder," written in April–May 1920, published in his *Collected Works*, Volume 31,

17–118, posted at https://www.marxists.org/archive/lenin/works/1920/lwc/ch09.htm. The most common variation of the Lenin quotation is this: "We must hate—hatred is the basis for communism." Among others, see this quotation published in the *Congressional Record* of April 1, 1933, 1538–39, inserted by Senator Arthur R. Robinson.

32 See Pipes, *Communism*, 29–30; and the entirety of Pipes, *The Unknown Lenin*.

33 See J. M. Bochenski, "Marxism-Leninism and Religion," in Bociurkiw, *Religion and Atheism*, 11.

34 Alexander Solzhenitsyn, "Men Have Forgotten God," Templeton Prize Award speech, May 10, 1983.

35 Sheen, *The Church, Communism and Democracy*, 61, 122, 138.

36 "Open Letter to Browder By Editors," *The Catholic Worker*, Vol. VI, No. 4, September 1938, 1–2.

37 Dodd, *School of Darkness*, 224.

38 Lenin's address to the Third All-Russia Congress of the Russian Young Communist League took place in Moscow on October 2, 1920. The transcript was published in *Pravda* on October 5, 6, and 7, 1920. See Lenin's *Collected Works*, volume 31, posted at: https://www.marxists.org/archive/lenin/works/1920/oct/02.htm.

39 Testimony of Bella Dodd, "Subversive Influence in the Educational Process," US Senate, Subcommittee to Investigate the Administration of the Internal Security Act and Other Internal Security Laws of the Committee on the Judiciary, February 24, 1953, 652.

40 Testimony of Bella V. Dodd, US Senate, Subcommittee to Investigate the Administration of the Internal Security Act and Other Internal Security Laws, Committee on the Judiciary, March 10, 1953, 521.

41 Quoted by Trotsky, *The History of the Russian Revolution*, 395.

42 Testimony of Bella Dodd, "Subversive Influence in the Educational Process," US Senate, March 10, 1953, 519–20.

43 The first FOIA request from Marshall and Judicial Watch was submitted in April 2019.

44 Email correspondence with Bill Marshall, September 17, 2020.

45 Among the documents stating this in Dodd's FBI file is a September 13, 1954 official FBI memorandum prepared by FBI agent R. R. Roach, page 2 of which states that Dodd "was on the Security Index."

46 That FBI assessment appears on page 1 of R. R. Roach's September 13, 1954 official memo on Dodd.

47 The "Communist Political Association" was a name change for Communist Party USA adopted in 1944 (it was not a permanent change).

48 "Communist Trends," FBI, NYC office, October 6, 1944.

49 Bella said this on a number of occasions cited in the pages ahead, including a May 14, 1962 speech in Omaha, Nebraska.

50 Email correspondence with Bill Marshall, March 4, 2021.

[51] The Honorable John R. Rarick, *The Congressional Record—Extensions of Remarks*, May 15, 1969, E4036.

[52] Testimony of Bella Dodd, "Hearing before the Committee on Rules and Administration," US Senate, August 13, 1954, 1345.

[53] See Kengor, *The Devil and Karl Marx*, 163–320.

[54] See Kengor, *The Devil and Karl Marx*, 185–218.

[55] Bella Dodd, "Counterattack," address to the Christian Anti-Communist Crusade, Detroit, Michigan, September 1, 1961. Hereafter cited as "Bella Dodd address, Detroit, September 1, 1961."

[56] Dodd, *School of Darkness*, 240–45.

[57] Testimony of Bella V. Dodd, US Senate, Subcommittee to Investigate the Administration of the Internal Security Act and Other Internal Security Laws, Committee on the Judiciary, March 10, 1953, 521.

[58] Pope Pius IX, *Qui Pluribus (On Faith and Religion)*, November 9, 1846.

[59] For an in-depth examination, see Kengor, *Takedown*.

[60] Dodd, *School of Darkness*, 153–62.

[61] Testimony of Bella V. Dodd, US Senate, Subcommittee to Investigate the Administration of the Internal Security Act and Other Internal Security Laws, Committee on the Judiciary, March 10, 1953, 511–46.

[62] Charles Cogen, "Review of *School of Darkness*," *The Call*, 1955.

[63] See, among others, the description published in the *New York Graphic*, June 12, 1969, 1.

[64] Testimony of Bella V. Dodd, US Senate, Subcommittee to Investigate the Administration of the Internal Security Act and Other Internal Security Laws, Committee on the Judiciary, March 10, 1953, 535. Also, see the very revealing book by CPUSA head William Z. Foster *Toward Soviet America*. In this testimony, Dodd several times referred to the "Soviet America" goal of Foster and the Communist Party USA leadership.

[65] Testimony of Bella Dodd, "Subversive Influence in the Educational Process," US Senate, March 10, 1953, 520.

[66] Courtois, *Black Book of Communism*, 4. For a review of various death estimates, see Kengor, *The Devil and Karl Marx*, xvi–xviii.

[67] Jordan Peterson lecture, posted at https://www.youtube.com/watch?v=XPf WThToClo, accessed July 25, 2021.

[68] Testimony of Bella Dodd, *Scope of Soviet Activity in the United States*, Subcommittee to Investigate the Administration of the Internal Security Act and Other Internal Security Laws, U.S. Congress, House Committee on the Judiciary, 84th Congress, Second Session, June 12, 1956, 1481.

[69] Testimony of Bella Dodd, *Investigation of Communist Activities in the Philadelphia Area*, Part I, US Congress, House, Committee on Un-American Activities, November 16, 1953, 2900.

[70] Testimony of Bella V. Dodd, US Senate, Subcommittee to Investigate the Administration of the Internal Security Act and Other Internal Security Laws, Committee on the Judiciary, March 10, 1953, 545.

71 Testimony of Bella V. Dodd, 545.
72 Dodd, *School of Darkness*, 220.
73 Bella is included in an FBI document, "Purge Victims of the Communist Party USA," Federal Bureau of Investigation, United States Department of Justice, posted at https://archive.org/details/PurgeVictimsOfCPUSA/mode /2up?view=theater.
74 Louis Schaeffer, "Conversation with Bella Dodd," *New Leader*, Vol. 32, August 1949.
75 Schaeffer, "Conversation with Bella Dodd."
76 "Expulsion of Bella Dodd Approved by State CP," *Daily Worker*, June 20, 1949, 9.
77 "Expulsion of Bella Dodd Approved by State CP," 9.
78 Testimony of Bella Dodd, "Subversive Influence in the Educational Process," US Senate, March 10, 1953, 534–35.
79 Testimony of Bella Dodd, March 10, 1953, 540.
80 Testimony of Bella Dodd, March 10, 1953, 531.
81 Testimony of Bella Dodd, "Hearing before the Committee on Rules and Administration," US Senate, August 13, 1954, 1356.
82 Testimony of Bella Dodd, "Subversive Influence in the Educational Process," US Senate, March 10, 1953, 541.
83 Testimony of Bella Dodd, March 10, 1953, 541.
84 Testimony of Bella Dodd, March 10, 1953, 541.
85 Testimony of Bella Dodd, "Hearing before the Committee on Rules and Administration," US Senate, August 13, 1954, 1359–62.
86 Testimony of Bella Dodd, August 13, 1954, 1361–62.
87 See Peters, *The Communist Party*, 122.
88 Testimony of Bella Dodd, "Hearing before the Committee on Rules and Administration," US Senate, August 13, 1954, 1370–76.
89 Davis joined CPUSA most likely in 1943, the same year that Bella joined. See discussion in Kengor, *The Communist*, 91–93. On Davis and CPUSA as "the Church," see 283–84.
90 Testimony of Bella Dodd, "Subversive Influence in the Educational Process," US Senate, March 10, 1953, 540.
91 Testimony of Bella Dodd, "Hearing before the Committee on Rules and Administration," US Senate, August 13, 1954, 1345.
92 Testimony of Bella Dodd, "Subversive Influence in the Educational Process," US Senate, Committee on the Judiciary, Subcommittee to Investigate the Administration of the Internal Security Act and Other Internal Security Laws, 82nd Congress, Second Session, September 8, 1952.
93 Dodd, *School of Darkness*, 221.
94 Dodd, 222.
95 Bella Dodd address, Detroit, September 1, 1961.
96 Testimony of Bella Dodd, "Subversive Influence in the Educational Process," US Senate, March 10, 1953, 540.

97   Dodd, *School of Darkness*, 222.

98   Dodd, 222.

99   Dodd, 223.

100   This group of attorneys also represented William Z. Foster and Eugene Dennis, who were indicted for "conspiracy to advocate the overthrow and destruction of the government by force and violence."

101   Testimony of John Lautner, Subcommittee to Investigate the Administration of the Internal Security Act and Other Internal Security Laws, US Congress, House Committee on the Judiciary, 84th Congress, Second Session, 1956, 6229.

102   Dodd, *School of Darkness*, 68, 74, 139.

103   The cadre is that core within the formal Communist Parties which represents Lenin's "organization of professional revolutionaries." Meyer, *The Moulding of Communists*, 4.

104   Meyer, 4.

105   Meyer, 16.

106   Koestler, T*he God That Failed*, 26.

107   Meyer, *The Moulding of Communists*, 21.

108   Meyer, 26.

109   Meyer, 25.

110   Dodd, *School of Darkness*, 223.

111   Dodd, 223.

112   Dodd, 223.

113   Dodd, 223.

114   Dodd, 223–24.

115   Dodd, 230.

116   Dodd, 230.

117   Dodd, 1–2.

118   Bella Dodd address, Detroit, September 1, 1961.

119   Dodd, *School of Darkness*, 6.

120   Dodd, 6.

121   Dodd, 9.

122   Dodd, 9–10.

123   Dodd, 10.

124   Dodd, 10.

125   Soup schools were for the poor and named such because they served soup as a main lunch menu item.

126   Bella Dodd, "I Found Sanctuary," in O'Brien, *Roads to Rome*, 44.

127   Dodd, 44.

128   Bella Dodd address, Detroit, September 1, 1961.

129   Dodd, "I Found Sanctuary," in O'Brien, *Roads to Rome*, 44.

130   Dodd, 45. The principal was a Dr. Condon from P.S. (Public School) 12 near her house.

131 Avelino de Almeida, *O Seculo*, May 15, 1917. Quoted in Socci, *The Fourth Secret of Fatima*, 12.

132 Kondor, *Fatima in Lucia's Own Words*, 124.

133 Kevin Symonds, "Fatima and Russia's 'Errors,'" National Review Online, May 13, 1917.

134 Sheen, *Communism and the Conscience of the West*, 200.

135 A non-FBI source, Israel Amter, testified in the 1941 Rapp-Coudert Committee hearings that there were twenty-five thousand communists in New York State. See Testimony Israel Amter, Rapp-Coudert Hearings, Kheel Center Library, Cornell University, Files of the Teachers Union of the City of New York, Box 71a, Folder 1, 1766.

136 This document was an inter-office "Office Memorandum: United States Government," basically an official internal FBI document, written by J. P. Coyne to "Mr. Ladd," who was D. M. Ladd. Both were high-level government officials. Ladd was the FBI's assistant director.

137 Dodd, "I Found Sanctuary," in O'Brien, *Roads to Rome*, 45.

138 In 1935, a communist shop paper, *The Challenge*, appeared, published by the Young Communist League at the school. See *New York Journal American*, December 4, 1935. *The Challenge* was mentioned in congressional hearings. Tima Ludins, a teacher at Evander Childs, also a graduate of Hunter, was asked "Have you or have you not ever edited a Communist publication named and called *The Challenge?*" She refused to answer. See Testimony of Bella Dodd, "Subversive Influence in the Educational Process," US Senate, March 10, 1953, 509.

139 The lead counsel was Robert Morris. See Testimony of Bella Dodd, "Subversive Influence in the Educational Process," US Senate, March 10, 1953, 519–20.

140 Masthead of *The Call*.

141 Dodd, *School of Darkness*, 22. *The Call* contained the first articles on birth control to appear in an American newspaper. See Johnson, *Marxism in United States History*, 95.

142 See Louis C. Fraina, "Bolsheviki Power Comes From Masses, Says Louis C. Fraina," *The Evening Call* 11, no. 35 (February 11, 1918): 7, http://www.marxisthistory.org/history/usa/parties/spusa/1918/0209-fraina-powerfrommasses.pdf.

143 John Reed was instrumental in the formation of the Communist Party of America. See Testimony of Ben Gitlow, *Investigation of Un-American Propaganda in the United States*, US Congress, House Special Committee on Un-American Activities, 76th Congress, First Session, September 7, 1939, 4530.

144 *The Evening Call* 11, no. 25 (January 13, 1918): 1, 3, https://www.marxists.org/history/usa/parties/spusa/1918/0130-call-reednamedconsul.pdf.

145 *The New York Call Magazine*, March 25, 1917, 6, http://www.marxisthistory.org/history/usa/parties/spusa/1917/0325-hillquit-russiaisfree.pdf.

146 *The Evening Call* 11, no. 125 (May 26, 1918): 6, http://www.marxisthistory
.org/history/usa/parties/spusa/1918/0526-pippa-rosepastorstokes.pdf.

147 "Bolshevism v. Democracy in Education," *The Call*, 17 October 1918, 5,
https://www.marxists.org/archive/paul/1918/10/17.htm.

148 Smedley, the lover of the spy Richard Sorge, was "perhaps the most effective
secret agent in Soviet History." She is mentioned in *Witness* by Whittaker
Chambers as active in the first espionage apparatus in the East. See Evans,
Stalin's Secret Agents, 91. Demonstrating the pervasive connections between
Stalin's spy apparatus and the cultural Marxism that penetrated the United
States, Richard Sorge was an assistant at the Frankfurt School's Institute of
Social Research.

149 *The Call* was subsidized by the radical American Fund for Public Service,
known as the Garland Fund. See Samson, *The American Fund for Public
Service*, 67.

150 Dodd, *School of Darkness*, pp. 23–24.

151 Bella Dodd, "I Was a Communist Teacher," *The American Weekly*, May 3,
1953, 4. One must wonder whether the atmosphere at Evander Childs combined with her exposure to *The Call* contributed to the eroding of religion in
Bella's mind and heart.

152 Dodd, "I Found Sanctuary," in O'Brien, *Roads to Rome*, 46.

153 Bella Dodd address, September 1, 1961, Detroit. Babbitts was a term used
by Sinclair Lewis, a socialist, in his novel of the same name. It was a dis-
paraging term for someone in the middle class, particularly a conformist
businessman.

154 Dodd, "I Found Sanctuary," in O'Brien, *Roads to Rome*, 45.

155 Dodd, 44–45.

156 Dodd, 47.

157 Dodd, *School of Darkness*, 24.

158 Dodd, 30–31.

159 Bella Dodd address, September 1, 1961, Detroit.

160 Lenin, "Socialism and Religion," *Novaya Zhizn*, December 3, 1905.

161 Dodd, *School of Darkness*, 28–29.

162 Karl Marx, "The Communism of the *Rheinischer Beobachter*," *Deutsche-
Brusseler-Zeitung*, September 12, 1847, published as Marx, "The Social Principles of Christianity," in Padover, *On Religion: Karl Marx*, 93–94.

163 Marx wrote this in his 1844 *Estranged Labor*. See Raines, *Marx on Religion*,
11; and version posted online at https://www.marxists.org/archive/marx/wo
rks/1844/manuscripts/labour.htm/.

164 Bella Dodd, "I Was a Communist Teacher," *The American Weekly*, May 3,
1953, 4.

165 Bella Dodd address, September 1, 1961, Detroit.

166 Address by Bella Dodd, "Communism in Education," First Annual Hoosier
Counter-Subversive Seminar, Indianapolis, Indiana, October 1954. Eagle

Forum Library and Archives. Hereafter cited as "Bella Dodd address, Indianapolis, October 1954."

167 Bella Dodd address, Indianapolis, October 1954.

168 Dodd, *School of Darkness*, 28.

169 Dodd, 28.

170 Dodd, 239.

171 Bella Dodd, "I Was a Communist Teacher," *The American Weekly*, May 3,
1953, 4. Strong, like Barrows, worked in the US Education Office. She was
a journalist and activist, named Moscow correspondent for the International
News Service, and wrote for *The Nation*. She lived and traveled throughout
Russia and China. See http://depts.washington.edu/labhist/cpproject/Anna
Strong.shtm.

172 Testimony of Bella Dodd, "Subversive Influence in the Educational Process,"
US Senate, March 10, 1953, 18.

173 Testimony of Bella Dodd, 18.

174 Bella Dodd address, Utica, New York, May 23, 1961, available at https://
www.youtube.com/watch?v=pKBj0s6OZec. Hereafter cited as "Bella Dodd
address, Utica, New York, May 23, 1961."

175 The National Women's Trade Union League was organized in 1903 to support women's groups that wanted to organize labor unions. They fought for
safer factory conditions, and Eleanor Roosevelt was a member. WTUL organized the First International Congress of Working Women in Washington,
DC, October 28, 1919. Margaret Dreir Robins was President of WTUL
from 1907 to 1922. Her name is prominent in the Soviet Bureau Report and
the Lusk Committee files. For additional information, see http://ocp.hul.har
vard.edu/ww/nwtul.html.

176 *Hunter Bulletin*, "New Debate Award to Be Tried for Annually," Archives of
Hunter College, 1872–2008, Box 29, Folder 1, Archives & Special Collec-
tions, Hunter College Libraries, Hunter College of the City University of
New York, New York City, October 3, 1924, 1.

177 *Hunter Bulletin*, "Miss Parks to Address Discussion Club," Archives of Hunt-
er College, 1872–2008, Box 29, Folder 1, Archives & Special Collections,
Hunter College Libraries, Hunter College of the City University of New
York, New York City, April 17, 1924, 2.

178 Class collaboration was a term used by Lenin and others to signify cooperation with capitalists, as opposed to "class struggle" against them. See https://
www.marxist.com/class-collaboration-with-capital-or-class-struggle-against
-capital.htm.

179 Hunter Bulletin, Archives of Hunter College, 1872–2008, Box 29, Folder 1,
Archives & Special Collections, Hunter College Libraries, Hunter College
of the City University of New York, New York City, "Final Ottinger Night
on Class Collaboration," November 19, 1925, 3.

180 Testimony of Mildred R. Garvin, "Subversive Influence in the Educational
Process," US Senate, Committee on the Judiciary, Subcommittee to Inves-

tigate the Administration of the Internal Security Act and Other Internal Security Laws, 82nd Congress, Second Session, September 8, 1952, 126–27.

181 Dodd, *School of Darkness*, 28.

182 Dodd, 30.

183 Dodd, "I Found Sanctuary," in O'Brien, *Roads to Rome*, 45.

184 Dodd, *School of Darkness*, 27.

185 Bella V. Dodd as featured guest on State of the Nation, interviewed by Hardy Burt and Ralph de Toledano, *Facts Forum*, February 1955, 35.

186 Dodd, *School of Darkness*, 28. *The Nation* magazine was edited or greatly influenced by people in close "collaboration with Willi Münzenberg and his men. See Koch, *Double Lives*, 27.

187 Dodd, *School of Darkness*, 31.

188 Dodd, 33.

189 Dodd, "I Found Sanctuary," in O'Brien, *Roads to Rome*, 46.

190 Dodd, *School of Darkness*, 22.

191 Dodd, 30.

192 *Vassar Miscellany* IX, no. 7 (October 14, 1924): 1.

193 *Vassar Miscellany* IX, no. 7 (October 14, 1924): 4.

194 The social hygiene movement arose from a progressive crusade against prostitution and venereal disease. *Social Diseases and Marriage* (1904) by Dr. Prince A. Morrow (1846–1913), a New York dermatologist, became the central document for the American Social Hygiene Association, a union of public-health physicians, educators, and anti-prostitution activists funded by John D. Rockefeller. The modern movement to place sex education grew out of this. See Boyer, *The Oxford Companion to United States History*.

195 Dodd, *School of Darkness*, 32.

196 Bella Dodd address, Utica, New York, May 23, 1961.

197 Bella Dodd address, Indianapolis, October 1954.

198 Dodd, *School of Darkness*, 27.

199 Dodd, "I Found Sanctuary," in O'Brien, *Roads to Rome*, 47.

200 *Hunter Bulletin*, Archives of Hunter College, 1872–2008, Box 29, Folder 1, Archives & Special Collections, Hunter College Libraries, Hunter College of the City University of New York, New York City, March 6, 1924, Vol. XI, No. 19, 1.

201 *Hunter Bulletin*, Archives of Hunter College, 1872–2008, Box 29, Folder 1, Archives & Special Collections, Hunter College Libraries, Hunter College of the City University of New York, New York City, April 23, 1925, Vol. XII, No. 26, 9.

202 *Hunter Bulletin*, Archives of Hunter College, 1872–2008, Box 29, Folder 1, Archives & Special Collections, Hunter College Libraries, Hunter College of the City University of New York, New York City, October 3, 1924, 1.

203 *Hunter Bulletin*, Archives of Hunter College, 1872–2008, Box 29, Folder 1, Archives & Special Collections, Hunter College Libraries, Hunter College

of the City University of New York, New York City, June 25, 1925, Vol. XII, no. 32, "Year's Activities Reviewed at Council Day Chapel," 1.

204 See Goldsborough, *The Days of Bella Dodd*.

205 See, among others, S. Doniger, "Soviet Education and Children's Literature," *The Journal of Educational Sociology* 8, no. 3 (1934): 162–67; and Barry Popkin, "Give me four years to teach the children," December 16, 2013, https://www.barrypopik.com/index.php/new_york_city/entry/give_me_fo ur_years_to_teach_the_children.

206 Some scholars argue that there was an early Marxist party in the United States. Oakley Johnson stated: "The United States was the world's second country to have a functioning Marxist party. The Workingmen's Party of the United States was organized on July 19-23, 1876, in Philadelphia." See Johnson, *Marxism in United States History*, 17. See also Bella Dodd address, September 1, 1961, Detroit.

207 Hillquit, *History of Socialism in the United States*, 17.

208 Johnson, *Marxism in United States History*, 2. Oakley was a communist. Correspondence from Bella enclosed a list of people for him to contact at Hunter. Letter from Bella Dodd to Oakley Johnson, June 11, 1934, Department of Special Collections, Oakley Johnson Collection, Box 13, Stony Brook University.

209 Hilquit, *History of Socialism in the United States*, 55–56. Owen's philosophy had an impact on European Marxists, and Engels called him one of the great utopians who "worked out his proposals for the removal of class distinction systematically and in direct relation to French materialism." See Engels, *Socialism*, 51–52.

210 Marx, *Capital*, 353.

211 See Noyes, *History of American Socialisms*, 39; and Kengor, *Takedown*, 14–17.

212 Kengor, *Takedown*, 14–16.

213 Wright believed that the goal of education should be "rational, republican education; free for all at the expense of all; conducted under the guardianship of the state, at the expense of the state, for the honor, the happiness, the virtue, the salvation of the state." See Blumenfeld, *NEA Trojan Horse in American Education*; and Carlton, "The Workingmen's Party of New York City, 1829-31," 401–15.

214 Van Der Sears, *My Friends at Brook Farm*, 6.

215 See Flynn, *A Conservative History of the American Left*, 52–62.

216 See Flynn, *A Conservative History of the American Left*, 19; and also discussion in Kengor, *Takedown*, 14–31.

217 Later, nearly thirty Fourierist communities were established throughout America during the 1840s.

218 Ralph Waldo Emerson, "Fourierism and the Socialists," http://www.emerso ncentral.com/fourierFourierism_and_the_socialists.htm Internet.

219 Brownson, *The Works of Orestes A. Brownson*, 441–42.

[220]   Brownson, 441–42.

[221]   See Power, *Religion and Public Schools.*

[222]   Bella mentioned Horace Mann in one of her addresses: "Of course, Antioch has long been an extremely liberal college from the time it was founded by Horace Mann and there has (sic) been Communists at Antioch, there has been a unit at Antioch since the days when I was active in the Teachers Union." Bella Dodd address, Indianapolis, October 1954.

[223]   Karl Marx, *New York Daily Tribune*, September 27, 1853, https://www.marxists.org/archive/marx/works/1853/02/25.htm.

[224]   Karl Marx, "Articles On China, 1853-1860," *New York Daily Tribune* June 14, 1853, https://www.marxists.org/archive/marx/works/1853/06/14.htm.

[225]   Karl Marx, "On Strikes and the Value of Labor," *New York Daily Tribune*, September 27, 1853, https://www.marxists.org/archive/marx/works/1853/09/27.htm.

[226]   Karl Marx, "Trade or Opium," *New York Daily Tribune*, September 20, 1858, https://www.marxists.org/archive/marx/works/1858/09/20.htm.

[227]   Marx, *The Communist Manifesto*, 71.

[228]   Marx, 71–72, 75.

[229]   See the long and in-depth discussion of Dewey by Paul Kengor in *Dupes*, 80–91.

[230]   See the analysis by Richard Weikart, "Marx, Engels, and the Abolition of the Family," 665–66.

[231]   Engels, *The Origin of the Family*, 67.

[232]   See, among others Geiger, *The Family in Soviet Russia*, 11; and Weikart, "Marx, Engels, and the Abolition of the Family," 657.

[233]   Bella Dodd address, Indianapolis, October, 1954.

[234]   Foster, *History of the Communist Party of the United States*; and Bella Dodd address, Indianapolis, October 1954.

[235]   *Vassar Miscellany* XLIV, no. 4 (February 19, 1915): 3; *Vassar Miscellany* I, no. X (November 10, 1915): 4.

[236]   *Columbia Spectator* XLIX, no. 23 (December 20, 1900): 4

[237]   *Vassar Miscellany* XLIV, no. 4 (February 19, 1915): 3; *Vassar Miscellany* XII, no. 17 (3 December 1927): 2. It said the letters "Tell Story of Mild Massachusetts Utopia of Cultured Farmers."

[238]   See, for example, *The Nation* 37, no. 947 (August 23, 1883): 168.

[239]   Bell, *Marxian Socialism in the United States*, 17.

[240]   Chambers, *Witness*, 741–42.

[241]   The 46th Annual Report of the Fabian Society ended March 31, 1929.

[242]   The White Sea Canal was one of Stalin's pet projects which had 300,000 slave laborers rounded up by the OGPU. Solzhenitsyn estimated that during the winter of 1931–1932 alone, 100,000 of these slaves perished in the horrific ravine, frozen to death. Since the numbers were too large to conceal, it received bad press. Enter Willi Münzenberg, who was taken to the Moscow-Volga canal. By the end of summer, leading writers were writing about the

marvels of socialist engineering. Shortly after, leading lights such as the Webbs gushed about this example of socialist compassion. See Koch, *Double Lives*, 29.

243   The Fabian Society was named after Quintus Fabius Maximus, a Roman general whose strategies of wearing down opponents by delays led to the Roman victory over Hannibal. Shaw distinguished "the highly respectable Fabian Society" from other radical groups. Yet the Fabians' creed remained radical: its goal was the "reorganization of society" with the extinction of private property and industrial capital from individual and class ownership, redistributing them to the "community for the general benefit." See Stormer, *None Dare Call It Treason*, 26. Also see Martin, *Fabian Freeway*, 24, 29.

244   Venture, Fabian Colonial Bureau, March 1949, quoted in Martin, *Fabian Freeway*, 85.

245   Martin, *Fabian Freeway*, 29.

246   Martin, 29.

247   Martin, 29.

248   Martin, 29.

249   Pease, *The History of the Fabian Society*, 7.

250   Shaw, *The Fabian Society*, 3.

251   See Shaw, *The Rationalization of Russia*, 112.

252   Shaw, 73, 76, 80–81, 109, 132n.

253   Shaw wrote this in a letter to the editor of *The Manchester Guardian*, published March 2, 1933. He was the author and lead signatory of the letter, followed by twenty other signers. As the letter itself stated, Shaw and all of the twenty others had been "recent visitors to the USSR."

254   Wells, *An Experiment in Autobiography*, 215, 667, 687–89. Wells made several trips to the USSR in the 1920s and 1930s. See Wells, *Russia in the Shadows*, 160–62.

255   Initiated by Rev. WDP Bliss, he founded the American Fabian society, in association with Shaw, "to unite social reforms and lead the way to a conception of socialism." Bliss, *Encyclopedia of Social Reform*, 578.

256   Martin suggested that any serious consideration of Fabian Socialism needed to address "the very real possibility that Communists early saw their opportunity to introduce communism into America through the Anglo-Saxon tradition." Martin, *Fabian Freeway*, 127.

257   Bella Dodd address, Utica, New York, May 23, 1961.

258   Bella Dodd address, Detroit, September 1, 1961. See also "Barack Obama, Fabian Socialist," *Forbes*, November 3, 2008.

259   Bella Dodd address, Indianapolis, October 1954.

260   Professor Herron, a Congregationalist pastor, joined with Eugene Debs in 1900 to organize the Socialist Party of America. His wealthy mother-in-law, Mrs. Carrie Rand, established the endowment for the founding of the Rand School of Social Science. Johnson, *Marxism in United States History*, 105.

261   Hubbard, *Political and Economic Structures*, 112; Johnson, *Marxism in United States History*, 12.

262   *The Intercollegiate Socialist*, October-November 1915.

263   Martin, *Fabian Freeway*, 179–180.

264   Martin, *Fabian Freeway*, 190.

265   Laski wrote in his "Appreciation of the Communist Manifesto" for the Labour Party, "Who, remembering these [policies of high taxation and centralization of credit] were the demands of the Manifesto [issued by Marx and Engels in 1848], can doubt their inspiration[?]"

266   "Socialist Society Will Convene Here Intercollegiate Organization to Hold Annual Session—Hillquit to Speak," *Columbia Daily Spectator* LX, no. 64 (December 14, 1916); and "Socialist to Discuss Trust Problems," *Columbia Daily Spectator* LV, no. 98 (February 14, 1912). Perhaps the most significant notice appeared in the January 19, 1918, edition of the *Columbia Daily Spectator* announcing that J. Sack, Director of the Russian Information Bureau, would speak on the Russian Revolution. Also see *Columbia Daily Spectator* XLI, no. 68 (January 17, 1918): 4.

267   *New York Call*, November 19, 1921. Otto Kahn, the financial titan, capitalist, and director of the American International Corp, in a speech to the League for Industrial Democracy, offered the socialist revolutionaries a friendly hand and shared goals: "What you radicals and we who hold opposing views differ about is not so much the end as the means, not so much what should be brought about as how it should, and can, be brought about." See Sutton, *Wall Street and the Bolshevik Revolution*, 21.

268   Dodd, *School of Darkness*, 64.

269   After the war, the Intercollegiate Socialist Society faced declining membership. Members reoriented the society from a purely educational group to education plus activism. "Production for Use and Not for Profit" is an expression *Vassar Miscellany* used to describe the "progressive" program of Norman Thomas in 1924.

270   Johnpoll, *The League for Industrial Democracy*, 22. In correspondence of the League for Industrial Democracy, they addressed each other as "comrade." See Correspondence of Morton Alexander to Harry Laidler, 10/12/27, Tamiment holdings, the Tamiment Library & Robert F. Wagner Labor Archives; Printed Ephemera, Box 12 "Humanity," TAM 49, Box 2, Folder 1; Correspondence Laidler to Berger, 9/29/27, 9/12/27; Correspondence Scott Goelal to Laidler, 10/12/27; Correspondence Goodman to Laidler, 1/20/28; Laidler to Goodman, 9/2/27; Henry to Laidler, 10/22/27; and Laidler Letters, See Tamiment holdings, the Tamiment Library & Robert F. Wagner Labor Archives, New York NY. TAM 49, Box 2, Folder 1.

271   Testimony of Whittaker Chambers, Hiss trial, quoted in Chambers, *Witness*, 693.

272   Merton, mercifully, would not remain a communist. Chambers, however, took a terrible trajectory, to the point of becoming a Soviet spy.

273   Merton, *The Seven Storey Mountain*, 153–57.

274   Merton, 194.

275   Edwards, *The Dewey School*, 436.

276   Edwards, 437.

277   John Dewey, "Schools of Utopia," *New York Times*, April 23, 1933.

278   As a measure of their influence, Bowers estimated that Kilpatrick alone taught almost thirty-five thousand students between 1909 and 1938. See Bowers, *The Progressive Educator and the Depression*, 11.

279   Quoted by Carson, *A Basic History of the United States*, 91.

280   Mann, "Lectures and Annual Reports on Education," 210.

281   Hall, *Life and Confessions of a Psychologist*, 219.

282   Dennis Cuddy, "The Conditioning of America," *The Christian News*, December 11, 1989.

283   Sutton, *America's Secret Establishment*, 84. It is interesting the Wundt studied in Tugingen, where later debates among the Frankfurt School developed.

284   Lionni, *The Leipzig Connection*, 8.

285   Anderson, *Encyclopedia of Activism and Social Justice*, 451.

286   Martin, *The Education of John Dewey*, 67–70.

287   Louis Budenz, also a defector, commented on John Dewey's pragmatism: "While not a communist philosophy, [it] serves as a convenient cover under which the Reds may operate and also under which they may win allies in the educational field. It rejects the supernatural and declares there is no absolute good or absolute truth."

288   Mayhew, *The Dewey School*, 436, 428; Dewey, *A Common Faith*, 87.

289   National Education Association, Bulletin 41, Recommendations of the NEA regarding the teaching of history, 1913.

290   Dewey, *Democracy and Education*, 82.

291   Dewey, 63.

292   Ryan, *John Dewey and the High Tide of American Liberalism*, 284.

293   See the chapter, "The Redemption of John Dewey," in Kengor, *Dupes*, 104–9, which covers the Dewey Commission involving Leon Trotsky.

294   The article was John Dewey, "Why I Am Not a Communist," *Modern Monthly* VIII (April 1934): 135–7. It was reprinted in Hook, *The Meaning of Marx*, 89.

295   See Rockefeller, *John Dewey*, 439. Also for insights on this, see Diggins, *The Promise of Pragmatism*, 399; and Westbrook, *John Dewey and American Democracy*, 468–69.

296   For an in-depth examination of this subject, see the three chapters on Dewey in Kengor, *Dupes*, 80–109.

297   Kilpatrick was a prominent academic who rose to the level of a college president. He got his doctorate in the philosophy of education from Columbia Teachers College and then also ended up as a full professor there (1918), where he became a protégé and expert on Dewey's work. Kilpatrick lived a long life (1871–1965). Though less prominent, Thomas Woody was also

respected. Woody earned an MA and PhD in the history of education from Columbia Teachers College in 1918.

298   Professor Brickman, who died in 1986, was a specialist in comparative and international education. He taught for roughly twenty years each at New York University and University of Pennsylvania, and did seminars and courses at numerous other colleges, including Columbia.

299   Brickman, *John Dewey's Impressions*, 17.

300   Brickman, 17–18.

301   Brickman, 18.

302   Brickman, 18.

303   See Edmondson, *John Dewey and the Decline of American Education*, 10–11.

304   Strong's trip took place either in 1922 or 1923.

305   Brickman, *John Dewey's Impressions*, 19.

306   Pinkevich, *The New Education in the Soviet Republic*, vi.

307   See Woody, *New Minds, New Men?* 47–48.

308   During his trip to the USSR in the summer of 1928, Dewey attended an educational conference organized by Professor Kalashnikov. They apparently hit it off quite well. It was ten days after the conference that Kalashnikov sent Dewey the two-volume encyclopedia.

309   Quoted in Martin, *The Education of John Dewey*, 354.

310   Brickman, *John Dewey's Impressions*, 19–20, 58n.

311   For a recent popular book that underscored one such important case, which included (as usual) a number of Columbia people, see Shlaes, *The Forgotten Man*, 47–84, particularly page 50.

312   Brickman, *John Dewey's Impressions*, 72.

313   The collection of essays was published in 1929 by The New Republic, Inc., as well as in subsequent Dewey writings and a later (1964) volume edited by William W. Brickman, produced and published by the Teachers College at Columbia University. The quotes cited herein are taken from the Brickman edition. See earlier note for full citation.

314   See the extended discussion in Kengor, *Dupes*.

315   Brickman, *John Dewey's Impressions*, 74, 89.

316   Brickman, 47, 74–75, 99.

317   Brickman, 74–75.

318   Brickman, 79.

319   Bella Dodd address, Detroit, September 1, 1961.

320   Dodd, *School of Darkness*, 43, 58.

321   George Counts was the author of many books, but especially illuminating were *American Education Through the Soviet Looking Glass, The Challenge of Soviet Education; Khrushchev and the Central Committee Speak on Education; America, Russia and the Communist Party in the Post-War World; The Challenge of Soviet Education, New Russia's Primer* and *I Want to Be Like Stalin*. From 1927 to 1932, Counts was associate director of International Education at Columbia. Under its auspices, he traveled to the Soviet Union in

1927 and 1929. In 1933 and 1934, the Institute sponsored school sessions at Moscow University when he was on the advisory council. The program worked in cooperation with the Soviet Union's commissariat of education and its official tourist agency, Intourist. At the Moscow sessions, hundreds of American educators were propagandized by Communist experts. See Gannon, *Biographical Dictionary of the Left*, 289.

322   George Counts was in the First American Trade Union Delegation to Soviet Russia in 1927. See *Pravda*, September 15, 1927, posted at https://www.mar xists.org/reference/archive/stalin/works/1927/09/15.htm.

323   Social Frontier/Frontiers of Democracy, https://www.tcrecord.org/frontiers. Professor George W. Hartman said that "*Social Frontier* was under the direct financial control of the Progressive Educational Association, one of the most important professional bodies of the United States." See Testimony, George W. Hartman, Associate Professor of Educational Psychology, Teachers College, Columbia University, Hearings before a Special Committee on Un-American Activities, *Investigation of Un-American Propaganda Activities in the United States*, US Congress, House, Committee on Un-American Activities, 76th Congress, First Session, 1939, 6849.

324   William H. Kilpatrick, "Launching the Social Frontier," *Social Frontier* 1, no. 1 (1934): 2.

325   C. A. Bowers, "The Ideologies of Progressive Education," *History of Education Quarterly* 7, no. 4 (1967): 465.

326   Theodore Brameld, "Karl Marx and the American Teacher," *Social Frontier* II, no. 2 (November 1935): 53–56. Brameld was an outstanding supporter of the communist front, the American League Against War and Fascism.

327   Dodd, *School of Darkness*, 42–43.

328   Dodd, 175. On the NEA, see Blumenfeld, *NEA Trojan Horse in American Education*.

329   Bella Dodd address, Detroit, September 1, 1961.

330   Bella Dodd address, Detroit, September 1, 1961.

331   Bella Dodd address, Indianapolis, October 1954.

332   Bella Dodd address, Indianapolis, October 1954.

333   Foster, *Toward Soviet America*, 316.

334   Testimony of Bella Dodd, "Subversive Influence in the Educational Process," US Senate, Committee on the Judiciary, Subcommittee to Investigate the Administration of the Internal Security Act and Other Internal Security Laws, 82nd Congress, Second Session, September 8, 1952, 7.

335   Bella Dodd address, Indianapolis, October 1954.

336   "Progressive School Called Tool of Reds," *New York Times*, January 18, 1953, 24.

337   Bella Dodd address, Detroit, September 1, 1961.

338   "Trial of an Ex-Communist," *Tidings*, November 23, 1956.

339   Bella Dodd, "I Was a Communist Teacher," *The American Weekly*, May 3, 1953, 4.

340   Wittner, *Conquest of the American Mind*, 39, quoted in Skousen, *The Naked Capitalist*, 70.

341   *The American Weekly*, "I Was a Communist Teacher," Bella Dodd, May 3, 1953, 5.

342   Dodd, *School of Darkness*, 40.

343   Academic Records confirmed from the Office of the Registrar of Columbia University.

344   Dodd, *School of Darkness*, 43.

345   From 1900 to 1903, William Beveridge was the director of the London School of Economics and future father of the welfare state and the National Health Service.

346   Dodd, *School of Darkness*, 39.

347   Dodd, 44.

348   Dodd, 44.

349   Chambers, *Witness*, 463–69; Weinstein, *Perjury*, 70.

350   Harry Dexter White was responsible for (among other things) establishing a hostile US policy toward prewar Japan in order to draw the United States into war as an ally of Soviet Russia and for delaying financial support to Generalissimo Chiang Kai-Shek, causing the triumph of Chairman Mao Tse Tung's Communist regime. He also handed over to the Soviets the Allied Military mark plates, causing a $250,000,000 deficit paid out by the US Treasury. White was the most important member of the Silvermaster spy ring and the most highly placed asset the Soviets possessed in the American government.

351   Columbia University Bulletin of Information, Twenty-third Series no. 26, March 25, 1933, 22. Columbia University, Rare Books & Manuscript Library. History, Economics, Public Law and Social Science, Courses Offered by the Faculty of Political Science for Winter and Spring 1933–1934.

352   Moley came into prominence as the personal adviser to President Roosevelt and his special delegate to the London Conference, 1933. Together with Rexford Tugwell (*The Emerging Constitution*), he is considered one of the leading liberals to push for national planning and collective responsibility. After a time, Moley broke with Roosevelt and published "Propaganda vs. Education," a July 13, 1953 essay, in *Newsweek*.

353   Columbia University Bulletin of Information, Twenty-third Series no. 26, March 25, 1933, 24. Columbia University, Rare Books & Manuscript Library. History, Economics, Public Law and Social Science, Courses Offered by the Faculty of Political Science for Winter and Spring 1933–1934.

354   Columbia University Bulletin of Information, Twenty-third Series no. 26, March 25, 1933. Columbia University, Rare Books & Manuscript Library. History, Economics, Public Law and Social Science, Courses Offered by the Faculty of Political Science for Winter and Spring 1933–1934. Shotwell was a member of the Advisory Committee of Postwar Foreign Policy, "a secretive committee created on February 12, 1942, to prepare recommen-

dations for President Franklin D. Roosevelt on post World War II foreign policy. The committee appointed various subcommittees. Chairman of the committee was Secretary of State Cordell Hull; vice chairman, Under Secretary of State Sumner Welles, Dr. Leo Pasvolsky (director of the Division of Special Research) was appointed Executive Officer. The committee included Dean Acheson, Ester C. Brunauer, Lauchlin Currie, Laurence Duggan, Alger Hiss, Harry Hopkins, Philip Jessup, Archibald MacLeish, George C. Marshall, Henry Wadleigh, Henry Agard Wallace, and Harry Dexter White. Several experts were brought in from outside the State Department, such as Hamilton Fish Armstrong, Isaiah Bowman, Benjamin V. Cohen, Norman H. Davis, and James T. Shotwell." "Advisory Committee of Postwar Foreign Policy," Conservapedia, July 23, 2019, https://www.conservapedia.com/Advisory_Committee_of_Postwar_Foreign_Policy.

355   Martin, *Fabian Freeway*, 508.

356   FBI Files accessed January 26, 2018, https://www.fbi.gov/. See also Gary Bullert, "The Frankfurt School Demythologized?" *The Journal of Social, Political, and Economic Studies* (Spring 2011): 90–100, which discusses Lynd's FBI files.

357   Root, *Collectivism on the Campus*, 102. Professor Lynd's name came up in the Rapp-Coudert hearings, where it was remarked that at a meeting of the Committee for the Defense of Public Education that he assailed by innuendo the capitalist basis of the US economy and that fascist powers are the bulwark of capitalism. Committee for the Defense of Public Education, Investigation Files of the Rapp-Coudert Committee. See Tamiment holdings, the Tamiment Library & Robert F. Wagner Labor Archives, New York. Tamiment Library R-7860, "Report of Memorandum Nov. 11, 1940." See Lewis S. Feuer, "The Frankfurt Marxists and the Columbia Liberals," *Survey* (Summer 1980): 156–76. See also Thomas Wheatland, "The Frankfurt School's Invitation from Columbia University: How the Horkheimer Circle Settled on Morningside Heights," *German Politics & Society* 22, no. 3 (72), (Fall 2004): 1–32.

358   Correspondence from the Institute of Social Science to Dr. Frank Fackenthal, Columbia University Archives, Box 549, Folder 8.

359   Through the IPR, Jessup was associated with Alger Hiss, Harry Dexter White, Frederick Vanderbilt Field, and Lauchlin Currie. He was assistant secretary-general of the United Nations Refugee and Rehabilitation Administration (UNRRA) conference in 1943 and the Bretton Woods Conference in 1944. He was also a member of the Council on Foreign Relations. A member of the American delegation to the San Francisco United Nations charter conference in 1945, he was also the US representative on the United Nations committee that drafted the World Court statute. Continuing as a technical expert and adviser to various UN commissions, Jessup prepared the State Department's "White Paper" on China, when the CCP were overrunning the mainland of China, and later became one of the early advo-

cates for the admission of PRC to the United Nations. President Truman appointed Jessup as United States delegate to the United Nations in 1951. His appointment was not approved by the Senate because of Jessup's openly pro-Communist record. President Truman circumvented the Senate action by assigning Jessup to the United Nations on an "interim appointment." When the Eisenhower administration took office, the State Department approved the appointment of Jessup as US candidate for the UN World Court, where he served from 1961 until 1970. US Congress, Senate, Committee on the Judiciary, Subcommittee to Investigate the Administration of the Internal Security Act and Other Internal Security Laws, *Institute of Pacific Relations.*, 82ⁿᵈ Congress, First Session.

Philip Jessup was "Chairman of the Institute for Pacific Relations (IPR) American council from 1939 to 1940 and chairman of its Pacific council from 1939 to 1942. Both councils were high-level policy-making bodies. The Senate Internal Security Subcommittee found in 1954 that "the IPR has been considered by the American Communists and by Soviet officials as an instrument of Communist policy, propaganda and military intelligence. . . . A small core of officials and staff members carried the main burden of IPR activities and directed its administration and policies. Members of the small core of officials and staff members who controlled the IPR were either Communists or pro-Communists." Through the IPR, Jessup was closely associated with Alger Hiss, Harry Dexter White, Frederick Vanderbilt Field and Lauchlin Currie. "Philip Jessup," Conservapedia, May 26, 2022, https://www.conservapedia.com/Philip_Jessup.

Dodd spoke of Jessup in an address in Detroit: "At present the World Court on which we have one member and that member Philip Jessup of Amerasia fame if you remember. Amerasia fame was that Philip Jessup helped Jaffe [note] to get two rooms full of documents from the State Department. Philip Jessup is the one American on the world court 15 judges." Bella Dodd address, Detroit, September 1, 1961.

360   Evans, *Blacklisted by History*, 399.

361   Bernstein, *The Frankfurt School*, 45.

362   Bernstein, 45.

363   Jay, *The Dialectical Imagination*, 3–4.

364   The "Institute," which in German is rendered "Institut," is alternately called the "Institute *of* Social Research" and the "Institute *for* Social Research." Wikipedia has long used the latter, whereas leading academic historians of the Institute, such as Martin Jay and Rolf Wiggershaus, have used the former. Consistent with the leading authorities, in this book we use "Institute of Social Research."

365   Jay, *The Dialectical Imagination*, 39.

366   Wiggershaus, *The Frankfurt School*, 144-45.

367   Wiggershaus, 145.

368   Jay, *The Dialectical Imagination*, 39.

369 Wiggershaus, *The Frankfurt School*, 146.

370 See Jay, *The Dialectical Imagination*, xxix; and Wiggershaus, *The Frankfurt School*, 402–3.

371 Columbia University, Central Files, Institute of Social Research, Box 549, Folder 8, 1942–1947, Correspondence Dr. Pollock to Dr. Fackenthal, June 1, 1942. The term "Critical Theory" was adopted by the Institute during its World War II exile at Columbia University as a "cover word for the Institute's commitment to the study of Marxism." Chandler, *Shadow World*, 23. In 1933, when Nazis came to power in Germany, the members of the Frankfurt School fled. Most came to New York City, and the Institute was re-established there in 1933 with help from Columbia University. The members of the Institute connected with Columbia University included Max Horkheimer, Frederick Pollock, Theodor W. Adorno, and Herbert Marcuse, among others. These members, gradually through the 1930s, though many of them remained writing in German, shifted their focus from Critical Theory about German society to destructive criticism about every aspect of that society to Critical Theory directed toward American society. Another important transition came with the onset of war. Some worked for the government, including Herbert Marcuse, who became a key figure in the OSS (the predecessor to the CIA). Horkheimer and Adorno moved to Hollywood. See Correspondence of Frederick Pollock to Dr. Fackenthal, June 1, 1942, Columbia University, Rare Books & Manuscript Library, Correspondence, Institute of Social Science research Central Files, University Archives #001, Box 549, Folder 8. Adorno was a graduate of the Tavistock Institute. See " Tavistock – Why America Folded Like a Cheap Tenet," henrymakow.com, August 2, 2021, https://www.henrymakow.com/2021/08/tavistock-why -america-folded.html?_ga=2.39931041.2005330966.1628014996-332419 165.1626369449.

372 Columbia University, Central Files, Institute of Social Research, Box 549, Folder 8, 1942–1947, "Ten Years on Morningside Heights, A Report on the Institute's History 1934-1944." Adorno was to play a significant part in US history when the Truman administration charged McCarthy with "hysteria and witch hunting," noting that this phenomenon occurred periodically in American history. This was at the beginning of Senator Tydings's committee to investigate McCarthy's charges of sabotage.

In 1954, Columbia University held a seminar on McCarthyism, and the historian Richard Hofstadter, using Theodor Adorno's tract "The Authoritarian Personality," explained that the phenomenon was a projection onto society of groundless fears. Hofstadter followed up with "The Paranoid Style in American Politics" in 1964, which was to become the left's bible for explaining McCarthyism. See Evans, *Blacklisted by History*.

A prominent radical who came under the influence of the Frankfurt School icon Herbert Marcuse is Angela Davis (mentioned earlier), a devotee of the Black Panthers. Like many leftist intellectuals, she was a professor at

UCLA. The Soviet dissident Bukovsky recalls that while jailed in Vladimir Prison, he read the *Pravda* headlines: "Free Angela Davis!" He said that reading it alone was comical when people were sentenced to prison for a word of criticism. To him, the scenario was "clear as crystal, a straightforward case of being an accomplice to murder. She gave her Black Panther boyfriend the arms with which he killed court officials and policemen in order to escape." Then, the stinger from *Pravda*: "Member of the Central Committee of the Communist Party of the USA, Angela Davis."

373   Root, *Collectivism on the Campus*, 46.

374   Root, 102.

375   Dodd, *School of Darkness*, 41.

376   Academic records confirmed from the Office of the Registrar of Columbia University.

377   Dodd, *School of Darkness*, 44–45.

378   Dodd, 47.

379   Dodd, 52.

380   Dodd, 51.

381   Dodd, 239.

382   Dodd, 51.

383   "A Belated Tribute," *Hunter Bulletin*, Archives of Hunter College, 1872–2008, Box 29, Folder 1, Archives & Special Collections, Hunter College Libraries, Hunter College of the City University of New York, New York City, Vol. 15, no. 19, Feb. 23, 1928.

384   Dodd, *School of Darkness*, 52.

385   Address by Bella Dodd, Utica, New York, May 23, 1961.

386   Address by Bella Dodd, Utica, New York, May 23, 1961.

387   Dodd, *School of Darkness*, 53.

388   Dodd, 53.

389   Dodd, 55.

390   Dodd, 54.

391   Dodd, 56–57.

392   Dodd, 56.

393   Dodd, 57.

394   US Congress, House, Committee on Education and Labor, Special Subcommittee of the Committee on Education and Labor House of Representatives, *Investigation of Teachers Union Local No. 555 UPWA-CIO*, 80th Congress, Second Session, September 29, 1948, 355. See also Address by Bella Dodd, Utica, New York, May 23, 1961.

395   Dodd, *School of Darkness*, 58.

396   Dodd, 59.

397   Dodd, 60.

398   Dodd, 60.

399   Dodd, 60.

400   Bella Dodd address, Detroit, September 1, 1961.

401 Bella Dodd address, Detroit, September 1, 1961.

402 Karl Marx and Friedrich Engels, *Manifesto of the Communist Party* (Redford, Virginia: Wilders Publications, 2007), 27.

403 Testimony of Bella Dodd, "Subversive Influence in the Educational Process," US Senate, Committee on the Judiciary, Subcommittee to Investigate the Administration of the Internal Security Act and Other Internal Security Laws, 82nd Congress, Second Session, September 8, 1952, 28.

404 Testimony of Bella Dodd, "Subversive Influence in the Educational Process," US Senate, March 10, 1953, 18.

405 Mary Nicholas interview with Frank Vasile, January 14, 2016. Vasile gave an interview with Dr. Stanley Monteith (†2014) of *Liberty Radio* on April 20, 2011, together with Dr. Edgar Lucidi (who also knew Dodd). The interview is available on *YouTube* in four parts by user "Eclipse 1958" in April 2011.

406 Dodd, *School of Darkness*, 162.

407 "Mother, Ex-Red, Denied Custody of 5 Children," *The Morning Herald*, July 1, 1955, 6.

408 Bella Dodd address, Detroit, September 1, 1961.

409 Sheen, *Communism and the Conscience of the West*, 141.

410 Lincoln, *Red Victory*, 476–77.

411 See Geiger, *The Family in Soviet Russia*, 253–54.

412 Geiger, 253–54.

413 See lengthy discussion in Kengor, *Takedown*, 32–52.

414 Vladimir Lenin stated this in *Pravda*, June 16, 1913, republished according to the original *Pravda* text in *Lenin, Collected Works*, Vol. 19, 235–57.

415 See chapter 7 of Trotsky's classic *The Revolution Betrayed*.

416 See Geiger, *The Family in Soviet Russia*, 254. The figure on some Soviet women having as many as twenty abortions is breathtaking but no doubt accurate.

417 See Kengor, *Takedown*, 32–36.

418 Kengor, 19–30.

419 Alexandra Kollontai, "International Women's Day," *International Socialist Review*, January-February 2013, 29–34.

420 Kollontai, *Communism and the Family*, 10, cited in Geiger, *The Family in Soviet Russia*, 51.

421 Pope Pius XI, *Divini Redemptoris*.

422 See Taylor Sullivan, "Election Special: The Politics of Margaret Sanger," Margaret Sanger Papers Project, October 31, 2016, https://sangerpapers.wordpress.com/tag/socialism/.

423 Foster, *The Twilight of World Capitalism*, 150.

424 *Investigation of Communist Activities in the Philadelphia Area*, Part I, US Congress, House Committee on Un-American Activities, November 16, 1953, 2904–5.

425 *Investigation of Communist Activities in the Philadelphia Area*, Part I, US Congress, House Committee on Un-American Activities, November 16, 1953, 2904–5.

[426] Bella Dodd address, Indianapolis, October 1954.

[427] Dodd, *School of Darkness*, 59–61.

[428] Testimony of Bella Dodd, "Subversive Influence in the Educational Process," US Senate, March 10, 1953, 511–13.

[429] As stated by Howard Selsam: "It is a tenet of Marxism-Leninism that a follower thereof must accept the discipline of the Communist Party . . . and that in so accepting Party discipline one must abide by and adhere to decisions, positions, and interpretations of the Party." See, among others, *Herbert Brownell Jr., Attorney General of the U.S., Peititioner, v. Jefferson School of Social Science*, 1955, Testimony of Howard Selsam, 41.

[430] Testimony of Bella Dodd, *Investigation of Communist Activities in the Philadelphia Area*, Part I, US Congress, House Committee on Un-American Activities, 83rd Congress, June 17, 1953, 2887.

[431] Testimony of Bella Dodd, 1747.

[432] Testimony of Bella V. Dodd, US Senate, Subcommittee to Investigate the Administration of the Internal Security Act and Other Internal Security Laws, Committee on the Judiciary, March 10, 1953, 512.

[433] Testimony of Bella Dodd, *Investigation of Communist Activities in the Philadelphia Area*, Part I, US Congress, House Committee on Un-American Activities, 83rd Congress, June 17, 1953, 2888.

[434] Hitler also confessed that he had learnt from "their [the Bolshevik] methods . . . the workers' sports clubs, the industrial cells, the mass demonstrations, the propaganda leaflets written especially for the comprehension of the masses; all of these new methods of political struggle are essentially Marxist in origin All I had to do was to take over these methods and adapt them to our purpose." Rauschning, *Hitler Speaks*, 185–86.

[435] Martin (M.Y.) Latsis, the ferocious Latvian. In *The Red Terror in Russia*, published in Berlin in 1924, the Russian historian and socialist Sergei Melgunov cited Latsis, one of the first leaders of the Cheka, as giving this order to his thugs on November 1, 1918. This quote has been cited by a number of sources. Most recently, see Courtois, *Black Book*, 8. Among other sources that cite this quote, see Brown, *Doomsday 1917*, 173; and Leggett, *The Cheka*, 463–68.

[436] Testimony of Bella Dodd, *Investigation of Communist Activities in the Philadelphia Area*, Part I, US Congress, House Committee on Un-American Activities, 83rd Congress, June 17, 1953, 2904

[437] Bella Dodd address, Utica, New York, May 23, 1961.

[438] Reeves, *America's Bishop*, 131–32.

[439] Reeves, 132.

[440] Riley, *Fulton J. Sheen*, 109.

[441] Reeves, *America's Bishop*, 145.

[442] Riley, *Fulton J. Sheen*, 114.

[443] Reeves, *America's Bishop*, 134.

[444] Riley, *Fulton J. Sheen*, 114.

445 Koch, *Double Lives*, 47.

446 Bella Dodd address, Indianapolis, October 1954. Testimony of Bella V.
     Dodd, US Senate, Subcommittee to Investigate the Administration of the
     Internal Security Act and Other Internal Security Laws, Committee on the
     Judiciary, March 10, 1953, 2896. See also *Herbert Brownell, Attorney General
     of the U.S. v Jefferson School of Social Science*, 17.

447 Testimony of Bella Dodd, *Investigation of Communist Activities in the Colum-
     bus, Ohio Area*, US Congress, House Committee on Un-American Activi-
     ties, 83rd Congress, First Session, June 17, 1953, 1746.

448 Sources: "Investigation of Un-American Propaganda Activities in the United
     States," Special Committee on Un-American Activities, House of Represen-
     tatives, 78th Congress, Second Session, on H. Res. 282, App. Part IX, Vol. 1
     (Washington, DC: GPO, 1944), 431; and "Guide to Subversive Organiza-
     tions and Publications (and Appendices), revised and published December
     1, 1961, to supersede Guide published on January 2, 1957 (including In-
     dex), prepared and released by the Committee on Un-American Activities,
     U.S. House of Representatives, Washington, DC, 87th Congress, 2nd Session,
     House Document No, 398, 26–88.

449 Engdahl was in Europe propagandizing the Scottsboro case. Cf. Dodd,
     School of Darkness, 66. Also see Samson, *The American Fund for Public Ser-
     vice*, 88–89. Engdahl died in Moscow in 1932.

450 Dodd, *Roads to Rome*, 43.

451 Dodd, *School of Darkness*, 67.

452 Silverman was an international operative for the Soviet Union. Testimony
     of Bella Dodd, *Investigation of Communist Activities in the Columbus, Ohio
     Area*, U.S. Congress, House Committee on Un-American Activities, 83rd
     Congress, First Session, June 17, 1953, p. 1746. See also Matthews collec-
     tion, Officers of the American Peace Mobilization, *Daily Worker*, Sept. 2.

453 See Tamiment holdings, the Tamiment Library & Robert F. Wagner Labor
     Archives, New York, PE.036, Printed Ephemera, Box 12.

454 Tamiment holdings, Box 12.

455 Earl Browder was Former General Secretary of the Central Committee of
     the Communist Party of the Soviet Union, General Secretary of the Com-
     munist Party of the United States, and a member of the Central Executive
     Committee, a member of the presidium of the Communist Internation-
     al. Dispelling any pretense of independence of the American Communist
     Party from the USSR, in sworn testimony before Congress, he admitted
     that *all* Communist Parties followed "one single line" of the Comintern (the
     Communist International) and are in "full agreement on their main line of
     approach to the world situation." Investigation of Un-American Propaganda
     Activities in the U.S. Special Committee on Un-American Activities, House
     of Representatives, Seventy-Sixth Congress, First Session on H. Res. 282, to
     Investigate the Extent, Character, and Objects of Un-American Propaganda
     Activities in the U.S., Appendix, Vol. 1, 1940, 830.

456   Testimony of Bella V. Dodd, US Senate, Subcommittee to Investigate the Administration of the Internal Security Act and Other Internal Security Laws, Committee on the Judiciary, March 10, 1953, 4.

457   Dodd, *School of Darkness*, 69.

458   Dodd, 86.

459   Koch, *Double Lives*, 30.

460   Koch, 30–32.

461   Koestler, *The Invisible Writing*, 208. Koestler regarded Münzenberg as the equivalent of Goebbels (p. 212). See also David Caute's informative study *The Fellow-Travellers* on the concept of fellow travelers, in which Caute goes into detail on the remote-control radicalism developed among intellectuals during the interwar era.

462   Hawkins, *Communism Challenge to America*, 34.

463   Investigation of Un-American Propaganda Activities in the United States, Special Committee on Un-American Activities, House of Representatives, Second Session on H. Res. 282, Appendix IX, Communist Front Organizations, Washington, DC, 1944, 261–62.

464   Bella belonged to the following fronts: American Peace Mobilization; American Youth Congress, Celebration of 15 Years of Biro Bidjan, Conference on Constitutional Liberties in America, Consumers National Federation, Greater New York Emergency Conference on Inalienable Rights, the Summer Milk Fund (Labor Defender), Win the War Programs, Jefferson School of Social Science, (School for Democracy), Joint Committee for Trade Union Rights, Armistice Day Peace Rally, Mobilize for Peace, International Labor Defense, The Teachers Non-Partisan Committee for the Election of Isidore Begun, Call to Conference on Constitutional Liberties in America, National Federation for Constitutional Liberties, Negro Labor Victory Committee, New Masses, Keep America Out of War (New York Peace Association), Progressive Committee to Rebuild the American Labor Party, Schappes Defense Committee, Trade Union Committee for the Continuation of the Work Projects Administration, Wartime Budget Conference, The Care of Children in Wartime.

465   "Liberty in Chains," *Daily Worker*, August 23, 1940, 3.

466   *Columbia Spectator* L, no.38 (October 10, 1926), 1. Flynn was a founding member of the ACLU and a member of the IWW.

467   *New Masses* 3, no. 6 (October 1927), 1.

468   "Massachusetts the Murderer," *The Nation*, August 31, 1927.

469   "80th Anniversary of Legal Lynching Lesson of the Fight to Free Sacco and Vanzetti Free Mumia Abu-Jamal! Free All Class-War Prisioners!" Rachel Wolkenstein (blog), http://www.rachelwolkenstein.net/sacco-and-vanzetti -trial.html.

470   Felix Frankfurter, "The Case of Sacco and Vanzetti," *The Atlantic*, March 1927, https://www.theatlantic.com/magazine/archive/1927/03/the-case-of -sacco-and-vanzetti/306625/.

471 Bella Dodd address, Utica, New York, May 23, 1961.

472 Bella Dodd address, Utica, New York, May 23, 1961.

473 Bella Dodd, *School of Darkness*, 228.

474 Frank Vasile, Radio Liberty, April 20, 2011, https://www.youtube.com/wa tch?v=AEmzdQrlAZI. Personal Interview of the author with Frank Vasile, January 14, 2016. Vasile was a friend of Bella Dodd's and gave an interview with Dr. Stanley Monteith of *Liberty Radio* on April 20, 2011, together with Dr. Edgar Lucidi (who also knew Dodd). The interview is available on *You-Tube* in four parts by user "Eclipse 1958" in April, 2011. *Radio Liberty* has a record of the interview as well, posted at http://www.radioliberty.com/apr11 .htm.

475 Bella V. Dodd as featured guest on State of the Nation, interviewed by Hardy Burt and Ralph de Toledano, *Facts Forum*, February 1955, 35. This was confirmed by Robert Goldsborough: "Bella Dodd and the other leaders were told that if this communications line broke down during World War II, that they could go to the three very wealthy capitalists who lived in the Waldorf Astoria Towers in New York City and that any one of these three men could give her, could give them, the leadership of the Communist Party USA, direct orders on what to do. They did not have to, they did not need to go through the Kremlin." Robert Goldsborough, president of the American Research Foundation, author of several books, "The Days of Bella Dodd," Youtube video, April 29, 2012, posted by 88kmitchell, https://www.youtu be.com/watch?v=Yyw-M8k9UEw.

476 Skousen, *The Naked Capitalist*, 1. Notes by Skousen after several interviews with Dr. Dodd in 1968. Those handwritten notes are in the possession of Mary Nicholas.

477 Dodd, *School of Darkness*, 73.

478 Testimony of Bella V. Dodd, US Senate, Subcommittee to Investigate the Administration of the Internal Security Act and Other Internal Security Laws, Committee on the Judiciary, March 10, 1953, 308.

479 Taylor, *Reds at the Blackboard*, 18.

480 The members of the American Party voted to create the Trade Union Unity League in 1929, obediently responding to the Sixth World Congress's order that Communist parties create revolutionary unions to compete with the conservative AFL. See Taylor, *Reds at the Blackboard*, 18. Dodd called this the Classroom Teachers Association. See Taylor, *Reds at the Blackboard*, 16, 21; and Dodd, *School of Darkness*, 72. Note the phrase "victimized teachers." These were teachers accused of propagating communist philosophy in the schools, demonstrating a common technique of the left.

481 Rank and File Slate, June 6, 1934, Kheel Center Library, Cornell University, Files of the Teachers Union of the City of New York, Box 25, Folder 9.

482 See multiple testimonies in *Subversive Influence in the Educational Process*, US Congress, Senate Committee on the Judiciary, Subcommittee to Investigate the Administration of the Internal Security Act and Other Internal

Security Laws, 83rd Congress, First Session, March 26, 27, 30, and April 1, 1953, 663–793.

483   Testimony of Bella Dodd, *Investigation of Communist Activities in the Philadelphia Area*, Part I, US Congress, House, Committee on Un-American Activities, November 16, 1953, 2905.

484   Testimony of Bella Dodd, "Subversive Influence in the Educational Process," US Senate, Committee on the Judiciary, Subcommittee to Investigate the Administration of the Internal Security Act and Other Internal Security Laws, 82nd Congress, Second Session, September 8, 1952, 527.

485   Testimony of Bella Dodd, 20–21.

486   Dodd, *School of Darkness*, 72.

487   "Teachers Protest Payless Furlough," *New York Times*, January 6, 1934, 1.

488   "School Teachers Besiege City Hall," *New York Times*, January 16, 1934, 23.

489   Dodd, *School of Darkness*, 73–74.

490   Testimony of Bella Dodd, "Subversive Influence in the Educational Process," US Senate, Committee on the Judiciary, Subcommittee to Investigate the Administration of the Internal Security Act and Other Internal Security Laws, 82nd Congress, Second Session, September 8, 1952, 19.

491   Bella Dodd, "Uninformed Idealists Soft Touch for Reds," *Saturday Evening Post*, 1953, 10.

492   Dodd, *School of Darkness*, 139.

493   Dodd, 22.

494   Testimony of Bella V. Dodd, US Senate, Subcommittee to Investigate the Administration of the Internal Security Act and Other Internal Security Laws, Committee on the Judiciary, March 10, 1953, 518.

495   Testimony of Bella V. Dodd, 513. Shortly after he began work at the *Daily Worker*, a comrade pulled Louis Budenz aside and let him in on the secret of the "real party." "That is the term he used one day in what seemed a sudden burst of confidence. 'There is a conspiratorial apparatus in the Party,' he said in a quiet and even oily manner. Then he compared the Communist organization to a submarine, in which the part seen by the people and the press was the periscope. The major part of the Party — 'not in numbers, but in responsibility' —was hidden beneath the waves of anonymity and aliases."

496   Dodd, *School of Darkness*, 73, 43.

497   Bella Dodd address, Detroit, September 1, 1961.

498   "Frown on Big 'Hunger March,'" The Sideliner, *The Pittsburgh Courier*, December 3, 1932, 6; and "Hunger March Halted at Gate of White House," *The Baltimore Afro-American*, December 3, 1932, 2.

499   "The Results of 'The Five –Year Plan in Four Years' in Agriculture." S. V. Kosior, general secretary of the Central Committee of the Ukrainian Communist Party, January 22, 1933, Document 180–187, https://msuweb.montclair.edu/~furrg/research/ukfaminedocs97.pdf. The single best film that shows both the story of the kulaks and the rest of people of Russia is *The Russian*

Story by Edvins Snore. With some narration by survivors of the Holodomor, https://www.imdb.com/title/tt1305871/.

[500] Walter Duranty, "Russians Hungry, but Not Starving," *New York Times*, March 31, 1933, 13.

[501] Walter Duranty, "Big Soviet Crop Follows Famine," *New York Times*, September 16, 1933, 14.

[502] See Douglas McCollam, "Should This Pulitzer Be Pulled?" *Columbia Journalism Review*, November/December 2003; Conquest, *The Harvest of Sorrow*, 308–9; Taylor, *Stalin's Apologist*, 205; and Levin, *Unfreedom of the Press*, 166–70.

[503] Dodd, *Roads to Rome*, 48.

[504] Shaw in Statement to the London General Press, 1932, quoted in Conquest, *Harvest of Sorrow*, 316.

[505] Bella Dodd address, Utica, New York, May 23, 1961.

[506] See Barron, *Operation Solo*, xv, 339–40.

[507] Dodd, *School of Darkness*, 140.

[508] Lenin's address to the Third All-Russia Congress of the Russian Young Communist League took place in Moscow on October 2, 1920. See Lenin's *Collected Works*, volume 31, https://www.marxists.org/archive/lenin/works/1920/oct/02.htm.

[509] Bella Dodd address, Detroit, September 1, 1961.

[510] Iversen, *The Communists and the Schools*, 59.

[511] Linville was a radical and expressed the desire to "De-Kaiserize education." See Board of Education the City of New York to the Board of the Superintendents, December 27, 1920, Kheel Center Library, Cornell University, Files of the Teachers Union of the City of New York, 5015, Box 42, Folder 2.

[512] Bella Dodd address, Detroit, September 1, 1961.

[513] The Wikipedia entry (retrieved February 24, 2022) states: "The New York City Teachers Union or "TU" (1916–1964) was the first New York labor union for teachers, formed as 'AFT Local 5' of the American Federation of Teachers, which found itself hounded throughout its history due largely to co-membership of many of its members in the Communist Party USA (CPUSA)."

[514] "Subversive Influence in the Educational Process," US Senate, Committee on the Judiciary, Subcommittee to Investigate the Administration of the Internal Security Act and Other Internal Security Laws, 82nd Congress, Second Session, September 8, 1952, 342.

[515] Testimony of Henry R. Linville, executive director, New York Teachers Guild, Investigation of Un-American Propaganda Activities in the United States, Hearings before a Special Committee on Un-American Activities, House of Representatives, 76th Congress, First Session, on H. Res. 282, Volume 8, 1939, 6859. See Draper, *The Roots of American Communism*, 315–18.

516   Testimony of Bella Dodd, "Subversive Influence in the Educational Process," US Senate, Committee on the Judiciary, Subcommittee to Investigate the Administration of the Internal Security Act and Other Internal Security Laws, 82nd Congress, Second Session, September 8, 1952, 343.

517   Testimony of Henry R. Linville, executive director, New York Teachers Guild, Investigation of Un-American Propaganda Activities in the United States, Hearings before a Special Committee on Un-American Activities, House of Representatives, 76th Congress, First Session, on H. Res. 282, Volume 8, 1939, 6859. See Draper, *The Roots of American Communism*, 6872–78.

518   See Iversen, *The Communists and the Schools*, 21. Whittaker Chambers said Scott Nearing was in his study group, which met in the Rand School on East 15th Street. Nearing had been a socialist instructor of economics at the University of Pennsylvania and was dismissed. He visited the Soviet Union, lived in Moscow for a time, and, believing that the Soviet system worked, joined the American Communist Party. He eventually left it due to the party discipline and factionalism. Benjamin Mandel left teaching and by 1935 was on the payroll of the Communist Party. See Taylor, *Reds at the Blackboard*, 14. He "went into full-time Party work as Industrial Organizer of District 2 and helped organize the New Jersey textile strike in 1926." Iversen, *The Communists in the Schools*, 22. Whittaker Chambers knew him under the name Bert Miller. In 1925, Mandel signed Chambers's Party card on entrance into the Party and worked closely with Chambers when "Miller" was business manager of the *Daily Worker*. He joined Linville in the 1935–36 Teachers Union fight and joined him in the Teachers Guild. Later, expelled from the Party, he became a strong anti-communist and researcher for the Special House Committee on Un-American Activities in 1939, when Chambers and Mandel would again meet as Mandel questioned Chambers during the Hiss-Chambers case. He later joined the staff of the Rapp-Coudert Committee. Chambers, *Witness*, 207.

519   *Monthly Review*, The Education Workers' International, October 1928, 33.

520   Testimony of Bella Dodd, "Subversive Influence in the Educational Process," US Senate, Committee on the Judiciary, Subcommittee to Investigate the Administration of the Internal Security Act and Other Internal Security Laws, 82nd Congress, Second Session, September 8, 1952, 13–17.

521   Myra Page, "Fascism in American Education," Educational Workers' International, no. 2 (October 1928), 32.

522   *Daily Worker* II, no. 207 (Nov. 19, 1924), 3.

523   Taylor, *Reds at the Blackboard*, 14.

524   Testimony of Bella Dodd, "Subversive Influence in the Educational Process," US Senate, Committee on the Judiciary, Subcommittee to Investigate the Administration of the Internal Security Act and Other Internal Security Laws, 82nd Congress, Second Session, September 8, 1952.

525   *The Union Teacher* IX, no. 9 (May 1932).

526   Testimony of Henry R. Linville, executive director, New York Teachers Guild, Investigation of Un-American Propaganda Activities in the United States, Hearings before a Special Committee on Un-American Activities, House of Representatives, 76th Congress, First Session, on H. Res. 282, Volume 8, 1939, 6859. See Draper, *The Roots of American Communism*, 6860.

527   Iversen, *The Communists and the Schools*, 22; and Testimony of Henry R. Linville, executive director, New York Teachers Guild, Investigation of Un-American Propaganda Activities in the United States, Hearings before a Special Committee on Un-American Activities, House of Representatives, 76th Congress, First Session, on H. Res. 282, Volume 8, 1939, 6859. See Draper, *The Roots of American Communism*, 6860.

528   "Why the Education Workers League," *The Education Worker* 1, no. 1 (May 1931), 1. Children were seen not as individuals or part of a family, but as a class to be haggled over.

529   Why the Education Workers League," 3.

530   Dodd, *School of Darkness*, 73.

531   Testimony of Bella V. Dodd, US Senate, Subcommittee to Investigate the Administration of the Internal Security Act and Other Internal Security Laws, Committee on the Judiciary, March 10, 1953, 518.

532   Testimony of Bella Dodd, "Subversive Influence in the Educational Process," US Senate, Committee on the Judiciary, Subcommittee to Investigate the Administration of the Internal Security Act and Other Internal Security Laws, 82nd Congress, Second Session, September 8, 1952, 20.

533   Testimony of Bella V. Dodd, US Senate, Subcommittee to Investigate the Administration of the Internal Security Act and Other Internal Security Laws, Committee on the Judiciary, March 10, 1953, 518.

534   Testimony, Bella Dodd, Subversive Influence in the Educational Process, Hearings before the Subcommittee to Investigate the Administration of the Internal Security Act and Other Internal Laws to the Committee on the Judiciary, US Senate, 82nd Congress, Second Session, September 8, 1952, 6.

535   Dodd, *School of Darkness*, 81

536   Testimony of Bella Dodd, *Investigation of Communist Activities in the Columbus, Ohio Area*, US Congress, House Committee on Un-American Activities, 83rd Congress, First Session, June 17, 1953, 1745.

537   June 16, 1932, meeting of the Executive Board.

538   US Congress, House, Committee on Un-American Activities, *Investigation of Un-American Propaganda Activities in the U.S., 76th Congress*, First Session, 1939, 6872–73. Report of the Special Grievance Committee of the Teachers' Union, on H. Res. 282, Volume 8.

539   Asked if the Communist Party was like any other political party, Dodd insisted: "No; it isn't. The Communist Party in America is a conspiracy. It is both a legal and an extra-legal and an illegal apparatus. It is a mechanism for bringing about the preconditions for a Marxist-Leninist victory in America." Senator Ferguson: "Then it is revolutionary and believes in revolution

to accomplish its purpose; that is, the overthrow of this Government; is that correct?" Mrs. Dodd: "There is no doubt about that. And when the Communist Party issues statements all it does is to wait for the reactionaries in this country to create the preconditions and to establish violence, and all they do then is to defend themselves against the violence, that is a complete hoax and a farce." Testimony of Bella Dodd, "Subversive Influence in the Educational Process," US Senate, Committee on the Judiciary, Subcommittee to Investigate the Administration of the Internal Security Act and Other Internal Security Laws, 82nd Congress, Second Session, September 8, 1952, 29.

540   Testimony of Rebecca Simonson, The UFT Story, part 3, accessed November 11, 2014, http://www.uft.org/your-union-then-now/class-struggles-uft-story-part-3.

541   Testimony of Rebecca Simonson.

542   Report of the Special Grievance Committee of the Teachers' Union, Investigation of Un-American Propaganda Activities in the United States, Hearings before a Special Committee on Un-American Activities, House of Representatives, 76th Congress, First Session on H. Res. 282, Volume 8, 1939, 6882.

543   Testimony of Bella Dodd, "Subversive Influence in the Educational Process," US Senate, Committee on the Judiciary, Subcommittee to Investigate the Administration of the Internal Security Act and Other Internal Security Laws, 82nd Congress, Second Session, September 8, 1952, 514.

544   Testimony of Bella Dodd, 516.

545   Testimony of Bella Dodd, 516.

546   Testimony of Bella Dodd, 5.

547   Zysman was a physical education teacher in New York City. According to Chambers, around "1941, Zysman's party membership was suspected or discovered. He was eased out of the schools in an incident that made a day's headlines. Later he went to work for the Communist Labor Research Group." Chambers, Witness, 213.

548   Schrecker, No Ivory Tower McCarthyism and the Universities, 52.

549   Dodd, School of Darkness, 123.

550   Educational Vanguard 1, no. 3 (July 23, 1936), 1.

551   Educational Vanguard 1, no. 3, 5.

552   Teacher-Worker I, no. 12 (March 1936), 4.

553   Teacher-Worker I, no. 13 (April 1935), 2.

554   "Teachers Plan College Drive at Convention," The Daily Worker, August 22, 1939, 4.

555   "Free School System in Danger," The Daily Worker, August 22, 1939, 4.

556   Iversen, The Communists and the Schools, 115.

557   New York Times, August 22, 1939, 1.

558   "The Soviet Union and Non-Aggression," Daily Worker XVI, no. 201 (August 23, 1939), 1.

559   New York Times, August 24, 1939, 23.

560 Dodd, *School of Darkness*, 125.

561 Haynes, *In Denial*, 30.

562 Taylor, *Reds at the Blackboard*, 35.

563 "The Executive Council's Proposal to Save the AFT," *American Teacher* XV, no. 8 (April 1941), 6.

564 Committee on Un-American Activities, US House of Representatives, Guide to Subversive Organizations and Publications (and Appendixes): Revised and Published December 1, 1961 to Supersede Guide Published on January 2, 1957: (Including Index). Washington: US Government Printing Office, 1962.

565 Testimony of Bella Dodd, *Investigation of Communist Activities in the Columbus, Ohio Area*, US Congress, House Committee on Un-American Activities, 83rd Congress, First Session, June 17, 18, and 19, 1953, 1752.

566 This was not entirely unusual. Barack Obama mentor Frank Marshall Davis joined CPUSA most likely in 1943, the same year that Bella joined. See discussion in Kengor, *The Communist*, 91–93. On Davis and CPUSA as "the Church," see 283–84.

567 Dodd, *School of Darkness*, 118.

568 Dodd, 118.

569 See Tamiment holdings, the Tamiment Library & Robert F. Wagner Labor Archives, New York. Teachers Union Minutes of the Executive Board Meeting, October 19, Folder 1.

570 Bella Dodd address, Detroit, September 1, 1961.

571 See Education Data Initiative, https://educationdata.org/high-school-dropo ut-rate. About 25 percent of high school freshmen fail to graduate from high school on time.

572 Elizabeth Leyva, David J. Purpura, and Emily Solari, "Why are so many 12th graders not proficient in reading and math?" *The Conversation*, February 10, 2021, https://theconversation.com/why-are-so-many-12th-graders-not-pro ficient-in-reading-and-math-149514.

573 Leyva, "Why are so many 12th graders not proficient in reading and math?" https://theconversation.com/why-are-so-many-12th-graders-not-profici ent-in-reading-and-math-149514. These figures were all taken prior to the Covid "pandemic" and lockdowns.

574 See Comintern Archives on Communist Party USA, 1936, fond 515, opis 1, delo 3971, Library of Congress.

575 Proceedings, 10th Convention, Communist Party New York State, May 20–23, 1938.

576 Stalin, *Foundations of Leninism*, vol. XXV, 282–83.

577 The manual, titled *The Communist Party: A Manual on Organization*, authored by J. Peters and published in July 1935, is available online at https:// www.marxists.org/history/usa/parties/cpusa/1935/07/organisers-manual/in dex.htm. The Communist Party of the United States was not an indepen-

dent political party but was under the control of an espionage arm of the Soviet Union.

578   Testimony of Bella Dodd, *Investigation of Communist Activities in the Columbus, Ohio Area*, US Congress, House Committee on Un-American Activities, 83rd Congress, First Session, June 17, 1953, 1752–53. Also see Bella's similar testimony on Peters to the US Senate, "Subversive Influence in the Educational Process," March 10, 1953, 516.

579   Testimony of Bella Dodd, 528–29, 538–39.

580   Testimony of Bella Dodd, 543.

581   Testimony of Bella Dodd, 543–44.

582   Bella explained the role of the control commission: It "is the internal police of the Communist Party in any country that there is. The control commission is the disciplinary commission. Remember, I said that communism is a government within a government. . . . If I commit an offense against the communist movement, either by thought, word, or action, I get brought before the control commission, and there I am tried, to a certain extent, and I am given certain penalties." Testimony of Bella Dodd, 528–29.

583   Testimony of Bella Dodd, "Subversive Influence in the Educational Process," US Senate, Committee on the Judiciary, Subcommittee to Investigate the Administration of the Internal Security Act and Other Internal Security Laws, 82nd Congress, Second Session, September 8, 1952, 466.

584   See Hook, *Heresy Yes, Conspiracy No*, 178.

585   Danny Postel, "Sidney Hook, an Intellectual Street Fighter," *Chronicles of Higher Education*, November 8, 2000. In the Rapp-Coudert hearings, he revealed that Earl Browder had tried to enroll him in the Party, saying he would be valuable in "building a strong following in the cultural and educational fields."

586   See Tamiment holdings, the Tamiment Library & Robert F. Wagner Labor Archives, New York. Rapp-Coudert Files, R-7860, Testimony of Sidney Hook before the Rapp-Coudert Committee, May 1941. Later, in an article in the *New York Times*, Hook argued that membership in the Communist Party was "*prima facie* evidence that a teacher does not believe in or practice academic freedom." Sidney Hook, "Should Communists Be Permitted to Teach in American Colleges?" *New York Times*, February 27, 1949. See also Bella Dodd address, Detroit, September 1, 1961.

587   Hook, *Heresy Yes, Conspiracy No*, 180.

588   Dodd, *School of Darkness*, 62.

589   Bella Dodd address, "Communism, Students and Labor," Omaha, Nebraska, May 10, 1962, at the Counterattack Freedom School, sponsored by Education for American Freedom.

590   See Haynes, *Spies*, 534–35.

591   As noted by Herb Romerstein and Stanislav Lechenko, "The Soviet Intelligence Service has had many names. Today's KGB was yesterday's Cheka,

GPU, OGPU, NKVD, MGB and MVD." See Romerstein, *The KGB against the "Main Enemy."*

592   Carlo Tresca, "Where is Juliet Stuart Poyntz?" *The Modern Monthly* 10, no. 11 (March, 1938), 12–13.

593   See Chambers, *Witness*, 36.

594   Elizabeth Bentley, a graduate of Vassar, who, before she defected from the Communist Party, ran one of the most effective spy rings, was the lover of Jacob Golos, and was introduced to Juliet Poyntz. When discussing Poyntz with Golos, he told her: "Poyntz was a traitor and had been liquidated by the Soviet intelligence service." See Romerstein, *The Venona Secrets*, 149.

595   Clarence Hathaway was a founding member of CPUSA and studied at the Lenin School in Moscow. See Testimony of Louis Budenz, House Committee on Un-American Activities, November 22, 1946, 18.

596   Federal aid to education was presented as follows: "Whereas the President's Advisory Committee on Education has completed its investigation and report which stated 'no sound plan of local or state taxation can be devised and instituted that will support in every local community a school system which meets minimum acceptable standards. Unless the Federal government participates in the financial support of the schools and related services, several millions of the children in the United States will continue to be largely denied the educational opportunities that should be regarded as their birthright." The union urged the president and Congress to give full support to the Harrison-Thomas-Larrabee bill for federal aid to education. Teachers Union, Local 5, June 1940, Kheel Center Library, Cornell University, Files of the Teachers Union of the City of New York, Box 25, Folder 9.

597   Dodd, *School of Darkness*, 98.

598   Bella Dodd address, Detroit, September 1, 1961.

599   Testimony of George W. Hartman, Associate Professor of Educational Psychology, Teachers College, Columbia University, Hearings before a Special Committee on Un-American Activities, *Investigation of Un-American Propaganda Activities in the United States*, US Congress, House Committee on Un-American Activities, 76th Congress, First Session, 1939, 6849.

600   Dodd, *School of Darkness*, 98.

601   Testimony of Bella Dodd, "Subversive Influence in the Educational Process," US Senate, Committee on the Judiciary, Subcommittee to Investigate the Administration of the Internal Security Act and Other Internal Security Laws, 82nd Congress, Second Session, September 8, 1952, 15.

602   Testimony of Bella V. Dodd, US Senate, Subcommittee to Investigate the Administration of the Internal Security Act and Other Internal Security Laws, Committee on the Judiciary, March 10, 1953, 15.

603   Testimony of Bella V. Dodd, 15–16.

604   "*Bella Dodd Reports*," *New York Teacher* 6, no. 1 (October 1941), 7.

605   Dodd, *School of Darkness*, 175.

606   Bella Dodd address, Omaha, Nebraska, May 10, 1962.

607 Testimony of Bella Dodd, *Investigation of Communist Activities in the Philadelphia Area*, 83rd Congress, First Session, September 16, 1953, 2896.

608 Bella Dodd, "I Was a Communist Teacher," *American Weekly*, Budd Schulberg Papers, Dartmouth University, Box 21, folder 44.

609 Testimony of Bella Dodd, *Investigation of Communist Activities in the Columbus, Ohio Area*, US Congress, House Committee on Un-American Activities, 83rd Congress, First Session, June 17, 18, and 19, 1953, 1752; Richard Frank, "The Schools and the People's Front," *The Communist*, May 1937, 432–45. Richard Frank was a graduate of the University of Virginia and became a functionary of the Communist Party.

610 Bella Dodd address, Detroit, September 1, 1961.

611 Bella Dodd address, Indianapolis, October 1954.

612 Slesinger, *Education and the Class Struggle*, 274.

613 Richard Frank, "The Schools and the People's Front," *The Communist*, May 1937, 432–45.

614 Quoted in Clum, *Making Socialists Out of College Students*, 3.

615 Lenin, *Imperialism the Highest Stage of Capitalism*, 7.

616 Bella Dodd address, Indianapolis, October 1954.

617 *New Masses* (1926–1948) was begun with funds from the American Fund for Public Service, commonly known as the Garland Fund. It provided an outlet for radical artists and writers. Samson, *The American Fund for Public Service*, xiv.

618 *The Times*, Hammond, IN., October 20, 1942, 377.

619 Bella Dodd, *School of Darkness*, 158, and Bella Dodd address, Detroit, September 1, 1961.

620 "From Bella Dodd," *New Masses*, March 16, 1943.

621 Testimony of Bella Dodd, Investigation of Communist Activities in the Columbus, Ohio Area, Part I, Hearing Before the Committee on Un-American Activities, House of Representatives, 83rd Congress, First Session, June 17, 1953, 1747.

622 Lenin, *The Soviets at Work*, 1918.

623 Friedrich Engels, *The Principles of Communism*, October-November 1847, https://www.marxists.org/archive/marx/works/1847/11/prin-com.htm.

624 Bella Dodd testimony to the US Senate, March 10, 1953, 534.

625 Bella Dodd address, Detroit, September 1, 1961.

626 See earlier full citation in introduction. This particular passage of the speech can be heard online at the 1:09:35 marker: https://www.youtube.com/watch?v=37HgRWTsGs0.

627 Budenz, *The Techniques of Communism*, 57–58.

628 *Daily Worker*, April 23, 1937, 1; *Daily Worker*, April 9, 1937, 3; and *Daily Worker*, June 6, 1936, 1.

629 Testimony of Louis Budenz, US Congress, Hearings before the House Committee on Un-American Activities, House of Representatives, 82nd Con-

gress, June 9, 1952, "The Role of the Communist Press in the Communist Conspiracy," 2211–12

630 In the language of the day, "Negroes" was the commonly used term by both blacks and whites. The term "African American" was not a common term yet.

631 Bella Dodd address, Indianapolis, October 1954.

632 Koch, *Double Lives*, 31, 42.

633 See Teachers Union pamphlet, "The Jerome Davis Case," 1937. Final Report of an Investigation conducted by the American Federation of Teachers."

634 See Kheel Center Library, Cornell University, Files of the Teachers Union of the City of New York Center for Labor-Management Documentation & Archives.

635 Dodd, *School of Darkness*, 103; "Teachers in Cap and Gown Picket Yale in Union Protest Over Davis Dismissal," *The New York Times*, June 13, 1937, 2.

636 "Students Will Picket at Yale This Saturday," *The Vassar Miscellany News* XXI, May 5, 1937, 1. Notices were placed in *New York Teacher* by the union for teachers to go to Yale, urging them to bring caps and gowns.

637 Dodd, *School of Darkness*, 102.

638 "Angell Denies Davis Charges," *New York Times*, October 22, 1936, 2.

639 Document 13 and Document 114 from *Russian Revelations from the Russian Archives: A Report from the Library of Congress* (Washington, DC, 1993), edited by Diane P. Koenker and Ronald D. Bachman, 22, 227.

640 The National Federation for Constitutional Liberties was cited by Attorney General Francis Biddle as "part of what Lenin called the solar system of organizations, ostensibly having no connection with the Communist Party, by which Communists attempt to create sympathizers and supporters of their program." *Congressional Record*, September 24, 1942, 7687. The Special Committee on Un-American Activities cited the National Federation as "one of the viciously subversive organizations of the Communist Party." Report of March 29, 1944, 50. The Committee on Un-American Activities reported that it was among a "maze of organizations" which were "spawned for the alleged purpose of defending civil liberties in general but actually intended to protect Communist subversion from any penalties under the law." Report of September 2, 1947, 3.

641 Lenin, *The Emancipation of Women*.

642 House, House Un-American Activities, Report on the Congress of American Women, October 23, 1949, Committee on Un-American Activities, US House of Representatives, United States, Government Printing Office, Washington: 1950, 1.

643 California Senate, Fourth Report Un-American Activities in California, Communist Front Organizations, 1948, Report on the Joint Fact-Finding Committee to the Regular California Legislature, Sacramento, 1948, 228.

644   US Congress, House, House Un-American Activities, Report on the Congress of American Women, October 23, 1949, Committee on Un-American Activities, US House of Representatives, United States, Government Printing Office, Washington: 1950, 3.

645   See House on Un-American Activities, Report on the Congress of American Women, October 23, 1949, Committee on Un-American Activities, US House of Representatives, United States, Government Printing Office, Washington: 1950, 5; and *The Daily Worker*, "Congress of American Women," April 21, 1949, 10.

646   Testimony of Bella Dodd, *Investigation of Communist Activities in the Philadelphia Area*, Part I, US Congress, House, Committee on Un-American Activities, November 16, 1953, 2891–92.

647   Testimony of Bella Dodd, 2891–92.

648   Newspapers during her period in the Party document the many functions at which she was a speaker; for example, "Dr. Bella Dodd Gives Address Over WMFF" (a radio station), *Plattsburg Daily Republican*, June 28, 1939, 3; "People of Harlem 'Indict' School Board," *Pittsburgh Courier*, January 23, 1937, 23; and "Vassar to Hold 3-Day Meeting on Education and Democracy," *New York Herald Tribune*, February 2, 1941, A9.

649   Bella Dodd, House Un-American Activities Hearings, "Investigation of Communist Activities in the Philadelphia Area, Part I, November 16, 1953, 2887. A partial list of other Committees to which Bella belonged follows: Women's Committee, Labor Committee, and Education; Women's Trade Union Committee for Peace ("In 1940 the CP assigned Bella V. Dodd to head a new labor antiwar front group, the Women's Trade Union Committee for Peace, which sent a mass delegation to Washington, D.C., to lobby Congress against sending aid to Britain. Dodd recalled that she and other Communists associated with the new front group 'went on the air with pro-German speakers.'" Norwood, *Antisemitism and the American Far Left*, 65); the Schappes Defense Committee (Dodd, *School of Darkness*, 128–30); *Daily Worker*, Thursday, April 9, 1946, "300 Communist Party Clubs in Special Meeting This Week," "Speakers for Kings County: Bella Dodd." *Daily Worker*, Sept. 2, 1940, "Officers of the American Peace Mobilization," Bella is listed as an officer. She was also a sponsor of the National Conference on Constitutional Liberties. McMichael Exhibit no. 21, 2731, Hearings Regarding Jack R. McMichael, House on Un-American Activities, House of Representatives, 83rd Congress, First Session, July 30 and 31, 1953, and Committee and US Congress. House. Committee on the Judiciary. Subcommittee to Investigate the Administration of the Internal Security Act and Other Internal Security Laws, 1956. *Scope of Soviet Activity in the U.S.*, 84th Congress, Second Session, June 12 and June 14, 1956, 1481, (Testimony of Bella Dodd).

650   The term "fellow traveler" was first used by Max Lerner, who defined it as "someone who does not accept all your aims but has enough in common

with you to accompany you in a comradely fashion part of the way. In this campaign both Mr. Landon and Mr. Roosevelt have acquired fellow-travelers." "Roosevelt and His Fellow Travelers," *Nation* 143, no. 17) October 24, 1936), 71.

651   Testimony of Bella Dodd, "Subversive Influence in the Educational Process," US Senate, March 10, 1953, 3.

652   Bella Dodd address, Detroit, September 1, 1961.

653   Testimony of Bella V. Dodd, US Senate, Subcommittee to Investigate the Administration of the Internal Security Act and Other Internal Security Laws, Committee on the Judiciary, March 10, 1953, 513.

654   Testimony of Dr. Abraham Lefkowitz, US Congress, House, Committee on Education and Labor, Special Subcommittee of the Committee on Education and Labor House of Representatives, *Investigation of Teachers Union Local No. 555 UPWA-CIO,* 80th Congress, Second Session, Sept. 29, 1948, 355.

655   "Dr. Dodd Demands Examiners End Anti-Communist Board Inquiry," *Daily Worker,* Feb. 20, 1946.

656   *The New York Teacher* II, no. 2 (March 1937), 5. An exposé of Stalin's legion in the Spanish Civil War can be found in Romerstein *Heroic Victims.*

657   Committee on Un-American Activities, US House of Representatives, Guide to Subversive Organizations and Publications (and Appendixes): Revised and Published December 1, 1961 to Supersede Guide Published on January 2, 1957 (Washington: US Government Printing Office, 1962).

658   Dodd, *School of Darkness,* 86.

659   Dodd, 87.

660   Romerstein, *Heroic Victims,* 4–6; and Bella Dodd address, Detroit, September 1, 1961.

661   Dodd, *School of Darkness,* 91.

662   Romerstein, *Heroic Victims,* 4.

663   Committee on Un-American Activities, US House of Representatives, Guide to Subversive Organizations and Publications (and Appendixes): Revised and Published December 1, 1961 to Supersede Guide Published on January 2, 1957 (Washington: US Government Printing Office, 1962).

664   Bella Dodd address, Indianapolis, October 1954.

665   Testimony of Bella Dodd, *Investigation of Communist Activities in the Philadelphia Area,* Part I, US Congress, House, Committee on Un-American Activities, November 16, 1953, 2900.

666   Dodd, *School of Darkness,* 98.

667   Dodd, 102.

668   Dodd, 101.

669   Dodd, 101–2.

670   Dodd, 101–3.

671   Dodd, 102–3.

672 Testimony of Bella Dodd, *Investigation of Communist Activities in the Columbus, Ohio Area*, US Congress, House Committee on Un-American Activities, 83rd Congress, First Session, June 17, 1953, 1745.

673 Taylor, *Reds at the Blackboard*, 273.

674 Klehr, *The Heyday of American Communism*, 238.

675 Taylor, *Reds at the Blackboard*, 274.

676 Bella Dodd, Legislative Representative, Federation of Teachers Unions, October 26, 1937, Kheel Center Library, Cornell University, Files of the Teachers Union of the City of New York, Box 63, Folder 6.

677 Taylor, *Reds at the Blackboard*, 274

678 Dodd, *School of Darkness*, 110.

679 Dodd, 110.

680 "Teachers to Plead for Substitute Bill," *The New York Times*, April 26, 1937, 11.

681 "Teachers Urge Lehman to Sign Bill," *Brooklyn Daily Eagle*, June 6, 1937, 11.

682 "Substitutes' Fight Wins Wide Support," *The New York Times*, March 28, 1937, 37.

683 "Need More Teachers," *Brooklyn Daily Eagle*, October 14, 1937, 3.

684 Dodd, *School of Darkness*, 112.

685 Testimony of Bella V. Dodd, US Senate, Subcommittee to Investigate the Administration of the Internal Security Act and Other Internal Security Laws, Committee on the Judiciary, March 10, 1953, 524.

686 "Parade for Dr. Dodd Tonight," *New York Times*, November 4, 1938, 14; and "Political Slates Are Shifted Here," *New York Times*, August 4, 1938, 12.

687 "College Teachers Form a Union Here," *The New York Times*, January 15, 1938, 16.

688 Testimony of Bella Dodd, *Investigation of Communist Activities in the Columbus, Ohio Area*, US Congress, House Committee on Un-American Activities, 83rd Congress, First Session, June 17, 1953, 1749.

689 Bella Dodd address, Detroit, September 1, 1961.

690 Bella Dodd address, Indianapolis, October 1954.

691 Bella Dodd address, Detroit, September 1, 1961.

692 Photographs, *New York Teacher* VI, no. 6 (March 1941), 23; and "Foes of School Cut Go to Albany Today," *The New York Times*, February 12, 1941, 16.

693 Testimony of Bella V. Dodd, US Senate, Subcommittee to Investigate the Administration of the Internal Security Act and Other Internal Security Laws, Committee on the Judiciary, March 10, 1953, 542.

694 Dodd, *School of Darkness*, 111.

695 Dodd, *Roads to Rome*, 43.

696 Dodd, 43.

697 Iversen, *The Communists and the Schools*, 204.

698   "The Executive Council's Proposal to Save the AFT," *American Teacher* XV, no. 8 (April 1941), 4.

699   Tenth Convocation of the Communist Party of New York State, May 20–23, 1938.

700   Robert Iversen confirmed this statement about the *New York Teacher*. After the takeover of the union, the administration saw to it that the position of opposition members "was never stated in the *New York Teacher*." It made sure "that this monthly journal was purely a house organ of the Communist group by removing from the editorial board any members who were discovered to be members of the opposition." Iversen, *The Communists in the Schools*, 111.

701   Affidavit of Manning Johnson, March 13, 1941, quoted in "The Executive Council's Proposal to Save the AFT," *American Teacher* XV, no. 8 (April 1941), 5.

702   Testimony of Bella Dodd, "Subversive Influence in the Educational Process," US Senate, Committee on the Judiciary, Subcommittee to Investigate the Administration of the Internal Security Act and Other Internal Security Laws, 82nd Congress, Second Session, September 8, 1952, 7.

703   Bella Dodd address, Detroit, September 1, 1961.

704   George Counts is an enigma. In his anti-communist book with Nucia Lodge, *The Country of the Blind: The Soviet System of Mind Control* (p. x), he commented: "The forces of democracy cannot cooperate or form a united front with any totalitarian movement or Party, however loudly it may announce its devolution to the cause of democracy. In particular does this means that the Communist Party as an instrument of popular advance, is completely repudiated? My experience convinces me that it poisons everything that it touches." Later, however, he proposed that people "be prepared as a last resort to follow the method of revolution.'" Iversen, *The Communists and the Schools*, 65.

705   See *CALL*, American People's Meeting, New York City, April 5–6, 1941. (Rubinstein Library, J.B. Matthews Collection, signed by Bella Dodd.)

706   Romerstein, *The Venona Secrets*, 325.

707   Trotsky was murdered in Mexico with an ax in 1940. It was a plot hatched in Moscow but carried out through comrades of the CPUSA in the United States and Canada, including Louis Budenz, editor of the *Daily Worker*, soon to defect from the Party.

708   "The Executive Council's Proposal to Save the AFT," *The American Teacher* XXV, no. 8 (April 1941), 2.

709   Testimony of Bella V. Dodd, US Senate, Subcommittee to Investigate the Administration of the Internal Security Act and Other Internal Security Laws, Committee on the Judiciary, March 10, 1953, 534–35.

710   "Bella Dodd Reports," *New York Teacher* 6, no. 1 (October 1941), 7.

711   "Lusk Wins His Anti-Sedition Fight," State Bulletin, New York State Association, Vols. 1-2, April 21, 1921, 12.

712   Hamilton Fish, "The Menace of Communism," *Annals of the American Academy of Political and Social Science*, 1931, 54–61. Fish stated: "Not only is Soviet Russia trying to wipe out all forms of religion, but it is successful in doing it. Not only are the leaders undermining the faith of 10 or 12 million children in Russia, but they are actually successful in teaching hatred of God and all religious beliefs to such an extent that the children at school must hold their parents in contempt and disobey them if the parents have the temerity to maintain any religious belief."

713   See "School Reds Curbed, Fish Inquiry Hears," *New York Times*, July 16, 1930, 1, 5. The late Herbert Romerstein, a defector from the Communist Party, illustrated the problem in New York schools with a child named Harry Eisman, a communist-trained youth, similar to the "Hitler youth." In the 1920s, school administrators in New York were plagued by Eisman, who became a communist agitator in 1924 at the age of eleven. "He organized school strikes and was arrested a number of times by the police in Communist demonstrations. Finally at sixteen, he was sent to a reform school. When he was paroled six months later, he was immediately re-arrested in a Communist riot. Eventually, Harry was permitted to leave the reform school provided he would go to Soviet Russia where he went on a nationwide speaking tour telling children there how bad conditions were in the United States." See Romerstein, *Communism and Your Child*, 28.

714   New York State Legislature, Investigation Files of the Rapp-Coudert Committee L0260-09, 1.

715   "Opening Statement of Paul Windels, Counsel, at the First Public Hearing of Joint Legislative Committee to investigate the Educational System of the City of New York Held in County Court House, New York County on Monday," December 2, 1940, at 2:30 P.M.

716   "Hearing Held at 165 Broadway, New York, NY, February 20, 1941, In the Matter of the Investigation into the Educational System of the State of New York Pursuant to Joint Resolution of the Senate and Assembly," adopted March 9, 1940, 3. Investigation Files of the Rapp-Coudert Committee, Tamiment Library, R-7860, Frame 0194, Bella Dodd (Custodian of Chapter Records) and Robert K. Speer (President of the Chapter).

717   Proceedings of the Tenth Convention of the Communist Party of New York State, New York City May 20-23, 1938 Tamiment Library, CPUSA Records, Box 225, Folder 39, 299. Morris Schappes was present at this convention and testified to this effect.

718   Amter was a charter member of the Communist Party and became New York State chairman. He joined the Socialist Party in 1901 and moved to Germany in 1903, where he remained until 1914, studying music at the Leipzig Conservatory and participating in the Social Democratic Party. On his return to the United States, Amter rejoined the Socialist Party and was a professional musician in New York until joining the communist movement in 1919. For several years, he was a leading advocate of an underground

party and held a leading post in the Friends of the Soviet Union. Amter held various Party jobs, including district organizer in Chicago.

719   Jack Stachel was a member of the National Organizing Secretary, a long-time member of the National Committee, and the US Politburo. At one time, he was in charge of national education and also oversaw the editorial content of the *Daily Worker*. Chambers said he was "one of the Party's top men in trade-union work." See Chambers, *Witness*, 342.

720   Charles Krumbein was state secretary of the Communist Party of New York.

721   Dodd, *School of Darkness*, 118.

722   Dodd, 117.

723   Dodd, 117.

724   Dodd, 120.

725   "Bella Dodd Reports," *New York Teacher* 6, no. 2 (November 1940), 3.

726   Testimony of Bella Dodd, "Subversive Influence in the Educational Process," US Senate, Committee on the Judiciary, Subcommittee to Investigate the Administration of the Internal Security Act and Other Internal Security Laws, 82nd Congress, Second Session, September 8, 1952, 361.

727   Dodd, *School of Darkness*, 121–22.

728   Dodd, 121–22.

729   Testimony of Harry G. Albaum, "Subversive Influence in the Educational Process," US Senate, Committee on the Judiciary, Subcommittee to Investigate the Administration of the Internal Security Act and Other Internal Security Laws, 82nd Congress, Second Session, September 8, 1952, 225–26.

730   Dodd, *School of Darkness*, 122.

731   Bella Dodd, Address in Seattle, Washington, 1962, SR-24-1.

732   As noted by Herb Romerstein and Eric Breindel, "Venona was the top-secret name given by the United States government to an extensive program to break Soviet codes and read intercepted communications between Moscow and its intelligence stations in the West. The Program was launched in February 1943 by the U.S. Army's Signal Intelligence Service, the forerunner of the National Security Agency." See Romerstein, *The Venona Secrets*, 3. In the Venona documents, Chester is mentioned in more than three dozen messages from 1944 and 1945. Venona documents citing Schuster are in appendix A of Haynes and Klehr's book. "In line with Fitin's directive of September 1943, the New York KGB used Schuster as its intermediary with Earl Browder rather than meeting with him directly, as had been done earlier, and often checked with Moscow first when it needed to approach Browder through Schuster." Haynes, *Venona*, 222–23.

733   Dodd, *School of Darkness*, 122–23.

734   Committee for the Defense of Public Education, *Education Defense Bulletin*, no. 3, December 8, 1940, 1.

735   "Graft Corruption Seen," *The New York Times*, August 12, 1941.

736   "Teachers Assail Inquiry Leaders Say They Want Publicity," *The New York Times*, March 31, 1941.

[737] "Teachers Assail Coudert Inquiry Federation at Detroit Says Twin Jobs Put Doubt on Committee's Purposes," *The New York Times*.

[738] Dodd, *School of Darkness*, 119–20.

[739] Dodd, 119–20.

[740] "Bella Dodd Reports," *New York Teacher* 6, no. 7 (Apr. 1941), 3.

[741] Dodd, *School of Darkness*, 124.

[742] Dodd, 123–24.

[743] Committee for Defense of Public Education, *Winter Soldiers, 1941. The Story of a Conspiracy Against the Schools*, 1. This was described as the "invisible effects of the witch-hunts in the schools" and "warning by the victims of the legislative smearkrieg."

[744] Dodd, *School of Darkness*, 125.

[745] Additional publications included "The Conspiracy Against the Schools: An Analysis of Rapp-Coudert," "For the Defense of the Schools—a United Teachers Union," "Academic Freedom Is in the Tombs," and "The Case of Ingram Bender: And Why You Must Act at Once." "It Is Happening in New York!," and "The Case of Ingram Bender: And Why You Must Act at Once." Bella Dodd address, Detroit, September 1, 1961.

[746] Dodd, *School of Darkness*, 120–21.

[747] Dodd, 119.

[748] "Hearings In the Matter of the Investigation into the Educational System of the State of New York Pursuant to Joint Resolution of the Senate and Assembly," formally adopted March 9, 1940, p. 3. See: Investigation Files of the Rapp-Coudert Committee, Tamiment Library R-7860, Frame 0194, Bella Dodd (Custodian of Chapter Records) and Robert K. Speer (President of Chapter).

[749] "Hearings In the Matter…," formally adopted March 9, 1940, 7. Investigation Files of the Rapp-Coudert Committee, Tamiment Library R-7860, Frame 0198.

[750] "Hearing Held at 165 Broadway, New York, NY, February 20, 1941, In the Matter of the Investigation into the Educational System of the State of New York Pursuant to Joint Resolution of the Senate and Assembly," adopted March 9, 1940, 3. Investigation Files of the Rapp-Coudert Committee, Tamiment Library R-7860, Frame 0235, Bella Dodd (Custodian of Chapter Records) and Robert K. Speer (President of Chapter), May 3, 1941. Frame 0235 and 0236.

[751] "Hearing Held at 165 Broadway," 3. Also see Iversen, *The Communists in the Schools*, 210.

[752] See Iversen, *The Communists in the Schools*, 265. According to Andrew Hartman, "sixty-nine teachers were publicly named as Communists before the committee, eleven resigned, six had no tenure and were not reappointed, nine were dismissed without a trial, and twenty were later tried and forced out." Hartman, *Education and the Cold War*, 42.

[753] Iversen, *The Communists and the School*, 209.

754   Iversen, 265.

755   Morris Schappes taught at City College and was faculty adviser for the Marxist Cultural Society. The *Young Communist Review* noted that such Karl Marx Societies "can become centers for stimulating the study of Marxism. They present ideas, the literature and the leaders of the Communist movement. Large numbers of students will be able actually to feel our movement and membership will be open to all who are interested in this study." Iversen, *The Communists in the Schools*, 159.

     When Schappes was dismissed, the Party rallied around him. Leaflets were handed out by students, and three hours after his dismissal, several thousand student leaders were outside the president's office—the first student sit-in. Schrecker, *No Ivory Tower McCarthyism and the Universities*, 66.

756   Clarence Taylor, in *Reds at the Blackboard*, claimed that Schappes was fired "for his political affiliation" and refusing to cooperate with the Rapp-Coudert Committee. He was convicted of perjury, which the *Daily Worker* acknowledged.

757   Conquest, *The Great Terror*, xvi.

758   Earl Browder, "The Moscow Trials: A Statement by American Progressives," *New Masses*, May 3, 1938. See Andrew J. Bacevich, "American Stalinism Then and Now," *The American Conservative*, March 7, 2018.

759   *New Masses* XXX (October 29, 1941), 23.

760   Morris U. Schappes, "Teachers in Handcuffs," *New Masses*, May 6, 1941, 9–11.

761   Dodd, *School of Darkness*, 128.

762   Dodd, 128.

763   Dodd, 251.

764   Testimony of Bella Dodd, "Subversive Influence in the Educational Process," US Senate, Committee on the Judiciary, Subcommittee to Investigate the Administration of the Internal Security Act and Other Internal Security Laws, 82nd Congress, Second Session, September 8, 1952, 12.

765   Herbert Brownell, Jr., *Attorney General of the United States, petitioner, v. Jefferson School of Social Science, respondent*, Report of the Subversive Activities Control Board, June 30, 1955, 41, https://babel.hathitrust.org/cgi/pt?id=mdp.39015031435723&view=1up&seq=5&skin=2021&q1=dr.%20selsam%20testified%20in%20substance.

766   Dodd, *School of Darkness*, 148.

767   Course Offerings School for Democracy, January 1941, Tamiment Library, Miscellaneous Pamphlets, Vol. 74.

768   Course Offerings School for Democracy, January 1941.

769   Course Offerings School for Democracy, January 1941.

770   Course Offerings School for Democracy, January 1941.

771   Herbert Brownell, Jr., *Attorney General of the United States, Petitioner v. Jefferson School of Social Science, Respondent*, Docket No. 107–53, 3, 5–7.

772   Dodd, *School of Darkness*, 149.

773 Dodd, 7.

774 Dodd, 149–50.

775 For a detailed treatment of how the Communist Party did this, see Kengor, *The Communist*, 181–93.

776 Dodd, *School of Darkness*, 150.

777 Dodd, 83, 93–94.

778 Dodd, 130. Also see Bella Dodd testimony to the US Senate, "Subversive Influence in the Educational Process," March 10, 1953, 517.

779 Dodd, *School of Darkness*, 94.

780 Notarized statement of Johnine Leininger and Paul Leininger, who were present for Bella Dodd's presentation in California, dated March 25, 2002. Also see Testimony of Bella Dodd, "Subversive Influence in the Educational Process," US Senate, Committee on the Judiciary, Subcommittee to Investigate the Administration of the Internal Security Act and Other Internal Security Laws, 82nd Congress, Second Session, September 8, 1952, 17.

781 Bella Dodd testimony to the US Senate, "Subversive Influence in the Educational Process," March 10, 1953, 516.

782 See Kengor, *The Devil and Karl Marx*, 219–74.

783 Hearing Before the Committee on Un-American Activities, US House of Representatives, 83rd Congress, First Session, "Investigation of Communist Activities in the New York City Area—Part 7 (Based on the Testimony of Manning Johnson)," July 8, 1953 (Washington, DC: US Government Printing Office, 1953), 2145–79.

784 Hearing Before the Committee on Un-American Activities, 2145–79.

785 Browder, *Communism in the United States*, 335.

786 See Kengor, *The Devil and Karl Marx*, part 4, "Infiltration and Manipulation," 163–320.

787 Sheen, *Communism and the Conscience of the West*, 67.

788 Testimony of Bella V. Dodd, US Senate, Subcommittee to Investigate the Administration of the Internal Security Act and Other Internal Security Laws, Committee on the Judiciary, March 10, 1953, 27.

789 Lenin, *Collected Works* (2nd Russian ed.), Vol. XIV, 68–69.

790 Another translation of the word is "necrophily." Lenin, Letter to Maxim Gorky, written November 13 or 14, 1913. First published in *Pravda*, No. 51, March 2, 1924. Translation taken from Lenin, *Collected Works*, Vol. 35, 121–24. See www.marxists.org/archive/lenin/works/1913/nov/00mg.htm.

791 See chapter 11, "Communism and Religion," in Bukharin's *The ABC of Communism*, written in 1920, first published in English in 1922, published by Penguin Books in 1969, and posted online at https://www.marxists.org/archive/bukharin/works/1920/abc/11.htm.

792 "The Programme of the Communist International," Comintern Sixth Congress 1929, posted at https://www.marxists.org/history/international/comintern/6th-congress/ch04.htm.

793 Foster, *Toward Soviet America*, 113. See the extended analysis of Foster and religion in Kengor, *The Devil and Karl Marx*, 163–84.

794 US Congress, House, Committee on Un-American Activities, *Investigation of Un-American Propaganda in the U.S.*, 75th Congress, Third Session, Oct. 20, 1938, 1564. (Testimony of Mr. Luhrs.)

795 See *The Catholic News*, "Personal Scale Comes to Balance," November 21, 1968, 13.

796 Mary Van Kleeck, a graduate of Smith College with a JD from St. Lawrence University, was director of industrial studies at the Russell Sage Foundation. Quoted in US Congress, House, Committee on Un-American Activities, *Investigation of Un-American Propaganda Activities in the U.S., 75th Congress,* Third Session, 1938, 1654–55.

797 Yaroslovsky, *Religion in the USSR*, 36.

798 Yaroslovsky, 36.

799 Ralph Kane, *Daily Worker*, March 16, 1937, 5.

800 Kane, 5.

801 "Communism Puts Ideals of Christ into Practice, *The Educational Vanguard* 1, no. 3 (July 23, 1936), 2.

802 Sheen, *Communism and the Conscience of the West*, 24.

803 "The changes (in the policy of the French Communist Party—ed.) originated entirely in Moscow." Borkenau, *European Communism*, 123.

804 See "Thorez Calls Catholics to Join in Fellowship Against the Fascist Enemy," *Daily Worker*, November 22, 1937, 3; and Thorez, *Oeuvres*, 11:215–16, quoted in Murphy, *Communists and Catholics in France*, 16.

805 Browder, *A Message to Catholics*. Document is available online at https://www.marxists.org/archive/browder/message-catholics.pdf.

806 See, among others, "Browder Offers Aid to Catholics," *The New York Times*, May 29, 1938.

807 Browder, *A Message to Catholics*, 12. In it, he admits the truth and results of this propaganda ploy that "these good intentions have strengthened the French People's Front. The French democracy ... was happy over the inner harmony of that resulted from this collaboration of the millions of Catholic democrats at home." Browder, 3.

808 Browder, 12.

809 Browder, 3.

810 Budenz, *This Is My Story*, 153–54.

811 Dodd, *School of Darkness*, 232.

812 La Documentation catholique, no. 800, June 13, 1936, col. 1480, quoted in Murphy, *Communists and Catholics in France*, 22.

813 Murphy, 23. In his decree against Communism, Pope Pius XII on July 1, 1949, specifically condemned any collaboration with communists and they were, consequently, excommunicated.

814 See Thorez, *Catholics and Communists*, 19–20; and Sheen, *Communism and Religion*, 6–7.

815 Communists often referred to convents and monasteries as "communist." *Daily Worker*, November 22, 1937, 6.

816 *Daily Worker*, December 28, 1937, 4

817 *Daily Worker*, December 29, 1937, 6

818 Murphy, *Communists and Catholics in France*, 103.

819 The Australian Catholic Truth Society published "The People's Front" by Gregory Parable, which included a section on the outstretched hand. The work explained: "The idea of the Clenched Fist, the communist symbol of aggressive hatred, being held out in friendliness to Catholics, the particular subjects of communist attack, is an accurate representation of communist thought, design and practice. For the one excludes the other. . . . If the communist hand is outstretched, the other hand is clenched; and the clenched fist is clenched to strike a blow." See Parable, The People's Front, 4.

820 Testimony of Manning Johnson, US Congress, Hearing before the House Committee on Un-American Activities House of Representatives, *Investigation of Hearings in the New York City Area*, Part 7, House of Representatives, 83rd Congress, First Session, July 8, 1953, 2166.

821 William Z. Foster, "Secondary Aspects of Mass Organizations," *The Communist*, August 1939, 702–3.

822 Melish was the editor of the *Reporter*, a CPUSA biweekly publication, published by the National Council of American-Soviet Friendship, Inc.

823 "Subversive Influence in the Educational Process," US Senate, Committee on the Judiciary, Subcommittee to Investigate the Administration of the Internal Security Act and Other Internal Security Laws, 82nd Congress, Second Session, September 8, 1952, 290.

824 See Romerstein, *The Venona Secrets*, 413.

825 Herbert Romerstein collection, Hoover Institute, Box 415, Folder 6.

826 Joseph Pronechen, "This Marian Pope Popularized Fatima—And It's Not Who You Think," *National Catholic Register*, August 27, 2017.

827 David Platt, "'Miracle of Fatima' Film Aids Pentagon War Drive," *Daily Worker*, September 2, 1952, 7.

828 Our colleague Kevin Symonds cautions that Martindale, being the good Jesuit that he was, was here perhaps following the historical-critical methodology with respect to Fatima. The *Daily Worker* twisted Martindale's points and theological background in order to serve its purposes.

829 *Daily Worker*, September 2, 1952, 7.

830 First and Second Secrets of Fatima, published by the Vatican in 1942. Santos, *Fatima in Lucia's Own Words*, 123–24.

831 Testimony of Bella Dodd, "Subversive Influence in the Educational Process," US Senate, Committee on the Judiciary, Subcommittee to Investigate the Administration of the Internal Security Act and Other Internal Security Laws, 82nd Congress, Second Session, September 9, 1952, 27–28.

832 Testimony of Bella Dodd, 27–27.

833   That reference appears on page 777. Unfortunately, it says virtually nothing about the group.

834   "Subversive Influence in the Educational Process," US Senate, Committee on the Judiciary, Subcommittee to Investigate the Administration of the Internal Security Act and Other Internal Security Laws, 82nd Congress, Second Session, September 9, 1952, 27–28.

835   Westbrook Pegler, "Reds and Church," *The Post-Standard* (Syracuse, New York), August 4, 1953, 11. Pegler's column was syndicated.

836   Pegler, "Reds and Church."

837   Pegler, "Reds and Church."

838   NCWC News Service, 20, Oct. 1947, Issued by the Press Department, National Catholic Welfare Conference, Washington, D.C., 46.

839   NCWC News Service, 20, Oct. 1947, 46.

840   "Catholic Group Renamed," *The New York Times*, August 17, 1939, 17.

841   Westbrook Pegler, "Reds and Church," *The Post-Standard* (Syracuse, New York), August 4, 1953, 11.

842   "Catholic Group Renamed," *The New York Times*, August 17, 1939, 17.

843   "Reds and Catholics," *The Tablet*, Managing Editor's Desk, July 18, 1953, 33.

844   Historical Note, *The Tablet*, Managing Editor's Desk, 13 June, 1953, 27.

845   Historical Note, *The Tablet*, Managing Editor's Desk, 13 June, 1953, 27.

846   US Congress, Senate, Committee on the Judiciary. Subcommittee to Investigate the Administration of the Internal Security Act and Other Internal Security Laws, 1952, *Subversive Influence in the Educational Process* 82nd Congress, Second Session, 84th Congress, First Session, April 7, 8, 1953, 1068–74.

847   "Senators Study Communist Cell Among Catholics," *The Tablet*, June 13, 1953, 1.

848   Testimony of Manning Johnson, July 8, 1953, 2145–79.

849   Gitlow, *I Confess*; and Gitlow, *The Whole of Their Lives*.

850   See Kengor, *The Devil and Karl Marx*.

851   Born Gilbert Greenberg in September 1906, "Gil Green" was a native of Chicago and became a very prominent and militant Party leader.

852   Testimony of Herbert Philbrick, US Congress, Senate Committee on the Judiciary, Subcommittee to Investigate the Administration of the Internal Security Act and Other Internal Security Laws, *Subversive Influence in the Educational Process*, 82nd Congress, Second Session, April 7, 1953, 739–69.

853   Testimony of Herbert Philbrick, 757.

854   Testimony of Herbert Philbrick, 759, 762.

855   Philbrick, *I Led 3 Lives*, 91. Also see 56–57, 84, 86, 90.

856   Testimony of Herbert Philbrick, US Congress, Senate Committee on the Judiciary, Subcommittee to Investigate the Administration of the Internal Security Act and Other Internal Security Laws, *Subversive Influence in the Educational Process*, 82nd Congress, Second Session, April 7, 1953, 752.

857   United States. Congress, House, Committee on Un-American Activities (1948), *100 things you should know about communism ...: a series on the communist conspiracy and its influence in this country as a whole, on religion, on education, on labor and on our government*, Washington: [U.S. Government Printing Office].

858   Committee on Un-American Activities, *100 things you should know about communism*, 1, 11–15.

859   Mary Nicholas recalls a conversation between her mother, then a recent convert to Catholicism, and Elise French Johnston, an aunt who had extensive knowledge of the techniques of communism from a former government professional: "Barbara, they have infiltrated every church in America; don't think they won't infiltrate yours."

860   See Reeves, *America's Bishop*, 170–73.

861   Budenz's testimony before the House Committee on Un-American Activities came on November 22, 1946. The key part of his testimony excerpted here from the official transcript runs from the bottom of page 31 to the middle of page 33.

862   Budenz had written in the *Daily Worker* a lengthy piece posing eight questions to Monsignor Sheen, then a professor of philosophy at the Catholic University of America, and already well-known on radio, in media, and for public lectures, which is why Budenz endeavored to take him on. Sheen responded to each question in detail, answering them with strictly communist sources. He let communism speak for itself. Sheen's answers were published in a small book by the Paulist Press titled *Communism Answers Questions of a Communist*. See Sheen, *Communism Answers Questions of a Communist*.

863   Mignot, *Les Fumées de Satan*, 45. This directive would likely have been addressed to multiple comrades in the United States and throughout the world. Thus, it is probable that Bella Dodd was one of many following this order.

864   Dodd, *School of Darkness*, 240–45.

865   Is it possible that Sheen heard it from Bella in the confessional? Of course, the priest is restricted as to what he can share, given the seal of confession. Being in New York, the epicenter of American communism, and being the most well-known Catholic priest in America, with a special interest in communism, he may have heard these things from not only Bella Dodd (in or out of the confessional) but from elsewhere. Bella could have said something to Sheen on numerous occasions during her personal instruction into the Church.

866   Dodd, *School of Darkness*, 85.

867   Dodd, 78–83.

868   "The Technique of Soviet Propaganda," A Study Presented by the Subcommittee to Investigate the Administration of the Internal Security Act and Other Internal Security Laws, Committee on the Judiciary, US Senate, 86th Congress, Second Session (Washington, DC: US Government Printing Of-

fice, 1960), 7. See link posted at https://babel.hathitrust.org/cgi/pt?id=uiug
.30112039644817;view=1up;seq=3.

869 "The Technique of Soviet Propaganda," Committee on the Judiciary, US
Senate, 8.

870 "Fulton Sheen Will Be Canonized—But When?" *Catholic Herald*, October
4, 2015.

871 In her memoirs, Alice von Hildebrand says that she and Dietrich met Bella
in the fall of 1965 or 1966. See Von Hildebrand, *Memoirs of a Happy Failure*,
82.

872 Mary Nicholas interview with Dr. Alice von Hildebrand, October 20, 2013.

873 Sheen biographer Tom Reeves writes: "Pius XI had told him to study Karl
Marx and communism, and never to speak in public during his pontificate
without exposing their fallacies." Reeves, *America's Bishop*, 86–87.

874 "Present at the Demolition," an interview with Dr. Alice von Hildebrand,
The Latin Mass Magazine, summer 2001, http://www.latinmassmagazine
.com/articles/articles_2001_su_hildebran.html.

875 "Exclusive Interview with Alice von Hildebrand," Michael Voris, Church-
Militant.com, January 28, 2016, YouTube, https://www.youtube.com/wat
ch?v=CKLBvvlabgw.

876 See Von Hildebrand, *Memoirs of a Happy Failure*, 82.

877 For instance, Symonds has scrutinized (among others) Taylor Marshall's
book *Infiltration*, which he finds lacking in its documentation on this specific question of an infiltration of seminaries.

878 Sherry was not comfortable sharing the name of the host couple without
their permission. The husband was a local dentist. It was not clear to us if
both the husband and wife are still living.

879 The text is over fourteen thousand words in length.

880 The authors thank Kevin Symonds for this transcript.

881 Paul Kengor received an email from one academic who used that one section
of that speech by Bella Dodd to essentially wipe out every other claim or alleged claim by Bella on the subject. The correct approach for any historian is
to measure that Detroit statement with all others. Most important, as known
by historians and public speakers alike, is to not put too much weight in the
words of a live presentation when a speaker can be imprecise. Individuals
very frequently misspeak or lack precision when addressing questions off the
cuff in live dialogues. To be sure, we do not ignore such statements, but we
also balance them against everything else.

882 Ronald Radosh, "'Naming names: A new witch hunt?" *New York Post*, April
26, 2012.

883 To this day, researchers of the Communist Party struggle to find lists of
Party members, membership numbers coupled to names of members, and
any clear documentation regarding individuals. The Party protected such
information with severe diligence.

884   US Congress, Senate, Committee on the Judiciary, Subcommittee to Investigate the Administration of the Internal Security Act and Other Internal Security Laws, 1953, *Subversive Influence in the Educational Process* 82nd Congress, First Session, September 9, 1952, 29–30.

885   Bella Dodd's address in Detroit, Michigan, September 1, 1961.

886   This data, first presented in *The Devil and Karl Marx*, comes from the Official Catholic Directory and was provided by The Rev. Donald Paul Sullins, MDiv, PhD, Research Associate Professor of Sociology at The Catholic University of America in emails April 14–15, 2019. We are grateful to Dr. Sullins for his assistance. For more data, see "Clergy and Religious," USCCB, http://www.usccb.org/about/public-affairs/backgrounders/clergy-religious.cfm. On statistics, since 1970, when there were 59,192 total priests, see the data maintained by Georgetown's Center for Applied Research in the Apostolate: "Frequently Requested Church Statistics," CARA, http://cara.georgetown.edu/frequently-requested-church-statistics/.

887   Email to Paul Kengor from Dr. Paul Sullins, April 15, 2019.

888   Also see discussion in Kevin Symonds, "Rethinking Bella Dodd and Infiltration of Catholic Priesthood," *Homiletic & Pastoral Review*, December 24, 2021.

889   Crosby, *Thank God Ahead of Time*, 1.

890   Letter published in Crosby, *Thank God Ahead of Time*, 193.

891   "Present at the Demolition," Interview with Alice Von Hildebrand, *Latin Mass Magazine*, Summer 2001.

892   "A Jesuit Goes Communist," *Life Magazine* 32, no. 21 (May 26, 1952), 47.

893   "Jesuit Joins Communists, Calls Church 'Outdated,'" *The New York Times*, April 26, 1952, 20.

894   Robert A. Graham, "Vatican, the Story of Bugging at the Vatican," *Columbian* XLIX, no. 10 (November 1969), 28.

895   Koehler, *Spies in the Vatican*, 153–54.

896   Koehler, 136–51.

897   Elisabeth Braw interviewed on "Kresta in the Afternoon," Ave Maria Radio Network, September 16, 2019.

898   Braw on "Kresta in the Afternoon."

899   Polish security services coverage of the meetings of the Second Vatican Council, Oct. 1–21, 1963, classified top secret. Copy of KGB report furnished by the East German Ministry for State Security (Stasi), BSTU No. 000001 27. Koehler, *Spies in the Vatican*, 1.

900   See the extensive treatment in Kengor, *A Pope and a President*.

901   Kengor, *A Pope and a President*.

902   Koehler, *Spies in the Vatican*, 9, 15, 169.

903   Koehler, 25.

904   Koehler, 155–56.

905   Koehler, 156.

906   Koehler, 156.

[907] Radecki, *Tumultuous Times*, 318.

[908] Amerio, *Iota Unum*, 76.

[909] Amerio, 76.

[910] Note by the chairman of the CROCA, Karpov, sent on March 14, 1959, to the assistant of the secretary of the Central Committee of the CPSU, E.A. Furceva, V.V. Zverev, CChSD, f.5, op. 33, d. 126, II, 43–44.

[911] Melloni, *Vatican II in Moscow*, 48–50.

[912] The authors are grateful to Kevin Symonds for this insight.

[913] Carmelo de Santa Teresa—Coimbra, *Um caminho sob o olhar de Maria: Biografia da Irmã Lúcia de Jesus e do Coração Imaculado, O.C.D.* (Coimbra, Portugal: Edições Carmelo, 2013), 275. English translation provided by Kevin J. Symonds. The Portuguese text reads: "É do conhecimento de Vossa Santidade a existência do chamado segredo de Fátima, fechado em envelope lacrado que poderá ser aberto após o início do ano 60. Embora não possa dizer o texto aí contido, porque o tempo se aproxima, devo dizer que, na era 60, o comunismo atingirá o ponto máximo, o qual pode ser diminuído quanto à intensidade e duração, e à qual se deverá seguir o triunfo do Imaculado Coração de Maria e o Reinado de Cristo."

[914] Carmelo de Santa Teresa—Coimbra, *Um caminho sob o olhar de Maria*, 275. The Portuguese text is: "Para conseguir este fim, quer Deus que se intensifiquem todos os trabalhos apostólicos, além dos quais quer que se faça ouvir no mundo, como o eco da Sua, a minha voz, expondo o que foi e o que é a Mensagem de Fátima em relação a Deus e às almas, ao tempo e à eternidade, a fim de elucidar os espíritos sobre o caminho da vida cristã que devem seguir e os erros dos quais se devem afastar, para que se não deixem enganar por falsas doutrinas."

[915] De Mattei, *The Second Vatican Council*, 159.

[916] AD II-II/3:775. (Acta Documenta Concilio Ecunenico Vaticano II, Series II, Volume II, part 3) Vatican City, Liberia Editrice Quoted in De Mattei, *The Second Vatican Council*, 153.

[917] See Paul Kengor, "Vatican II's Unpublished Condemnations of Communism," *Crisis*, November 2017.

[918] See Matthew Cullinan Hoffman, "Vatican II's Lost Condemnation of Communism."

[919] Martin, *The Jesuits*, 85–86.

[920] De Mattei, *The Second Vatican Council*, 154. A particularly soul-wrenching plea came from Cardinal Stepinac, from Croatia, who was unable to participate in the council who had served in prison and was at the time under house arrest: "A battle for life and death is being waged and it is not possible to retreat if we do not want to betray God. Bloody communism, too, knows very well that it will be destroyed down to its roots as soon as the opportunity presents itself to the people. There is no longer any power on earth capable of rehabilitating communism in the eyes of the masses, so odious, indeed it has made itself with its bloody violence, its pillaging its lies, its intrigues and

inhumane acts, which are unparalleled in world history. A true, living image of hell! . . . And yet in the West there are still naïve individuals who play with fire and in their naïveté believe in the possibility of coexistence with bloody communism." Quoted in De Mattei, *The Second Vatican Council*, 154–55.

921 Ferrara, *The Great Façade*, 96.

922 De Mattei, *The Second Vatican Council*, 154.

923 De Mattei, 469.

924 Amerio, *Iota Unum*, 76.

925 Malachi Martin, a former Jesuit, commented about Arrupe. See Martin, *The Jesuits*, 36, 44.

926 De Mattei, *The Second Vatican Council*, 471.

927 De Mattei, 471.

928 De Mattei, 471.

929 De Mattei, 471.

930 De Mattei, 471.

931 De Mattei, 471.

932 De Mattei, 471.

933 De Mattei, 471.

934 Wiltgen, *The Inside Story of Vatican II*, 421.

935 See *Gaudium et Spes*, December 7, 1965, http://www.vatican.va/archive/hist _councils/ii_vatican_council/documents/vat-ii_const_19651207_gaudium -et-spes_en.html.

936 Wiltgen, *The Inside Story of Vatican II*, 418.

937 To be clear, the authors are not saying that the likes of Baum are communists but that the wider infiltration of radical leftist thinking in the Church is represented by the likes of Baum.

938 "Tragedy at Winnipeg The Canadian Catholic Bishops' Statement on *Humanae Vitae*," Monsignor Vincent Foy, from Selected Writings of Monsignor Foy, posted at https://msgrfoy.com/2014/01/08/tragedy-at-winnipeg -the-canadian-catholic-bishops-statement-on-humanae-vitae-by-monsignor -vincent-foy/.

939 Wikipedia, s.v. "Gregory Baum," last modified March 27, 2022, https://en .wikipedia.org/wiki/Gregory_Baum.

940 Francis DeBernardo, "Theologian's Autobiography Explains His Gay Journey," New Ways Ministry, May 3, 2017, Theologian's Autobiography Explains His Gay Journey - New Ways Ministry.

941 See https://msgrfoy.com/2014/03/23/notes-on-gregory-baum-by-their-fruits -you-shall-know-them-by-monsignor-vincent-foy/.

942 Coleman added that, years later, it was discovered that Governor Smith, a staunch Catholic, had been "advised on issues of social justice" by Father Ryan, "an avowed Socialist planted on Smith by a Socialist-dominated National Catholic Welfare Council."

943 Arthur S. Meyers, "Social Justice Warrior," *Commonweal*, July 2, 2018, https://www.commonwealmagazine.org/social-justice-warrior.

944 "Former Soviet spy: We created Liberation Theology," *Catholic News Agency*, May 1, 2015, https://www.catholicnewsagency.com/news/former-soviet-spy -we-created-liberation-theology-83634.

945 "Former Soviet spy: We created Liberation Theology."

946 Pacepa, *Disinformation*, 106.

947 Pacepa, 106.

948 "Former Soviet spy: We created Liberation Theology," Catholic News Agency, May 1, 2015.

949 "Former Soviet spy: We created Liberation Theology."

950 Published in 2013, Paul Kengor wrote the foreword to this book.

951 Paul Kengor became friends with Pacepa and exchanged many emails with him and even co-authored articles with him. See Paul Kengor, "Death of a Defector: Ion Mihai Pacepa, RIP," *The American Spectator*, February 24, 2021.

952 De Mattei, *The Second Vatican Council: An unwritten story*, 523.

953 Martin, *The Keys of This Blood*, 261.

954 Martin, *The Jesuits*, 47.

955 Congregation for the Doctrine of the Faith, "Instruction On Certain Aspects of the Theology of Liberation," http://www.vatican.va/roman_curia /congregations/cfaith/documents/rc_con_cfaith_doc_19840806_theology -liberation_en.html.

956 Congregation for the Doctrine of the Faith, "Instruction On Certain Aspects of the Theology of Liberation."

957 Dodd, *School of Darkness*, 113.

958 Printed in "The Communist Party of the United States of America: What It Is, How It Works," Committee on the Judiciary, US Senate, 84th Congress, 2nd Session, April 23, 1956 (Washington, DC: GPO, 1956), 2.

959 Dodd, *School of Darkness*, 166–67.

960 Dodd, 166–67. A Party member had once said of Red: "He is a wonderful comrade to help make the revolution but after it is successful, we are going to have to kill him because he would immediately proceed to unmake it." Dodd, 70.

961 Dodd, 173.

962 Testimony of Bella Dodd, "Subversive Influence in the Educational Process," US Senate, Committee on the Judiciary, Subcommittee to Investigate the Administration of the Internal Security Act and Other Internal Security Laws, 82nd Congress, Second Session, September 8, 1952, 25.

963 Bella Dodd address, Indianapolis, October 1954.

964 Dodd, *Roads to Rome*, 45.

965 Testimony of Bella V. Dodd, US Senate, Subcommittee to Investigate the Administration of the Internal Security Act and Other Internal Security Laws, Committee on the Judiciary, March 10, 1953, 519–20, 528–29.

966 Dodd, *Roads to Rome*, 48.

967 Bella Dodd address, Utica, New York, May 23, 1961.

968   Dodd, *School of Darkness*, 186–87.

969   Dodd, 121.

970   Dodd, 199.

971   Dodd, *Roads to Rome*, 49.

972   Dodd, *School of Darkness*, 207.

973   Dodd, 208.

974   Dodd, 212.

975   Dodd, 212.

976   Dodd, 212.

977   Dodd, 212–13.

978   Dodd, 196. In congressional hearings, Bella explained that there were three levels within the Communist Party: "There is the party functionary, the person in unions or mass organizations who is just aware of the do-good principles of the Communist Party; and then there is the underground spy apparatus and police apparatus, with which I had nothing to do and knew nothing about. I learned much later that even in my union there were contacts with the teachers on the part of people like J. Peters, who later on I learned was an international spy." Testimony of Bella V. Dodd, US Senate, Subcommittee to Investigate the Administration of the Internal Security Act and Other Internal Security Laws, Committee on the Judiciary, March 10, 1953, 516. Whittaker Chambers identified J. Peters as the chief of the national underground of the Communist Party (cf. Chambers, *Witness*, 32).

979   Dodd, *School of Darkness*, 197.

980   Bella Dodd address, Detroit, September 1, 1961.

981   Bella Dodd address, Detroit, September 1, 1961.

982   A. R. Raskin, "Report on the Communist Party (U.S.A.)," *New York Times Magazine*, March 20, 1947.

983   Dodd, *School of Darkness*, 162. *The New York Times Magazine* agreed with Bella's assessment. Raskin described the "Report on the Communist Party (U.S.A.)," March 20, 1947.

984   Dodd, *School of Darkness*, 213–14.

985   For much more on Trachtenberg, see Klehr, *Venona Decoding Soviet Espionage in America*, 69, 403; and Klehr, *The Soviet World of American Communism*, 282.

986   Bella Dodd address, Indianapolis, October 1954.

987   Dodd, *School of Darkness*, 214.

988   Dodd, 214.

989   Dodd, 215.

990   Dodd, 216.

991   Dodd, *Roads to Rome*, 42.

992   Budenz, *The Techniques of Communism*, 27–37; and Testimony of Bella Dodd, March 10, 1953, United States Senate, Subcommittee To Investigate The Administration Of The Internal Security Act And Other Internal Security Laws.

993   Budenz, *The Techniques of Communism*, 37.

994   Draper, *American Communism and Soviet Russia*, 162.

995   Budenz, *The Techniques of Communism*, 27.

996   Dodd, *School of Darkness*, 217.

997   Dodd, 217.

998   Maxim Gorky, a famed writer of the revolution, penned "Proletarian Hatred," describing the right to hate capitalists.

999   Dodd, *School of Darkness*, 218.

1000 Dodd, 220.

1001 Dodd, 216–17.

1002 Dodd, 216–17.

1003 Bella Dodd address, Indianapolis, October 1954.

1004 Testimony of John Lautner, Testimony of Bella Dodd, "Subversive Influence in the Educational Process," U.S. Senate, Committee on the Judiciary, Subcommittee to Investigate the Administration of the Internal Security Act and Other Internal Security Laws, 82nd Congress, Second Session, September 8, 1952, pp. 251, 255. Lautner, a former member of the Communist Party, was an interesting witness, as he had been named as a "traitor" by the Party.

1005 Dodd, *School of Darkness*, 219.

1006 Dodd, *Roads to Rome*, 50.

1007 Dodd, *School of Darkness*, 219.

1008 Louis Schaeffer, "Conversation with Bella Dodd," *New Leader* 32, August 1949.

1009 Schaeffer, "Conversation with Bella Dodd."

1010 Testimony of Bella Dodd, *Investigation of Communist Activities in the Columbus, Ohio Area*, US Congress, House Committee on Un-American Activities, 83rd Congress, First Session, June 17, 1953, 1751.

1011 Dodd, *Roads to Rome*, 50.

1012 Testimony of Bella Dodd, *Investigation of Communist Activities in the Columbus, Ohio Area*, US Congress, House Committee on Un-American Activities, 83rd Congress, First Session, June 17, 1953, 1751.

1013 Dodd, *Roads to Rome*, 49.

1014 Dodd, 49.

1015 Bella Dodd address, Indianapolis, October 1954.

1016 Bella Dodd address, Indianapolis, October 1954.

1017 Dodd, *School of Darkness*, 143.

1018 Bella Dodd address, Utica, New York, May 23, 1961.

1019 Dodd, *School of Darkness*, 231.

1020 Dodd, 231.

1021 Dodd, 232.

1022 Dodd, *Roads to Rome*, 51.

1023 Dodd, *School of Darkness*, 231–37; and Sheen, *Treasure in Clay*, 263.

1024 Dodd, *School of Darkness*, 144–45.

1025 Bella Dodd address, Utica, New York, May 23, 1961.

[1026]   Dodd, *School of Darkness*, 231–33.

[1027]   Dodd, 236.

[1028]   Dodd, 237.

[1029]   Dodd, 149–50.

[1030]   Dodd, 150.

[1031]   Dodd, 151.

[1032]   Dodd, 152.

[1033]   Dodd, 152.

[1034]   Dodd, 152.

[1035]   Dodd, *Roads to Rome*, 42.

[1036]   Dodd, *School of Darkness*, 240–45.

[1037]   "Ex-Red Bella Dodd Rejoins Church," *Daily Mirror*, August 6, 1952, 2.

[1038]   "Ex-Red Bella Dodd Rejoins Church," *Daily Mirror*, August 6, 1952, 2.

[1039]   Dodd, *Roads to Rome*, 43.

[1040]   Dodd, *School of Darkness*, 240–45.

[1041]   Interview of Dr. Alice von Hildebrand by Mary Nicholas, October 20, 2013.

[1042]   Mary Nicholas interview with Robert H. Goldsborough, Staff Investigator for the House Un-American Activities under Congressman Walters of Pennsylvania, via telephone, October 30, 2015.

[1043]   "Trial of an Anti-Communist," *Tidings*, November 23, 1956.

[1044]   "Personal Scale Comes to Balance," *The Catholic News*, November 21, 1968, 15.

[1045]   Bella Dodd address, Indianapolis, October 1954.

[1046]   Bella Dodd address, Detroit, September 1, 1961.

[1047]   Testimony of Bella Dodd, "Subversive Influence in the Educational Process," US Senate, Committee on the Judiciary, Subcommittee to Investigate the Administration of the Internal Security Act and Other Internal Security Laws, 82nd Congress, Second Session, September 8, 1952, 12.

[1048]   Testimony of Bella Dodd, 527.

[1049]   Testimony of Bella Dodd, 12.

[1050]   *Guideposts*, November 1963.

[1051]   In *School of Darkness* (p. 179), Bella Dodd said that when the "Yalta conference had ended, the Communists prepared to support the United Nations Charter which was to be adopted at the San Francisco conference to be held in May and June, 1945. For this I organized a corps of speakers and we took to the street corners and held open-air meetings in the millinery and clothing sections of New York where thousands of people congregate at the lunch hour. We spoke of the need for world unity and in support of the Yalta decisions."

[1052]   Teachers College Bulletin, St. John's University, 1953-54.

[1053]   Teachers College Bulletin, St. John's University, 1953-54.

[1054]   Muriel Ward O'Brien, "Personal Scale Comes to Balance," *The Catholic News* 15 (Nov. 21, 1968), 15.

[1055]   O'Brien, "Personal Scale Comes to Balance," 15.

[1056] O'Brien, "Personal Scale Comes to Balance," 15.

[1057] Letter from Rosalind Frame to Norman Dodd, May 13, 1969, in possession of authors.

[1058] Frame lived in Savannah, Georgia.

[1059] Letter from Percy Greaves to Rosalind Frame, May 23, 1969, in possession of authors.

[1060] Letter from Ed Coey to Rosalind Frame, May 28, 1969, in possession of authors.

[1061] Lawrence Hall, "Bella Dodd, New Yorker, Fights On," *Sunday News*, October 16, 1966, M4.

[1062] *The Record of the Association of the Bar of the City of New York*, November 1964, Vol. 19, no. 8., 441.

[1063] "Personal Scale Comes to Balance," *The Catholic News*, November 21, 1968, 15.

[1064] "Personal Scale Comes to Balance," 15.

[1065] Hall, "Bella Dodd, New Yorker, Fights On."

[1066] "Personal Scale Comes to Balance," *The Catholic News*, November 21, 1968, 15.

[1067] According to Frank Vasile, a friend of Bella when she was a communist lawyer, "she never lost a case. After she left the Communist Party, she couldn't win a case." That, however, does not seem to be totally accurate. Frank Vasile, friend of Bella Dodd, telephone interview with Mary Nicholas, January 14, 2015.

[1068] Hall, "Bella Dodd, New Yorker, Fights On."

[1069] Ralph Clifford, "Crusader for Justice," *New York Graphic* II, no. 11 (June 12, 1969), 1.

[1070] The April 8 date is incorrect. According to Bella's memoirs (page 244), the correct date is April 7, 1952.

[1071] "Personal Scale Comes Home to Balance," *The Catholic News*, November 21, 1968.

[1072] See FBI files, the Vault, SA Lautner to FBI Director, "Bella Dodd Seriously Ill and Destitute," February 5, 1964; and "Bella Dodd Reported Destitute," CNS, January 16, 1964, 15.

[1073] See FBI files, the Vault, SA Lautner to FBI Director, "Bella Dodd Seriously Ill and Destitute," February 5, 1964; and "Bella Dodd Reported Destitute," CNS, January 16, 1964, 15.

[1074] Editorial page, "Advises of Fund to Aid Bella Dodd," *Utica Observer-Dispatch*, January 31, 1964.

[1075] *Time Magazine*, May 9, 1969.

[1076] Timothy A. Mitchell, "The Penitent Years of Bella V. Dodd: A Personal Memoir by Timothy A. Mitchell," *Pro Ecclesia Magazine* XXXV, no. 1 (2004), 6, reprinted from the original October 1969 tribute by Mitchell in the *Social Justice Review*.

[1077] The exact date of Bella's birth in 1904 is not known.

1078   Ralph Clifford, "Crusader for Justice," *New York Graphic* II, no. 11 (June 12, 1969), 1.

1079   Timothy A. Mitchell, "The Penitent Years of Bella V. Dodd: A Personal Memoir by Timothy A. Mitchell," *Pro Ecclesia Magazine* XXXV, no. 1 (2004), 6.

1080   Source (as previously cited) is Robert Goldsborough.

BIBLIOGRAPHY

Allen, Naomi, ed. *The Challenge of the Left Opposition: 1923-1925.* New York: Pathfinder Press, 1975.

Amerio, Romano. *Iota Unum.* Kansas City, MO: Sarto House, 1996.

Anderson, Gary and Kathryn G. Herr. *Encyclopedia of Activism and Social Justice.* Thousand Islands, CA: Sage Publications, 2007.

Barron, John. *Operation Solo: The FBI's Man in the Kremlin.* Washington, DC: Regnery, 1996.

Bell, Daniel. *Marxian Socialism in the United States.* Ithaca, New York: Cornell University Press, 1952.

Bernstein, Jay. *The Frankfurt School: Critical Assessments.* New York: Routledge, 1994.

Berry, Faith. *Langston Hughes: Before and Beyond Harlem.* New York: Citadel Press, 1992.

Bliss, William D. P. *Encyclopedia of Social Reform.* New York: Funk and Wagnalls, 1897.

Blumenfeld, Samuel L. *NEA Trojan Horse in American Education.* Boise, ID: The Paradigm Co., 1984.

Bociurkiw, B. R., et al, eds. *Religion and Atheism in the USSR and Eastern Europe.* London: MacMillan, 1975.

Borkenau, Franz. *European Communism.* London, 1953.

Bowers, C. A. "The Ideologies of Progressive Education." *History of Education Quarterly* 7, no. 4 (1967).

———. *The Progressive Educator and the Depression; The Radical Years.* New York, Random House, 1969.

Boyer, Paul S. *The Oxford Companion to United States History.* New York: Oxford University Press, 2004.

Brameld, Theodore. "Karl Marx and the American Teacher." *Social Frontier* II, no. 2 (November 1935).

Braw, Elisabeth. *God's Spies: The Stasi's Cold War Espionage Operation Inside the Church.* Grand Rapids, MI: Eerdmans, 2019.

Brickman, William W., ed. *John Dewey's Impressions of Soviet Russia and the revolutionary world, Mexico-China-Turkey 1929.* New York: Bureau of Publications, Teachers College, Columbia University, 1964.

Browder, Earl. *Communism in the United States.* New York: International Publishers, 1935.

———. *A Message to Catholics.* New York: Workers Library Publishers, 1938.

Brownson, Henry A. *The Works of Orestes A. Brownson.* Detroit, MI: Thorndike Nourse, 1885.

Budenz, Louis. *The Techniques of Communism.* New York: Arno Press, 1977.

———. *This Is My Story.* New York: McGraw-Hill, 1947.

Bullert, Gary. "The Frankfurt School Demythologized?" *The Journal of Social, Political, and Economic Studies* (Spring 2011).

Carlton, Frank T. "The Workingmen's Party of New York City, 1829-31." *Political Science Quarterly* 22, no. 3 (September 1907).

Carmelo de Santa Teresa—Coimbra. *Um caminho sob o olhar de Maria: Biografia da Irmã Lúcia de Jesus e do Coração Imaculado, O.C.D.* Coimbra, Portugal: Edições Carmelo, 2013.

Carson, Clarence. *A Basic History of the United States: The Sections and the Civil War, 1826-1877.* Wadley, Alabama: American Textbook Committee, 1994.

Caute, David. *The Fellow-Travellers. Intellectual Friends of Communism.* New Haven, CT: Yale University Press, 1988.

Chambers, Whittaker. *Witness.* New York: Random House, 1952.

Chandler, Robert. *Shadow World.* Washington, DC: Regnery, 2008.

Clum, Woodworth. *Making Socialists Out of College Students.* Los Angeles: Better Federation of America, 1920.

Conquest, Robert. *The Great Terror: A Reassessment.* New York: Oxford University Press, 1990.

———. *The Harvest of Sorrow.* New York: Oxford University Press, 1986.

Counts, George and Nucia Lodge. *The Country of the Blind: The Soviet System of Mind Control.* Boston: Houghton Mifflin, 1949.

Courtois, Stephane, Nicolas Werth, Andrzej Paczkowski, Jean-Louis Margolin, Ehrhart Neubert, Karel Bartosek. *Black Book of Communism.* Cambridge, MA: Harvard University Press, 1991.

Crosby, Michael H. *Thank God Ahead of Time: The Life and Spirituality of Solanus Casey.* Cincinnati, OH: Franciscan Media, 2009.

De Mattei, Roberto. *The Second Vatican Council: An unwritten story.* Fitzwilliam, NH: Loreto, 2010.

Denning, Michael. *The Cultural Front: the Laboring of American Culture in the Twentieth Century.* New York: Verso, 2010.

Dewey, John. *A Common Faith.* New Haven, CT: Yale University Press, 1934.

———. *Democracy and Education.* New York: Macmillan Co., 1916.

Diggins, John Patrick. *The Promise of Pragmatism.* Chicago: University of Chicago Press, 1995.

Dodd, Bella V. *School of Darkness: The record of a life and of a conflict between two faiths.* New York: The Devin-Adair Company, 1954.

Doniger, S. "Soviet Education and Children's Literature." *The Journal of Educational Sociology* 8, no. 3 (1934).

Draper, Theodor. *American Communism and Soviet Russia.* New York: Routledge, 2004.

———. *The Roots of American Communism*. New Brunswick, NJ: Transaction Publishers, 2003.

Edwards, Anna. *The Dewey School The Laboratory School of the University of Chicago 1896-1903*. Piscataway, New Jersey: Transaction Publishers, 1966.

Engels, Frederick. *The Origin of the Family, Private Property and the State*. New York: International Publishers, 1942.

———. *Socialism: Utopian and Scientific*. Chicago: Charles Kerr & Co., 1908.

Evans, M. Stanton. *Blacklisted by History*. New York: Three Rivers Press, 2007.

Evans, M. Stanton and Herbert Romerstein. *Stalin's Secret Agents*. New York: Threshold Publications, 2012.

Ferrara, Christopher. *The Great Façade*. Kettering: Angelico Press, 2015.

Feuer, Lewis S. "The Frankfurt Marxists and the Columbia Liberals." *Survey* (Summer 1980).

Flynn, Daniel J. *A Conservative History of the American Left*. New York: Random House, Crown Forum, 2008.

Foster, William Z. *History of the Communist Party of the United States*. http://williamzfoster.blogspot.com/.

———. *Toward Soviet America*. New York: Coward-McCann, 1932.

———. *The Twilight of World Capitalism*. New York, International Publishers, 1949.

Fraina, Louis C. "Bolsheviki Power Comes From Masses, Says Louis C. Fraina." *The Evening Call* 11, no. 35 (February 11, 1918): 7, http://www.marxisthistory.org/history/usa/parties/spusa/1918/0209-fraina-powerfrommasses.pdf.

Gannon, Francis X. *Biographical Dictionary of the Left*, Vol. II. Boston: Western Islands, 1971.

Geiger, H. Kent. *The Family in Soviet Russia*. Cambridge, MA: Harvard University Press, 1968.

Gitlow, Benjamin. *I Confess: The Truth About American Communism*. New York: E.P. Dutton, 1940.

———. *The Whole of Their Lives*. New York: Scribner's, 1948.

Goldsborough, Robert, Jim Demers, and Tom Mehmel. "The Days of Bella Dodd." YouTube video. April 29, 2012. https://www.youtube.com/watch?v=Yyw-M8k9UEw.

Graham, Robert A. "Vatican, the Story of Bugging at the Vatican." *Columbian* XLIX, no. 10 (November 1969).

Hall, G. Stanley. *Life and Confessions of a Psychologist*. New York, New York: D. Appleton & Co., 1923.

Hartman, Andrew. *Education and the Cold War*. New York: MacMillan, 2008.

Hawkins, Carroll. *Communism Challenge to America*. East Lansing, MI: Michigan State College, 1953.

Haynes, John Earl and Harvey Klehr. *In Denial*. San Francisco: Encounter, 2003.

———. *Venona: Decoding Soviet Espionage in America*. New Haven, CT: Yale University Press, 1999.

Haynes, John Earl, Harvey Klehr, and Alexander Vassiliev. *Spies: The Rise and Fall of the KGB in America*. New Haven, CT: Yale University Press, 2009.

Hillquit, Morris. *History of Socialism in the United States*. New York: Funk and Wagnalls, 1903.

Hook, Sidney. *Heresy Yes, Conspiracy No*. New York: John Day Co., 1953.

———, ed. *The Meaning of Marx: A Symposium by Bertrand Russell, John Dewey, Morris Cohen, Sidney Hook, and Sherwood Eddy*. New York: Farrar & Rinehart, 1934.

Hubbard, Bela. *Political and Economic Structures*. Caldwell, ID: Caxton Printers, 1956.

Iversen, Robert W. *The Communists and the Schools*. New York: Harcourt Brace & Co. 1959.

Jay, Martin. *The Dialectical Imagination: A History of the Frankfurt School and the Institute of Social Research, 1923-1950*. Berkeley, CA: University of California Press, 1996.

Johnpoll, Bernard K. and Mark P. Yerburgh. *The League for Industrial Democracy: A Documentary History*. Westport: Greenwood Press, 1980.

Johnson, Oakley C. *Marxism in United States History Before the Russian Revolution*. New York: Humanities Press, 1974.

Kengor, Paul. *The Communist: Frank Marshall Davis: The Untold Story of Barack Obama's Mentor*. New York: Simon & Schuster, 2012.

———. *The Devil and Karl Marx*. Gastonia, NC: TAN Books, 2020.

———. *Dupes*. Wilmington, DE: ISI Books, 2010.

———. *A Pope and a President*: John Paul II, Ronald Reagan, and the Extraordinary Untold Story of the 20th Century. Wilmington, DE: ISI Books, 2017.

———. *Takedown: From Communists to Progressives, How the Left Has Sabotaged Family and Marriage*. Washington, DC: WND Books, 2015.

Kilpatrick, William H. "Launching the Social Frontier." *Social Frontier* 1, no. 1 (1934).

Klehr, Harvey. *The Heyday of American Communism*. New York: Basic Books, 1984.

Klehr, Haynes and Harvey Klehr. *Venona Decoding Soviet Espionage in America*. New Haven, CT: Yale University Press, 1999.

Klehr, Harvey, John Earl Haynes, and Kyril McAndrew. *The Soviet World of American Communism*. New Haven, CT: Yale University Press, 1995.

Koch, Stephen. *Double Lives: Spies and Writers in the Secret Soviet War of Ideas Against the West*. New York: The Free Press, 1994.

Koehler, John. *Spies in the Vatican: The Soviet Union's Cold War Against the Catholic Church*. New York: Pegasus Books, 2009.

Koestler, Arthur. *The Invisible Writing*. New York: Macmillan 1969.

Kollontai, Aleksandra M. *Communism and the Family*. New York: Andrade's Bookshop, 1920.

Kondor, Louis and Joaquin M. Alonso. *Fatima in Lucia's Own Words*. Fatima, Portugal: Fundacao Francisco E. Jacinta Marto, 2007.

Lenin, Nikola. *The Soviets at Work. The International Position of the Russian Soviet Republic and the Fundamental Problems of the Socialist Revolution.* New York: Rand School of Social Science.

Lenin, Vladimir. *Collected Works.* 45 Volumes. USSR: Progress Publishers, 1964.

———. *The Emancipation of Women.* New York: International Publishers.

———. *Imperialism the Highest Stage of Capitalism.* Mansfield Centre, CT: Martino Publishing, 2011.

Levin, Mark. *Unfreedom of the Press.* New York: Threshold Editions, Simon & Schuster, 2019.

Lincoln, W. Bruce. *Red Victory: A History of the Russian Civil War.* NY: Simon and Schuster, 1989.

Lionni, Paolo and Lance J. Klass. *The Leipzig Connection.* Portland, Heron Books, 1980.

Mann, Horace. "Lectures and Annual Reports on Education." Boston, MA: Lee and Shepard, 1872.

Martin, Jay. *The Education of John Dewey.* New York: Columbia University Press, 2003.

Martin, Malachi. *The Jesuits: The Society of Jesus and the Betrayal of the Roman Catholic Church.* New York: Simon & Schuster, 1987.

———. *The Keys of This Blood.* New York: Touchstone, 1990.

Martin, Rose. *Fabian Freeway.* Chicago, Heritage Foundation, 1966.

Marx, Karl. *Capital.* New York: International Publishers, 1934.

Marx, Karl and Friedrich Engels. *Communist Manifesto.* Edited by Martin Malia. New York: Penguin Signet Classics, 2001.

———. *Manifesto of the Communist Party.* Redford, VA: Wilders Publications, 2007.

Mayhew, Katherine Camp and Anna Edwards. *The Dewey School.* New York: D. Appleton-Century, 1936.

Melloni, A., ed. *Vatican II in Moscow,* (1959-1965). Leuven: Bibliotheek van de Faculteit Godgeleerdheig, 1997.

Merton, Thomas. *The Seven Storey Mountain.* NY: Harcourt Brace, 1948.

Meyer, Frank. *The Moulding of Communists the Training of the Communist Cadre.* New York: Harcourt Brace and Co., 1961.

Mignot, André. *Les Fumées de Satan.* Paris : La Table Ronde, 1976.

Murphy, Francis J. *Communists and Catholics in France, 1936-1939 The Politics of the Outstretched Hand.* Gainesville, University of Florida Press, 1989.

Norwood, Stephen H. *Antisemitism and the American Far Left.* New York: Cambridge University Press, 2013.

Noyes, John Humphrey. *History of American Socialisms.* Philadelphia: J.B. Lippincott, 1870.

O'Brien, John A. *Roads to Rome.* Notre Dame, IN: University of Notre Dame Press, 1960.

Pacepa, Ion Mihael and Ronald J. Rychlak. *Disinformation: Former Spy Chief Reveals Secret Strategies for Undermining Freedom, Attacking Religion, and Promoting Terrorism.* Washington, DC: World Net Daily, 2013.

Padover, Saul K., ed. *On Religion: Karl Marx.* Vol. 5 of, *The Karl Marx Library.* New York: McGraw-Hill Book Company, 1974.

Parable, Gregory. *The People's Front.* Melbourne: Australian Truth Society Record, 1939.

Pease, E. R. *The History of the Fabian Society.* New York: E. P. Dutton & Co., 1916.

Peters, J. *The Communist Party A Manual on Organization.* New York: Workers Library Publishers, 1935.

Philbrick, Herb. *I Led 3 Lives.* New York: McGraw-Hill, 1952.

Pinkevich, Albert P. *The New Education in the Soviet Republic.* New York: John Day, 1929.

Pipes, Richard. *Communism: A History.* New York: The Modern Library, 2001.

———. *The Unknown Lenin: From the Secret Archive.* New Haven, CT: Yale University Press, 1999.

Pope Pius IX. *Qui Pluribus (On Faith and Religion).* November 9, 1846.

Pope Pius XI. *Divini Redemptoris.* March 19, 1937.

Power, Edward J. *Religion and Public Schools in 19th Century America: The Contribution of Orestes A. Brownson.* New York: Paulist Press, 1996.

Radecki, Francisco and Dominic Radecki. *Tumultuous Times.* Wayne, MI: St. Joseph's Media, 2001.

Rauschning, Hermann. *Hitler Speaks.* New York: Putnam, 1940.

Reeves, Thomas C. *America's Bishop: The Life and Times of Fulton J. Sheen.* Encounter Books, 2001.

Rockefeller, Steven C. *John Dewey: Religious Faith and Democratic Humanism.* New York: Columbia University Press, 1991.

Romerstein, Herbert. *Communism and Your Child.* New York: The Bookmailer Inc, 1963.

———. *Heroic Victims.* Washington, DC: The Council for the Defense of Freedom, 1994.

Romerstein, Herbert and Eric Breindel. *The Venona Secrets.* Washington, DC: Regnery, 2000.

Romerstein, Herbert and Stanislav Lechenko. *The KGB against the "Main Enemy."* Lexington, MA: Lexington Books, 1989.

Root, E. Merrill. *Collectivism on the Campus.* New York: The Devin-Adair Co., 1955.

Ryan, Alan. *John Dewey and the High Tide of American Liberalism.* New York: Norton, 1995.

Samson, Gloria Garrett. *The American Fund for Public Service.* Westport, CT: Greenwood Press, 1996.

Santos, Lucia. *Fatima in Lucia's Own Words.* Secretariado dos Pastorinhos, Fátima, Portugal, 2003.

Schrecker, Ellen W. *No Ivory Tower McCarthyism and the Universities.* New York: Oxford University Publishing, 1986.

Shaw, George Bernard. *The Fabian Society: Its Early History.* London: The Fabian Society, 1892.

———. *The Rationalization of Russia.* Bloomington, IN: Indiana University Press, 1964.

Sheen, Fulton J. *The Church, Communism and Democracy.* New York: Dell, 1954.

———. *Communism and the Conscience of the West.* New York, New York: The Bobbs-Merrill Co., 1948.

———. *Communism and Religion.* New York: Paulist Press, 1948.

———. *Communism Answers Questions of a Communist.* New York: The Paulist Press, 1937.

———. *Treasure in Clay.* New York: Doubleday, 1980.

Shlaes, Amity. *The Forgotten Man: A New History of the Great Depression.* New York: HarperCollins, 2007.

Skousen, W. Cleon. *The Naked Capitalist.* Salt Lake City: Reviewer, 1970.

Slesinger, Zalmen. *Education and the Class Struggle.* Covici-Friede, 1937.

Socci, Antonio. *The Fourth Secret of Fatima.* Fitzwilliam, NH: Loreto Publications, 2006.

Stalin, J. V. *Foundations of Leninism,* vol. XXV. New York: Red Star Publishers, 2010.

Stalin, Josef. *Problems of Leninism.* Moscow: Foreign Languages Publishing House, 1945.

Stormer, John. *None Dare Call It Treason.* New York, Buccaneer Books, 1964.

Sutton, Antony. *America's Secret Establishment, An Introduction to the Order of Skull and Bones.* Walterville, OR: Triune Day, 2002.

———. *Wall Street and the Bolshevik Revolution.* New York: Arlington House, 1974.

Taylor, Clarence. *Reds at the Blackboard.* New York: Columbia University Press, 2011.

Taylor, S. J. *Stalin's Apologist.* New York: Oxford University Press, 1990.

Thorez, Maurice. *Catholics and Communists.* New York: Workers Library Publishers, 1938.

Tresca, Carlo. "Where is Juliet Stuart Poyntz?" *The Modern Monthly* 10, no. 11 (March, 1938).

Trotsky, Leon. *The History of the Russian Revolution.* Translated by Max Eastman. Ann Arbor: University of Michigan Press, 1932.

USSR Academy of Sciences, Maxim Gorky Institute of World Literature. *Maxim Gorky, Collected Works in Thirty Volumes.* Vol. 27. Moscow: Fiction Literature State Publishing House, 1953.

Van Der Sears, John. *My Friends at Brook Farm.* New York: Desmond Fitzgerald Inc, 1913.

Von Hildebrand, Alice. *Memoirs of a Happy Failure.* Charlotte, NC: St. Benedict Press, 2014.

Wagner, Jean. *Black Poets of the United States: From Paul Laurence Dunbar to Langston Hughes.* Chicago and Urbana: University of Illinois Press, 1973.

Weikart, Richard. "Marx, Engels, and the Abolition of the Family." *History of European Ideas* 18, no. 5 (1994).

Weinstein, Allen. *Perjury: The Hiss Chambers Case.* Stanford: Hoover Institution, 1978.

Wells, H. G. *An Experiment in Autobiography: Discoveries and Conclusions of a Very Ordinary Brain (Since 1866).* New York: Little, Brown & Co., 1984.

———. *Russia in the Shadows.* George H. Doran Company, 1921.

Westbrook, Robert B. *John Dewey and American Democracy.* Ithaca, NY: Cornell University Press, 1993

Wheatland, Thomas. "The Frankfurt School's Invitation from Columbia University: How the Horkheimer Circle Settled on Morningside Heights." *German Politics & Society* 22, no. 3 (72), (Fall 2004).

Wiggershaus, Rolf. *The Frankfurt School: Its History, Theories, and Political Significance.* Cambridge, MA: The MIT Press, 1994.

Wiltgen, Ralph. *The Inside Story of Vatican II.* Charlotte, NC: TAN Books, 2014.

Wittner, Felix. *Conquest of the American Mind.* Boston: Meador Publishing, 1959.

Woody, Thomas. *New Minds, New Men?* New York: Macmillan, 1932.

Yaroslovsky, A. *Religion in the USSR.* London: Modern Publishers, 1932.

INDEX

413

252, 255, 346, 348, 349, 351, 356, 366, 369, 373, 377, 379, 385, 386, 392, 399.

Communist Political Association, 14, 298–299, 324, 347.

Congress of American Women, 190–191, 381, 382.

Conquest, Robert, 146, 221, 373, 389.

Cooperative Commonwealth, 75.

Coudert Jr., Frederic René, 29, 202, 207–218, 220–224, 273, 308, 351, 363, 374, 378, 386, 388, 389.

Counts, George, 85, 93–94, 113, 114, 202, 204, 360, 361, 385.

Cowl, Margaret, 191.

Cripps, Stafford, 76.

Daily Worker, 26–27, 28, 29–30, 103, 132, 136, 152, 161–162, 175, 187, 232–237, 240–244, 257, 349, 369, 370, 374, 378, 380, 382, 383, 385, 387, 389, 391, 392, 394.

Dana, Charles, 69.

Davidson, Thomas, 76.

Davin, Tom, 245, 247–248.

Davis, Angela, 106, 365–366.

Davis, Ben, 300, 304.

Davis, Frank Marshall, 30, 349, 377.

Davis, Jerome, 188–189, 197, 222, 381.

Day, Dorothy, 10.

De Almeida, Avelino, 44, 351.

De Mattei, Roberto, 286, 295, 397, 398, 399.

Debs, Eugene, 49, 357.

Democracy and Education, 85, 88, 90, 359.

Dennis, Eugene, 103, 203, 350, 359.

Dettloff, Dean, 21.

Dewey, John, 70, 83–97, 103, 108, 114, 150, 156–157, 171, 204, 356, 359, 360.

Dickinson, Emily, 168.

Dies, Martin, 29.

Dissemond, Paul, 280.

Divini Redemptoris, 10, 18, 122, 290, 345, 367.

Dodd, Bella (see also Maria Assunta Isabella Visono), 1–24, 25–38, 39–44, 46–51, 53–65, 67, 70, 74, 78–82, 83, 85, 89–90, 93–99, 101–104, 107–114, 115–120, 122–125, 127–130, 132–134, 136–147, 149–152, 154–156, 158–159, 161–163, 165–173, 175–180, 183–187, 189–201, 204–206, 207–226, 227–232, 235–236, 238, 244–247, 253, 258–269, 271–276, 277, 280, 291, 293–296, 297–313, 315–322, 323–330, 333–338, 339–342, 345, 346, 347, 348, 349, 350, 351, 352, 353, 354, 355, 356, 357, 360, 361, 362, 364, 366, 367, 368, 369, 370, 371, 372, 373, 374, 375, 376, 377, 378, 379, 380, 381, 382, 383, 384, 385, 386, 387, 388, 389, 390, 392, 394, 395, 396, 399, 400, 401, 402, 403, 404.

Dodd, John F., 115–117.

Don Levine, Isaac, 102.

Dubinsky, David, 297.

Duranty, Walter, 145, 373.

Dzerlin, Frances, 26, 308–309.

Dzerzhinsky, Felix, 104.

Educational Workers' International (EWI), 152, 154, 374.

Egan, Hannah, 61–62.

Engdahl, John Louis, 132, 369.

Engels, Frederick, 6–7, 9, 13, 49, 72–73, 77, 104, 117, 119, 121–123, 166, 185, 333, 355, 356, 358, 367, 380.

Eros and Civilization, 106, 346.

Evander Childs, 44, 47–49, 51, 63, 351, 352.

Evans, M. Stanton, 103.

Evil Empire (speech), 5.